Making Minimum Wage

Studies in American Constitutional Heritage
Justin Wert and Kyle Harper, Series Editors

Making Minimum Wage

Elsie Parrish versus the
West Coast Hotel Company

Helen J. Knowles

University of Oklahoma Press : Norman

Library of Congress Cataloging-in-Publication Data

Names: Knowles, Helen J., 1973– author.
Title: Making minimum wage : Elsie Parrish versus the West Coast Hotel
    Company / Helen J. Knowles.
Description: Norman : University of Oklahoma Press, [2021] | Series: Studies
    in American constitutional heritage ; volume 4 | Includes bibliographical
    references and index. | Summary: "Tells the story behind the US Supreme
    Court's 1937 decision in West Coast Hotel v. Parrish upholding Washing-
    ton State's minimum wage law for women; illuminates the lives of those
    involved in the litigation and reveals the case's impact on local, state, and
    national levels"—Provided by publisher.
Identifiers: LCCN 2021001156 | ISBN 978-0-8061-6928-6 (hardcover) |
    ISBN 978-0-8061-6938-5 (paperback)
Subjects: LCSH: Parrish, Elsie, 1899–1980—Trials, litigation, etc. | West Coast
    Hotel Company—Trials, litigation, etc. | Minimum wage—Law
    and legislation—United States—Cases.
Classification: LCC KF228.P378 K56 2021 | DDC 344.7301/423—dc23
LC record available at https://lccn.loc.gov/2021001156

Making Minimum Wage: Elsie Parrish versus the West Coast Hotel Company is
Volume 4 in the Studies in American Constitutional Heritage series.

The paper in this book meets the guidelines for permanence and durability of
the Committee on Production Guidelines for Book Longevity of the Council
on Library Resources, Inc. ∞

For John

In loving memory of Jenny

There shall never be another season of silence until women have the same rights men have on this green earth.

—*Susan B. Anthony*

Nothing could be more revolutionary than to close the door to social experimentation. The whole subject of woman's entry into industry is an experiment. And surely the federal constitution—itself perhaps the greatest of human experiments—does not prohibit such modest attempts as the woman's minimum-wage act to reconcile the existing industrial system with our striving for social justice and the preservation of the race.

—*Louis D. Brandeis,* "The Constitution and the Minimum Wage"

[T]here was the sense, and there still is the sense, that nice girls don't speak up; nice girls don't make demands . . . um, well, too bad!

—*Sharron Frontiero*

Contents

Acknowledgments

I have traveled a long way, moved jobs and houses several times, and been distracted by countless other projects since I first began to think about the story of this case over a decade ago. I had no idea it was an untold story. Originally for me, its attraction was purely geographical, because I was a visiting professor at Whitman College in Walla Walla, Washington, and was interested in finding out more about the relationship between constitutional law and the state I would call home for two years. I knew about Justice William O. Douglas, the Whitman alum, and I soon became aware of another Whittie, Lucile Lomen, who was the first woman to work as a U.S. Supreme Court law clerk (for Justice Douglas, 1944–45). I was well acquainted with the decision in *West Coast Hotel v. Parrish* because of its place in the Supreme Court's New Deal jurisprudence; at that time, however, to me, Elsie Parrish was simply the name of one of the parties in that case.

My perception of *Parrish* began to change, and the idea for the project that became this book was born one evening in October 2010 when I read over the research paper outlines submitted by two of my constitutional law students. The assignment prompt asked them to consider the backstories of the cases that they were studying, and these students wanted to find out more about *Parrish* because the case was "local." I *think* I knew before then that the case had originated in Wenatchee, 180 miles northwest of Walla

Walla. I certainly knew afterward. My interest piqued, I began to research Elsie's story; at the same time the students began to write their papers. Special recognition goes to those students, Tom Everett (Whitman '12) and Ethan Robertson (Whitman '13), for writing inspiring research papers about the *Parrish* case.

After uncovering precious little about the stories behind *Parrish*, I sought information from several primary research sources. I do not recall when I began to cross email paths with members of Elsie's family and the grandchildren of the lawyers involved in the case. What I do know, however, is that I am deeply indebted to those descendants for sharing their family histories with me. As Jim Sargent has observed: "One must go to many sources to put together a family history. One has to dig into every possible information repository to pull out useful bits that will bring days gone past into focus. . . . The genealogist [or any other kind of historian] who has more than names and dates enjoys a richer understanding of the people involved."[1] Oftentimes I have had little more than "names and dates" to work with. Therefore, it is no exaggeration to say that without the aid of Chris Conner, the granddaughter of C. B. Conner, Elsie's lawyer; Ross Crollard and Sydney Crollard Ranney, the grandson and granddaughter of Fred Crollard, the attorney for the West Coast Hotel Company; Bill Murray and Barbara Roberts—Elsie was their great-aunt; and Debra Parrish Stewart, Elsie's great-granddaughter, this book could not have been written. It was a true delight to have the opportunity in March 2018 to interview Barbara Roberts. The first female governor of Oregon, Barbara has spent her entire political career as a pioneering trailblazer—Elsie would be very proud of her great-niece!

My initial email paths led directly to Wenatchee and into the welcoming arms of a wonderful community, many members of which have provided me with invaluable information and assistance. I am especially grateful to Chris Rader and Darlene Spargo, both retired from the Wenatchee Valley Museum and Cultural Center (WVMCC); Chuck Holberg, for taking Chris, Darlene, and myself on a special tour of the Cascadian building in April 2012; Paul Moseley, for taking Darlene and myself on an extended tour of the Cascadian building in January 2020; Selina Danko, WVMCC; Melanie Wachholder, curator at the WVMCC; Rufus and Wilfred Woods at the *Wenatchee Daily World*; Kris Bassett, a font of historical preservation knowledge; and Susan Hart, for wonderful reminiscences about her sisters' lives in Wenatchee.

When interviewed by the *Oregonian* newspaper in 1991, Roy Turnbaugh (who served as the Oregon state archivist from 1985 to 2005) astutely observed that "government records . . . are records of everybody, rather than just the distinguished, the prominent, or the wealthy. There's a very democratic quality to these records."[2] As anyone who has undertaken archival research well knows, it is impossible to gain an adequate understanding of—or appreciation for—the extent of the "democratic quality" of records contained in any one repository without the help of the dedicated archivists who oversee their administration. While undertaking the research for this book, I have benefited from the assistance of the following individuals: Susan Boeggeman, deputy court clerk for Chelan County; Brigid Clift, Washington State Archives; Laura Edmonston, Washington State Law Library; Robert Ellis, National Archives; Andrea Faling, Nebraska State Archives; Lin Fredericksen, Kansas Historical Society; Betty Gaeng, League of Snohomish County Heritage Organizations; Kerry Gelb, Wenatchee Library; Barry George, Okanogan County Historical Society; Cheryl Gunselman, Washington State University Library, Special Collections; Natasha Hollenbach, Montana Historical Society; Caitlin Jones, Massachusetts Archives; Dwight King, University of Notre Dame Law School Library; Jen Laine, Washington State Law Library; Virginia Lewick, Franklin D. Roosevelt Presidential Library; Rebecca McLain, Oneida County History Center; Nancy Mulhern, Wisconsin Historical Society; Lynne Palombo, State of Oregon Law Library; Cheryl Ravagni, Seattle Public Library—Business, Science and Technology section; Catherine Romano, research librarian, Supreme Court of the United States; Molly Rooney, Washington State Archives; Daniel Sauerwein, State Historical Society of North Dakota; David Schmidtke, Minnesota Legislative Reference Library; Patrizia Sione, Kheel Center for Labor-Management Documentation & Archives in Cornell University's Catherwood Library; Emily Venemon, Washington State Archives; Megan Weiss, Research Center of the Utah State Archives and Utah State History; Bob Young, Legacy Washington, Office of the Secretary of State, Washington; and the staffs of the Manuscript Division at the Library of Congress, the Central Washington University Archives and Special Collections,

the Arthur and Elizabeth Schlesinger Library on the History of
Women in America at Harvard University, the Center for Pacific
Northwest Studies at Western Washington University, the Division
of Rare and Manuscript Collections at Cornell University's Carl A.
Kroch Library, Microform & Newspaper Collections at the University of Washington's Suzzallo Library, and the Records Office at the
King County Superior Court in Seattle. A special shout-out must
go to the Interlibrary Loan Department of the Penfield Library at
SUNY Oswego, the staff of which never ceases to amaze me with
its ability to fill my constant barrage of requests for obscure historical materials.

I could not have undertaken the research at the King County
Superior Court without the amazing research help provided by
Emma Rodman, with whom it has been a privilege subsequently to
coauthor a conference paper that drew upon the archival materials
we found. I am also grateful to Emma for "sharing" with me one of
her terrific undergraduate students at the University of Washington.
That individual, Aidan Killackey, did invaluable work for me at the
Seattle Central Library. As he explained to me, the experience he
gained from doing the research was multifaceted, including the fact
that, in his words, "I also feel that I now know how to run a hotel
in the 1930s." I also benefited from the excellent research skills
of Andre Nichols (SUNY Oswego '20), whose work for me was
funded by two separate SUNY Oswego Undergraduate Research
Assistant grants. Nicholas Stubba (SUNY Oswego '20) undertook
the essential task of proofreading and double-checking the bibliog-
raphy entries for me.

My article about a small part of Elsie's story appeared as
"'Omak's Minimum Pay Law Joan D'Arc': Telling the Local Story
of *West Coast Hotel v. Parrish* (1937)," *Journal of Supreme Court
History* 37 (2012): 283–304; and the following is my short article
highlighting some of the history of the Cascadian Hotel—"The
Cascadian: An 'Outstanding Small City Hotel,'" *The Confluence* 33,
no. 2 (2017): 13–15. Some material from this book appears in a
revised format in Helen J. Knowles and L. Darlene Spargo, *Images
of America: Cascadian Hotel* (Charleston, SC: Arcadia Press, 2020).
I have presented papers about the stories told in this book at the
annual meetings of the New England Political Science Association,
Western History Association, Western Political Science Association,
Pacific Northwest Political Science Association, Southern Political

Science Association, and American Journalism Historians Association. I have also had the distinct privilege of twice presenting at the WVMCC. For the feedback that I received at these conferences and events, and also for the feedback that I received from other individuals along the way, I am very grateful to Aaron Lorenz, Michael D. Cobb, James C. Foster, Mark Tushnet, Keith E. Whittington, Jason E. Whitehead, Lori Hausegger, Eric Waltenburg, and Paul Chen.

These individuals had faith in this project when another person (who will remain nameless) told me it should never see the light of day and belonged in the trashcan. How satisfying it is to prove him wrong.

Indeed, this was just one of the ways in which that unnamed scholar psychologically abused me for a number of years. The luxury that we academics call "tenure" enabled me to put an end to that torment. Hopefully my decision to forge ahead with this book, and this note I am writing, will serve to encourage junior academics (yes, I know, senior scholars can also be such victims, but in my experience the abusers disproportionately prey upon untenured faculty) to stand up for, and take pride in their work.

Jim Foster and Julie Novkov, the manuscript proposal reviewers solicited by Oklahoma, provided me with very useful comments that have made this a much stronger project. The following individuals also did me the honor of reading and providing exceptionally useful feedback on either the entire manuscript, or extensive portions of it: Beau Breslin, Keith Bybee, Barry Cushman, Aaron Lorenz, Bill Murray, Chris Rader, Sydney Crollard Ranney, Darlene Spargo, Deb Stewart, and Bob Young.

I am tremendously grateful to Adam Kane, an editor extraordinaire, who was the first person at Oklahoma Press (he is now director of the Naval Institute Press) to show interest in this project. I cannot thank him enough for having faith in my work and, it should be added, for coming up with a truly superb title for this book. I have also been blessed to work with the following staff members at Oklahoma, who did a wonderful job of getting my vision for this book into print (hopefully I have not left anyone out): Kent Calder, Steph Attia Evans, Amy Hernandez, Joe Schiller, and Sarah Stringfield. I also extend my gratitude to Bill Nelson for creating the maps for this volume. Finally, if Adam is an editor extraordinaire, then Kerin Tate is surely his copyediting equivalent. She did a fantastic job of casting an extremely careful eye over the entire manuscript. The remaining errors are of course mine, including those idiosyncrasies of the Queen's English that I, born and raised in Great Britain as I was, remain stubbornly attached to, more than twenty-five years of living in the United States notwithstanding.

This entire project benefited immeasurably from the 2017 weeklong summer seminar—on "The *Lochner* Era"—run by the Institute for Constitutional History (under the superb organizational leadership of Maeva Marcus). Barry Cushman conducted the seminar and masterfully took us on a dizzyingly (and dazzlingly) detailed and unbelievably energizing and educational journey through the literature and cases associated with this period in American constitutional history. That seminar had a profound impact on this book, and I am immensely grateful to Barry, Maeva, and my fellow seminarians.

This project was made possible by very generous research grants from the American Philosophical Society, the American Political Science Association, SUNY Oswego, and Whitman College.

The project has also been made possible by the love and support of my family. My mother, Rae, has been a constant source of encouragement. The mistakes that remain are, of course, solely my responsibility. Bingo (may she rest in peace), Clementine, Doc, Faith, Fiona, Smokey, and Toffee (Toffee reluctantly put his paw-pen signature to a coauthored request stipulating that their names be listed in alphabetical order) have kept me grounded, ensuring that pens playfully go missing, that cat hairs affectionately clog keyboards, and that dog walks and horse rides bring much needed physical and psychological breaks.

Finally, this volume is dedicated to two wonderful people.

First, it is dedicated to my stepdaughter, Jenny Dunbar Ramos, who in 2019 was taken from this world far, far, far, far too early.

Second, it is with immense pleasure that I dedicate this volume to my life partner, John Gardner. This book is a much better piece of work because of his love. He is my emotional support through good times and bad; writer's block times; and those oh-so-valuable times when I needed space to hammer away at the keyboard, forage through files, and dash off on research trips. I could not have asked for a more caring, loving person with whom to share this wonderful journey called life! Meow.

Prologue

"She is Mrs. Elsie Parrish"

Most of us have a breaking point. Elsie Parrish's occurred on May . . . [11], 1935, when she was fired by the Cascadian Hotel in Wenatchee.

—*Darlene Spargo, longtime resident and local historian of Wenatchee*

On December 17, 1936, it was unseasonably warm outside as Elsie Parrish went about her work, making beds and cleaning rooms at the Jim Hill Hotel in Omak. Temperatures were in the forties, no snow was forecast, and the winter sunshine bathed this small town nestled in the North Central region of Washington State, forty-five miles south of the Canadian border.[1] Elsie and her husband, Ernie, had moved to Omak, population 2,500, earlier that year.[2] Attracted by job opportunities at the Biles-Coleman sawmill, this was a chance for Ernie to return to his native Okanogan Highlands. For Elsie, relocating saw her return to life as a chambermaid, employment she had not been able to find since leaving the services of the Cascadian Hotel in the city of Wenatchee.

That same day, 2,600 miles and an entire world away from Omak, it also did not feel like winter had yet come to Washington, D.C., Attorney General Homer S. Cummings sat in his office and continued to ruminate over the contents of a letter sent to him the previous day by his friend and confidant, Edward S. Corwin. Outside,

1

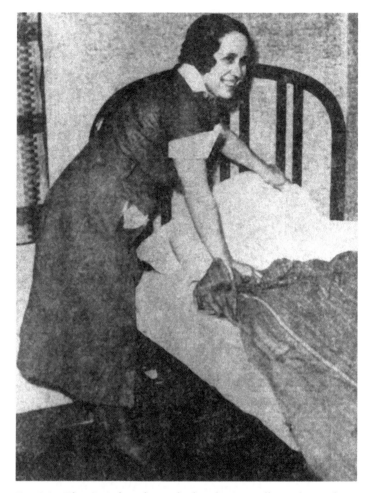

FIG. 0.1   Elsie Parrish making a bed at the Jim Hill Hotel, Omak, Washington, November 1936. Wenatchee Valley Museum and Cultural Center, 87-169-1.

the overnight rain began to dissipate, leaving the skies over the nation's capital partly cloudy and temperatures in the forties.[3] However, in the weeks leading up to Christmas that year, the nation's liberal intelligentsia felt nothing but cold winds blowing. They held out little hope that progressive change would come from within the walls of the U.S. Supreme Court, the conservative majority of which was obstructing the New Deal agenda at every turn. Corwin's letter expressed that pessimism. "It is probably Utopian," he wrote, "to hope that the Court will supply the needed remedy for a situation which it has itself created." Corwin (a politics professor at Princeton University) and Cummings were of one mind; a solution to the Court's progress-inhibiting, laissez-faire rulings would have to come in the form of action from the other branches of the federal government.[4]

History remembers Corwin's letter for one of its suggestions, because that suggestion would become President Franklin D. Roosevelt's plan to "pack" the Court with justices more sympathetic to his agenda. That plan was not unveiled to the public until February 1937. Two months earlier, on December 17, neither Corwin nor Cummings, nor the president for that matter, could have known that unfolding before the *existing* justices was the latest chapter in a story that would fundamentally change the Court-packing narrative, ultimately rendering the plan redundant. For December 17 was the second and concluding day of oral arguments in *West Coast Hotel v. Ernest and Elsie Parrish*.[5] It came exactly twenty-two years after the Court first heard oral arguments in a case involving the constitutionality of a minimum wage law for women,[6] and was a case whose decision on March 29, 1937, would "supply the needed remedy" that Corwin had once considered it "utopian" to hope for.

*   *   *

For three months during the late summer and early fall of 1933, Elsie Lee (née Murray) worked as a part-time employee of the Cascadian Hotel, one of the largest employers in Wenatchee, a city of eleven thousand people, situated one hundred miles south of Omak. Born in Kansas in 1899, Elsie moved to the Evergreen State in approximately 1930. She divorced Roy Lee, whom she had married when she was fifteen, shortly thereafter. Working as a chambermaid to support her large family, Elsie (who had six children with Roy, and was already a grandmother) initially received twenty-two and a half cents per hour with lunch provided. A raise later brought this up to twenty-five cents per hour (although, then she was expected to provide her own lunch). In 1934, when she married Ernest Parrish, she became a full-time member of the hotel's staff, working there regularly until May 11, 1935.[7]

During the Great Depression, any wages were better than no wages; however, the amount that Elsie received was in violation of

FIG. 0.2   The Cascadian Hotel, Wenatchee, Washington, circa 1930.
Wenatchee Valley Museum and Cultural Center, 98-86-1.

the law. In 1913 Washington State enacted a minimum wage law
for women. Under the terms of that law Elsie should have been
receiving considerably more money in her weekly pay packet.
When Willard E. Abel, manager of the Cascadian, discharged Elsie
on May 11 and presented her with a check for $17—the balance
of wages owed, Elsie refused to accept the money. The Depression had been slow to affect Wenatchee, the self-described "Apple
Capital of the World," but by 1935 residents had been enduring its
wrath for several years.[8] Nevertheless, Elsie knew that under state

law her family was owed far more than $17. To be precise, she was owed $216.19 (the equivalent of approximately $4,100 in 2020).

Life in Wenatchee became more difficult for the Parrish family in the summer of 1935 when Elsie and Ernie decided to do something about that situation. They walked into C. B. Conner's office on the third floor of the Doneen Building and asked for his assistance in suing the Cascadian. One of the city's most respected lawyers, Conner took the Parrishes' case pro bono and initiated a lawsuit on June 10, 1935, seeking to recover the amount of back wages that the Cascadian owed his clients.

The U.S. Supreme Court's 1937 decision in *West Coast Hotel v. Parrish*, upholding the Washington State law and handing Elsie a victory, has been the subject of an immense scholarly outpouring. It is, as Julie Novkov observes, "the case that launched a thousand law review articles."[9] This is because almost immediately, the ruling in *Parrish* was labeled "the switch in time that saved nine."[10] Implicit in that appellation was the belief that, when confronted with President Franklin Delano Roosevelt's threat to attempt to reform the judiciary with the Judicial Reorganization Act (the Court-packing plan), Justice Owen Roberts reversed course and voted, with his more liberal colleagues, to uphold a law that was very similar to the New York statute that a majority (including Roberts) had struck down the previous summer.[11]

The overwhelming majority of literature about *Parrish* continues to focus on that temporal relationship even though historians have long since shown that the case was decided before FDR's announcement of the plan.[12] Most scholars are cognizant of the real timeline and are careful not to perpetuate the "switch" myth. However, this does not stop them from mentioning the decision because of its relationship to the Court-packing controversy (a controversy which, given the amount of literature it has spawned, is the epitome of a "twice-told tale").[13] When we remove the connection to FDR and his Court-packing plan from the story of *Parrish*, several principal actors remain—Elsie Parrish, the Cascadian Hotel (operated by the West Coast Hotel Company), the 1913 Washington State Minimum Wages for Women law, Frederick M. Crollard (the West Coast Hotel Company's lawyer), and C. B. Conner (Elsie's lawyer). All of their stories, as they relate to the *Parrish* case, have gone untold.

*   *   *

In 1908, the *Wenatchee Daily World* (then, as now, Wenatchee's primary newspaper)[14] editorialized about the "ranks of mediocrity"—"the half-successful" in this world. Those ranks, it argued, "are crowded with people of fine natural abilities, who never rise above inferior stations because they never act independently. They are afraid to take the initiative in anything—to depend upon their own judgment and resources—and so let opportunity after opportunity pass them by."[15] Had Elsie Parrish decided not to sue for the back pay she was owed, and had Conner rejected her request for legal assistance, then perhaps history would have remembered another similarly situated Depression-era worker and her lawyer for successfully leading the 1930s charge to sustain minimum wage laws for women. But history need not do so because these two residents of Wenatchee were anything but members of the "half-successful." They were not about to let this "opportunity pass them by."

Eighty years after the *Wenatchee Daily World* article appeared, in 1988 Margie Jones, a Wenatchee native and local historian, observed that during the previous year "the 50th anniversary of the Parrish decision . . . passed virtually without recognition. Most of the people involved, including Elsie, are dead," she wrote. "They died without being given the honors they deserved. All of us are better off because a tired chambermaid wanted to be paid what was her rightful salary under the law. . . . From now on, when I look at the Cascadian," continued Jones, "I will remember Elsie Parrish and offer up a silent 'thank you.' Forever she will be a part of our history, but hopefully she will not be a lost part of it."[16]

Ultimately, minimum wage laws are "not an academic question or even a legal one, but [instead] a human problem."[17] I therefore share Jones's belief that Elsie's story deserves to be told. This book seeks to ensure that it is a story that will not be lost to time.

Introduction

Humanizing the People

> Few Americans can recollect the names of . . . people who
> began important Supreme Court cases. Hardly anyone,
> aside from family and friends, knows anything of their lives.
> —*Peter Irons*, The Courage of Their Convictions

In the foreword to Peter Irons's *A People's History of the Supreme
Court*, Howard Zinn lamented the fact that "[a]lthough the Preamble to the United States Constitution begins with the words 'We
the People . . . ,' the volumes upon volumes that deal with constitutional law are remarkably devoid of human beings."[1] This observation is consistent with what Irons experienced at law school:
"I read hundreds of Supreme Court opinions, and noticed the lack
of any description of the parties in most opinions. They were simply names on paper."[2] In these quotations, both men were referring
to the pages of the U.S. Reports that contain U.S. Supreme Court
opinions. However, both quotations appear within works that ask
us to take a broader view—a view that brings with it the realization
that the "people" are similarly missing from much of the scholarly
commentary about those Court opinions and decisions. As Zinn
rhetorically asked, "How many Americans, of the huge number
who have heard of *Brown v. Board of Education*, know that 'Brown'

refers to Oliver Brown and his eight-year-old daughter Linda in Topeka, or know anything about the long struggle of their family to bring the case before the highest court in the land?"[3] Together, Irons and Zinn were expressing their shared belief that not enough is known or learned about the people who bring the lawsuits that end up as U.S. Supreme Court decisions.

There is nothing uncharitable about saying that neither Edward Corwin, Homer Cummings, the justices of the Supreme Court, nor even the president of the United States probably cared much, if at all, about Elsie Parrish. She was not the focus of their attention when her case came before the nation's highest tribunal, and nor should she have been. Yes, Cummings and, indirectly, Corwin were part of an administration genuinely concerned about the working-man and woman. And yes, the members of the Supreme Court were in the business of dispensing justice. However, ultimately to the Court *West Coast Hotel v. Parrish* was about the law of mini-mum wages. It just happened to be a case involving a constitutional challenge brought by a chambermaid from Wenatchee, Washing-ton. What really mattered was this: that the case was [*no-name hotel in a state with a minimum wage law for women*] v. [*no-name female employee of that hotel, who was paid less than the minimum wage she was owed under a state's law*]. In this respect, *West Coast Hotel v. Parrish* is no different from the overwhelming majority of Supreme Court cases, "the notoriety of . . . [which] is matched by the obscu-rity of the people who began them."[4]

Why, then, should we care about Elsie Parrish, the Cascadian Hotel, and the Washington State 1913 law? Why should we devote extended scholarly treatment to their story? Surely it is the out-come we care about, not the story of how we got there. *Parrish* is famous because it was a turning point in the law of minimum wages; however, any such decision would have been famous for that rea-son. Therefore, perhaps the identities and stories of the individuals bringing the case are irrelevant. Indeed, one could make a very credible argument that all that the readers of the April 12, 1937, issue of *Life* magazine needed to know about the minimum wage worker from the *Parrish* case—and all that we need to know—was contained in the caption beneath the iconic picture of Elsie mak-ing a bed. That caption read: "A chambermaid brought the case on which the Supreme Court reversed itself. She is Mrs. Elsie Parrish (*above*), a grandmother at 37, who used to get $12 a week from her employer."[5]

There is, however, much more to the story than this.

Putting the People Back in "We the People"

In recent years there have been great advancements in the telling of the stories of constitutional law cases like *Parrish*, advancements that seek to fill the void lamented by Zinn.[6] Scholars have begun to "put . . . the people back in 'We the People.'"[7] In doing so, they have brought to our attention the lives of the people who displayed the "courage of their convictions" when they became involved in legal challenges (sometimes of their choosing, sometimes not).[8] When we learn about these lives, we do not simply learn more about those cases. We learn more about the society in which we live; the society that was home to the generations that came before us; and the society that we hope to leave for our posterity. And as the following examples make clear, we can learn about these lives regardless of whether they are associated with (a) cases that move forward because of structural interests and/or mobilization by sociolegal organizations, or (b) cases driven by the impetus of stubborn litigants.

For example, from Jim Foster's poignant treatment of *Morse v. Frederick* we learn about just how much more dauntingly complex the American judicial system is when two intelligent but stubborn forces shun a settlement in favor of defending the legal principles in which they believe.[9] Read the multiple opinions by the fractured justices in "messy *Morse*," and you will find, as Foster explains, that the "outcome results, in large part, from a failure of judicial imagination. Unable (because unwilling?) to conceive of a remedy in nondichotomous, relational terms, the *Morse* majority opinion contains no surprises."[10] However, unless you know the stories behind *Morse*, you will not be able to appreciate how in so many ways those opinions mirrored the nature of the battle that took place between Joe Frederick and his principal, Deborah Morse, at Juneau-Douglas High School. Nor will you realize that there was much more to this seminal freedom of speech case than the actions, one snowy day in Alaska, of a recalcitrant teenager who thumbed his nose at the authorities and made international headlines with a banner that many presumed to be an endorsement of recreational drugs.

Or what about the stories of Michael Hardwick, John Geddes Lawrence, and Tyron Garner? Anyone familiar with the U.S. Supreme Court's LGBTQ rights decisions will no doubt recognize the last names of these three men and will know the basic stories of their cases. However, there is much that is left unsaid in the opinions of the justices in *Bowers v. Hardwick* (1986) and *Lawrence v. Texas* (2003).[11] The writings of Irons, William N. Eskridge Jr., Hardwick himself, and Bill Moyers's 1987 PBS interview with Hardwick are all proof positive that there was much more to *Bowers* than met the eyes of the readers of the Court's opinions.[12] And Dale Carpenter's magnificent *Flagrant Conduct* is nothing short of an eye-opening book-length treatment of the *Lawrence* case, eye-opening not only for what it tells us about the stories behind this litigation, but for what those stories tell us about the factual inaccuracies contained within the pages of the various court decisions in the case.[13]

This is not to say that the pages of the U.S. Reports are totally devoid of U.S. Supreme Court opinions that cast the facts of a case in an unusually detailed and humanizing light.[14] However, it seems clear that such language is usually only inserted into an opinion because the author of the opinion very deliberately wants it to be there. The Court that he or she sits upon may at any one time be composed of justices more or less likely to produce emotional and humanizing opinions,[15] but that is usually beside the point. The decision to tell the stories of litigants is a personal choice. Of course, when such language appears in majority opinions, we must remember that it does so with the blessings of the justices who have joined that opinion. Authors of majority opinions must consider their colleagues' concerns during the drafting process; they are participants in a collegial and strategic process, and they "compose with tied hands."[16] Nevertheless, if any such concerns are raised by the justices, but then allayed by the opinion's author, that author will likely feel greater freedom to include his or her chosen language.

Parrish in the Law Books

So, what about the different judges who wrote majority opinions in *Parrish*? Did they humanize the facts of *Parrish*, giving us a substantive understanding of the story of the case? Although Chapters 4 and 6 provide detailed analytical answers to that question, a brief response can be provided here. The first judicial opinion handed down in the *Parrish* litigation was issued by Judge William O. Parr from the bench of the main courtroom of the Chelan County Superior Court in Wenatchee in October 1935. His "findings of fact and conclusions of law" is the only judicial opinion, at any level of the case, which mentions both Elsie Parrish and the Cascadian Hotel by name:

1. That the defendant, West Coast Hotel Company, is a corporation, doing business as a hotel company, and in the conduct of said business operates the Cascadian Hotel in city of Wenatchee, Chelan County, Washington, and did at all times during the period referred to in plaintiffs' Complaint.
2. That about August of 1933, the plaintiff Elsie Parrish, whose name at that time was Elsie Lee, was employed by the defendant through its Manager, to work as a chambermaid in the Cascadian Hotel in Wenatchee . . . [17]

Neither chambermaid nor hotel is named by Chief Justice William J. Millard in his opinion for the Washington State Supreme Court, the first level of appeals courts to hear the case. All that we are told of them in that opinion is that "[f]rom August, 1933, to May, 1935, when she was discharged, plaintiff was in the employ of defendant hotel corporation as a chambermaid at an agreed wage which was less than the minimum weekly wage of $14.50 as fixed by the Industrial Welfare Commission under section 3, chapter 174, Laws 1913 (page 602)."[18]

Elsie Parrish is mentioned only once in Chief Justice Charles Evans Hughes's opinion for the U.S. Supreme Court. After a pro forma summary of the principal constitutional question, and a listing of the relevant provisions of the 1913 Washington State law, the only paragraph of Hughes's opinion pertaining to the facts of the case reads, in part, as follows: "The appellant conducts a hotel. The appellee, Elsie Parrish, was employed as a chambermaid and (with her husband) brought this suit to recover the difference between the wages paid her and the minimum wage fixed pursuant to the state law."[19] The remainder of the opinion reads like any other majority opinion. It is heavy on the relevant legal rules and tests, and analysis and discussion of principles of jurisprudence and pertinent precedents, while light on any factual information (let alone humanizing factual information).

In summary, in the judicial opinions that were written in *Parrish*, a "description of the parties" is noticeable by its absence. Most times those parties are "simply names on paper";[20] and sometimes, as in *Parrish*, they are not even that.

*   *   *

To a certain extent it is inevitable that "[r]ules, not persons, are the ordinary subject matter of legal study."[21] Legal rules bring order to society. They both prescribe and proscribe certain behavior, and are accompanied by enforcement and compliance mechanisms. As Judge John T. Noonan Jr. observed, that "rules should be the ordinary stuff of legal analysis follows from their indispensability for social control and social construction."[22] Society does not, however, benefit if the rules are constructed, applied, interpreted, and construed in an excessively formalistic manner. The law is created and administered by people, and its effects are felt not only by its creators and administrators, but also by every other member of society. The law is not a "machine that would go of itself" (to borrow Michael Kammen's phrase).[23] As Noonan says:

> Rules of law are formed by human beings to shape the attitude and conduct of human beings and applied by human beings to human beings. The human beings are persons. The rules are communications uttered, comprehended, and responded to by persons. They affect attitude and conduct as communications from persons to persons. They exist as rules—not as words on paper—in the minds of persons.[24]

When the law constructs "masks" (to use Noonan's term) as "ways of classifying individual human beings so that their humanity is hidden and disavowed," law arguably makes a strongly negative statement about the way in which it sees its relationship to people. And because the law is a human creation, those legal "masks" are ultimately human creations too. What does it say about a society when some of the members create rules that suppress or distort other members? As Judge Noonan explains, "Indispensable but insufficient to the legal process, living only in the minds of persons and applied only in the interaction of persons, rules cannot be the sole or principal object of legal study, legal history, and legal philosophy without distortion. *What is distorted is the place of persons in the process.*"[25]

In other words, a strong case can be made that Elle Woods was right, and Aristotle wrong. The law cannot simply be a construct of dispassionate reason.[26] One cannot just apply "pure reason to legal problems"; from such an approach is missing "the nourishment essential to a healthy and vital rationality"—the "passion" which is the "range of emotional and intuitive responses to a given set of facts or arguments, responses which often speed into our consciousness far ahead of the lumbering syllogisms of reason."[27]

Parrish in the Secondary Literature

Whether they are used by jurists within the confines of an official court opinion, by journalists in accounts written up during or after the various stages of the litigation in a case, or by historians reflecting upon a particular legal dispute at a particular moment in time, words that humanize the parties to a case by elucidating upon their life stories help to unmask the law. What we find with *West Coast Hotel v. Parrish* is that the stories of the lives of the participants have remained hidden from view in not only the official court opinions, but also the secondary literature.

Some scholarly analyses of the case provide more than fleeting references to the parties in the case.[28] However, prior to the publication of this book, the only substantive treatments of the subject matter were the articles that I published in 2012 in the *Journal of Supreme Court History*, and in 2017 in *The Confluence* (the magazine of the Wenatchee Valley Museum and Cultural Center).[29] When scholars mention the *Parrish* case, they do so because of the decision's jurisprudential implications, and not because they seek to educate us about the stories behind the case.[30] In so doing, they only tell us about what the Court, the *final* actor in the story, did. *Why*, *how*, and *when* the case began; *why* it worked its way through the lower courts in the way it did; *what* forces the parties encountered along the way; and *how* the decision affected (or did not affect) the lives of the parties involved are all ignored if the focus is solely upon the jurisprudential implications.

Indeed, such is the paucity of information about the *Parrish* stories, that on more than one occasion, when presenting iterations of this work at academic conferences, professors (from both law schools and political science departments) have revealed to me that they had always taught *Parrish* as a case involving a chambermaid who worked at the West Coast Hotel. This is an innocent and perfectly understandable mistake because Chief Justice Hughes simply tells us that "[t]he appellant conducts a hotel."[31] And when reprinting excerpts of that decision, the overwhelming majority of law school and undergraduate constitutional law textbooks, from which the aforementioned professors teach, do not provide accompanying commentary that tells the reader the name of the hotel.[32] For those curious about the case, a simple internet search easily reveals that Elsie Parrish worked for the Cascadian Hotel. However, imagine trying to find out that information before Google. The documents in the case do not provide the researcher with very much assistance. As will become clear, in so many ways the story of the Cascadian is just as important to the story of *Parrish* as the story of Elsie Parrish herself. However, the hotel's story is even less well known than the story of its former chambermaid. You can count on the fingers of one hand the number of law journal articles that actually mention that it was the "Cascadian Hotel" (and not, for example, the "West Coast Hotel") for whom Elsie worked.[33]

The Roadmap of This Book

That story of the Cascadian began in 1928 when the initial plans were formulated to bring a brand new, state-of-the-art hotel to the city of Wenatchee. Told in chapter 1, it is a story of a hotel that opened to great fanfare at the beginning of August 1929. It was not until two months later that the operators realized that this was an inauspicious time in American history to embark upon a new business venture. The onset of the Great Depression notwithstanding, the Cascadian immediately became an integral part of the community. Over time, its role as a Main Street meeting place only strengthened. Staffed as it was, by members of the region's hospitality industry whose prestigious reputations preceded them, it is easy to understand why, when Elsie initiated her litigation in 1935, she forever doomed her chances of working in Wenatchee again.

Initiate, she did, though; therefore, chapter 1 also explains what life was like for Elsie (and her family) before she came to the North Central region of Washington State, and why that life shaped her desire to gamble with her employment opportunities during the depths of the Depression.

Chapter 2 then follows the story of the 1913 law, situating it within the sociopolitical context of (generally) other Progressive Era developments and (specifically) the minimum wages for women movement that had strong roots in the Pacific Northwest. Before examining the *Parrish* litigation in detail (in chapters 4, 5, and 6), chapter 3 explains the principal legal decisions that constituted the constitutional landscape that the *Parrish* litigants had to traverse.

After analyzing the U.S. Supreme Court's decision in *Parrish*, chapter 6 focuses on the way in which it generated a "flood" of minimum wage lawsuits filed by women workers in Seattle.

These chapters are followed by a conclusion, and then an epilogue; the latter allows the reader to trace the fortunes of the Cascadian Hotel until 1971 when it ceased to be a place of lodging for visitors to Wenatchee; and to learn of the paths taken by the myriad people who made appearances in the preceding chapters. That cast of characters includes, of course, Elsie Parrish, who died in Anaheim, California, on April 3, 1980 (five days after the forty-third anniversary of *Parrish*). She died surrounded by her family, neighbors, and acquaintances, who were for the most part unaware that their mild-mannered friend made American constitutional history in 1937 in a way that led her to be dubbed the "Minimum Pay Law Joan d'Arc" of Omak, Washington.[34]

* * *

As part of her inaugural address in January 1991, Oregon governor Barbara Roberts observed that "each generation has but one chance to be judged by future generations, and this is our time."[35] Elsie Parrish—Barbara's great aunt—was part of a generation for whom the prime of life was unmistakably defined by the Great Depression. In Wenatchee, in 1935, Elsie's decision to bring suit against the Cascadian Hotel was one that would earn her the judgment of future generations. By contrast, the focus of the next chapter is the judgment that her litigation decision brought upon her by her *own* generation. It was a judgment that compelled her and Ernie to relocate to Omak in 1936. In November of that year, when journalists sought her out, they found that time had been kind to Elsie Parrish. Her wholesome good looks, and head of carefully coiffed naturally warm brunette hair, in which one could not find a gray hair, belied the hard life she had led.[36]

1 "For each generation has but one chance to be judged"

Women's world-old timidity due to their inferior strength has gone with them into the industrial world. Thus protective laws for women are harder to enforce because of their dislike of a fight and of the notoriety attached to a court action. Where they have others dependent upon them, their spirit of self-sacrifice inclines them to put up with abuse rather than to subject their dependents to possible suffering by refusing to suffer themselves.

—*Sister Miriam Theresa*, Bulletin of the Women's Bureau, No. 90 *(1931)*

Sister Miriam Theresa devoted her life to social reform and education in Oregon and played a central role in the advocacy for, and administration of, the minimum wage law for women enacted by that state in 1913.[1] However, as this quotation demonstrates, Sister Theresa was very much aware that one could not simply enact a minimum wages for women law at this moment in American history and expect it to break down the roles that women, and women workers, traditionally played. Women were still widely viewed as the inferior sex, and this made it easier for (predominantly male) employers to coerce them into accepting unfair terms of employment. They were safe in the knowledge that their female employees would not challenge those terms because, as Sister Theresa observed, women "dislike[d] . . . a fight and . . . the notoriety attached to a court action," and had "others dependent upon them . . . [which] inclines them to put up with abuse rather than to subject their dependents to possible suffering."[2]

Elsie Parrish ignored both of these barriers. By choosing to sue the Cascadian Hotel, she ran toward, rather than away from a "fight," and "the notoriety" that would surely come with taking one of Wenatchee's most prominent employers to court. Why Elsie made this choice, and what she was risking, is the subject of this chapter.

The Murray Family

Elsie's father, Edward H. Murray, was born on December 17, 1862, in the rural township of Hire, in McDonough County in western Illinois, the fourth and final child of Alexander Hamilton Murray (who went by Hamilton) and Elizabeth (Sullivan) Murray. Like all their neighbors, the Murrays were farmers. On August 19, 1880, four months shy of his seventeenth birthday, in a ceremony performed in Kansas, Edward married Emma Sarah Sallee. Emma was also born and raised in Illinois; although, she hailed from Donovan, a small town two hundred miles east of Hire, close to the Indiana border. Emma was born on December 28, 1864, the eighth of Samuel and Elizabeth (Clear) Sallee's nine children. She would never know two of her older brothers, Joel and William, who both died in the Civil War. She entered the world six months after eighteen-year-old William, a private in the Illinois infantry, was killed in action at Big Shanty when General Sherman took that location during the Atlanta Campaign.

Born on March 17, 1899, in Reno County in central Kansas, the farmland that she would call home until she was almost fifteen, Elsie Deliah Murray was the tenth (and last) child born to Edward and Emma.[3] Six of those children lived into adulthood (beyond the age of sixteen). Elsie experienced familial tragedies—and the disruption they bring—at a very young age. Her mother became a widow, and Elsie and her siblings fatherless, when Edward was killed in a horrific farming accident in July 1900. As the local newspaper reported, it was "[o]ne of the most deplorable and horrible accidents which has ever occurred in Reno county."[4] This was an ominous sign for those local readers of the article, readers who were

FIG. 1.1   Edward and Emma Murray with three of their children (*from left to right*) Minnie, Grover, and Earl. Courtesy of Bill Murray.

intimately familiar with the hard work and occupational hazards of the scrappy agricultural existence of this time and place in American history. The report of the accident makes for gruesome reading, and Edward's death came as "a great shock to the people of Bell, his home township, and to many of the citizens all over the county":

> When the accident occurred Mr. Murray had walked across the top of the thresher. The cap over the cylinder had been removed by some one, a fact of which Mr. Murray was ignorant. The top of the machine was covered with straw and believing that the cylinder was covered the owner of the thresher stepped directly into the cylinder while the machine was in motion. Instantly his leg was nearly torn from his body. With almost superhuman strength he strugled [*sic*] from the machine and had pulled himself free from the cylinder before any help reached him.

This might have been "a circumstance which seemed a miracle to those who witnessed it," but it was not enough to save the life of Edward. The only miracle (if one can call it that) is that Edward lived for only another few hours (in what must have been excruciating pain) before finally succumbing to the extent of his injuries.[5]

Emma suddenly found herself having to raise seven children on her own. Life did not get any easier when, less than a year later, death again came knocking at the family door when Elsie's sixteen-year-old brother, Grover Leroy (Roy), the de facto head of the household, was taken in a drowning accident. The friend with whom he was swimming in the local millpond concluded that Roy, a good swimmer, must have succumbed to a sudden cramp.[6] Elsie's brother was buried alongside their father in the Lerado town cemetery. Although Emma was an exceptionally strong and determined woman, until she remarried in 1907, she found it necessary to rely upon the support of the Bell Township community for help in raising her frontier family.

When Samuel Sallee, Emma's father, passed away on January 20, 1909, his death set in motion a chain of legal events whose outcome limited the already sparse financial options of Emma and her second husband, Blair Corley. Samuel's will stipulated that his Kansas homestead (and/or any proceeds from its sale) be divided equally among his six surviving children (of whom Emma was the youngest). Potentially standing in the way of Emma's inheritance was her brother-in-law's judgment against her in an earlier legal case. After the death of Edward, Emma inherited his 160 acres of land in Bell Township. The immediate neighbor to her north was her father, who also owned 160 acres. To the immediate northwest were eighty acres owned by another member of the Murray family.[7] It appears that Emma had difficulty maintaining her late husband's land. She was forced to transfer to the Penalosa State Bank all her rights to the land she had inherited from her father; this was in order to help satisfy other debts. This made a bad financial situation worse for Emma (and Blair) because of the money she also owed her brother-in-law, James F. Murray. After Samuel's death, James sought to recoup some of that money by exercising a lien against the inherited property. The bank (which now owned the property) secured an injunction, contending that Emma had only ever had rights to the proceeds if the land were sold; she herself had never had a right to the property (and the concomitant right to sell that land). The Kansas Supreme Court finally resolved the resulting lawsuit in 1912, interpreting Samuel's will as intending to extend physical ownership of the land to his children. This handed a victory to James, who was now able to exercise that lien against the land adjudged to have been lawfully owned by Emma at the time she transferred rights to it to the bank.[8]

The Lee Family

Named after General Jesse L. Reno, a Union army commander killed during the Civil War in 1862 at the Battle of South Mountain, at the turn of the century Reno was one of the most populous counties in Kansas, home to approximately thirty thousand people.[9] The county seat, Hutchinson, accounted for one-third of those residents. The remainder of families—disproportionately farmers— were scattered throughout myriad rural locations such as Lerado or Bell Township. In 1910, the census for Bell Township was taken by Vernon Lee, whose family, like the overwhelming majority of their neighbors, migrated to the Great Plains from the Midwest (the Lee family hailed from Ohio). At the Murray home, Vernon enumerated the details of forty-five-year-old Emma, her second husband Blair, and Blair's four stepchildren, including ten-year-old Elsie.[10]

In neighboring Langdon Township, James Holland was gathering census data on his allocated residences. At one house he took the details of Noah and Mary Lee, and their two teenage sons, Roy and Ray W.[11] Less than five years later Roy would marry Elsie Murray. We do not know how Elsie and Roy met, but what we do know is that Elsie and Roy clearly knew each other when, in 1913, Roy left Kansas with his parents and his brother Ray, bound for parts northwest. By early 1914 the Lees had crossed the border into Montana, reaching the Bighorn River. Shortly thereafter, they pressed on to their final destination—Coffee Creek, a newly established community built around a station on the Milwaukee Road (the Chicago, Milwaukee, St. Paul, and Pacific Railroad). This was a foreign destination for the Lees, but not for the Corley-Murrays, who followed their Kansan neighbors west a few months later. The Corley-Murray family members were relocating to a family homestead located on the outskirts of Coffee Creek. Elsie's elder brothers Fred and Earl had established the Murray homestead in 1909.[12]

FIG. 1.2   Roy and Elsie Lee. Used with permission of the Lee family.

With the written consent of her mother,[13] Elsie married Roy Lee in 1914. Although the marriage records have not survived, all the evidence points to the couple exchanging vows in Big Horn, after which Elsie left her parents behind and headed two hundred and fifty miles farther into Big Sky Country, finally making a home with her new husband (and in-laws) in Coffee Creek. It would be some time before Elsie would once again have the comfort of close proximity to her parents. In the meantime, the teenage Elsie faced a tough life, juggling the demands of being a mother, wife to an alcoholic spouse, and daughter-in-law. (For the entirety of their married life Roy and Elsie lived with Roy's parents.) And what a demanding life this was, because when Elsie and Roy Lee welcomed their first child into the world on March 12, 1915, Elsie was five days shy of her sixteenth birthday. Vera Ethel was the first of Elsie and Roy's seven children. (Six lived into adulthood.) Their four girls and three boys were born between 1915 and 1928.

Montana: "Too Poor to Move, But Always Rich"

Over the course of four decades spanning the end of the nineteenth century and the beginning of the twentieth century, Montana experienced a truly dramatic population increase (see graph 1.1). The passage of the Homestead Act of 1862 helps to explain why the number of residents of the territory (Montana did not gain statehood until 1889) almost doubled between 1870 and 1880. However, the maximum land claim under that law was 160 acres. Not until the passage of the Desert Land Act of 1877, which better addressed the needs of those who wanted to farm the more arid western land (such as that found on the plains of Montana) by permitting land claims up to 640 acres, did the area's population explode, increasing by over 250 percent between 1880 and 1890.[14] At the dawn of the twentieth century, these governmental policies, together with settlement campaigns such as that conducted by the Great Northern Railway led by James J. Hill, federally supported efforts to bring better irrigation to the region, and other technological advances all helped to make farming this landscape more attractive, thereby fueling further population growth (albeit at a more modest pace).[15]

The Murray and Lee families were part of a significant wave of migrants at the end of the first decade of the twentieth century who were attracted by all the above factors but also, importantly, by the enactment of the Enlarged Homestead Act in 1909. This new law did exactly what its name suggested—it doubled the amount of *free* land available to homesteading claimants from 160 to 320 acres. Elsie's brother Earl married Elmo Smail in Penalosa,

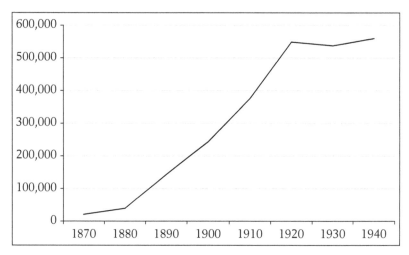

GRAPH 1.1   Population change in Montana, 1870–1940. Compiled using U.S. Census Bureau data.

Kansas, in January 1908, and the couple moved to Montana the following year, taking advantage of the new law and establishing a homestead in Fergus County, in the town that would become Coffee Creek.[16] Earl's brother, E. V. (Stub) Murray, followed the next year.[17] The Lee family followed not far behind. Noah and Mary (Roy's parents) lived in Coffee Creek until their deaths in 1945 and 1947 respectively. The Lee and Murray families contributed to the 114,620 homestead claims filed in Montana between 1909 and 1923, claims for approximately 25 million acres of land. They were part of what Michael P. Malone, Richard B. Roeder, and William L. Lang describe, in their history of the state, as "[t]he great Montana land rush."[18]

These two families were typical homesteaders. Many of the farmers attracted by the 1877 law neither improved the land nor stayed for the long term;[19] and the subsequent buying up of land by the railroads and other speculators—which amounted to the acquisition of approximately nine times as many plots of farmland as those purchased/claimed by "bona fide farmer[s]"[20]—oftentimes had profoundly negative consequences (both short and long term).[21] The Murrays and Lees, however, were in this for the long haul, come what may.

Although Elsie rarely talked about the time she spent living in Montana,[22] it is possible to establish a picture of what life must have been like for her during those fifteen years. This is because there were certain things that almost all homesteaders had to deal with—such as unscrupulous land speculators (who all too frequently made promises to their unsuspecting clients that would not—or could not—be delivered upon), a scarcity of basic necessities such as water (for both irrigation and drinking) and wood (for construction and fuel), the unpredictability of mother nature, the impact of federal government policies, and national and international events.[23] Yes, the Murray and Lee families came to Montana with a significant advantage over a great many of their fellow homesteaders who were lured out west by the promise of agricultural riches, because they were already well acquainted with the trials and tribulations associated with farming frontier land.[24] However, that experience did not make one immune to the effects of the aforementioned challenges; all it did was to sometimes make it easier to cope with these hardships.

It is also important to remember (although for a methodological rather than historiographical reason) that *female* homesteaders had to endure these financial, meteorological, political, and subsistence-related challenges just as much, if not more so, than their male family members. As Susan Armitage emphasizes, we must disabuse ourselves of the notion that the West, at this time in American history, was "Hisland . . . a magnificent western landscape, under perpetually cloudless western skies," wherein "a cast of heroic characters engages in dramatic combat." That is the stuff of "folklore: the legendary Wild West" where "women . . . are strictly stereotyped" into "three common images: the refined lady, the helpmate, and the bad woman."[25] Armitage further describes these categories in the following way:

> The lady, who may be a schoolteacher, a missionary, or merely a woman with some civilized tastes, is defined as being too genteel for the rough and ready West. She is either uncomfortable, unhappy, or is driven literally crazy by the frontier. Apparently the only way she can prove her gentility is to become a victim. On the other hand, the strong and uncomplaining helpmate adapts to the West, but in the process becomes a work-worn superwoman, losing all her individuality. The bad woman has both glamour and power, but loses them along with her life as she comes rapidly to her appropriate end—a bad one.[26]

Everything that we as historians *know* about the realities of life in the American West in the early decades of the twentieth century (which is distinct from everything that many people have *wanted to believe* about that region) tells us that categorizing the life of western women in this way is wholly inadequate. Elsie Parrish's life in Montana cannot be shoehorned into any one of these boxes, and there is no indication that this makes her western life experiences particularly unusual. Her life, as a hardworking frontier mother and wife, should be considered the rule; the women of "Hisland" are the exceptions to that rule.

In the 1970s, on and off during her teenage years and into early adulthood, Debra Parrish Stewart lived with Elsie and Ernest (known to the family as Ernie), her great-grandparents, in Southern California. Her memories of those years tell us much about what homesteading life must have been like for Elsie in Montana decades earlier, and they serve to reinforce Armitage's observation that the frontier women of "folklore" were just that; myth rather than reality. Debra recalls that Elsie enjoyed and excelled at cooking and crocheting, and could easily turn her hand (using the sewing machine she took everywhere) to making clothes.[27] From an early age Elsie also developed a passion for baseball, a sport that the entire family took very seriously.[28] Two of Elsie's older brothers, Earl and Fred Murray, were mainstays of the Penalosa, Kansas, baseball team, and Elsie frequently joined them for pick-up games.[29] This family tradition was maintained in Montana, where Earl, Fred, and another brother, Samuel, were frequent starters (at second base and in the outfield, respectively) for the Coffee Creek team.[30]

For the Murrays, baseball was an important part of their homesteading social life. Just like their neighbors, the Murrays and Lees made it a point to break up the monotony of their working days, weeks, and months—dominated by weather and the agricultural calendar—with vibrant "[s]ocial gatherings [that] were well spaced and looked forward to for much time in advance."[31] As Katherine Harris explains, "Community-wide family attendance characterized the secular as well as the religious gatherings of homesteaders. Dances, picnics, box suppers, spelling bees, baseball games, card parties, 'literaries,' and other events involved the whole family."[32] While Harris's case study was northeastern Colorado between 1873 and 1920, there is every reason to believe that her observations are equally applicable to homesteading life during that same time period in Montana.[33]

*　*　*

Whenever he recalled life in Montana in the 1920s and 1930s, Jim Sargent's father summarized it in this simple but meaningful way: "We were too poor to move, but always rich." Writing of his parents' struggles to make ends meet in Big Sky Country, Sargent observes that "[t]he depression, drought, and accompanying despair put people under challenges that are hard, if not impossible, to comprehend today."[34] The 1910s brought failed federal government wartime agriculture price policies that ultimately led to inflation and then a postwar financial crash. Subsequently, beginning in 1917, there was a cycle of devastating natural disasters—droughts, followed by, "[i]n 1919, perhaps the most calamitous year," forest fires, and "hordes of gophers and swarms of locusts."[35]

For Elsie and Roy, homesteading life became particularly challenging in 1927 and 1928. On September 28, 1927, tragedy struck when eight-year-old Glen died of an internal abdominal hernia.[36] Almost nine months later, Elsie and Roy welcomed their seventh and final child into the world when (Lester) Dean was born on May 30, 1928 in Coffee Creek. For reasons that remain unknown, shortly thereafter Elsie and Roy moved their family approximately 650 miles west to Nappel (later renamed Moses Lake) in Washington State. They left Montana just in time, because 1931 was a truly miserable year for that state's residents (including the Murray and Lee family members that Elsie and Roy left behind). Half of the state's counties sought Red Cross aid in 1931, and things only got worse as the decade progressed, with "more searing droughts and frightening, dust-laden winds" wreaking havoc in 1934, 1936, and 1937.[37] Sometime between 1930 and 1933, the Lee family once again relocated, this time making the seventy-mile journey northwest to Wenatchee. Perhaps Elsie felt she had arrived in a place that would give her family the comfort, shelter, and support they needed. Or perhaps the stresses of the Great Depression proved to be the final straw for her, because by 1933 she had divorced the alcoholic man to whom she had been tied since she was a teenager.[38]

The Great Depression Comes to Wenatchee:
When Dollars No Longer Grew on Trees

When Elsie arrived in Wenatchee in the early 1930s, she found a city that was slow to be affected by the Great Depression. In 1930 Wenatchee was rightly described as "about the most prosperous community in the northwest,"[39] and the Washington State Apple Blossom Festival, held every year in Wenatchee beginning in 1920, set attendance records in 1931. As late as the middle of 1931 Wenatchee was still booming; the self-described "Apple Capital of the World" was the exciting "big-city" destination that children from the surrounding rural valleys looked forward to visiting. Bruce Foxworthy recalls that "[t]he multistory buildings and the expanse of grassy park in front of the courthouse seemed so grand."[40]

Just as in Montana, the railroad was responsible for the establishment of numerous communities in Washington, including Wenatchee. As Chris Rader and Mark Behler explain: "The coming of the Great Northern Railway Company to Wenatchee in 1892 was probably the most significant event in the town's history. . . . From St. Paul, Minnesota, across the Rockies to Spokane, the tracks crossed the Columbia River at Rock Island (a few miles south of Wenatchee), paralleled the river through Wenatchee, then veered westward along the Wenatchee River and across Stevens Pass to Seattle."[41] In 1900 approximately 450 people lived in Wenatchee. Over the course of the first decade of the twentieth century, that population increased by almost 800 percent; thereafter, the population grew by 56 percent between 1910 and 1920, and then again by 84 percent between 1920 and 1930 (see graph 1.2).

By 1914 the value of apple orchard land in Wenatchee had skyrocketed to a staggering average of $1,925 per acre (approximately $50,000 in 2020). It was little wonder that the Wenatchee Commercial Club produced booster brochures describing the city as "The Home of the Big Red Apple, Where Dollars Grow on Trees." The brochures proclaimed that Wenatchee was "a place to make money with less effort and worry than in other occupations, and with a moderate investment a good income for life can be obtained. An apple orchard provides as sure income as government bonds and more than 25 percent on the investment."[42]

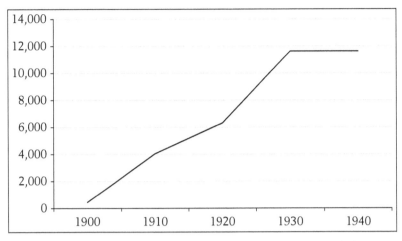

GRAPH 1.2   Population change in Wenatchee, 1900–1940. Compiled using U.S. Census Bureau data.

The first commercial apple orchard was planted in Wenatchee in 1884, but it is the arrival of the railroad, eight years later, that explains the subsequent economic growth of the area. The railroad opened up endless possibilities for apple growers. In 1890 Washington and Oregon combined to produce 622,000 barrels of apples; by 1917 that number had increased tenfold. Wenatchee apples were first shipped by rail across Stevens Pass to Seattle in 1901. Within ten years approximately 2,400 carloads of apples left the city in a single year (with nearly six times as many heading east than were sent to the Pacific Coast). Of course, the strength of this local apple-driven economy could only be maintained if the national economy stayed strong.[43]

The impact of the Great Depression on Wenatchee was ultimately devastating because at the time Wenatchee was "supported almost 100% by agriculture."[44] As the nationwide market for fresh produce declined, agriculturally reliant communities were hit particularly hard. In October 1931 Clyde Pangborn and Hugh Herndon Jr. used Wenatchee as the site for landing their plane, the Miss Veedol, at the end of their successful quest to make the first nonstop flight across the Pacific Ocean. (Landing there was one of their backup plans.) Although their exploits "put Wenatchee on the map," the accompanying hoopla could not stop the Great

Depression from coming to town. The effects began to be felt that autumn as apple prices finally fell. The city had no choice but to cancel the 1932 Apple Blossom Festival. This was a devastating blow for an area "made" and "maintain[ed]" by apples, an area "surrounded by a sea of orchards, covered in spring with a pink foam of blossoms, mile upon mile, filling the valleys and covering the slopes."[45]

In 1930 approximately 10 percent of the 11,627 people living in Wenatchee were out of work; by January 1935 the unemployment rate had jumped to 24 percent.[46] Despite the fact that a quarter of the area's workers were now jobless, in August the *Washington State Labor News* proudly reported on the recent upswing of union activity that more favorable "business conditions" had brought to the Wenatchee Valley.[47] In late October 1935, however, a sudden deep freeze destroyed many of the area's orchard crops, giving residents of the Wenatchee Valley every reason to be far less optimistic about the prospects for an imminent economic recovery.[48]

Elsie Parrish was one of the thousands of Wenatcheeites who found themselves unemployed in the fall of 1935. She had been unable to find work after being let go by the Cascadian Hotel in May (having worked there since August 1933), and her employment prospects were not helped by her decision to sue that mighty institution.

Built in 1929 at a cost of $500,000, the ten-story Cascadian, an impressive mixture of Art Moderne and Beaux Arts styles, was the tallest building in town (and retains that elevation honor to this day). After its grand opening it quickly became a landmark institution in the area, and an important part of the social life of Wenatcheeites. Across the country, "[v]irtually no new hotels were built for six years after 1930; occupancy averaged 51 percent in 1932, the lowest in the industry's history; and 80 percent of the nation's hotels were in receivership by 1935."[49] During the Depression the Cascadian bucked this trend and became the go-to gathering place for events in Wenatchee. Like other Main Street hotels, it was "thought of as [a] community center," somewhere "to conduct business, discuss politics, and generally socialize."[50] It was a building everyone was invested in, because it was a building that the entire community played a role in building. And that community was not about to see its reputation torn down by one lowly, *former* chambermaid, "who was not, by any measure, in a position of influence" in Wenatchee.[51]

The Cascadian: An "Outstanding Small City Hotel"

When J. Edward Ferguson, one of the pioneer settlers of Wenatchee, rode into the valley for the first time in 1897, from atop his horse he saw a great expanse of territory laid out before him, territory upon which a small frontier outpost was beginning to take shape. Today, Wenatchee is a vibrant city that is home to approximately thirty-five thousand people. For all its growth, however, its basic layout continues to be dictated by the same two features that dominated the landscape in the late nineteenth century: the Columbia River and the railroad tracks that run parallel to the river.

John Jakle and Keith Sculle do not mention Wenatchee in their book about Main Street hotels, but their description of the typical layout of a small railroad boomtown easily applies to the Apple City:

> A town's Main Street either paralleled the tracks, often a block or two away, or crossed the tracks on the perpendicular. Most railroad-era hotels were located in business districts close to but, nonetheless, comfortably distanced from the smoke and noise of railroading. Although distances might be short, hotel-owned, horse-drawn "hacks" met all trains to solicit business and, importantly, convey would-be guests quickly and conveniently to a hotel's front door.[52]

In Wenatchee, such transportation existed courtesy of the Bell Hotel, which opened in 1897. In addition to operating a horse and cart transportation service to take guests to and from the Great Northern railroad depot, the Bell used a thrice-daily dinner triangle to inform the lodgers that their meals were ready for consumption.[53]

During the rapid growth of the late nineteenth and early twentieth century, numerous hotels sprang up in Wenatchee. In 1914 it was home to thirteen; by 1928 that number had risen to twenty-five.[54] For many years, the grandest hotel in town was the Wenatchee Hotel on Wenatchee Avenue, the town's main thoroughfare. That changed in 1929 when the Cascadian was constructed at the corner of North Wenatchee Avenue and First Street.[55] Thirty-two years after he arrived in Wenatchee, Edward Ferguson became one of the first people to stay at the Cascadian. "I never expected to live to see such a magnificent hotel . . . actually built in Wenatchee," he told the *Wenatchee Daily World*.[56] Ferguson was not the only Wenatcheeite in awe of the new building, as the opening ceremonies demonstrated.

The human spider that scaled the façade of the Cascadian Hotel was the featured attraction of the Cascadian's opening. To the gathered crowd's gasps and shouts of delight, he/she (the spider's name is not known) topped the official festivities on August 9, 1929, literally and figuratively. Shielding their eyes from the summer sun, the town's residents craned their necks for a better view of the gravity-defying attraction. Hundreds of sweltering onlookers marveled at the spider's ability to ascend the ten stories effortlessly and seemingly immune to the effects of the 98-degree heat. When the stunt reached its spectacular climax, it drew whoops of terrified excitement, accompanied by a musical crescendo courtesy of the Washington State Band and the American Legion drum and bugle corps, which performed at the ceremony for over an hour. A majority of the crowd were either first- or second-generation pioneers, a hardy group who had seen and heard many things while experiencing Wenatchee's growth. Yet, it was not every day that a new building opened with such an elaborate ceremony, let alone one that culminated with the spider performing a handstand on the flagpole, 127 feet up.[57] The Cascadian was widely viewed as "a success from the day it opened."[58] Therefore, Elsie Parrish's decision to sue its parent company in 1935 was a bold and brave move; she and her husband were gambling with their futures in Wenatchee.

A Hotel Is Born

The Wenatchee City Council gave its formal blessing to the hotel early in 1929. A number of prominent residents had already pledged to purchase $50,000 in preferred stock from the hotel's operating company, and the council was satisfied that a further $20,000 could be found from other funding sources. The West Coast Hotel Company duly filed its Articles of Incorporation with state authorities in Olympia, and purchased the plot of land where the Cascadian would be built.[59] As Grover C. Winn, owner of the Seattle-based investment firm backing the development, observed in a boosterish January 1929 article in the *Daily World*, there were grand plans for the hotel. "Wenatchee is ideally located for the handling of conventions and with the building of this new hotel, the

city will be in a position to invite and entertain many of the organizations, which, because of lack of accommodations, have been
compelled to go to other cities."[60] This was an accurate assessment,
for over the course of the next four decades regional newspapers
regularly reported on the large number of meetings of community
and civic groups, and conferences of out-of-town organizations,
held at the Cascadian.

The groundbreaking ceremony for the ten stories, 133 guest
rooms, coffee shop, and social hall was held on February 27, 1929.[61]
By April, the building finally had a name. After much speculation,
and "hundreds" of suggestions, the investors settled upon "The
Cascadian."[62] Like so many of the names given to American Main
Street hotels constructed in the first three decades of the twentieth century, this was deliberately designed to have a local and/or
regional theme.[63]

"And Now We'll Go into . . . The Cascadian"

On Tuesday, August 13, 1929, for those Wenatcheeites who had
been unable to attend the Cascadian's grand opening, the *Daily
World* produced a thirty-page special edition devoted to boosting
the hotel. In between congratulatory advertisements from almost
one hundred merchants[64] were articles describing and illustrat-
ing every last detail of the building, its contents, and its principal
staff.[65] That special edition shows us why it was not just the building, but also its features—two in particular—that made it a source
of regional pride. Neither of these features will strike the twenty-
first-century reader or hotel guest as remarkable. For their time,
however, they made the Cascadian a very important addition to
the area, a local landmark whose reputation would be threatened
by Elsie Parrish's lawsuit.[66]

The first standout feature of the Cascadian was its innovative
air conditioning system. From the foyer into which they entered,
visitors to the Cascadian saw an impressive and sophisticated lobby
featuring a gleaming floor of terrazzo. They were greeted by comfortable armchairs in which they could sit and rest in a relaxing and
"metropolitan" atmosphere, an environment that the Cascadian's
designers and operators took immense satisfaction in maintaining
at a year-round, comfortable temperature of seventy-five degrees
using a unique air-cooling system which was undoubtedly "one of

the greatest features of the hostelry."[67] Today we take air conditioning for granted, but prior to the 1920s it was primarily used in factories, "where its role was to produce not human comfort but manufacturing consistency." A century ago, it was very rare to find it installed in places of public accommodation.[68] Five years after the Cascadian opened, Ray W. Clark, the hotel's first manager, was still able to reliably inform the trade magazine *Hotel Monthly* that this was "one of the few one hundred percent air-conditioned hotels on the Pacific Coast."[69]

Using an analogy that many of its readers could understand, the *Daily World* observed that the system, involving two air washers, two exhaust fans, and one roof-mounted supply fan, "resembles that of an apple washing machine with a large spray on the inside through which the air is forced." The supply fan brought air into the washers, from which emerged the fresh, washed, cooled air that circulated throughout the hotel, before being removed by the exhaust fans. Operating constantly (and able to be converted into a heating system for the winter), this technology ensured a "complete change of air" in the hotel every sixty seconds (the washer water was changed every four days), and guests could adjust the temperatures of their rooms using the individualized controls installed in "every bedroom and every public room, including the basement."[70]

The second important feature of the Cascadian was its coffee shop. Following the lead of other hotels, when it opened, the hotel only had a coffee shop. (It later added a restaurant—the famed "Apple Box.")[71] The elegance and style of the rest of the hotel (including the terrazzo floor) was seamlessly carried over into the coffee shop. With mahogany fixtures, the "model" coffee shop could seat 152, and was divided into three sections—a bar area, a section of dining tables and chairs, and, toward the rear, an area furnished with "tables with comfortable arm chairs."[72]

For the average Main Street hotel that functioned as a vital social center for its community, the coffee shop was frequently the hub of that center. Just as in many small towns today, where one can find small groups of friends, acquaintances, business partners, and politicians using their local coffee shop, sandwich bar, or diner to conduct business, it was the Main Street hotel coffee shop to which such people gravitated in the 1920s and 1930s. Prohibition made it essential that hoteliers replace the "male-dominated spaces where too often wayward behavior was conveniently blinked at" as people enjoyed the "vices of life," with a "home and club atmosphere." Coffee shops were the dominant solution, and this was certainly true of the one housed at the Cascadian.[73] It became yet another way for the hotel to cement its stature as a pillar of the community.

Under the watchful eye of James Kinsella, the chief of the coffee shop when the hotel first opened, guests ate the food prepared by executive chef Bill Dal Bon, who came to the Cascadian with an impressive résumé that included extensive culinary experience as a hotel chef.[74] Dal Bon and his staff paid close attention to local tastes. They proudly maintained a policy of serving "common American food," not subjecting their diners to the faddish "'French' food" all too likely to dominate the culinary offerings of other institutions, notably those on the East Coast.[75] And, as the menus that have survived from the early to mid-1930s tell us, one could always expect to choose from dishes that proudly used local ingredients.[76]

A Hotelier Comes to Town

The Cascadian was neither the first hotel to come to Wenatchee, nor the only game in town. However, it was expected to be the grandest lodgings for many years to come; and the decision to hire Ray Clark as its first manager made a strong statement about the investors' expectations. After all, one would not bring a half-a-million-dollar hotel to a relatively small town in the middle of rural Washington State unless one believed it would succeed. The Cascadian was immediately expected to establish a reputation as a state-of-the-art establishment that could attract visitors through its attention to detail and outstanding service. *Hotel Monthly* announced Clark's hiring in its March 1929 issue and observed that he would "devote all of his time to supervising the construction and equipment of" the new hotel.[77]

Starting out in 1907 as a fifteen-year-old page at the Oregon (now the Benson) Hotel in Portland, Clark devoted his life to the hotel business and became "a live wire in his section" of the country.[78] A Washingtonian by birth, he rarely strayed far from the Pacific Northwest. After school, he worked as a bellboy at the Seattle Hotel in Seattle before returning to the Oregon Hotel. This was a "cruel world" to work in, but Clark was "incidentally learning the value of a dollar and acquiring some knowledge of the hotel business." In the 1910s he spent eighteen months working in San

Francisco, but he soon gravitated back north, landing in 1914 at the Fry Hotel in Seattle. At the Multnomah Hotel in Portland, he worked his way up from mail clerk to an assistant managerial position in charge of publicity and promotion. Over the next decade he held three more managerial positions—at the Umpqua Hotel (in Roseburg, Oregon, and where he also oversaw catering), the Olympian (Olympia, Washington), and the Winthrop (Tacoma, Washington).[79]

For the five years that he worked there, Clark was fiercely loyal to the Cascadian. Early on in his career he developed a well-defined understanding of the way a hotel should be run. In 1921, while working at the Hotel Umpqua, he wrote a letter to the editor of the trade publication *The Hotel World*, in which he argued that hotel managers should hold regular meetings with their department heads, and that the department heads should hold regular meetings with their employees. This would improve income and guests' favorable views and ratings.[80] Clark brought this organizational, tight-ship mentality to the Cascadian, a mentality that would brook minimal dissent and strongly encourage one to be the consummate team player.

To Ray Clark, the Cascadian was more than just the next position on his career ladder. He sought to ensure that the hotel survived the nation's economic crisis and constantly served as a booster for the establishment whose financial well-being he had a three-pronged interest in maintaining. Refusing to comply with the requirements of the state's minimum wage law for his female employees was one way for Clark to balance the books of both the Cascadian and the West Coast Hotel Company. In so doing, he protected (a) his employment, (b) the stock that he held in the West Coast Hotel Company (by virtue of being its secretary), and (c) the employment of his family—his wife, Kathryn, was in charge of the housekeeping department, and for a period of time his mother-in-law, Edith Baldwin, was employed as a secretary at the Cascadian.[81] It was the Cascadian's second manager, Willard E. Abel, who on May 11, 1935, made what turned out to be the fateful decision to terminate the employment of Elsie Parrish.[82] A "tall, debonair" man who was "strong on financing, tax structures, and insurance requirements," Abel held some prominent community positions in Wenatchee (such as president of the Toastmasters club—which held its regular meetings at the Cascadian).[83] However, there is every reason to believe that when Abel fired Elsie, he was simply following the company policies put in place by Clark.

In the fall of 1936 Clark was one of eleven men that Harry Gowman appointed to the newly formed Executive Committee of the Washington State Hotel Association (WSHA), of which Gowman was president. When the group met in Seattle that October, Elsie Parrish's pending Cascadian litigation was one of the most pressing items on the agenda. *Hotel News of the West*, "The Official Organ of the Washington State Hotel Association," would later comment that "[p]robably all hotel operators are familiar with the case."[84] It is worth quoting, at length, from that magazine's report of the October 1936 meeting:

> They discussed the appeal of the minimum wage case . . . taking an hour to consider all the different phases of this problem, finally deciding to go through with the appeal, which has been set for the week of December 7th. The question of financing this matter was the most perplexing phase that had to be considered, but a plan was finally worked out to finance it out of the regular dues making it unnecessary to call on the members to put up any additional funds. This decision was arrived at after a most careful study of the income and expenses of the association, which required an analysis of every item. By maintaining the present income and curtailing on certain items, a sufficient amount of money will be available to take care of this expense, amounting to $2500, without asking any member to put up more than his regular dues.[85]

There is no evidence that the WSHA was involved in the *Parrish* litigation in any formal way. It did not file an amicus brief in the case (as discussed in chapter 5, this is a "friend of the Court" brief filed by an interested party that is not one of the parties to the litigation); and the lawyers for the West Coast Hotel Company do not appear to have been connected to the organization.[86] Consequently, it is not at all clear (a) what the magazine meant when it reported that the WSHA would "go through with the appeal," or (b) why the organization was trying to gather together such a large sum of money. Nevertheless, while these questions remain unanswered, it is very clear that from the outset the WSHA strongly disagreed with Elsie Parrish's contention that the state minimum wage law for women was valid and that she therefore was legally entitled to back pay. Indeed, at the September 1935 meeting WSHA members concluded that "a very dangerous situation will exist if she [Elsie Parrish] is successful." The details of the Parrish lawsuit were "reviewed" and "discussed at considerable length," and the editors of *Hotel News of the West* made it clear that the WSHA would actively attempt to defeat the Cascadian's former chambermaid and the state's minimum wage law.[87]

That publication later devoted almost an entire page to covering the ruling of Judge William O. Parr (Chelan County Superior Court), who issued the first judicial decision in the *Parrish* case (discussed in chapter 4) in October 1935. The first paragraph of the editorial disingenuously concluded that Parr's decision "may have a far reaching effect upon the working women of the state." This language would have been appropriate in an article criticizing the ruling, but in this article, which lauded Parr's action, it strikes the reader as an unfortunate statement that shows limited concern for the welfare of female employees. That conclusion is further substantiated by the next paragraph, wherein the editors of the magazine explained that "[t]he decision was a great relief to the hotel operators of the state." In its closing paragraph, the article explained that "[t]he majority of the hotel operators believe in paying a living wage to their employees and many of them have been paying the state wage or more." There was also little reason to believe that, even during the Great Depression, "any great number will take advantage of the decision [by Parr] and disregard [wage] standards altogether." It was what the article said next, however, that should make the reader pause to consider whether there was genuine concern for the wages plight of female employees. "Pay your employees all that the traffic will bear," the article said, "and your actions will pay big dividends, *but if you can't pay them a living wage, both will be better off if you ceased operations as you are headed for trouble any way.*"[88] In other words, this suggests the WSHA was of the view that an employer's failure/refusal to pay his or her employees the state-mandated minimum wage was problematic not because of the hardship it would cause the employees, but rather because a poorly paid employee should be grateful for the job she had, and not risk causing her employer to go out of business by demanding that he or she pay her a "living wage." When the Washington Supreme Court decided in Elsie Parrish's favor on

April 2, 1936 (also discussed in detail in chapter 4), that ruling was not well received by the WSHA.[89]

Two months later, the U.S. Supreme Court decided *Morehead v. Tipaldo*, striking down New York's minimum wage law for women.[90] News of that decision—which was far more pleasing to the WSHA, reached the editors of *Hotel News of the West* just in time for them to announce the ruling in their June 1 issue. The news flash announcement appeared next to an article indicating the intent of the organization's executive committee to become involved in the appealing of the Washington Supreme Court's decision.[91] Although, as discussed above, there is no evidence of such involvement, it is worth remembering that Ray Clark was intimately involved with the highest levels of WSHA decision-making. This further confirms that he was unwilling to pay his female Cascadian staff the state-mandated minimum wage because he considered the law unconstitutional (and would therefore take a dim view of any employee who raised the fact that she was being underpaid).

* * *

In 1937 James A. Wood was a very well-respected associate editor for the *Seattle Times*, a position he had held for a decade.[92] He brought both formal legal training and extensive journalism experience to his writing.[93] However, even the best newspapermen sometimes present incorrect interpretations of facts. This was true of the *Seattle Times* editorial that ran two weeks after the U.S. Supreme Court's decision in *Parrish*. In it Wood concluded that the ruling was "welcome in this state. . . . Even the one case finally carried to the highest court was more a test case for the purpose of dispelling doubt of the law's validity . . . than a move against evasive and delinquent employers."[94] Wood could not have been more wrong; the litigation that Elsie Parrish initiated against the Cascadian Hotel in Wenatchee was everything that Wood said it was not, because it *was* "a move against [an] evasive and delinquent employer."

"I needed the work so bad"

As Elsie later observed, when working at the Cascadian she "took what they gave me because I needed the work so bad and I figured

they would pay what was right."[95] Like the majority of the unemployed in America during the Depression, she sought "work at any
price."[96] She did not enter into any formal contract of employment
(written or verbal) that told her what she would be paid for her
labors. "She did not ask what the wages would be; they did not tell
her what the wages would be; and no word was spoken on that
subject."[97] In the depths of the Depression, the Cascadian held all
of the employment bargaining power. This was the kind of sce-
nario that Justice George Sutherland had failed to comprehend in
Adkins v. Children's Hospital in 1923,[98] and it was exactly the type
of situation that minimum wage laws were designed to address
(as we will see in detail in the next chapter)—laws including the
1913 statute enacted by Washington State. As the Parrishes' lawyer, C. B. Conner, remarked in his memoir: "The statute was written to take care of situations just like this. These laborers evidently
needed the work or they would not have been there; and the fact
that they accepted a smaller sum than the statutory price was
due not to their agreement to take that sum, but to the necessity
which drove them to do the work and the fear and knowledge
that in case they raised a question about it they would lose their
jobs."[99] It was because she "raised" such "a question" that Elsie lost
her job at the Cascadian in May 1935, a job that had provided her
with steady, albeit underpaid employment since the summer of
1933.[100] For a forty-eight-hour workweek she should have been
receiving $14.50. The wage that the Cascadian actually paid her
began at $10.80 and then increased to $12. Today, accounting for
inflation, the difference between receiving $12 rather than $14.50
per week is the difference between receiving approximately $225
rather than $272.

Ernest Parrish

On Saturday July 28, 1934, at 8:15 P.M., after working her 7.5-hour
shift at the Cascadian, Elsie was joined in wedlock to Ernest Everett Parrish; she was thirty-five, he had just turned twenty-seven.[101]
How the two met remains a family mystery;[102] however, one thing
is very clear, this was a refreshing and liberating second chance at
romance for Elsie. Ernie and Elsie remained together until April 3,
1980, when Elsie died.

As Debra Parrish Stewart emphasizes, Elsie wore the trousers in the relationship.[103] Take, for example, the automobile financing lawsuit in which the couple found themselves embroiled during the winter of 1935–36. In April 1935 Ernie and Elsie purchased a used car from the Wenatchee Auto Exchange. After receiving a $50 credit for the vehicle they traded in, the remaining balance due required them to make monthly payments of $11.91 through April 1936. October 1935 was a very difficult month for the Parrish family; Elsie encountered defeat (at the Chelan County Superior Court) in the first round of her minimum wage litigation, and the family finally decided that it was no longer willing to make payments on its car.

The precise details of the litigation are shrouded in mystery because of significant factual inconsistencies between the documents filed by the lawyers for the two parties—the Pacific Finance Corporation of California, and the Parrishes—and the contents of a letter that Ernie wrote to the Washington State attorney general, Garrison Hamilton.[104] One week before Christmas 1935, Chelan County sheriff Thomas H. Cannon executed a court order and seized the Parrishes' car for Pacific Finance. That same day, Ernie and Elsie were served with a summons and a complaint laying out the reasons why Pacific Finance had ordered the repossession.[105] Elsie immediately headed to Conner's office (we will hear much more about him in subsequent chapters) to inform the lawyer that the case was far more complex than the court filings indicated. The affidavit that she signed on December 21, three days after the seizure of the car, indicates that the Parrishes' failure to make payments was not the result of any financial struggles; instead, it was an entirely voluntary decision not to pay. As Elsie explained to Conner, when she and Ernie purchased the car from the Wenatchee Auto Exchange, the salesman, J. K. Terry, gave them a signed contract, which was accompanied by a verbal agreement that Terry would provide the couple with the necessary title and registration documents for the vehicle. Terry's failure to do this, despite "repeated demands" from Ernie and Elsie, meant that the couple could not obtain a state license to operate the vehicle. It was this that led them to cease making payments.[106]

On April 2, 1936, Ernie wrote his aforementioned letter to the Washington State attorney general Hamilton.[107] It is a piece of correspondence that helps to explain why Ernie and Elsie ultimately decided to stop making their car payments. However, none of the details that Ernie lays out in that letter appear anywhere in the court documents. Why? The answer to that question has been lost to the sands of time. What we do know, however, is that the contents of Ernie's letter were far from clear and, themselves, generated more questions than answers. Ernie states that Terry did not give the couple the relevant documents because he was unable to obtain them from the previous owner of the vehicle because that individual was incarcerated in the Idaho state penitentiary. (Why didn't that individual give Terry the papers with the vehicle?) A set of vehicle documents subsequently materialized. (Where did these papers come from? The letter suggests that the finance company produced them.) However, Ernie and Elsie were very concerned about the veracity of the documents because the name of the supposed "previous owner" did not match the name of the individual incarcerated. (However, the difference in spelling was certainly not an egregious one.) This led the couple to conclude that the documents had been forged, hence their decision to stop making payments on the car. Whatever we make of the disputed facts of this particular automobile financing case, one thing remains clear: Judge Parr ruled that the sale of the car to the Parrishes had violated the law, but the final judgment would be against the couple because instead of refusing to make their payments, they should have initiated legal action.[108] It was this ruling that prompted Ernie to write to the state's chief law enforcement officer. However, with regard to this litigation, this was the only piece of paper to which Ernie put his signature. It is Elsie's signature that appears on all the briefs filed by Conner. Taking the litigation lead was not something that Elsie shied away from.

On to Omak

Elsie and Ernie moved to Omak sometime in 1936. On April 2, when Ernie wrote to the Washington State attorney general about the aforementioned repossession of their automobile, they were still living at 724 North Chelan Avenue in Wenatchee. When the 1936 edition of *Polk's Wenatchee City and Chelan County (Washington) Directory* appeared, Ernie and Elsie appeared in its listings as residents of that address. That volume indicates that Ernie was employed as a warehouseman for Biles-Coleman.[109] This employment opportunity presented itself to Ernie in mid-May, when approximately 350 workers went out on strike at the Biles-Coleman sawmill in Omak.[110] It appears that Ernie, who was from the Omak area, was immediately able to find work there as the sawmill sought nonunion workers to keep the facility operating. In accepting this work, Ernest had to leave his wife behind in Wenatchee. However, the separation was only temporary because Elsie had moved to Omak by November 1936 (when the *World* newspaper interviewed her). When the U.S. Supreme Court decided her case in March 1937, she was no longer employed at the Jim Hill Hotel; she was instead working at the Model Laundry & Cleaners.

The headline in the April 6, 1937, issue of the *Wenatchee Daily World* newspaper declared that Elsie Parrish was "Omak's Minimum Pay Law Joan d'Arc." The accompanying text references an article, including a photograph of her, which appeared in that newspaper sometime during the fall of 1936.[111] The identity of this article and photograph remains unclear, but what we do know is that on Monday, November 16, 1936, four weeks before the U.S. Supreme Court heard oral arguments in her case, Elsie was contacted by a clerk working at the Jim Hill Hotel. A reporter and photographer from the *World* wanted to interview her and take pictures for a feature story. Newspapers across the country subsequently ran Associated Press stories about, or summaries of, the *Parrish* case, articles that were often accompanied by one of two photographs—the iconographic picture of Elsie making a bed at the Jim Hill (the photograph presumably taken in November 1936), or a headshot of her projecting a beaming smile.[112] Elsie found this media attention utterly "flabbergasting,"[113] and after the Supreme Court's decision in her case, she acknowledged that while she did not regret her decision to sue the Cascadian, it was a decision that had negatively affected her ability to find work in Omak (and, obviously, Wenatchee).[114]

2   Fulfilling "an obvious and desperate human need"

It is all very well to say of a woman that "she is working for her living," but suppose she is working and not making her living. What are you to say then? You can remark that you are indeed very sorry, and leave the matter there. Or you can say with more piety than wisdom that wages are determined by natural laws which man must let alone. Or you can insist that she is being sweated; that a business which does not pay a living wage is not paying its labor costs; that such businesses are humanly insolvent, for in paying less than a living wage they are guilty of as bad business practice and far worse moral practice than if they were paying dividends out of assets.

—Walter Lippmann, "Campaign against Sweating" (1915)

A few weeks before oral arguments in *West Coast Hotel v. Parrish*, an article about the U.S. Supreme Court and minimum wage laws appeared in the November 1936 issue of *Harper's Magazine*. This widely distributed and much-discussed piece of commentary by journalist Irving Dilliard pointed out that between 1917 and 1936, seventeen of the Court's justices had participated and cast votes in cases involving minimum wage laws for women. When tallied up, there had been ten votes to uphold the laws, and seven to strike them down (see table 2.1).[1] Of course, a majority of these justices did not coalesce around the position that minimum wage laws for

TABLE 2.1   The U.S. Supreme Court justices who, between 1917 and 1936, voted for or against minimum wage laws

FOR (10)	AGAINST (7)
Hughes, New York	Van Devanter, Wyoming
Stone, New York	McReynolds, Tennessee
Cardozo, New York	Sutherland, Utah
Holmes, Massachusetts	Butler, Minnesota
Brandeis, Massachusetts	White, Louisiana
Taft, Ohio	McKenna, California
Clarke, Ohio	Roberts, Pennsylvania
Day, Ohio	
Pitney, New Jersey	
Sanford, Tennessee	

Source: This is a replication of the table in Irving Dilliard, "A Supreme Court Majority? The Court and Minimum-Wage Legislation," Harper's Magazine, November 1936, p. 600.

women were constitutional *in any one case* until *Parrish*. Nevertheless, Dilliard's observation suggests that there is more to the story of the constitutionality of such laws than simply saying that finally by 1937, a majority was now willing to uphold them (when, ten months earlier, it had declined to do so).

There is indeed more to that story, much more. This chapter tells the *first* half of that story of jurisprudential twists and turns, a first half that ends in 1913 with the enactment of a slew of state laws (including Washington State's) that provided minimum wages for women workers.

"Liberty of Contract"

Between February and July 1913, eight states enacted minimum wage laws for women. All these laws were borne of the "questioning spirit" of the Progressive Era,[2] and their legislative contours were defined by a large number of people and organizations that brought diverse knowledge, interests, and expertise to this endeavor. Many things united these advocates. However, for the purposes of telling the story of *Parrish*, the place to start is with the constitutional concept of "liberty of contract." As Vivien Hart astutely observes, using "landmarks of judicial review" to "[b]lock . . . out minimum wage history . . . is convenient but carries the wrong message—that the courts made the running. The law both constrained minimum wagers and was a political resource to take hold of and use."[3] This is undoubtedly true, but it is equally important to keep in mind that the concept of "liberty of contract," as it was interpreted in the opinions of various U.S. Supreme Court justices, significantly influenced the way in which reformers approached and defended the task of creating minimum wage laws for women workers in America. Indeed, as Hart has compellingly demonstrated, the history of minimum wage laws for women in the United States is, more than anything, defined by the United States Constitution. It was the "one factor above all" that "steered the crucial decision—*who* should benefit from minimum wage policy" in America, and it was also the principal factor that determined whether *anyone* would be able to benefit from this protective legislation.[4]

Contractual Liberty

A free person is, among other things, a person who owns his or her own labor and the fruits of that labor—that is, their property.[5] When Congress enacted the Civil Rights Act in 1866, it recognized that bound up in the free labor of man is the right "to make and enforce contracts"—so much so, that this was the first right that it listed as protected by Section I of that law which said, in part:

> [A]ll persons born in the United States and not subject to any foreign power, excluding Indians not taxed, are hereby declared to be citizens of the United States; and such citizens, of every race and color, without regard to any previous condition of slavery or involuntary servitude, except as a punishment for crime whereof the party shall have been duly convicted, *shall have the same right, in every State and Territory in the United States, to make and enforce contracts*, to sue, be parties, and give evidence, to inherit, purchase, lease, sell, hold, and convey real and personal property, and to full and equal benefit of all laws and proceedings for the security of person and property, as is enjoyed by white citizens.[6]

Today, far more familiar to Americans is Section I of the Fourteenth Amendment, which reads as follows:

All persons born or naturalized in the United States and subject to the jurisdiction thereof, are citizens of the United States
and of the State wherein they reside. No State shall make or
enforce any law which shall abridge the privileges or immunities of citizens of the United States; *nor shall any State deprive
any person of life, liberty, or property, without due process of law*;
nor deny to any person within its jurisdiction the equal protection of the laws.[7]

Ratified two years after the Civil Rights Act was passed, the amendment's citizenship language mirrors that of the 1866 law, and its
due process clause contains the spirit of the liberty and property
protections spelled out in that act. This is no coincidence. There
were concerns that the 1866 law would not be able to withstand
a constitutional challenge, and those concerns weighed heavily on
the minds of some of the members of Congress who participated in
writing and passing the amendment. In this respect, therefore, the
Fourteenth Amendment can be said to have constitutionalized the
1866 law.[8] Importantly, as we will see, this gave rise to a belief that
the Fourteenth Amendment constitutionalizes a liberty of contract.
However, a number of crucial questions remained. For example,
just what did a right "to make and enforce contracts" include? In
other words, what was the scope of this right? In order to understand how the Court answered those questions, and how those
answers eventually led it to the decision in *West Coast Hotel v. Parrish*, the best place to start is post–Civil War Chicago.

Munn v. Illinois

In 1870, if you wanted to transport grain using the nation's railroads, you had little choice but to go through Chicago; the city
was the indisputable center of the nation's distribution network.
If you were sending this product (a dietary staple, no less) from
one "of [the] seven or eight great States of the West" to one of the
"four or five of the States on the seashore," your business had to go
through the Windy City, and you were therefore at the commercial
mercy of the operators of the grain elevators that lined the railroad
yards.[9] Recognizing that the problems associated with this monopoly needed to be addressed, and that they were clearly a matter of

public concern, when Illinois adopted its new state constitution in 1870, it included a section declaring that "[a]ll elevators or store-houses where grain or other property is stored for a compensation, whether the property stored be kept separate or not, are declared to be public warehouses."[10] This meant that grain elevators were no longer considered private property under state law. Consequently, the following year the state legislature was free to enact a law imposing a maximum price that could be charged for the storage of grain in the elevator. "The maximum charge of storage and han-dling of grain, including the cost of receiving and delivering," the law read, "shall be for the first thirty days or part thereof two cents per bushel, and for each fifteen days or part thereof, after the first thirty days, one-half of one cent per bushel."[11] When confronted with a challenge to that law, the U.S. Supreme Court held that it did not unconstitutionally deprive the warehouse owners and oper-ators of any "property" protected by the Fourteenth Amendment. From an analysis of the Court's reasoning in that decision in *Munn v. Illinois* (1876), three important points of law emerge.

1. "Due process of law"
The language of the due process clauses of the Fifth and Fourteenth Amendments is deceptively simple.[12] The linguistic simplicity is deceptive because "due process of law" is susceptible to multiple meanings. Least controversially, we can think of it as a procedural protection—ensuring that we receive the *process we are due*. In other words, this understanding of *procedural due process* guarantees that the government will follow the proper legal procedures when depriving you of your "life, liberty, or property." For example, if the government believes you have committed a capital crime, but simply acts upon its belief by shooting (effectively imposing the death penalty) you dead in the street, that would be an egregious violation of due process because the government failed to follow the proper procedures involved—arrest, jury trial, and so on. Under this *procedural* understanding of the clauses, then, there can be no due process challenge to the types of laws enacted (only challenges to the post-passage enforcement of the laws). Procedural due pro-cess cannot be a constitutional mechanism for preventing a leg-islature from passing laws that are silly, asinine, discriminatory, or arbitrary (to mention just four things).

Today, however, we are accustomed to thinking about due process not only in a procedural sense, but also as a *substantive* protection of rights. This allows us to challenge (as a violation of due process) the *substance* of the law that is being enforced against us, regardless of whether it is being enforced using the correct legal procedures. *Substantive due process* enables us to challenge, as a violation of our life, liberty, or property, laws that are silly, asinine, discriminatory, or arbitrary. It is from this concept of substantive due process that a woman has received the constitutionally protected liberty to choose to terminate her pregnancy,[13] and same-sex couples have received the constitutionally protected liberty to engage in intimate sexual relations[14]—to name just two examples.

Late nineteenth- and early twentieth-century constitutional scholars and judges, however, did not hold the same understanding of substantive due process as we do today.[15] At the time of *Munn*, substantive due process was best understood not as substantive due process *per se*, but as a protection of life, liberty, and property *by separating the powers of the different branches of government*.[16] This understanding meant that the due process clauses were viewed as guaranteeing *judicial* process. (Note the emphasis on judicial, rather than just common or garden legal process.) This is because the Fourteenth Amendment says you are entitled to due process according to the law of the land. Consequently, as long as the legislature is not doing something that deprives you of property rights that you are entitled to, your only recourse to its action is legislative, not judicial. In *Munn*, Chief Justice Morrison Waite expressed this principle in the following way:

Rights of property which have been created by the common law cannot be taken away without due process; *but the law itself, as a rule of conduct, may be changed at the will, or even at the whim, of the legislature, unless prevented by constitutional limitations.* Indeed, the great office of statutes is to remedy defects in the common law as they are developed, and to adapt it to the changes of time and circumstances. *To limit the rate of charge for services rendered in a public employment, or for the use of property in which the public has an interest, is only changing a regulation which existed before.* It establishes no new principle in the law, but only gives a new effect to an old one. We know

that this is a power which may be abused, but that is no argument against its existence. *For protection against abuses by legislatures, the people must resort to the polls, not to the courts.*[17]

As Waite indicates, in America's constitutional democracy the
power to make laws lies with the people *through their elected representatives.* This majoritarian decision-making process might produce laws that are unwise, imprudent, and even silly; and it might
well produce laws borne of a majoritarian whim, a knee-jerk reaction to something upon which a majority frowns. However, if the
people believe that the legislature has overstepped the mark and
abused the power that the people gave it, the power to change
comes from within—from the people voting at the ballot box—
"the polls"; it does not come from without—from the "courts."

As Waite indicates, however, there is one important exception:
change can be initiated (or driven) by the judiciary when a law vio-
lates "constitutional limitations." This, of course, begs the question—
what are the relevant "constitutional limitations"? In *Munn,* the grain
elevator owners and operators contended that the answer to this
question could be found in the due process clause of the Fourteenth
Amendment. In the passage printed above, Waite has already given
us a partial answer as to why he and six of his colleagues rejected
this Fourteenth Amendment claim: "To limit the rate of charge for
services rendered in a public employment, or for the use of property
in which the public has an interest, is only changing a regulation
which existed before." The *public* had an interest in the property,
so there was no private property deprivation. Of course, on its own
that answer does not get us very far because it suggests that the legislature could deprive people of their property (by imposing maximum prices) because it—the legislature—had stated that the public
had an interest in that property. On its own, that answer smacks of
legislative omnipotence. This leads us to the second important point
to take away from *Munn.*

2. Bundles of rights
In *Munn,* the Court held that a law could only deprive you of
property rights without due process if it deprives you of something that is part of your bundle of property rights in the first
place. This is basic social contract theory, the political theory that
was handed down to us by (most prominently) John Locke and

Thomas Hobbes. It is the political theory that strongly influenced the thinking of the Framers of the U.S. Constitution,[18] and it was, as Mark Graber describes it, "the philosophical glue for melding popular sovereignty and fundamental law when the Constitution of the United States was framed and ratified."[19] Civil society exists, so this theory explains, in order to protect our inalienable rights (to borrow language from the Declaration of Independence); this is achieved by, for example, creating a governing system where there exists a neutral arbiter for the resolution of rights disputes. If Phyllis kills James and takes all the property that James claimed was his, the upside is that the property dispute between these two individuals has been resolved; the downside, of course, is that James is now dead. This is not only a fundamental violation of James's right to life, but under this precedent there is now nothing to stop Phyllis from going on a killing spree and taking the property of Collin and Dexter (unless one of them kills her first). Consequently, under this societal setup no one's property is safe. Hence the social contract theory that one's freedom will be better preserved in a society where one gives up part of one's freedom in order to mutually coexist with others. (At the heart of that freedom are—as Locke made clear—one's rights to acquire, hold, and protect property.) So, Phyllis (just like everyone else in the society) gives up her freedom to randomly kill people with whom she has property disputes in favor of a system of neutral governing organizations whose judges will arbitrate those property disagreements. As Waite put it in *Munn*, "When one becomes a member of society, he necessarily parts with some rights or privileges which, as an individual not affected by his relations to others, he might retain."[20]

However, that member of society does not part with the power "to control [his or her] rights which are purely and exclusively private."[21] The government is authorized to enact "laws requiring each citizen to conduct himself, and so use his own property, as not unnecessarily to injure another." As Waite went on to say, "This is the very essence of government." You may use your property so as long as you do not harm another in the process ("*sic utere tuo ut alienum non lædas*"),[22] because the right to use one's property to harm another is not part of the bundle of rights attaching to that property. Hence what is known as the "police power" of the states—the power of a state to regulate for the health, safety, welfare, and morals of its citizens.

This brings us to the third of the three important points of law that *Munn* gives us as we set out on our contractual liberty journey to *Parrish*.

3. "Affected with a public interest"
In *Munn*, the Court concludes that there is an additional, important limitation to the common law property right protected by the Fourteenth Amendment. Not only is the government empowered to limit the use of your *private* property so as to avoid harm to others, but also it is authorized to place far greater limits on your use of that property when that "private property is 'affected with a public interest.'" For it is at that point that "it ceases to be *juris privati* only."[23] This is because:

> Property does become clothed with a public interest when used in a manner to make it of public consequence and affect the community at large. *When, therefore, one devotes his property to a use in which the public has an interest, he, in effect, grants to the public an interest in that use, and must submit to be controlled by the public for the common good, to the extent of the interest he has thus created.*[24]

There was never any doubt, in the minds of the *Munn* majority, that the Chicago grain elevators and warehouses were "affected with a public interest" and therefore permissibly subject to the Illinois price regulations. Chicago's geographical location, at the crossroads of the nation's grain distribution network, gave the elevator and warehouse operators a "'virtual' monopoly."[25] As Waite wrote, "They stand . . . in the very 'gateway of commerce,' and take toll from all who pass. . . . Certainly, if any business can be clothed 'with a public interest, and cease to be *juris privati* only,' this has been."[26]

The grain elevators were "affected with a public interest" and represented a "virtual [nationwide] monopoly"; consequently this *public* property could be constitutionally subjected to state legislation regulating the prices charged (in the name of the welfare of the public—covered by the state's police power); and if the aggrieved residents of Illinois wanted to do something about this, they needed to vote the bums in Springfield out of office.

*   *   *

In *Munn*, the Court addressed the scope of property rights protected under the Fourteenth Amendment. In another decision, a generation later, it again passed judgment on the relationship between property rights and the police power of the states. In so doing, it issued a ruling that would become one of the most controversial decisions ever reached by that tribunal, a decision that would have the dubious distinction of giving its name (misleadingly) to an entire "era" of the Supreme Court's history.

Lochner—Bakers Are Not Special

In *Lochner v. New York* (1905), a five-justice majority of the Court struck down the provision of the 1897 New York State Bakeshop Act that prohibited bakers from working in excess of sixty hours a week, or for more than ten hours each day. A bakery owner could not lawfully contract bakers to work in excess of these maximum hours, and similarly a baker could not lawfully choose to enter into such a contract.[27] The Court considered this provision a violation of contractual liberty, concluding that employers and employees had a constitutional right to enter into labor contracts free of "interfering" state regulations such as those imposed by the New York law. "Both property and liberty," wrote Justice Rufus Peckham in his opinion for the *Lochner* majority, "are held on such reasonable conditions as may be imposed by the governing power of the State in the exercise of" the "certain powers, existing in the sovereignty of each State in the Union, somewhat vaguely termed [as] police powers."[28] Concomitant to these limits on individual property and liberty are limits on the powers of the state. *Lochner* tells us that property can only be regulated if the state action (using the police power) in question is "fair, reasonable and appropriate" and not "an unreasonable, unnecessary and arbitrary interference with the right of the individual to his personal liberty or to enter into those contracts in relation to labor which may seem to him appropriate or necessary for the support of himself and his family."[29] However, when does one know that the line has been crossed? The answer comes from an evaluation of two things—(a) "the kind of employment," and (b) "the character of the employes [sic] in such kinds of labor."[30]

In 1898, in *Holden v. Hardy*, the Court upheld a Utah law that limited the number of hours per day that underground miners

Joseph F. Lochner

248–250 South Street   Utica, N. Y.

LOCHNER'S

is one of the oldest and most reliable

Bakeries

in Central New York

We pride ourselves on Uniformity, Purity, Cleanliness

FIG. 2.1   Advertisement for Joseph Lochner's home bakeries in the 1914 Utica (N.Y.) Steber Directory. Courtesy of the Oneida County History Center.

and ores and metals smelters could work. The Court, in that case, observed that the Industrial Revolution had inevitably wrought an expansion of the valid scope of the police power because of "an enormous increase in the number of occupations which are dangerous, or so far detrimental to the health of employees as to

FIG. 2.2   Joseph Lochner's home bakery, 1947. Courtesy of the Oneida County History Center.

demand special precautions for their well-being and protection, or the safety of adjacent property."[31] Inherently hazardous occupations could be regulated using the police power because the health of the employees (and therefore the public) was negatively affected by working excessively long hours. In other words, there was a rational relationship between the exercise of that power and the ends—health, safety, welfare, and morals—that were to be achieved with that legislative means.

In the eyes of the *Lochner* majority, there was a world of difference between the mines of Utah and Joseph Lochner's bakery in Utica. Thumbing its nose at the extensive data it received in the case briefs about the negative health effects of working long hours in such establishments, the majority feared that upholding the New York law would set society upon a slippery slope toward an illiberal and excessively paternalistic state because "[i]t is unfortunately true that labor, even in any department, may possibly carry with it the seeds of unhealthiness."[32] Additionally:

> There is no contention that bakers as a class are not equal in intelligence and capacity to men in other trades or manual occupations. . . . They are in no sense wards of the State. *Viewed in the light of a purely labor law, with no reference whatever to the question of health, we think that a law like the one before us involves neither the safety, the morals nor the welfare of the public, and that the interest of the public is not in the slightest degree affected by such an act.*[33]

In other words, the New York Bakeshop Act was a constitutional failure on two counts. First, it was "an unreasonable, unnecessary and arbitrary interference with the right of the individual to his personal liberty or to enter into those contracts in relation to labor which may seem to him appropriate or necessary for the support of himself and his family."[34] Second, bakers were not engaged in a business "affected with a public interest."[35]

Together, *Munn* and *Lochner* established a consistent set of doctrinal rules for dealing with the property and contractual liberty rights protected by the Fourteenth Amendment. The states were only permitted to use their police powers to regulate private property (including a person's right to labor freely) when either (a) that property was "affected with a public interest," or (b) when a reasonable case could be made that the property/liberty needed to be regulated to prevent harm to the health, safety, morals, and/or welfare of a citizenry. And if your state is permitted to regulate your property/liberty on these grounds, you need to direct your complaints to the legislature, not the courts. That is the very essence of the due process guaranteed to you by the U.S. Constitution. What did this mean for those Progressive Era individuals who advocated for minimum wage laws for the nation's women workers?[36] The U.S. Supreme Court *appeared* to provide an answer to that question three years after *Lochner*, but appearances can be deceptive.

Women Are Special

The progressive push to establish minimum wages for women was just one part of a much larger effort to enact two types of protective legislation, an effort whose "various incarnations . . . extend[ed] over an astonishingly long period of time."[37] The first category of laws limited the types of jobs some members of the workforce could legally undertake. For example, beginning in 1881 with California, many states prevented women from working in establishments that sold alcohol;[38] and other statutes, representing similar concerns about the mental and physical welfare of women, prohibited them, for example, from being messengers, driving taxis, or working at night.[39]

While these laws undoubtedly play an important role in understanding the history of the nation's protective legislation,[40] it is the second category of laws that concerns us here. This category *regulated*, rather than *restricted*, the work of women and "aimed to preserve the worker's independence by providing safe and clean working conditions, minimizing health hazards, putting a floor under wages, shortening hours, and eventually compensating workers for job-related accidents."[41] In this respect, the laws that imposed maximum working hours and those that provided minimum wages were statutory siblings. However, for reasons that will become clear, maximum hours laws were enacted well in advance of those that imposed minimum wages; and for a long time the Court declined to view the two types of legislation as belonging in the same constitutional category.

The first minimum wage law was not enacted until 1912. By contrast, in 1896 twelve states already had hours laws in place (see map 2.1). The laws were of varying enforceability and effectiveness, but the basic point remains the same—"Women's hour legislation" was "one of the simplest and most generally accepted types of state activity for the protection of the wage earner" over the course of the late nineteenth and early twentieth century. By 1933 that "general acceptability" had spread to forty-two of the forty-eight states (see map 2.2).[42]

After 1905, state legislatures rarely hesitated to enact maximum hours laws for categories of workers whose occupations were clearly controlled by the decision in *Holden* rather than *Lochner*. However, the general acceptability of hours legislation for *women* came in the aftermath of another Supreme Court decision—*Muller v. Oregon* (1908), which limited *Lochner* (much like *Holden* did) and gave advocates of women's protective legislation an important constitutional ray of hope.[43] It was a decision that "electrified" those who advocated for the passage of wage laws.[44] However, it was a ray of hope for women who did not mind being confined

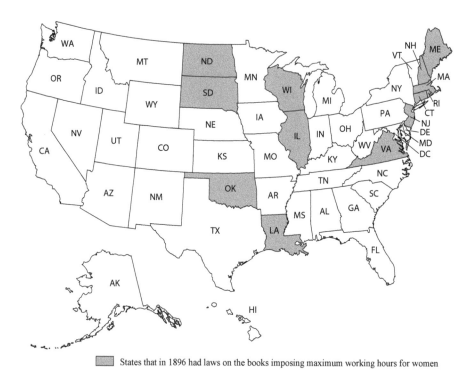

States that in 1896 had laws on the books imposing maximum working hours for women

MAP 2.1   Map showing the twelve states (identified with shading) that in 1896 had laws on the books imposing maximum working hours for women. In 1896 Oklahoma did have such a law on its books (which is why it is shaded), but it did not become a state until 1907. Compiled using data from Elizabeth Brandeis, "Labor Legislation," in *History of Labor in the United States, 1896–1932,* ed. John R. Commons (New York: Macmillan, 1935), 457n1. Map by Bill Nelson.

to the traditional sphere of domesticity that subsequent developments, such as the Nineteenth Amendment, were designed to lift them out of. As such, it helps to explain why the advocates and designers of protective legislation for women approached this particular policymaking task in the way they did.

Muller v. Oregon

When a large crowd of Oregonians gathered in Portland's Cedar Park on Monday, September 4, 1905, for that year's Labor Day celebration, they were grateful for some respite from the brutal late

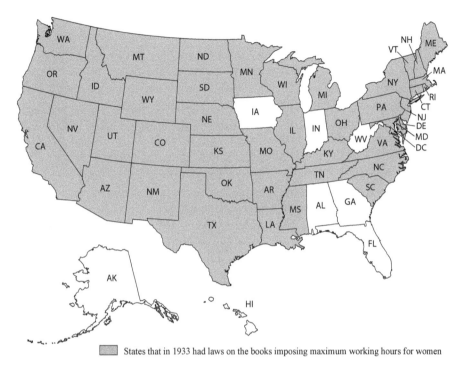

States that in 1933 had laws on the books imposing maximum working hours for women

MAP 2.2   Map showing the forty-two states (identified with shading) that in 1933 had laws on the books imposing maximum working hours for women. Compiled using data from Elizabeth Brandeis, "Labor Legislation," in *History of Labor in the United States, 1896–1932*, ed. John R. Commons (New York: Macmillan, 1935), 458n5. Map by Bill Nelson.

summer sun that had mercilessly baked the city for the past few days.[45] Although it was still a very warm eighty-two degrees, this was better than the ninety-five degrees to which the mercury had soared three days earlier. One thing celebrated at the Labor Day gathering was the state statute, enacted two years earlier, which limited the employment of women—"in any mechanical establishment, or factory, or laundry"—to a maximum of ten hours over the course of any one twenty-four hour period.[46] As the labor leader Avery Moore observed, that law was designed to alleviate some of the ills of the "system which makes the happiness and well-being of [workers] subject to the caprice of an individual, or association."[47] The law deliberately focused on the laundry industry. At the turn of the century 40 percent of eighteen thousand adult women who

were wage earners in Oregon toiled in Portland, the state's largest city, and approximately 20 percent of them were employed in
industries categorized as either "manufacturing" or "mechanical." Of
those industries, only the garment industry could claim more female
employees than the laundry industry. Over the course of the first
decade of the twentieth century, those numbers steadily increased.[48]

These numbers included the workers at the Grand Laundry,
who were unable to attend the Labor Day gathering because the
laundry's owner, Curt Muller, refused to grant them a reduced
schedule for the holiday. He instructed one of his overseers, Joe
Haselbock, to require his female employees to work more than ten
hours that September 4. Numerous signs point to the conclusion
that Muller expected—and indeed hoped—that he would be pun-
ished to the fullest extent of the law for this violation of the 1903
statute, thus enabling him to bring a test case challenging its constitutionality.[49] After losing at both the trial court level and the Oregon Supreme Court, Muller appealed his case to the U.S. Supreme
Court. He contended that the law violated his "liberty of contract,"
and given the decision a mere three years earlier in *Lochner*, he
expected to win. But there was just one problem for Muller; his
employees were *women*.

Writing for a unanimous Supreme Court, Justice David Brewer
observed that "[i]n the matter of personal and contractual rights,"
all individuals "stand on the same plane," regardless of their sex.
The state is no more entitled to violate those rights possessed by a
woman than it is to violate those held by a man.[50] It could not, for
example, rule one way for a Curt Muller and the opposite way for
a Catherine Muller. However, while the "personal and contractual"
rights of the sexes were theoretically "on the same plane," that theory had to coexist with reality. This was a reality that "everyone"
knew to be both true and obvious—that the woman in society had
always been and still was in need of "especial care [so] that her
rights may be preserved."[51] This is because women have a specific
physical attribute that men do not possess, an attribute that means
they will play a role in society that men will not—they have the
ability to bear children. There is, as Brewer observed, a "widespread
belief that woman's physical structure"—that structure that consists of the female reproductive organs—"and the functions she per-
forms in consequence thereof, justify special legislation restricting
or qualifying the conditions under which she should be permitted

to toil."[52] This conclusion cannot have come as much surprise to the nation's legislatures, twenty of which (including Oregon) had, by 1908, enacted statutes regulating the working hours laws of their female employees.[53]

Continuing, Brewer concluded that in terms of her "effort to maintain an independent position in life," a woman "is not upon an equality" because of the burdens that are placed upon her by "her physical structure and a proper discharge of her maternal functions— having in view not merely her own health, but the well-being of the race." And because she is "[d]ifferentiated by these matters from the other sex, she is properly placed in a *class* by herself, and [*class*] legislation designed for her protection may be sustained."[54] The Court upheld the state restrictions on the employment hours of women in laundries for the same reason that it upheld the equivalent limits imposed on the mining industry in Utah in *Holden v. Hardy*. Laundry work was one of those "occupations which are dangerous, or so far detrimental to the health of employees as to demand special precautions for their well-being and protection, or the safety of adjacent property."[55] Only, however, if the employees in question are women, because "woman's physical structure and the performance of maternal functions place her at a disadvantage in the struggle for subsistence . . . by abundant testimony of the medical fraternity, continuance for a long time on her feet at work, repeating this from day to day, tends to injurious effects upon the body." This was devastating for women and society as a whole because "healthy mothers are essential to vigorous offspring." Therefore, "the physical well-being of woman becomes an object of public interest and care in order to preserve the strength and vigor of the race."[56] The Court reached its decision in *Muller* very quickly (only thirty-nine days elapsed between the oral argument and announcement of the judgment), because of the fact (as "history discloses") "that woman has always been dependent upon man."[57]

This observation strikes the twenty-first-century reader as the embodiment of Victorian-era sexism and paternalism. However, in 1908 this perception of female inferiority was indeed "widespread," and the statute books reflected that belief because their pages were filled with laws that, in one way or another, "protected" women.[58] Additionally, as Nancy Erickson persuasively argues, *Muller* was not a jurisprudential outlier; its gendered origins were deeply rooted and could clearly be seen in Fourteenth Amendment cases decided on consecutive days a generation earlier in 1873: the *Slaughter-House Cases* and *Bradwell v. Illinois*.[59] At issue in the *Slaughter-House Cases* was an 1869 Louisiana law empowering the City of New Orleans to incorporate a slaughterhouse company that would centralize and monopolize the meat-slaughtering business in the city.[60] The members of the Butchers' Benevolent Association who challenged the constitutionality of the law argued that it prevented them from exercising their common law right to engage in their chosen profession (by giving one corporation a monopoly over that trade). The Fourteenth Amendment, they contended, made it unconstitutional for states to deprive them of this right. Although that labor right clearly exists, a bare majority of the Court concluded that the provision of the Fourteenth Amendment, which says that "[n]o State shall make or enforce any law which shall abridge the privileges or immunities of citizens of the United States," only applies to U.S. citizens; therefore it only protects a limited number of rights already expressly or implicitly stated in the Constitution. All four dissenters—Chief Justice Salmon P. Chase and Justices Noah H. Swayne, Stephen J. Field, and Joseph P. Bradley—agreed that the Fourteenth Amendment did indeed give protection to the right to pursue lawful employment. As Erickson points out, one would have then expected those justices similarly to dissent from the decision the following day in *Bradwell*, in which the Court hewed to its *Slaughter-House* position in holding that the right to pursue employment as a lawyer was not one of the constitutionally protected "privileges or immunities."[61]

At issue in *Bradwell* was Myra Bradwell's challenge to the Illinois Supreme Court's decision to deny her admission to the state bar based on her sex, the fact that she met all the statutory requirements for admission notwithstanding. The decision in *Bradwell* was 8–1, and the only *Slaughter-House* dissenter who did not join the majority was Chief Justice Chase. Justices Swayne and Field joined Justice Bradley's separate opinion, which left the reader with absolutely no doubt as to why these three men viewed *Bradwell* as an entirely different type of case. In language that would be echoed in *Muller*, these justices expressed a gendered reading of the Fourteenth Amendment. As Bradley emphasized, they considered it obvious that the right "to pursue any lawful employment for a livelihood (the practice of law included)" had never "been established as one of the fundamental privileges and immunities of the [female] sex," and this was "an historical fact."[62] Indeed, he continued, "the civil law, as well as nature herself, has always recognized a wide difference in the respective spheres and destinies of man and woman," because "[m]an is, or should be, woman's protector and defender. The natural and proper timidity and delicacy which belongs to the female sex evidently unfits it for many of the occupations of civil life."[63] It is in the dissenting opinion in the *Slaughter-House Cases* that we find the intellectual jurisprudential foundations of the doctrine of contractual liberty. However, *Bradwell* demonstrated that the "doctrine was clearly sex-based at its inception."[64]

*　*　*

Of course, this doctrine, as it was expressed in *Muller*, left some pressing questions unanswered. Would its reasoning extend to laws that prescribed minimum wages for women? When confronted with a statute that regulated the *wages*, rather than *hours*, of women workers, how would the Court rule? Which would be the prevailing precedent? *Lochner* or *Muller*?[65] As we will see in the next chapter, the answer would come in the decision in *Adkins v. Children's Hospital* (1923), in which the Court struck down a law that provided minimum wages for women workers in the District of Columbia.[66]

Borne of a "questioning spirit"

In a speech that he gave in Olympia on April 10, 1923, Louis F. Hart, the governor of Washington State, described *Adkins* as "a new Dred Scott decision." As he told one of his aides, he "'didn't give a damn' what the Supreme Court thought." The judgment in that case, announced by the Court the previous day, threatened the very existence of the minimum wage laws for women enacted by states such as his. Hart was determined to defend this part of the legislative legacy of his predecessor, Governor Ernest Lister.[67]

When Lister signed into law the 1913 bill that would guarantee minimum wages to women workers in Washington State, he did not make national legislative history. Massachusetts is forever enshrined in the annals of that history, famous for becoming the first state in the nation to enact a minimum wages for women law. However, that law had far more bark than bite; it was only a temporal trailblazer. In 1911, the Massachusetts legislature asked the governor to form a commission "to study the matter of wages of women and minors, and to report on the advisability of establishing . . . [wage] boards."[68] The resulting minimum wages law (which did not reflect many of the commission's recommendations) enacted the following year was exceptionally weak. The welfare of the employers, as well as the employees, was taken into account so as to ensure that the minimum wages set would not have a significantly deleterious effect on a particular industry. And, most notably, compliance with the law was not mandatory; the "enforcement" provision stipulated that any employer who did not pay the required minimum wages would only be held accountable by having their names published in local newspapers.[69] Nevertheless, for all of that law's ineffectiveness it was encouraging that in 1912 *any* statute providing minimum wages for women workers had been enacted by an American state legislature.

The real substantive state-level legislative trailblazing came out of the Pacific Northwest when Governor Oswald West signed Oregon's minimum wages for women bill into law on February 17, 1913, followed shortly thereafter (on March 24) by Lister, his counterpart to the north. This meant that four states now had such laws on their books.[70] However, none of those laws sprang forth like Athena, fully formed and clothed in armor, ready to "deal with" this particular part of "the human wreckage of industrial capitalism."[71] Nor were they unique, never-before-seen means of achieving (or attempting to achieve) that socially progressive end. In order to understand the real intellectual ancestry of the state minimum wages for women laws enacted in 1913, we have to look far beyond the shores of the United States, and much further back in time than the 1910s.

In New Zealand the 1894 Industrial Conciliation and Arbitration Act empowered an arbitration court to impose minimum wages, but it was the Factories and Shop Act, enacted two years later by the Victoria legislature in Australia, that proved to be the globally pioneering minimum wage law. It established six Wage Boards, made up of representatives of employers *and* employees (in equal numbers), each responsible for overseeing a different industry and determining the minimum wages that should be established for workers in those industries.[72] Although this particular Victorian system quickly "became the centre of" and was ultimately ended by "a political tug-o'-war,"[73] it established a broad policy precedent that influenced the passage in Great Britain of a similar minimum wages law—the 1909 Trade Boards Act.[74] The enactment of this law was one of the three things to which Louis D. Brandeis pointed as being responsible for the proliferation of minimum wages laws that were passed in the United States in 1913. The other two factors he identified were the 1912 Massachusetts statute, and the nineteen-volume report into the working conditions of women and children that was published by the United States Department of Labor and Commerce between 1910 and 1913.[75] That report, heavily laden with statistical data, epitomized the progressive approach to the crafting of minimum wages laws.

The Numbers Didn't Lie

Progressive reformers were disproportionately drawn from the middle classes. As Richard Hofstadter observes in his 1955 Pulitzer Prize-winning book *The Age of Reform*, "[T]he growth of middle-class reform sentiment, the contributions of professionals and education men, made Progressive thought more informed, more moderate, more complex than Populist thought had been."[76] Many of these individuals were the products of academic departments (such as economics, political science, and sociology) that had experienced the intellectually revolutionary changes that swept across the social sciences at the turn of the twentieth century. Among other things, these changes brought a new reverence for quantitative methodology.[77] This new focus on statistical data had a profound impact on many aspects of society, including the work of progressive reformers. In May 1883 Lord Kelvin opened his lecture at the Institution of Civil Engineers with the following observation: "I often say that when you can measure what you are speaking about, and express it in numbers, you know something about it; but when you cannot express it in numbers, your knowledge is of a meager and unsatisfactory kind; it may be the beginning of knowledge, but you have scarcely in your thoughts, advanced to the stage of science, whatever the matter may be."[78] This sentiment was shared by a great many of the progressive reformers.

Much has been written about who these men and women were and what drove them to achieve their social policy goals. There is broad scholarly agreement that those who specifically campaigned for *wages laws for women* were middle class, just like the typical progressive reformer,[79] and that they received limited support from labor unions.[80] These are important observations, and they reflect the value of remembering that "[t]he basic riddle in progressivism is not what drove groups apart, but what made them seek common cause."[81] In her study of Pacific Northwest history, Dorothy Johansen emphasizes that it would be wrong "[t]o ascribe ideological consistency to progressives." However, there was "one factor" that "appear[ed] . . . common to all who called themselves progressive: they seemed to believe or profess that superior to private interests was a public interest which could best be served by extended public participation in lawmaking processes."[82]

The uniting refrain that brought all progressive reformers together in pursuit of a public interest was "corporate arrogance."[83] As the historian Robert Wiebe describes it, this was a period of crisis during which Americans engaged in a "search for order." They searched for order in a society wherein they saw a grave threat to the American dream of individual advancement of "opportunity." That threat came from the "great corporations" that were viewed by progressive reformers as social enemy number one because they were systematically destroying "every American's birthright"—the "dream" that "included a fair chance to win his pot of gold." This had, "if anything, grown even more powerful in the expansive years after the Civil War," but it was a dream that was dying at the hands of corporate robber barons.[84] Unlike populists, who responded to problems that primarily affected the "rural and provincial," progressives addressed ills faced by urban residents across the country, residents who were increasingly crammed into tight quarters, as the urban population in 1910 was approximately seven times larger than that of 1860.[85] And it was undeniable that sweating epitomized those ills, especially for affected women workers.

In his 1897 *Encyclopedia of Social Reform*, one such reformer, William D. P. Bliss, succinctly described the sweating system as: "the production of goods for sale, particularly prevailing in the clothing trades, whereby the wholesalers buy their goods off middlemen (or sweaters), who employ men, women, or children to manufacture the goods at the lowest possible wages, either in hot small rooms (sweatshops) belonging to the sweater, or taking the materials to their own homes and making them there for usually still lower prices."[86] Although the demographics of those who were sweated in

Great Britain and the United States were very similar, and in both countries reformers defended state-based remedies in terms of their economic and broader societal benefits, only in the latter were those defenses distinctively and consciously couched in gendered terms.[87]

When women's groups in California campaigned for a minimum wage for women in 1913, their slogan was: "Employed womanhood must be protected in order to foster the motherhood of the race."[88] In *Muller*, the Supreme Court said that legally, women were in "a class by themselves" and the government was therefore justified in limiting their hours of work. Minimum wage advocates took this limitation and used it to further expand the protection of those who would bear and raise future generations. Yes, they were constrained by the Constitution (and judicial interpretations of that document),[89] but they were also empowered by those constraints—an empowerment that perhaps seemed fitting given that the Preamble of that document spoke of "secur[ing] the Blessings of Liberty to ourselves *and our Posterity*."[90]

*   *   *

Writing in the October 1913 edition of the *Atlantic Monthly*, J. Laurence Laughlin lamented these laws. A professor of political economy at the University of Chicago, Laughlin was a staunch opponent of this type of legislation, and he derogatorily described it as resulting from a fit of "hysterical agitation" by, and on behalf of women workers "interested chiefly in getting some cheap political notoriety."[91] In other words, he believed the laws were borne of the unprincipled, irrational, impulsive, and careless activism of uneducated and ill-advised groups in society. Nothing could have been further from the truth. Above all else, the "demand" for such laws "was not self-interest but social conscience," and the far-from-ill-advised group that made the greatest such "demand" was the National Consumers' League (NCL).[92]

The National Consumers' League: Investigating, Agitating, Legislating

With its origins in the consumers' leagues established in New York, Massachusetts, Pennsylvania, and Illinois earlier in the decade, the NCL was formed in 1899 when these different state-level groups united to create a single, national organization whose motto was "Investigate, agitate, legislate."[93] Its creation, and the goals it pursued, reflected the impact of industrialization on American society. It appealed to the women—especially white, middle-class women—who increasingly became consumers, rather than producers, of the goods they used in their homes. As the twentieth century dawned, many of the goods that were once made within the home were now produced by factories. The workforce experienced significant demographic changes as, beginning in the 1890s, married women, who were bearing fewer children and having to spend less time at home because of technological laborsaving innovations, far more frequently ventured into the labor market. However, these were disproportionately working-class women because, unlike their middle- and upper-class counterparts, they were not "confined to the home in accord with the prevailing dictates of the 'Cult of True Womanhood,' which stressed domesticity and submissiveness as the correct womanly characteristics." The middle-class women—those to whom the NCL principally appealed—were the primary consumers. These were the women who once made all the clothing and canned all the foodstuffs for their families but now went to stores to buy these items.[94] They were the intended recipients of the NCL's "call for ethical consumption."[95]

Writing in 1899, Florence Kelley described the NCL's approach and the choice of its targeted audience as "very natural":

> Since the exodus of manufacture from the home, the one great industrial function of women has been that of the purchaser. Not only all the foods used in private families, but a very large proportion of the furniture and books, as well as the clothing for men, women, and children, is prepared with the direct object in view of being sold to women. It is, therefore, very natural that the first effort to educate the great body of miscellaneous purchasers concerning the power of the purchaser should have been undertaken by women, among women, on behalf of women and children.[96]

This approach ultimately became a two-pronged one. The NCL first encouraged women to exert ethically driven consumer power. Second, it sought to bring improvements to the working conditions of those individuals who bore the disproportionate burden of

FIG. 2.3   Florence Kelley, general secretary of the National
Consumers' League (1910). Library of Congress.

making those consumer goods—hence its campaign for the enactment of minimum wage laws for women (and children).

"The heart of the NCL was always its general secretary" (for
at least the first forty years of its existence),[97] and that heart beat
stronger than it might otherwise have done and gave the minimum wages for women movement the cardiological strength it
needed, because the NCL's first general secretary was the indomitable Florence Kelley. Serving in that capacity for thirty-three years,
until her death in 1932, Kelley is universally lauded by both historians and those who worked alongside her. She was "the bearer
of a message"—and just like that message (and oftentimes because
of it), she "made her generation think."[98] She "personified . . . the

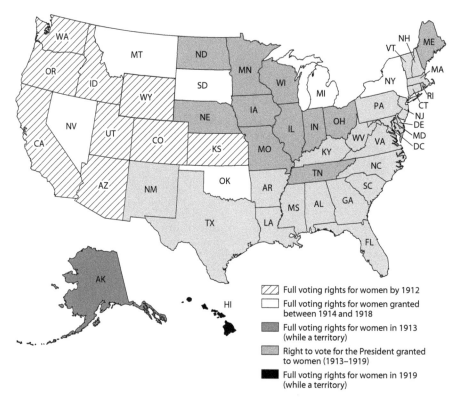

MAP 2.3   Map showing the twenty-six states (and one territory—Alaska) that granted women full or partial (for president) voting rights before ratification of the Nineteenth Amendment in 1920. Compiled using data from "Centuries of Citizenship: A Constitutional Timeline," National Constitution Center, accessed December 31, 2018, https://constitutioncenter.org/timeline /html/cw08_12159.html. Map by Bill Nelson.

quickening of women's concern for the humanizing of industry in this epoch change," and was the kind of person about whom "[i]t was said that, when she entered a room, 'everyone was brave.'"[99] In short, there was much truth to Felix Frankfurter's description of Kelley as the "woman who had probably the largest single share in shaping the social history of the United States during the first thirty years" of the twentieth century.[100]

For the first five years of the NCL's existence, most of its sixty-four branches were established in twenty Northeast and Midwest states, but at the numerical height of its membership in 1916, its fifteen thousand members were spread over forty-three states.[101]

This geographical expansion can largely be explained by the decision in *Muller*, which "both regenerated and reoriented" the NCL.[102] In doing so, it enabled the organization to break down some of the geographical barriers that impeded the progress of other social reform movements. In the 1910s, for example, the woman's suffrage movement was negatively affected by an "old East-West antagonism" that saw many western women bristle at the work of the principally eastern-run National American Woman Suffrage Association. As map 2.3 shows, many westerners already had voting rights and "wondered why the easterners should tell them what to do."[103] By contrast, when the NCL led the post-*Muller* crusade for minimum wage laws, it was working with a blank slate because no state had such a statute in place. Yes, every state had its own distinct "political culture," and the state "constitutions and traditions of judicial interpretation" were all very different.[104] Therefore, the nine state minimum wage laws for women enacted in 1912 and 1913 all had distinctive features representative of these geographical political differences. However, it is also important to note that the nine state legislatures all resoundingly approved these new additions to their statute books. And there is no doubt that the NCL played a significant unifying role without which it is doubtful that any states would have enacted meaningful minimum wage laws as early as they did.

One of the ways in which the NCL achieved this goal was to produce a model minimum wage law based on the Trade Boards Act passed by Great Britain. The preamble of this 1910 NCL document read as follows: "The welfare of the State of _____ demands that women and minors be protected from conditions of labor which have a pernicious effect on their health and morale."[105] The language of this model became the basis for laws enacted by numerous states, including Washington.[106]

Taking the Pacific Northwest Initiative:
"It couldn't be done but here it is"

In the late nineteenth and early twentieth century, the transcontinental railroads brought unprecedented expansion of domestic and international commerce to the Pacific Northwest, with accompanying population booms.[107] Between 1890 and 1910 the population grew by 112 percent in Oregon, and in Washington by

220 percent; and in cities like Portland and Seattle, the numbers of women workers grew exponentially. (Those numbers grew by almost 700 percent in Seattle between 1900 and 1920; the increase in the percentage of *married* women entering the workforce during the same period of time was 900 percent.)[108]

When they took up the question of minimum wage laws in early 1913, progressive legislators in Oregon and Washington benefited in a way that their counterparts in Massachusetts had not done. For a start, the legislative landscape was quite different in the Pacific Northwest. The degree of industrialization in Oregon and Washington did not even remotely compare to that of the eastern states; women made up a far smaller percentage of the workforce (and particularly in manufacturing, where only 4 percent of Washingtonians were female); and there was "regional isolation from competition," which limited the number of industries economically interested in opposing minimum wage laws. (Because of the prohibitively high costs of transporting certain goods across the country by railroad, only those industries "that came into direct competition with the products of eastern sweatshops—cracker and candy producers and elements of the garment and box trades" challenged the legislation.) Consequently, there was much less business-led obstruction to the passage of minimum wage laws.[109]

There was also "a greater readiness to 'give women a chance'"[110] in Oregon and Washington because neither state was a stranger to taking the national progressive policymaking lead. For example, in 1902 Oregon became the first state to introduce "fully functioning" direct democracy when voters approved a ballot measure empowering the direct citizenry proposal of amendments to the state constitution and the passage of new state laws (initiatives), and enabling Oregonians to put questions on the ballot that proposed the overturning of state statutes (referenda). The voters overwhelmingly supported what became known as the "Oregon system": 62,024 voted in favor of it, and only 5,668 individuals rejected it.[111] Oregon subsequently led the way with countless progressive reforms (including the 1903 maximum hours law upheld in *Muller*).[112] To the north, in 1911 the Washington legislature passed the "Waitresses' Bill," imposing an eight-hour workday for women (the previous limit, imposed in 1901, was ten hours), and in 1912 a voter-approved law gave the state's citizens the initiative and referendum power.[113] This Pacific Northwest spirit of policymaking initiative was captured in a 1923 booster publication jointly produced by the Chicago, Burlington & Quincy Railroad, the Northern Pacific Railway, and the Great Northern Railway: "If there is one impression that goes deeper than any other as you travel through the Pacific Northwest today, it is that nothing is too big to be undertaken in this land of surpassing achievements. The war-time slogan of the Shipping Board fits . . . 'It couldn't be done but here it is.'"[114]

For both Oregon and Washington, it was entirely in keeping with their progressive histories for them to be out ahead of most of the pack when it came to enacting minimum wage laws for women. Reformers in both states realized that hours and wages laws should go hand in hand. As Father Edwin V. O'Hara observed when testifying in support of wages legislation in Oregon, it was pointless and socially irresponsible to have one without the other. Overworking and underpaying women subjected them to twin evils:

> Not wages alone, which are insufficient to give the worker a full, nourishing meal three times a day, and call for close, unhealthful sleeping quarters; not hours alone which strain her to a point of exhaustion to finish the day's demands; but these two together, combining with unsanitary, dirty, and distasteful conditions under which girls work, are responsible for much of the inefficiency, sickness, and degeneracy that is found among women wage earners.[115]

When O'Hara received an honorary doctorate of laws from the University of Notre Dame in 1917, the citation on the certificate read: "To a learned and zealous priest, author of the 'Minimum Wage Law in the State of Oregon,' a vindicator of popular rights and a vigorous champion of the Church."[116] This description was no exaggeration. When Father O'Hara testified, Oregon's legislators listened, and when the 1913 session of the legislature opened, one of the first orders of business was for the Senate president, Dan J. Malarkey, to introduce a minimum wage bill. "On February 11, 1913, it took the [state] house just 12 minutes . . . to pass . . . [that] bill," and when it came up for a final vote, there were only four "nays" cast.[117] It was a similar story in Washington State.

Piper's Music

In his inauguration speech on Wednesday, January 15, 1913, Governor Lister gave the Washington state legislature some advice. It was important to achieve progressive policymaking goals, but only by *"follow[ing] safe and sane lines."* The preferred course of action was *"to follow public opinion rather than to rush in advance of it."* A law guaranteeing minimum wages for the state's women workers was not, however, something that Lister desired to see advanced through the legislature slowly, and it is widely agreed that Lister's support for the legislation was a major factor in securing its passage that spring.[118] This was not the elected state representatives "rushing" to "advance" something. After all, 1913 did not represent the first year in which such a bill was brought to the floor of that body. In 1909, after the decision in *Muller*, various organizations— including the Washington State Federation of Labor and the Federation of Women's Clubs—unsuccessfully attempted to get such a law passed.[119] Nor was the bill that became the 1913 law—the bill introduced by Senator George U. Piper—the first of its kind to be brought up for debate by a state legislator during that session.

Writing the Music

For the first time in its history, in 1913 the Washington state assembly welcomed female members into its ranks after Nena J. Croake (Progressive) and Frances C. Axtell (Republican) were both elected to the state House in 1912.[120] Both women had a limited legislative impact, but this had as much to do with entrenched "separate spheres for the sexes" attitudes in the legislature as it did with the fact that both women only served one term in office.[121] For example, Croake's principal campaign issue was the need for a mother's pension law because, as she said, it was "of special interest to women, and the human side of it as well as the economic value it possesses is sweeping the continent as a great wave."[122] While the 1913 legislature did pass such a bill, it was different from the one envisioned by Croake. A similar fate befell the first bill that she introduced, a bill providing for minimum wages for women. She was given the honor of introducing the session's very first bill, which proposed a guaranteed $1.25 daily wage (or hourly rate of 16 cents) for women workers, but the bill went nowhere.[123]

The *Seattle Union Record*, a weekly labor union newspaper published by the Central Labor Council of Seattle and Vicinity, and self-described "official Organ of the Washington State Federation of Labor," closely followed the debates over and final passage of Senator Piper's bill (in addition to reporting extensively on minimum wage developments in other states). It began its reporting on January 18 (the first issue published after the legislative session began) by blasting Croake's proposed bill. "Any woman who would place other women in a position where their salaries would be fixed at a minimum of $7.50 has but little conception of what it takes to support a woman who is compelled to work," the newspaper stated. "An adequate bill will be introduced by some other member of the legislature, and to that member should be given the credit of securing the passage of the bill." It was clear that "persons resident in Seattle" were encouraged to steer well clear of Croake, who "had an object in view in introducing a bill with a low provision for women who work." The article concluded that "before the legislature adjourns she will be smoked out."[124]

Perhaps there are traces of sexism and classism in this reporting (as a successful osteopath, Croake defied many stereotypes of her time), but it would be inaccurate to ascribe such motives to the writer of this article. The newspaper wholeheartedly agreed with Croake about the need for a minimum wage for women—it was a "primal" need for reasons that were reminiscent of the Court's reasoning in *Muller*. As the newspaper rhetorically asked: "[H]ow can we expect a sturdy race from mothers who suffer the hardship of overwork and undernourishment due to lack of sufficient pay with which to provide the commonest necessities of life?"[125] It did not, however, believe that this goal could be achieved with a flat-rate minimum wage. Such provisions were generally unpopular. Of the seventeen minimum wage laws enacted between 1912 and 1919,[126] only Utah (1913), Arizona (1917), and Puerto Rico (1919) provided for an "inflexible" wage.[127] All the others specified that wage scales would be established for different industries, usually through the creation of a commission tasked with investigating working conditions across the state.

When the Washington state assembly House and Senate committees on labor came together for a special joint hearing in early February 1913, they compared the two minimum wage law bills introduced by Representative Croake and Senator Piper. The NCL

had been "instrumental in drafting" the latter, and as a result the proposed legislation looked very much like the other ones (such as Oregon's) that this organization played a role in composing. The forces
in attendance at the hearing (including Father O'Hara and other
individuals from Portland) overwhelmingly supported the Piper bill.
O'Hara emphasized its "element of fairness," something that he did
not believe could be said of flat-rate laws.[128] His concern—that such
legislatively determined rates would become outdated after a very
short period of time—was echoed by many of those who testified
in support of Piper's bill. Indeed, this was the standard fear that
drove opponents of flat-rate bills. As Elizabeth Brandeis—Louis
Brandeis's daughter—observed in her detailed study of minimum
wage laws, such laws were considered useless because "in a period
of rapidly rising prices the rates set were soon below existing wages
and played no part in ameliorating conditions."[129] Defending her
bill, Croake expressed the concern that wages set by a commission
would be anything but fair because "the commission would have an
ear to the call of 'its master'"—in other words, it would be beholden
to employers, at the expense of women workers. This argument
found little to no support, and the committee voted to recommend
passage of Piper's bill.[130]

When that legislation passed the Senate, the final February 21
vote indicated the extent to which minimum wages for women
had legislative support in Washington in 1913. As the *Union Record*
reported:

> There was much skirmishing by a few who opposed the mea-
> sure to tack on amendments that would destroy the purpose
> of the bill, but they were strongly voted down each time. Sen-
> ator [Josiah] Collins of King [County], who always stands for
> the chamber of commerce crowd, was the chief opponent of
> the bill, but the only thing that he succeeded in doing was to
> prepare the way for his political funeral, which is scheduled to
> take place the next occasion upon which he aspires for politi-
> cal office.[131]

Such opponents were few and far between. The final vote in the
Senate was 36–2. When the bill came up for a final vote in the
House on March 12, there was greater opposition, but it still passed

with the support of what the *Union Record* described as "a good strong majority to its credit" (the vote was 82–12).[132]

As Section 1 of the new law stated, it was intended to protect women and minors from the "conditions of labor which have a pernicious effect on their health and morals," namely "inadequate wages and unsanitary conditions."[133] It therefore provided for the establishment of an Industrial Welfare Commission (IWC) that would identify the minimum wages appropriate for achieving these goals for workers in various different industries.[134] Joining the state commissioner of labor, who would sit as an *ex-officio* member of the commission, were four gubernatorial appointees with staggered terms (varying from six to thirty months). Their replacements would serve fixed four-year terms. Interestingly, there was no requirement that the members be appointed from any specific segments of society (no requirement, for example, that they equally represent the interests of employers and employees). The only people ineligible for appointment were those who were "or shall have been at any time within the five years prior to the date of such appointment a member of any manufacturers or employers association *or of any labor union*." Significantly, the commissioners were unpaid.[135]

If, after using the extensive investigative powers bestowed upon them by the 1913 law, the commissioners found cause to implement a minimum wage in any particular industry, they would do so by establishing a conference which, unlike the commission, would be "composed of an equal number of representatives of employers and employes [*sic*] in the occupation or industry in question, together with one or more disinterested persons representing the public."[136] Upon accepting the minimum wage recommendation of a conference, the commission would then issue mandatory orders, violation of which carried three different forms of penalty: (1) discharging an employee who testified, or who was about to testify, at what an employer believed to be an investigative meeting of the commission; (2) paying an employee less than the legal minimum wage established by the commission, of which both were criminal misdemeanors, with potential fines of up to one hundred dollars; and (3) Section 18 of the law permitted aggrieved employees to bring a civil suit against their employer in order to secure back pay *"notwithstanding any agreement to work for such lesser wage.*"[137] It was of course the existence of this section that, in 1935, enabled Elsie Parrish to file suit against the West Coast Hotel Company.

Playing the Music

The 1913 law took effect on June 12. Exactly one month later Governor Lister named his chosen appointments to the commission. Eleven days after that, those members met in Olympia for the first time.[138] Their initial task was to gather the data needed to determine the wage schedules that would be set for different industries. They quickly realized that this would be easier said than done. It was one thing to print thirty thousand blank forms that, upon completion, would furnish the commission with information about the family status of, wages and working conditions of, and estimates of the costs of living and expenses faced by female wage earners across the state. How one would get these forms into the hands of employers and employees and then ensure that they were completed and returned to Olympia was another task completely. It was not as if there existed any kind of list of women workers, and although various labor and women's organizations were able to assist with the distribution of the forms, the commission also found it necessary to send investigators out to the state's five largest cities. In light of these logistical obstacles, it is particularly impressive that the commission received 11,059 completed forms from employees and 138 from employers.[139] Many of the women workers who returned the forms chose to provide additional information about "individual struggles . . . and the attitude of employers toward minimum wage legislation" by writing on the backs of blank cost of living forms.[140] When collated, the data told a grim story, but these individual recollections did something that the numbers simply could not do. They personalized the suffering.

In order to put the immense amount of data into some semblance of order, the commission sought out and temporarily secured the services of Caroline Gleason, the secretary of the IWC of Oregon.[141] In 1914 Gleason published a one-hundred-page report for the Washington commission. It provided detailed summaries of the data gathered, highlighting the problems—wage-related and otherwise—faced by women workers in the state.[142] Eighteen months later, writing for *The Survey*, a prominent social work journal, Frances K. Headlee (secretary of Washington's IWC), provided a national audience with an overview of that data. Not only was it abundantly clear that women were being systematically very poorly paid, but also there were glaring disparities between the different industries (which came as no surprise to any of the advocates of minimum wage laws). For example, Headlee reported that while 55.6 percent of mercantile employees made less than ten dollars per week, the percentages were far higher for factory workers (71.2 percent) and laundresses (72.4 percent).[143]

"Somewhat at a loss"

Headlee also reported that after the commission began setting minimum wage scales in the summer of 1914, some employers resisted the changes but ultimately "recogniz[ed] in its provisions a legal standard which eliminates unfair competition. Results of a survey made late in 1914," Headlee continued, "show that none of the doleful predictions that were made by the opposers of the measure have come true." Contrary to the predictions of some opponents of minimum wage laws, "experienced workers are not being replaced by inexperienced. Neither does there appear to be any tendency for the minimum of law to become the maximum of custom, for many of the groups of women receiving more than the legal wage show an increase in number in 1914 after the wage became effective."[144]

Two decades later, Alma Lutz, a prominent member of the National Woman's Party (NWP), wanted to know whether things had changed. Over time, had the 1913 law actually hindered the advancement and employment of women in Washington State? Seeking an answer to this question, in 1933 Lutz wrote to Gersha V. Haney, supervisor of Women in Industry for the State of Washington.[145] Lutz was seeking factual ammunition that the NWP could use in a campaign to shoot down protective legislation. It viewed such laws as public albatrosses around the necks of the nation's women. When Lutz received Haney's letter, she used a red pen to make a mark in the margin next to what she considered to be the most important sentence. "In some cases," Haney had written, "boys and men have replaced women" because there was no state statute requiring males to be paid a minimum wage.[146] It did not matter that Haney went on to emphasize that such instances were very rare. *Any* evidence that minimum wage laws hurt, rather than helped, women was useful for the NWP.

While it was this sentence of Haney's letter that piqued Lutz's interest (as shown by the marking in red pen), the story of *Parrish* finds far greater interest in the paragraph that followed it, a paragraph that reads as follows:

> We are in rather a difficult position at the present time due to the fact that about a year ago the Assistant Attorney General [of Washington State] sent this office a copy of an opinion that he had made in regard to the minimum wage law. He cited the decision given by the United States Supreme Court in 1923 in "Adkins vs. Children's Hospital." The Attorney General has kindly refrained, at our request, from giving any publicity to his opinion, and we have only spoken of it where absolutely necessary. To give it any publicity would only work a hardship upon the women who are employed.[147]

The rendering of an "Opinion"—the providing of advice on a question of law when asked to do so by a public official—is one of the formal duties of an attorney general at both the state and federal levels. Interestingly, the Opinion to which Haney refers appears to have been an informal statement of views, because there is no record of such an Opinion having been issued. However, Haney's letter does strongly suggest that the Opinion stated that while the 1913 state law was still on the books, there existed a decision, from the nation's highest court, that made it legally difficult for the statute to be enforced to its fullest extent. This conclusion is confirmed by correspondence from the files of the Washington attorney general's office, correspondence penned in the immediate aftermath of *Parrish*. Namely, the July 1937 letter that a firm of lawyers in Minneapolis sent to Attorney General George W. Hamilton asking for information about Washington's minimum wage and maximum hours laws. Replying on Hamilton's behalf, Assistant Attorney General Wilbur A. Toner described both the relevant statutory provisions and the state court decisions upholding them. It was what he wrote next that was particularly instructive: "Due . . . to the fact that our [welfare] commission was *somewhat at a loss after the decision of the supreme court of the United States in the case of Adkins v. Children's Hospital, not many hearings have been held in the last fifteen years.*"[148]

Washington was not the only state with a minimum wages for women law on its books that found itself "somewhat at a loss" after *Adkins*. The laws had been enacted out of a profound belief, on the part of legislators and other advocates such as the NCL, that there was "an obvious and desperate human need" to provide minimum wages for women workers.[149] One important question remained, however. Would a majority of the U.S. Supreme Court consider such laws constitutional?

3   Creating a Legal "no [wo]man's land"

New policies are usually tentative in their beginnings, advance in firmness as they advance in acceptance. They do not at a particular moment of time spring full-perfect in extent or means from the legislative brain.

—*Justice Joseph McKenna*, Bunting v. Oregon *(1917)*

Would a majority of the U.S. Supreme Court consider state minimum wage laws for women constitutional? Oregon's 1913 minimum wages law pushed the Court to answer that question sooner rather than later. However, when the Court finally did so in 1917, the justices were hopelessly deadlocked; by a vote of 4–4, they automatically affirmed the lower court's decision, an outcome without precedential value.[1] That nondecision in *Stettler v. O'Hara* was just one of three cases that year in which the Court managed to avoid determining which of its prior decisions—*Lochner v. New York* (1905) or *Muller v. Oregon* (1908)—controlled the question of whether minimum wage laws for women were constitutional.[2] This stalemate ended in 1923 when the Court reached one of the "all-time peaks" in its own "conservatism" in *Adkins v. Children's Hospital*, in which a stridently self-confident quintet of justices unequivocally stated its belief that laws providing minimum wages for women ran afoul of the U.S. Constitution.[3]

Adkins held firm for almost exactly fourteen years. During that time the Court did decide two cases (not involving the

82

regulation of wages) whose opinions potentially laid the jurisprudential groundwork for overturning *Adkins* (as discussed in chapter 5). However, on June 1, 1936, a five-justice majority of the Court stubbornly upheld *Adkins* when it struck down New York State's minimum wage law for women in *Morehead v. New York ex rel. Tipaldo*.[4] Defenders of such laws would have to wait another nine months, until *West Coast Hotel v. Parrish*, for the Court finally to overturn *Adkins*.[5] The path that the Court took to get to its decisions in *Adkins* and *Tipaldo*, and how that path and those decisions affected the enactment, implementation, and enforcement of state minimum wage laws across the nation, is the story told in this chapter. It is the second half of the story, begun in the previous chapter, about jurisprudential twists and turns.

A Loss of Momentum

In May 1921, while she was working with the National Women's Trade Union League of America (NWTUL), Alice Henry, the prominent Australian suffragist and trade union activist, put her own words to "The Song of the Shirt," the poem penned in 1843 by the Englishman Thomas Wood:[6]

> Work, work, work,
> Till our backs are ready to creak
> Work, work, work,
> For a pittance at end of the week.
> In morning's old chill
> To factory and mill
> We hurry along the dark street;
> In laundry's [*sic*] compete
> Midst the steam and the heat
> For the wages
> That makes up our share:
> Unfairly divided,
> Its blessings one-sided,
> A pittance at the end of the week.
>
> Work, work, work,
> Till drudgery burdens us down,

Work, work, work,
With patience that merits a crown,
O where is the glory
One hears in the story
Of honor in labor and toil?
We're weak, unprotected,
Our freedom subjected
Because to our job
We must cling.
We need that one-sided,
Unfairly divided
Poor pittance at end of the week.

Work, work, work,
A light in the distance we see.
Work, work, work,
In the future a reckoning there'll be.
O, you legislators,
Combaters, debaters,
Hearken at once to our cry,
You're strong
We are weak,
Your aid now we seek,
A minimum wage
Our budget to gage
We demand as our pittance a week.

Work, work, work,
On that bill for morning to night,
Work, work, work,
Till our wrongs are buried in right.
Rise up in your might
Be ready to fight,
Our vote put you here just as theirs.
And we're the foundation
Of this very nation
Without us you can't turn a wheel.
Add to your page a minimum wage
As our pittance at end of the week.[7]

Henry's words perfectly described the sweatshop conditions whose ultimate eradication was the goal of those campaigning for the passage of minimum wage laws for women (and children). Those activists knew that there was much work to be done even after the successful enactment of nine such state laws in 1912 and 1913. Those laws needed to be implemented and enforced; every other state needed to pass, implement, and enforce this kind of statute; and these laws needed to survive constitutional challenges. Between 1915 and the 1923 decision in *Adkins* six more states enacted laws guaranteeing minimum wages for women workers; and in 1918 and 1919 respectively, minimum wage laws were enacted that applied to women employed in the District of Columbia and Puerto Rico. To say, however, that this brought to seventeen the number of pre-*Adkins* minimum wage laws enacted to protect American women would be to oversimplify what was a far more complex reality, a reality defined by considerable legislative uncertainty and numerous obstacles. As Elizabeth Brandeis accurately observed, "After 1913 the minimum wage movement rapidly lost momentum," the passage of post-1913 laws notwithstanding.[8]

As table 3.1 shows, the laws enacting minimum wages for women in the 1910s suffered negative treatment for various different reasons. Some laws simply never went into effect (for myriad reasons), some were quickly repealed, and those statutes that provided for flat-rate wages soon became redundant as prices rose (exactly as the opponents of those types of laws had predicted). The majority of the laws, however, were temporarily put on hold until such time that the U.S. Supreme Court could issue a ruling about the constitutionality of minimum wage laws. Above all else, it is this U.S. Supreme Court uncertainty that explains both the gap, between 1915 and 1917, when no new wages laws were enacted, and the fate of the laws that had been enacted by 1917.[9]

On the Brink of War and Revolution

Stettler was one of the three cases, decided in 1917, in which the U.S. Supreme Court deftly managed to avoid deciding whether *Lochner* or *Muller* ultimately would determine the constitutional fate of minimum wage laws for women. Will Englund gave the subtitle "On the Brink of War and Revolution" to his book about the

TABLE 3.1 State minimum wage laws for women workers, enacted between 1913 and *Adkins*, that received negative treatment

State	Fate of minimum wage law for women
Arizona	Flat-rate law that quickly became redundant as prices rose.
California	Wage commission decided not to act until U.S. Supreme Court passed judgment on constitutionality of minimum wage laws.
Colorado	State never established a scale of minimum wages, and money never appropriated for law's enforcement; new law enacted 1917, but commission says it is inactive because of WWI and the absence of any complaints submitted.
Kansas	State decides not to act because of potential for a U.S. Supreme Court ruling on the subject; after *Stettler*, wage commission established in 1918.
Minnesota	1913 law enforced for one year until temporary injunction put law on hold until after *Stettler*; law upheld in 1918 by the state supreme court.
Nebraska	State never established a scale of minimum wages; law repealed in 1919.
North Dakota	Temporary injunction prevented enforcement of the law from 1920 to 1921 until resolution of lawsuit regarding the way in which wage orders were issued.
Puerto Rico	Flat-rate law that quickly became redundant as prices rose.
South Dakota	Flat-rate law that quickly became redundant as prices rose.
Texas	Law never operational, repealed in 1921.
Utah	Flat-rate law that quickly became redundant as prices rose; additionally, money was not appropriated for the law's enforcement.
Wisconsin	1913–17 wage commission decided not to act because of potential for a U.S. Supreme Court ruling on the subject; after *Stettler*, new minimum wage set and imposed, effective August 1919.

Source: Compiled using Elizabeth Brandeis, "Labor Legislation," in *History of Labor in the United States, 1896–1932*, ed. John R. Commons (New York: Macmillan, 1935), 504; Dorothy W. Douglas, "American Minimum Wage Laws at Work," *American Economic Review* 9 (December 1919): 711–12; and Alice S. Cheyney, "The Course of Minimum Wage Legislation in the United States," *International Labour Review* 38, no. 1 (July 1938): 28, 36–37.

turbulent events that took place in Russia and the United States in March 1917.[10] Conducting business in the Old Senate Chamber of the U.S. Capitol (the Supreme Court did not have its own building until 1935) in March and April 1917, the justices came to the brink of their own war about, and potential judicial revolution regarding, the legislative regulation of the wages of the nation's workers.

Wilson v. New: A Strikingly Different Case

First came the March 19 announcement of the decision in *Wilson v. New*. The case did not address the constitutionality of wage regulations that applied only to female employees.[11] Instead, it asked broader—and, in that respect, perhaps more important—questions about governmental interference with contractual relations. At issue in *New* was the Adamson Act, which was enacted by Congress in September 1916 in order to avert a national railroad strike. Its provision imposing an "eight-hour day for employees of carriers engaged in interstate and foreign commerce" was gender-neutral. However, it regulated a male-dominated business, so any question of whether the law violated the Constitution was a question of whether the contractual liberty of men could be interfered with in this manner.

Although the case divided the justices along familiar ideological lines, Chief Justice White's opinion suggested that—at least with regard to the hours provision of the law—this was an easy case to decide. This is because the statute acted to limit the employment conditions of workers in an industry over which the regulatory powers of the federal government unequivocally extended. The law could not possibly be considered unconstitutional, wrote White. Indeed, "we put" that "question . . . entirely out of view, on the ground that the authority to permanently establish it is so clearly sustained as to render the subject not disputable."[12] This is because Article I of the Constitution clearly gives Congress the power "[t]o regulate Commerce with foreign Nations, and among the several States, and with the Indian Tribes."[13] That power is of course not without limits; however, since 1819 the Court had said that "where a particular subject is within such authority, the extent of regulation depends on the nature and character of the subject and what is appropriate to its regulation."[14] It had been well established in *Munn v. Illinois*, and myriad cases thereafter, that the railroads constituted precisely the kind of "'virtual' monopoly" that would be designated "affected with a public interest."[15] As White emphasized, this was "settled by so many decisions, state and federal, and is illustrated by such a continuous exertion of state and federal legislative power as to leave no room for question on the subject."[16]

There was one question, however. It had been easy for the justices to determine the constitutional fate of the *hours* provision of the Adamson Act, but would they find one of the other challenged provisions of the law as simple to deal with? Section 3 stipulated that the railroads were temporarily (a) prevented from reducing their employees' wages below what they were currently being paid, and (b) they had to pay overtime "at a rate not less than the *pro rata* rate for" the "standard eight-hour workday." The terms of Section 3 were tied to those of Section 2, which read as follows:

> Sec. 2. That the President shall appoint a commission of three, which shall observe the operation and effects of the institution of the eight-hour standard workday as above defined and the facts and conditions affecting the relations between such common carriers and employees during a period of not less than six months nor more than nine months, in the discretion of the commission, and within thirty days thereafter such commission shall report its findings to the President and Congress.[17]

Prior to the enactment of this law, railroad employees typically worked ten-hour days. Consequently, the combined effect of Sections 2 and 3 of the Adamson Act was to ensure that for somewhere between six and nine months after the law took effect, those employees would be legally guaranteed to receive the same amount of wages for working ten hours as they would for working eight hours. As Justice James C. McReynolds observed at the beginning of his short but pointed solo dissenting opinion, "whatever else" the law did, it certainly did that.[18]

White and his colleagues were sympathetic to the argument that this wage regulation amounted to a governmental taking of the private property of the railroads. As White observed, "the right to fix by agreement between the carrier and its employees a standard of wages to control their relations is primarily private." The justices nevertheless concluded that the government could permissibly regulate that agreement here because not doing so threatened an "entire interruption of interstate commerce" (if the railroads struck), and that would cause an "infinite injury to the public interest which was imminent."[19] Not to mention the fact that the law only authorized the government to regulate the wages for a period of time "expressly limited"—thereby "leaving the employers and employees free as to the subject of wages to govern their relations by their *own* agreements after the specified time."[20] As the legal historian Barry Cushman summarizes, the railroads were "businesses affected with a public interest" and as such, "were under special duties to the public, and accordingly the contractual prerogatives of both the carriers and their employees had to yield to the public interest."[21]

In *Wilson v. New*, both *Munn* and the Commerce Clause gave the Court a way out of confronting the main "*Lochner or Muller?*" question. Avoiding addressing that question in the two other wage regulation decisions of 1917 would be much more difficult.

Hanging Out the Oregon *Bunting*

It should have come as no surprise to reformers that those two cases both involved challenges to the constitutionality of laws enacted by Oregon. As we saw in the previous chapter, during the first thirteen years of the twentieth century the Beaver State trail blazed the passage of progressive legislation. The "Oregon System" produced major social reforms. These included giving women the right to vote, bringing several elements of direct democracy to the state, and regulating the working conditions of women and children. The Court had already heard and rejected a challenge to one of those reforms when it upheld the maximum working hours for women law in *Muller*. Would the same fate befall challengers to the two 1913 laws that imposed maximum working hours (for men *and* women) and minimum wages (for women only)? This would be determined by the Court in *Bunting v. Oregon* (1917) and *Stettler v. O'Hara* (1917). There was little doubt that these were both cases "to which all industrial and social workers were looking with interest."[22]

In *Bunting*, the justices were confronted with a challenge to an Oregon law that limited employment "in any mill, factory or manufacturing establishment in this state [to no] more than ten hours in any one day, except watchmen and employees when engaged in making necessary repairs, or in case of emergency, where life or property is in imminent danger."[23] The challenge to this law came from Franklin O. Bunting, a supervisor at the Lake View Flouring Mills, located in Lake County in the south-central region of the state. Bunting was convicted for violating the law when he required one of the employees, George Hammersely, to work thirteen hours in one day. Bunting's lawyer, Oregon state senator W. Lair Thompson, contended that the law actually regulated wages, not hours. This is because an additional provision stated that an employee could work in excess of the stated maximum working hours if undertaking "overtime not to exceed three hours in any one day" *as long as* "payment be made for such overtime at the rate of time and one half of the regular wage."[24]

In a relatively short opinion that spoke for a five-justice majority, Justice Joseph McKenna upheld the law. He emphasized that the Court was neither bound to defer to a state supreme court's interpretation of a law, nor to accept the legislative rationale written into a law. However, in *Bunting* the Court did just this, its commitment to protecting contractual liberty notwithstanding (and without providing any clear explanation as to why). McKenna's opinion suggests that Senator Thompson badly overplayed his client's hand by focusing not on the ills of the maximum hours law (which *Lochner* would logically lead him to emphasize) but instead on the overtime pay provision. "[A]s to plaintiff in error's attack upon the law," wrote McKenna:

> He says: "The law is not a ten-hour law; it is a thirteen-hour law designed solely for the purpose of compelling the employer of labor in mills, factories and manufacturing establishments to pay more for labor than the actual market value thereof." And further: "It is a ten-hour law for the purpose of taking the employer's property from him and giving it to the employee; it is a thirteen-hour law for the purpose of protecting the health of the employee."[25]

Rejecting this argument and defending the difficult job of the legislature, which "it is to be borne in mind . . . was dealing with a matter in which many elements were to be considered," McKenna chastised Thompson for accusing the Oregon legislature of trying to slip a wages regulation in through the back door of a law regulating hours. "We are not required to be sure of the precise reasons for its exercise, or be convinced of the wisdom of its exercise. It is enough for our decision if the legislation under review was passed in the exercise of an admitted power of government."[26] And this law was passed in this manner because the Oregon Supreme Court had quite reasonably concluded that "[i]n view of the *well known fact* that the custom in our industries does not sanction a longer service than ten hours per day, it cannot be held as a matter of law that the legislative requirement is unreasonable or arbitrary as to hours of labor."[27] Even today, this reads as a remarkably deferential conclusion; that it came from a member of the *Lochner* majority makes it a truly stunning statement.

Although the 1913 statute in *Bunting* was very similar to the 1903 one that was upheld in *Muller*, there was a crucial difference between the two laws, a difference that must have given Bunting confidence that he would prevail. The 1913 law applied to *all* persons, male *or* female. Therefore, the law could not be upheld on the paternalistic/sexist grounds that it was needed to protect the vulnerable and fragile bearers of the nation's future generations (as in *Muller*). Additionally, insofar as it was a clear limitation on working hours, this law bore striking similarities to the New York Bakeshop Act that was struck down in *Lochner*. Finally, *Lochner* suggested that this Court would easily find the health rationale equally wanting as it related to the Oregon law. One could easily understand why Thompson thought his client would prevail. So, why did Bunting lose?

The answer to that question lies in the fact that there was one other way in which the 1913 Oregon law differed from the New York statute. Where Oregon's law had broad application, New York's was confined to "work[ers] in a biscuit, bread or cake bakery or confectionary establishment."[28] We can only speculate that this difference was important to the majority in *Bunting* because, curiously, references to *Lochner* are conspicuous by their absence from McKenna's opinion.[29] However, as Professor Cushman persuasively argues, the absence of *Lochner* in *Bunting*; McKenna's willingness to uphold the Oregon law in that case; and his subsequent decision to join the majority striking down a minimum wage law in *Adkins* all make sense if one steps back from the "liberty of contract dimensions" of *Lochner* and instead focuses on that majority's clear hostility to class legislation, the type of law that was *not* at issue in *Bunting* because of the statute's general applicability.[30]

* * *

On March 17, 1914, the day that the Oregon Supreme Court announced its judgment in *Bunting*,[31] it handed down its decision in another case that, unlike *Bunting*, squarely confronted the issue of wage regulation. There was no disputing the nature of the issue at hand in *Stettler v. O'Hara*, for it involved a constitutional challenge to the state's 1913 minimum wages for women law, a challenge that the Oregon Supreme Court unanimously rejected.[32] In choosing to appeal the case to the nation's highest court, Frank Stettler "would become the Curt Muller of the second phase of the . . . legal campaign" for minimum wage laws for women.[33]

Settling for *Stettler*

Leading the constitutional defense of the law in *Stettler*, just as he had done in *Muller* and *Bunting*, was the great progressive legal mind Louis D. Brandeis. It was in *Muller* that Brandeis first introduced the world of Supreme Court litigation to the groundbreaking type of extraordinarily detailed, heavy-on-social-science-rather-than-legal-citations brief that would come to bear his name (a type of brief that would also be prepared in *Bunting* and *Stettler*). Ringing in at 113 pages, only two of which laid out legal arguments, the "Brandeis brief" in *Muller* provided the justices with reams of data and statistics (primarily compiled by his sister-in-law Josephine Goldmark and other National Consumers' League [NCL] employees) that amply supported the contention that the 1903 law was an entirely reasonable statute. As the renowned Columbia University law professor Thomas Reed Powell observed in his article about *Stettler* (published within months of the Court's decision), such data are invaluable resources for the Court because the "due process of law" clauses in the Constitution do not "tell us what ends are public ends, nor what means are reasonable and what means are arbitrary." Continuing, wrote Powell, "Any judgment on such matters must be based on knowledge of actual conditions, on prognostications of the probable effect of any legislation on such conditions, and on views of what is desirable. In acquiring this knowledge and making these prognostications, and in forming judgments of what is desirable, recourse must be had to other sources than judicial precedents," sources such as the Brandeis brief.[34]

And that brief was truly revolutionary, for to this point when interpreting provisions of the Constitution (such as "due process of law") judges had either looked to *historical* sources (informing upon the original intent of the framers of the text) or *mechanical* ones (informing upon the original meaning of the words of which the text is composed).[35] These were two stick-in-the-mud sources that, by their very nature, left little or no room for accommodating the changing nature, circumstances, and condition of society. As Felix Frankfurter (who took over the minimum wage litigation NCL baton after Brandeis was appointed to the Supreme Court) observed, until Brandeis presented "his famous brief in *Muller* . . . social legislation was supported before the courts largely *in vacuo*— as an abstract dialectic between 'liberty' and 'police power,' unrelated to a world of trusts and unions, of large-scale industry and all its implications."[36] In *Muller*, "[f]or the first time the arguments and briefs breathed the air of reality."[37]

Although Brandeis briefs were also prepared in *Bunting* and *Stettler*, by the time the justices eventually decided both cases, President Woodrow Wilson had appointed Brandeis to the Court to replace Justice Joseph Lamar, who died in January 1916. On one level, Jennifer Friesen and Ronald K. L. Collins are right to say that *Bunting* and *Stettler* are both proof positive that "Louis Brandeis's legal talents, along with Josephine Goldmark's vast knowledge of industry, provided the winning combination that brought victory after victory for the N.C.L. between 1908 and 1918," even before a U.S. Supreme Court composed of many men deeply hostile to the idea of minimum wage and maximum hours laws.[38] However, on another level, one cannot ignore the fact that ultimately, it was Brandeis's appointment to the Court that led to the 4–4 stalemate in *Stettler*.[39]

Although the U.S. Supreme Court's final adjudication of Frank C. Stettler's lawsuit had no precedential value (because of the tie), it represented the first time that the nation's highest court had ruled on a minimum wage law for women. In the opinion of the advocates for the Oregon law, Stettler, a manufacturer of paper boxes in Portland, epitomized the problems that reformers sought to address. As Father Edwin V. O'Hara said, Stettler was "the most vicious of the parasites feeding on vulnerable women."[40] That feeling of enmity was mutual. When O'Hara, the Catholic priest who spearheaded the push for a minimum wage law for women in Oregon, was appointed by the governor to be chairman of the industrial commission established by the 1913 law, it was only a matter of time before Stettler would (a) lead the legal push to have the statute declared unconstitutional, and (b) turn that constitutional crusade into "a personal battle against O'Hara, whom he labeled a 'radical and socialist.'"[41] *Stettler* initiated his lawsuit on October 14, 1913, nine months after Governor Oswald West signed the bill into law. (The following year one of Stettler's employees, Elmira Simpson, initiated her own lawsuit challenging the law; her case, *Simpson v. O'Hara*, was decided by the Supreme Court together with *Stettler*.)[42] As if the hostility that O'Hara had publicly expressed regarding Stettler and his factory were not enough, the rift between the two men widened when Stettler discovered that he had inadvertently hired Caroline J. Gleason, the woman charged with undertaking O'Hara's survey of working conditions in the state. For three ten-hour days in the fall of 1912, Gleason sweated and toiled in the dismal environs of the factory, gluing labels on to shoeboxes. Among the multiple horrid aspects of this work were "[t]he odors wafting up from the hot glue." As Gleason reported in an understated manner, those fumes "were 'something less than pleasant.'" For her thirty hours of employment Gleason received $1.52 (which amounted to $0.05 per hour; accounting for inflation, that works out to approximately $1.34 per hour in 2020).[43] Of that factory, Gleason said, "It was the worst in the city. . . . The employer is dead now, God rest his soul."[44]

Gleason was not popular with many of the employers. (As she recalls, "Some of them ground their teeth at me and one good German, as big around as his pickle barrels, said of me, 'she iss a terrible voman. She is worse than a lawyer.'") Yet, for all the insults received, she steadfastly believed "firsthand experience was the best source of data . . . so she and her staff began to 'infiltrate' factories, stores, and offices where women were employed."[45] In January 1913, the "material Gleason collected" was incorporated into "a book published by O'Hara . . . and sent to public leaders, editors, and legislators."[46] This was precisely the kind of information from which a Brandeis brief was built.

When the U.S. Supreme Court heard arguments in *Stettler* on December 17, 1914, by all accounts "Brandeis's advocacy" as the lawyer in the case was just as powerful "as his brief writing." As William Hitz, a Department of Justice attorney, reflected:

> I have just heard Mr. Brandeis make one of the greatest argu-
> ments I have ever listened to, and I have heard many great argu-
> ments. . . . When Brandeis began to speak, the Court showed
> all the inertia and elemental hostility which Courts cherish for
> a new thought, or a new right, or even a new remedy for an
> old wrong, *but he visibly lifted all this burden, and without ora-*
> *tionizing or chewing of the rag he reached them all. . . . He not only*
> *reached the Court, but he dwarfed the Court.*[47]

Similarly:

> Charles Warren, a lawyer and constitutional historian, was in
> attendance that day and recalled how the Court had deferred
> to Brandeis. Chief Justice White gave each side an extra half
> hour, then gave Brandeis another half hour, and then said:
> "'Mr. Brandeis, your time is up but we will consider that the
> clock has stopped and you may continue.' The Clerk of the
> Court told me later that he never recalled such a thing ever
> before being done by a Chief Justice."[48]

However, it was one thing for the justices to "defer" to Brandeis during oral argument; it was another thing entirely for a majority of them to be *persuaded* by the lawyer's points of reasoning. And from the outset, a majority was not persuaded. Circumstances, some unclear,[49] some clear—such as Justice Lamar's death (January 1916), Brandeis's appointment to replace him (June 1916), Justice Hughes's resignation from the Court to run for the presidency (also June 1916), and the replacement of him with John Hessin Clarke (October 1916)—led to the original majority opinion (striking down the law) never being released, and the setting down of the case for reargument in January 1917 (proceedings from which Brandeis obviously had to recuse himself).[50] And so it was, that when the U.S. Supreme Court chose to announce its final judgments in *Bunting* and *Stettler* (on the same day—April 9, 1917), in only *Bunting* could a majority decision be mustered; the justices were hopelessly deadlocked in *Stettler*.

The 4–4 ties in *Stettler* (and *Simpson*) generated a traditional pro forma *per curiam* one-sentence decision—"Judgments [of the lower courts] affirmed with costs by an equally divided court."[51] This stalemate had profoundly important consequences for the immediate future of minimum wage laws for women in the United States. On the one hand the optimist could look at the decisions and take considerable heart from the fact that the Court had not struck down the Oregon law. However, on the other hand Frankfurter was right to lament the fact that "the vicissitudes of procedure . . . played no inconsiderable role in the drama" that was the Supreme Court's treatment of minimum wage laws for women between 1917 and 1937;[52] because in *Stettler* the Court came so near but remained oh so far away from declaring such laws constitutional in a manner that would have precedential force across the nation.

* * *

At the end of the second decade of the twentieth century, many minimum wage advocates believed the "legal tides were turning" in their favor.[53] This was a reasonable belief because in 1917 and 1918 the courts in Arkansas, Minnesota, and Washington all upheld minimum wage laws for women workers in their states.[54] However, the U.S. Supreme Court's 1923 decision in *Adkins v. Children's Hospital* subsequently put a serious dampener on the hopes of minimum wage advocates.

The *Adkins* Starvation Diet

In *Adkins* the Court struck down a 1918 federal law that established minimum wages for women and children in the District of Columbia. The statute (enacted by the Democratically controlled U.S. Congress, and signed into law by President Woodrow Wilson) created a Minimum Wage Board charged with establishing minimum wages for all female and child workers.[55] Two parties (one employer, one employee) challenged the law, claiming it violated the due process clause of the Fifth Amendment. The Children's Hospital of the District of Columbia considered the law an abridgment of its economic freedom to contract with its female employees, and twenty-one-year-old Willie Lyons contended that the law had caused her to lose her job as an elevator operator at the Congress Hall Hotel. She, her lawyers explained, was in no way an oppressed worker at the mercy of an unscrupulous employer. Reformers assumed that women would benefit from the paternalistic helping hand that protective legislation gave them because women *needed* that hand; without it, they would inevitably remain trapped in their sorry existences, enslaved by a vicious and unforgiving world ruled by uncompromising market forces. Lyons's lawyers sought to hold her up as the perfect example of a woman (and there were many such women in the workforce, they contended) who led a comfortable and fulfilling life earning far below statutorily prescribed minimum wages, the kind of independent individual whose constitutional liberty was no less important (and could be no more interfered with by price-fixing laws) than that of her male colleagues. And, indeed, not only had the 1918 law deprived her of her contractual liberty; it had also deprived her of her job (and negatively affected her ability to find another job).[56] Although we will probably never know the truth about Willie Lyons (she, like countless others, "became one of the many 'forgotten' litigants whose names are now relegated to footnotes in history books"), Peter Irons is rightly skeptical of the board's claim that she was not "induced to bring this action against her own interest."[57] After all, we are talking about her participating in a lawsuit that challenged the constitutionality of a law that would have compelled her employer to pay her twice what she had been receiving (with the obvious caveat that she allegedly lost her job because her employer did not want to pay her those additional wages).

In his opinion that spoke for the five-justice majority, Justice George Sutherland confidently concluded that women would applaud the liberating decision in *Adkins*. This was because of the "great—not to say revolutionary—changes which have taken place . . . in the contractual, political and civil status of women, culminating in the Nineteenth Amendment." The "differences" between the sexes of which *Muller* spoke "have now come, almost, if not quite, to the vanishing point," wrote Sutherland.[58] A woman no longer needed to be "placed in a *class* by herself, and [*class*] legislation designed for her protection" would no longer "be sustained."[59]

In response to the decision in *Muller*, the *Oregon Daily Journal* (a newspaper published in Portland) had concluded that "[t]he Supreme Court evidently takes the view that women are not citizens in the fullest sense of the term, as it sustains in full the Oregon statute limiting their right to make contracts."[60] In 1908 women in America were second-class citizens in many different ways, including, of course, the fact that they had no constitutionally guaranteed right to vote. That central component of citizenship would not become theirs until the ratification of the Nineteenth Amendment in 1920. In *Adkins*, Sutherland placed considerable emphasis on the enlightening and emboldening nature of this egalitarian constitutional development. However, reformers knew full well that while securing the right to vote was an immensely important, positive political development for women, it alone would not be able to bring about the degree of socioeconomic empowerment that female workers needed. It was a harsh but sad reality that for all the advances women had made over the past decade, American society was still very much one in which the "fairer sex" was seen as the "fragile sex," a sex still in need of "especial care [so] that her rights may be preserved," the "especial care" about which the Court had written in *Muller*.[61] Sutherland looked past this reality and crafted an opinion that the labor union leader Samuel Gompers condemned as the "logical next step in perfecting the doctrine that those who cannot help themselves shall not be helped."[62]

The fact that *Adkins* involved a disgruntled employer *and* a disgruntled employee suited Sutherland just fine. In his opinion he emphasized the way in which the 1918 law restricted the contractual liberty of both parties. He even went so far as to chastise the nation's lawmakers for enacting a statute that was "not confined to the great and powerful employers, but embraces those whose bargaining power may be as weak as that of the employee."[63] In one sense, he was of course right that liberty of contract "is as essential to the laborer as to the capitalist, to the poor as to the rich; for the vast majority of persons have no other honest way to begin to acquire property, save by working for money."[64] Therefore, the law did indeed distribute its burden equally. In *Muller*, Justice David Brewer looked beyond the fact that "in the matter of personal and contractual rights" women and men "stand on the same plane"[65] because the harsh reality of the situation was that both sexes clearly did not actually "stand on the same plane" in the workplace. In *Adkins*, Sutherland rejected the theory-reality distinction. He simply did not think that the sanctity of contractual liberty should be sacrificed at the altar of protective legislation. Liberty of contract could only be constitutionally limited under "exceptional circumstances,"[66] and the inequitable workplace conditions and employer-employee relations that defined much of the landscape of industrialized America in the early twentieth century simply did not amount to "exceptional circumstances." Sutherland justified these conclusions in part because he viewed the law in *Adkins* as doing something that was not simply *different* ("in every material respect") from all the other restrictions on contractual liberty the Court had previously upheld, but also far more *threatening* to that liberty. It was "simply and exclusively a price-fixing law" that struck at "the heart of the contract" by regulating "the amount of wages to be paid and received."[67]

This helped to explain the answer that the justices in *Adkins* gave to the "*Lochner* or *Muller*?" question. No longer avoiding that issue, in *Adkins* Sutherland's reasoning unequivocally demonstrated that at this point in time a majority of the justices considered *Lochner* the relevant referent. In part this was because of the aforementioned belief that women had made "revolutionary" socioeconomic and sociopolitical gains that had enhanced their workforce bargaining power.[68] However, Sutherland's use of reasoning that suggested *Muller* had been "laid to rest"[69] also reflected the crucial difference that he saw between the regulation of working hours and the regulation of wages. The latter posed a far greater constitutional threat because "[a] law forbidding work to continue beyond a given number of hours leaves the parties free to contract about wages, and thereby equalize whatever additional burdens may be imposed upon the employer as a result of the restrictions as to hours, by an adjustment in respect of the amount of wages."[70]

For Sutherland, any such "adjustment" would clearly strike at the heart of constitutionally protected liberty. The *actual* "adjustment" imposed by the 1918 law went one terrible step further. The minimum wage board was empowered "to ascertain and declare . . . the following things: . . . Standards of minimum wages for women in any occupation within the District of Columbia, and what wages are inadequate to supply the necessary cost of living to any such women workers to maintain them in good health and to protect their morals" for the stated "purposes . . . [which] are 'to protect the women . . . of the District from conditions detrimental to their health and morals, resulting from wages which are inadequate to maintain decent standards of living.'"[71]

Sutherland poured scorn on what he considered to be the plainly false justification for these provisions—"the assumed necessities of the employee." First, the law completely disregarded (and, in doing so, heaped paternalistic treatment upon) those female workers with "independent resources" (who Sutherland seemed to believe existed in relatively large numbers).[72] Why would independently wealthy, working women need the financial protection of a minimum wage law? Of course, the answer is that they probably would not. Therein lay Sutherland's point—not every woman in the District of Columbia needed and/or benefited from this law, yet it applied to and cramped the contractual liberty of all of them, and that was unconstitutional. Second, the law wrongly assumed "that well paid women safeguard their morals more carefully than those who are poorly paid"; and since there was "no such prevalent connection between" morals and wages, there could be no justification for such "a broad attempt to adjust the latter with reference to the former."[73] This did not mean that a "living wage" was an undesirable goal; indeed, Sutherland tentatively acknowledged that "every worker" had an "ethical right . . . to a living wage." But in America's constitutional democracy a law prescribing minimum wages was not a permissible means to achieving that end; and that, Sutherland pointedly observed, was not a conclusion that left workers high and dry. After all, what did American workers think that labor unions were for?[74]

This conclusion sat well with the individuals who chose to write letters praising the justice for his opinion in *Adkins*. While they came from various different quarters, those correspondents all made the same basic point. They were, as Henry W. Anderson put it, "delighted to see that the Court has the 'guts' (not quantity but quality!) to stand up in defense of personal liberty against the constant encroachment of government."[75] The "not quantity but quality" remark was inserted by hand after the letter was typed up, and of course referred to the fact that once again the Court was bitterly divided on liberty of contract questions.

The *Adkins* Dissents: "The power of Congress seems absolutely free from doubt"

As Peter Irons remarks, Chief Justice William Howard Taft "felt compelled to dissent" because "Sutherland's opinion was so reactionary."[76] In his dissent in *Adkins*, Taft offered a blistering rebuttal to many of the majority's key points. First, he simply could not understand how his colleagues could be blind to the working conditions that faced the nation's women, the women for whom minimum wage laws were passed. Unlike Sutherland, who felt that the burdens of protective legislation were borne by employer *and* employee alike, Taft recognized that no such reality existed. The industrialized workplace was not one within which either men and women, or employers and employees, entered and existed on equal footings. Conspicuous by its absence from Sutherland's opinion was any reference to sweatshops. By contrast, Taft introduced the "evils of the sweating system" into the second paragraph of his dissent in order to provide "well known" evidence in support of the conclusion that minimum wage laws for women represented entirely rational legislative choices founded in the realization "that employees, in the class receiving the least pay, are not upon a full level of equality of choice with their employer, and, in their necessitous circumstances, are prone to accept pretty much anything that is offered. They are peculiarly subject to the overreaching of the harsh and greedy employer."[77]

Second, Taft exasperatedly decried the fact that after *Adkins* a precedent that should have been controlling now seemed to be dead, and a precedent that should *not* have been controlling because it appeared dead had suddenly and magically been revived. Although it was clear that he was "sure" that they did not, Taft nevertheless expressed some uncertainty about whether his colleagues thought "the authority of *Muller v. Oregon* is shaken by the adoption of the Nineteenth Amendment." What *they thought* was ultimately irrelevant though, because *he knew* (as did so many others) that political empowerment "did not change the physical strength or limitations of women upon which the decision in *Muller* . . . rests."[78] And as for *Lochner*, why on Earth was that decision now very much alive when only six years earlier in *Bunting* it had, "supposed" Taft, been "overruled *sub silentio*"?[79] As discussed above, the differences between the applicability of the laws at issue in *Lochner* and *Bunting* might explain how those two decisions could peacefully coexist; but that is only a possibility. For Taft, any explanation for the apparent revival of *Lochner* lay in the majority's contention that minimum wage laws and maximum hours laws were two very different types of legislation. Although Taft expressed his "regret" that he was "at variance with the Court as to the substance of this distinction," there was nothing truly regretful about his dissent.[80]

By virtue of his seniority (as chief justice), Taft's dissenting opinion in *Adkins* appears as the first separate opinion printed in that case in the pages of the United States Reports. However, it is Justice Oliver Wendell Holmes Jr.'s dissenting opinion, which Taft admiringly described as "forcible," that unleashed the truly devastating attack on Sutherland's reasoning.[81] Just like Taft, Holmes ridiculed the Court's distinction between hours and wages and its Nineteenth Amendment and *Muller* arguments.[82] But unlike the chief justice, Holmes went much further in expressing his disbelief at what the majority had done. He was just as angry at the majority's refusal to defer to reasonable legislative judgments in *Adkins* as he had been in *Lochner*. He did not go so far as to call his colleagues stupid and unreasonable, but that was the implication of his words, which read as follows: "When so many *intelligent persons*, who have studied the matter [of minimum wages for women] more than any of us can, have thought that the means are effective and are worth the price, *it seems to me impossible to deny that the belief reasonably may be held by reasonable men.*"[83]

Taft believed that the very same illegitimate judicial motive that drove the majority to strike down the New York Bakeshop Act in *Lochner* underpinned the Court's decision in *Adkins*. Invoking one of the famous aphorisms from Holmes's dissent in *Lochner*, Taft reminded his colleagues that "it is not the function of this Court to hold congressional acts invalid simply because they are passed to carry out economic views which the Court believes to be unwise or unsound."[84]

In *Adkins*, Holmes did not feel the need to repeat that sentiment. However, the alternative way in which he chose to attack the Court made precisely the same point:

The earlier decisions upon the . . . [due process clause] in the Fourteenth Amendment began within our memory and went

no farther than an *unpretentious* assertion of the liberty to follow the ordinary callings. Later that *innocuous generality was
expanded into the dogma, Liberty of Contract.* Contract is not
specially mentioned in the text that we have to construe. It is
merely an example of doing what you want to do, embodied in
the word liberty. *But pretty much all law consists in forbidding
men to do some things that they want to do, and contract is no
more exempt from law than other acts.*[85]

Unless, as he had said in *Lochner,* a majority of the justices *wanted*
to exempt it because that exemption was consistent with their "economic theory," an "economic theory which," by the way, "a large part
of the country does not entertain."[86] He concluded that "the power
of Congress" to enact the 1918 law "seems absolutely free from
doubt."[87]

The "Shadow" or Specter of *Adkins*

As blistering as Holmes's dissent was, undoubtedly the most well-
known rhetorical indictment of *Adkins* came from outside the
Court—from the pen of the cartoonist Rollin Kirby, whose satirical
portrayal of the decision left nothing to the imagination. Justice
Sutherland is pictured enveloped in his black robes and standing
by a blank wall that has no distinguishing markings and would be
unknown to the viewer had not Kirby written the words "SUPREME
COURT"; Sutherland is handing a large piece of paper, complete
with a rosette-style official seal attached to it and bearing the words
"MINIMUM WAGE DECISION," to a petite, well-dressed woman whose
purse betrays her standing in life—for upon it Kirby has written
"WOMAN WAGE WORKER." The cartoon, which ran in the *New York
World,* bore the following, instantly famous caption: "This decision
affirms your constitutional right to starve."

   That the U.S. Supreme Court, the highest court in the land, had
declared that women had a "constitutional right to starve" became
a rallying cry for many labor activists both at the time of *Adkins*
and for many years afterward. For example, eleven days after the
Court's decision the NCL reprinted the Kirby cartoon and caption on the front page of the report of its nationwide conference,[88]
and Florence Kelley repeated it in her letter to Mrs. John Blair on
May 1: "The minimum wage law of the District of Columbia has

Nation Wide Conference
called by
National Consumers' League
on the

Minimum Wage Decision
of the Supreme Court of the United States

This decision affirms your constitutional right to starve

FIG. 3.1   National Consumers' League 1923 Conference program cover, featuring Rollin Kirby's cartoon about *Adkins v. Children's Hospital*. Library of Congress.

been held unconstitutional, and several thousand women have been assured of their constitutional right to starve, in the capital of our country."[89] Before *Adkins*, sufficient "legal uncertainty" existed that the minimum wage laws were repealed in several states, including Nebraska and Texas.[90] After *Adkins* no such "uncertainty" remained;

to the NCL, and to many other protective legislation advocates, the Court's decision "seemed like the death of m.w. legislation."[91]

Two more Supreme Court decisions (in October 1925 and January 1927) perfunctorily struck down minimum wage laws for women in Arizona and Arkansas with unsigned *per curiam* opinions that essentially said, "see *Adkins*." These appeared to confirm that reports of the constitutional demise of minimum wage laws for women were not at all exaggerated.[92] In the years that followed, the minimum wage laws of six other jurisdictions (California, Kansas, Massachusetts, Minnesota, Wisconsin, and Puerto Rico) were subjected to constitutional challenges. Only the Massachusetts statute—which, recall from chapter 2, was not a mandatory law—was upheld.[93] In Utah, the law was repealed in 1929 because of an assumption that it was unconstitutional; and in Ohio, "[i]n one of the longest games of 'wait and see,'" the legislature never acted upon the 1912 amendment to the state constitution which authorized it to regulate wages (including, but not limited to, the passage of minimum wage laws for women). It had waited to see how *Stettler* would play out; and then obviously *Adkins* derailed the plans of those legislators "who ironically had finally begun implementing such legislation." After *Adkins*, Ohio would not act on its constitutional mandate until 1933.[94] And it should be borne in mind that even in several states where minimum wage laws for women workers were not challenged in the courts, enforcement of the statutes encountered little opposition simply because the laws did not cover the industries where women were predominantly employed.[95]

Once again, the Pacific Northwest bucked the national trend.[96] The wage commissions of Oregon and Washington both had enforced their 1913 laws from the outset.[97] After *Adkins*, the Washington commission proved to be particularly "fearless," buoyed as it was by rulings from the Washington Supreme Court. For, in addition to a 1918 ruling in *Larsen v. Rice*, in 1926 that court said that while *Adkins* "probably has the effect of overruling . . . *Larsen*," that court was going to "ignore the question [of the law's constitutionality] . . . until, if ever, that question is urgently necessary in a proper case for decision."[98] This was the exception to the rule, though. For across the country it was widely accepted that *Adkins* had defined the constitutional landscape of minimum wages for women. Its "shadow . . . hung over all the minimum wage statutes."[99]

"[D]espite these limitations," the "minimum wage experiment" does "deserve . . . an important place in a history of labor legislation in the United States." Elizabeth Brandeis accurately emphasizes that "[t]he high hopes and ambitious program of the decade 1913 to 1923 have their significance" for it was "[i]n those years for the first time low wages were regarded as a matter of public concern and an attempt was made to devise governmental machinery to *mitigate the evil*."[100] In *Adkins*, the Sutherland-led majority disregarded the importance of that concern.

Ten years later, when the voters went to the polls on Tuesday, November 8, 1932, they handed the Democratic Party presidential nominee, Franklin Delano Roosevelt, a decisive victory over the incumbent Herbert Hoover. This victory was accompanied by massive congressional gains. Picking up ninety-seven seats in the House, the Democrats increased their control of that chamber; capturing twelve additional Senate seats gave them control of that chamber for the first time since 1919.[101] These gains were driven in large part by a popular desire to have in place a federal government that would view progressive policy measures, such as minimum wage laws, as a pressing "matter of public concern." The victories signaled that a majority of the American public wanted to see the economically depressed nation taken in a different direction than that which conservative judicial decisions, such as *Adkins*, had laid out.[102]

1933: "The thrill of creative effort"

In his inaugural address on March 4, 1933, the newly elected President Roosevelt admonished his audience to remember that "[h]appiness lies not in the mere possession of money; it lies in the joy of achievement, in the thrill of creative effort."[103] That same month, Al Smith (another prominent New Yorker and the Democratic Party's losing presidential candidate in 1928) penned "Democratic Leadership at the Crossroads" for the *New Outlook* magazine. The party, wrote Smith, "faces the most important decision in its history." Democrats might have claimed the White House, captured the Senate, and retained the House, but Smith was adamant—their ability to *govern* effectively, at a time when the country was desperate for *effective* leadership, could not be taken for granted:

The Democratic Party, in my opinion, must rid itself of the counsels of the minority of bigots, fanatics, populists, demagogues, mountebanks and crackpots who masquerade as leaders and give the party a bad name with sensible people—the fanatics who dragged religion and liquor into politics, the populists who blighted the party for so many years with their free silver and other economic heresies, the demagogues who support the opposing party more than half the time and who are without loyalty to person or principle, the mountebanks with their clownish antics and their irresponsible raving against millionaires and big business.

He refused to downplay the importance of this. "The future of the country," he wrote, "may well depend upon it."[104]

In the article, one of the six policies that Smith advocated was the minimum wage for women and minors—it was one of the things to which he believed the country should turn its "creative effort," the "creative effort" of which Roosevelt had spoken at his inauguration. However, the decision in *Adkins* hung, albatross-like, around the necks of all who had sought to enforce or enact state minimum wage laws in the intervening decade. And now, in the depths of the Depression *Adkins* was, in the words of Smith, "producing . . . logical results . . . [t]he sweat shop has returned in its worst form, and thousands of women are again singing 'The Song of the Shirt,'"[105] perhaps using the words of Alice Henry. It would take a special kind of "creative effort" to turn back this tide of oppressive employment practices. Roosevelt explicitly endorsed such an effort in the telegram that he sent to the governors of thirteen states (primarily located in New England and the Midwest) on April 12, 1933. He described the new minimum wage law, enacted in New York, as a "great forward step against lowering of wages, which constitutes a serious form of unfair competition against other employers, reduces the purchasing power of the workers and threatens the stability of industry." He "hope[d] that similar action can be taken by the other States for protection of the public interest."[106]

Two months earlier, a one-paragraph report that appeared in the Beloit, Kansas, *Call* newspaper indicated that the NCL was spearheading a "campaign in 44 states for minimum wage and restricted hours of labor for women workers." The newspaper was quick to caution its readers that the NCL "may not get anywhere in our generation." There was hope, though; "it's not going backward, at least."[107]

In 1933 seven states went forward with the passage of minimum wage laws for their women workers; most of the statutes were based on the new model law produced by the NCL.[108] This septet included five of the governors who had received the presidential telegram; all five signed into law statutes that did indeed mirror the New York legislation referenced by Roosevelt.[109] It is notable that one of the five was the governor of Ohio, the state that, as mentioned above, had since 1912 possessed the power, via an amendment to its own constitution, to enact such laws but had resisted doing so because of the uncertainty of the *Stettler* litigation and then the decision in *Adkins*.

A New York State of Mind

In *Adkins*, Justice Sutherland devoted extensive sections of his opinion to lamenting the absence, in the District of Columbia law, of any kind of relationship between wages and the value of the work performed for those wages. The new 1933 model NCL law was specifically designed to survive an *Adkins*-style constitutional challenge on these grounds, because it prohibited the employment of all women (except domestics and farm workers) at a wage that was "*both* less than the fair and reasonable value of the services rendered *and* less than sufficient to meet the minimum cost of living necessary for health."[110] Although that law did not directly confront *Adkins*, it certainly represented a major statutory challenge to that precedent. Two months earlier, the Albany *Times-Union* had expressed its support for the pending New York legislation, based on the NCL model. "Unemployment," the newspaper emphasized, "is depression's most tragical [sic] consequence. But hardly second to unemployment in its immediate poignancy, and sometimes worse in its lasting and baleful effects upon society, is the heartless exploitation of women and children in industry which times like these are so prone to bring forth. . . . Laws express the public spirit. In every community, let the social conscience be aroused."[111] As Marjorie McFarland (executive secretary of the Consumers' League of New York) observed in a letter to the Organizations in Labor Subcommittee of the State Assembly, "The deep issue of the case [of minimum wage laws] is whether the state has a right to protect itself and its citizens against conditions which undermine our whole democratic system."[112]

Whether such a right existed was a constitutional question that would ultimately be determined by the U.S. Supreme Court, and in 1933 the stakes could not have been higher—for minimum wage laws in particular, and more broadly the entire New Deal agenda. As Paul Hutchinson asked in *Forum and Century* magazine in September of that year. "What will happen to Mr. Roosevelt . . . if the program which he has mapped out for his Administration, and which has won him this unprecedented support, should be tossed into the constitutional wastebasket by the coming decision of the Supreme Court?"[113] He cautioned against sanguinity, and emphasized that constitutional challenges to the New Deal were not only inevitable but also likely to succeed because "a part of American industry will never allow the economic order to be revolutionized in this fashion [the New Deal laws] without shrieking 'Unconstitutional!' and rushing for the Supreme Court." Continuing, he expressed his belief that it was not "difficult to prophesy what arguments will be used to convince the Justices that unless they intervene, the heritage of our fathers (*vide* Mr. Hoover's Valley Forge speech!) will be destroyed."[114] Of course, the only way to find out whether Hutchinson was accurately predicting the constitutional fate of laws that provided minimum wages for women was to enact a bill such as New York's.

After that bill became law, there was an extensive period of data gathering by the state authorities that were charged with setting the appropriate wage rates. From the outset it had been New York's intention to make the laundry industry the first to be held accountable under the new law. The state had the broad support and promises of compliance from the New York State Laundry Owners Association and the Laundry Board of Trade.[115] Nevertheless, setting the rates was no simple procedure, as the aid that the New York Women's Trade Union League (NYWTUL) tried to lend to the process indicated. The NYWTUL hosted a series of meetings (the first of which took place just a few weeks after the law was enacted) that female laundry workers were encouraged to attend for the purposes of reporting just how little they were being paid. However, such efforts inevitably ran into the problem of fear, fear that one would be fired (and easily replaced with the next desperate unskilled worker in line), a fear even graver for those women (the majority of the workers in question) with small children at home.[116] A rate was finally settled upon, however, and on October 2 laundry owners were *directed* to pay their female workers a minimum hourly rate of 31 cents (in New York City).[117] That Directory Order changed to a *Mandatory* Order on August 6, 1934.

Morehead v. Tipaldo: Starched Judicial Resolve

Laundryman Joseph Tipaldo and three of his employees became the first people to be indicted and arrested for violating New York's minimum wages law after the authorities spent three months in "close observation" of their business. New York's industrial commissioner Elmer F. Andrews proudly professed his belief that the state had "developed an air-tight case" against the operator of Tipaldo's Bright Light Laundry, a one-floor establishment on 61st Street in Brooklyn.[118] Laundryman Tipaldo was an outlier in an industry whose members resoundingly supported the enactment and enforcement of the statute.[119] He had no qualms about neglecting to pay his female employees the mandated $12.40 for a forty-hour week, proudly justifying it as a financially prudent business practice that saved him over $60 every week and kept his untrustworthy girls in check.[120] Indeed, he made no effort to disguise his contempt for and distrust of his employees. Quoted after New York's highest court struck down the law, he said: "Now I can give work to beginners, girls who don't have jobs anyhow, at $10 a week. I get more production out of the girls too. Before this a Labor Department inspector could walk in any time and look over my books. This encouraged the girls to take it easy and loaf when they thought they had the inspector behind them."[121]

When the state authorities interviewed those girls brave enough to inform on their employer, their suspicion that Tipaldo was part of the "chiseling minority of unscrupulous or inefficient employers" that were failing to comply by, among other things, using fraudulent or kick-back practices, was confirmed.[122] Tipaldo's contempt for his employees extended to the way in which he paid them and covered up his lack of compliance with the minimum wage law. Whether they received ten dollars or as little as seven dollars a week (as some of the workers did), the process of payment was the same (and affidavits confirmed this had been a "*persistent violation of the law*"). To try and fool the authorities, Tipaldo paid wage checks into the bank—made out for the legally required minimum amount—which had been endorsed and surrendered by the employees. In return, however, those girls received far less *in cash*. It was no surprise that Tipaldo's bookkeeper, Nicoleta Somperisi, was indicted alongside her employer.[123]

Tipaldo Goes to Court

Over the course of the *Tipaldo* litigation, a total of seventeen judges ruled on the constitutional merits of the New York law, and there can be little doubt that all of them agreed with the sentiments in the last two sentences of the *Times-Union* piece quoted above. "Laws [*do*] express the public spirit" and "[i]n every community, [the democratic process] *does* let the social conscience be aroused." However, just as assuredly there are limits to the ways in which legislation can express the arousal of the public spirit and conscience of a society, and some of those limits are delineated in the U.S. Constitution including, after *Lochner* and *Adkins*, limits on infringements of "freedom of contract." Nine of the seventeen judges who presided over *Tipaldo*—including, most significantly, five U.S. Supreme Court justices—held that even though the New York law might be a statement of aroused democratic conscience, that was beside the constitutional point.

Justice Mitchell May (Supreme Court, Kings County, New York) issued the first judgment in *Tipaldo*. It was the only time that Joseph Tipaldo lost.[124] At the New York Court of Appeals (the state's highest court), he prevailed in a 4–3 decision that produced, from the pen of Chief Justice Frederick E. Crane, a majority opinion that Marjorie McFarland decried as a "legalistic" document that "maintained" contractual freedom "at whatever cost of misery, pauperism, and economic chaos." She was certain that "[t]he public, the workers, and the laundry employers themselves" instead "agree[d]" with the dissenting opinion authored by Justice Irving Lehman (who spoke for himself and Justices Leonard C. Crouch and John T. Loughran).[125]

It took Judge Crane a mere ten paragraphs to explain why the New York law was unconstitutional. He saw absolutely "no material difference" between it and the 1918 law struck down in

Adkins, rejecting as nothing more than "a difference in phraseology" the argument made in the brief submitted by New York attorney general John J. Bennett Jr., who explained that the New York law could be distinguished. Therefore, it could survive constitutional scrutiny, because it "provides a definite standard for wages paid. It provides that the worker is to be paid at least the value of the services rendered."[126] On the one hand, the logic of Crane's conclusion about the language of the New York law is sound. The state had made a concerted effort to craft a law that could survive *Adkins* because it had said that the minimum wage paid had to be linked to the "fair and reasonable value of the services rendered." However, as Crane noted, the law *also* said that wages had to "meet the minimum cost of living necessary for health." The language of the law made it clear that these two clauses were not mutually exclusive. "The minimum wage," wrote Crane, "must include both." In other words, New York had gone too far; had it only linked minimum wages to "the value of the services rendered," it might have been able to successfully defend its law because, at the very least, the law would then have been distinguishable from *Adkins*. On the other hand, however, what Crane said next made it very clear that even absent the "minimum cost of living necessary for health," the law would be considered unconstitutional. Indeed, his discussion of the linguistic differences between the two laws was completely unnecessary because he concluded that "the exercise of legislative power to fix wages in any employment is the same": "We should follow the law as given, and not speculate as to the changes which have come or are supposed to have come to economic conditions in the last decade."[127] What mattered most to Crane was not any differences between the language of the law struck down in *Adkins* and the myriad state minimum wage laws, but rather the wholly unconstitutional *principle* of wage fixing. In other words, Crane was deeply sympathetic to the argument made by Tipaldo's lawyers in the Appellant's Reply Brief, an argument that "any [wage] standard set by others than the parties to the contract must necessarily be an arbitrary compromise of individual opinion. Free men and women cannot be ruled in that way under our system."[128]

The day after the Court of Appeals issued its ruling, Elinore Herrick, the New York director of the National Labor Relations Board, hosted a strategy meeting at her house, a meeting attended by civic groups who all "fe[lt] strongly that the majority of the Court of

Appeals ha[d] missed the entire point of the minimum wage legislation."[129] Among labor activists, there was some expression of hope
that a victory could be secured on appeal to the nation's highest tribunal.[130] However, liberal observers of the Court's anti–New Deal
decisions knew that any such optimism was probably misplaced.
Responding to the decision by the New York Court of Appeals,
the *New Republic* captured the prevailing pessimism: "If evolution
toward a decently socialized society continues to be this slow, our
cities will be being dug up by archeologists before the most elementary reforms are realized."[131]

Attorney General Bennett appealed the Court of Appeals decision to the U.S. Supreme Court. Lawyers for the National Woman's
Party (NWP) believed that Bennett's petition for certiorari would
be granted. As Jane Norman Smith observed in her March 24 letter to Alma Lutz, the justices' "calendar is fairly clear and the case
may be reviewed within the next few weeks."[132] Smith and Lutz,
both prominent members of the NWP, were absolutely right; on
March 30 the justices agreed to hear the case.[133] Three weeks later,
on Tuesday, April 21, Justice Willis Van Devanter (whose vote
against the New York law was just about as sure as a sure thing
could be) wrote to one of his correspondents that "[s]pring is now
coming quite rapidly and soon will be in its best clothes."[134] With
the *Tipaldo* oral arguments scheduled for the following Tuesday,
Van Devanter's adversaries were about to find out whether the ill
wind that they had felt blowing through Washington was about to
relent in favor of a sunnier forecast. Put another way, the justices
were about to hear the case of a laundryman who would have "his
day [in court] as the darling of all those who believe in the freedom of the individual worker to sell his services for what the market will afford without coercion from any quarter."[135]

Justice Butler's Majority Opinion: "Strident and uncompromising"

Although the economic woes of the 1930s brought renewed legislative efforts to enact minimum wage laws, in *Tipaldo* the Court
took a dim view of the argument that times had changed (echoing
Justice Crane's Court of Appeals opinion). In his petition for certiorari, New York's attorney general Bennett had not asked the Court
to reconsider its decision in *Adkins*. Instead, he again contended
that New York's law was distinguishable from that struck down in

1923. Confining itself to the question of the reconcilability of the two laws, the U.S. Supreme Court followed Crane's lead.[136] Quoting extensively from the state jurist's opinion, Justice Butler agreed that the two components of the New York law had to be evaluated together, and that when that happened, it became clear that the statute was no different from the one in *Adkins*. In the Court's first ever use of the verb "to blink" as a synonym for "ignore," Butler wrote that there was "no blinking the fact that the state court construed the prescribed standard" in the state law "to include cost of living." There was also no blinking the fact that Butler wholeheartedly believed the Court's precedents gave it no choice but to defer to the state court's construction of the law.[137] The similarities between the opinions of Crane and Butler did not end there, though. What Butler wrote next indicated that the two men shared the same belief about the *principles* bound up in minimum wage laws for women. "Petitioner," he wrote, "does not attempt to support the act as construed by the state court. His claim is that it is to be tested here as if it did not include the cost of living and as if value of service was the sole standard." This claim did not resonate with Butler. *"If the state has power to single out for regulation the amount of wages to be paid women, the value of their services would be a material consideration. But that fact has no relevancy upon the question whether the state has any such power."*[138] In other words, the discussion about the linguistic components of the New York law ultimately played just as little role in Butler's opinion as it had done in Crane's.

Critics of the justices' pre-1937 New Deal decisions have described Butler's opinion in *Tipaldo* as "one of the Court's biggest mistakes" because of its "strident and uncompromising tone in the midst of the Great Depression."[139] At the time, the American public overwhelmingly agreed that the Court had taken a very wrong turn. In his survey of 344 newspaper editorials, the historian Arthur Schlesinger Jr. could find only ten that wrote favorably about what the justices had done.[140] Unsurprisingly, in Albany, New York, the decision was particularly badly received. Speaking of law as a general concept, the *Knickerbocker Press* newspaper ridiculed the decision: "the law that would jail any laundry-man for having an underfed horse," it opined, "should jail him for having an underfed girl employee."[141] As the historian Jeff Shesol observes, there was something about *Tipaldo* that was different; here, at last, was an anti–New Deal Court decision that could generate a comprehensive negative public reaction.[142] But why? Why this issue, why this decision, and why now? "With *Tipaldo*, the issue had finally transcended the New Deal. . . . For most Americans, 'the liberty of contract' was an abstraction; 'the liberty to starve,' as *The New Republic* put it, was, for many, reality."[143] To borrow language from a slightly different context, *Tipaldo* was a decision that could both "arouse . . . [the] popular conscience" *and* "sear . . . the conscience of the people's representatives."[144]

Justice Stone's Dissent: "Unless government is to be rendered impotent"

Many of the arguments that Chief Justice Hughes made in his dissenting opinion in *Tipaldo* would be repeated in the language of his majority opinion in *Parrish*, less than ten months later. While the Hughes dissent was forceful, and was joined by the other three dissenters—Justices Brandeis, Harlan Fiske Stone, and Benjamin Cardozo—the truly stinging repudiation of Butler's reasoning came in Justice Stone's separate dissent (which Hughes declined to join, but which was supported by Brandeis and Cardozo). Stone agreed with Hughes's opinion, but he wanted to go further because he was disinclined to make—as the chief had done—"the differences between the present statute and that involved in the *Adkins* Case the sole basis of decision."[145] Indeed, ultimately Stone agreed with Butler and Crane—the two laws did not contain statutorily significant differences.[146] Why, then, did Stone vote to uphold the New York law? The answer to that question speaks to the main principle at the heart of the justice's reasoning. While Butler and Crane believed that the judiciary was properly empowered to determine the constitutional fate of minimum wage laws, Stone vehemently believed that this was not the job of the courts: "No one doubts that the presence in the community of a large number of those compelled by economic necessity to accept a wage less than is needful for subsistence is a matter of grave public concern," he wrote. Indeed, he continued, "*It is difficult to imagine any grounds, other than our own personal economic predilections, for saying that the contract of employment is any the less an appropriate subject of legislation than are scores of others in dealing with which this Court has held that legislatures may curtail individual freedom in the public interest.*"[147]

And under the Court's precedents—precedents which the majority found it convenient to ignore—minimum wage laws represented policy judgments that had a "reasonable relation to a proper legislative purpose, and" were "neither arbitrary nor discriminatory." They therefore met "the requirements of due process."[148] Just as Holmes had done in *Lochner* and *Adkins*, Stone was accusing his colleagues of deciding cases in accordance with their own policy views. (Although, because of Stone's inaction discussed below, one could argue that he was just as guilty of this as his colleagues.)

In a memo dated May 29 (three days before the decision in *Tipaldo* was announced), Justice Stone informed his colleagues that he was substituting a full paragraph for what had originally been just a single sentence. The decision to insert this paragraph came after an exchange of notes between Stone and Chief Justice Hughes, an exchange that also led to a change in the language of Hughes's dissent, but not enough of a change to persuade Stone to join it.[149] The paragraph read as follows:

> I know of no rule or practice by which the arguments advanced in support of an application for certiorari restrict our choice between conflicting precedents in deciding a question of constitutional law which the petition, if granted, requires us to answer. Here the question which the petition specifically presents is whether the New York statute contravenes the Fourteenth Amendment. In addition, the petition assigns as a reason for granting it that "the construction and application of the Constitution of the United States and a prior decision" of this Court "are necessarily involved," and again, that "the circumstances prevailing under which the New York law was enacted call for a reconsideration of the *Adkins* Case in the light of the New York act and conditions aimed to be remedied thereby." **Unless we are now to construe and apply the Fourteenth Amendment without regard to our decisions since the *Adkins* Case, we could not rightly avoid its reconsideration even if it were not asked.** We should follow our decision in the *Nebbia* Case and leave the selection and the method of the solution of the problems to which the statute is addressed where it seems to me the Constitution has left them, to the legislative branch of the government. The judgment should be reversed.[150]

In *Nebbia v. New York* (1934), the Court laid out a test for evaluating whether laws could survive challenges based on the due process clause of the Fourteenth Amendment. It was that test—asking whether a law had a "reasonable relation to a proper legislative purpose, and" whether it was "neither arbitrary nor discriminatory"— that Stone had wanted to apply in *Tipaldo*.[151] As we will see in the next chapter, when the appeal in *West Coast Hotel v. Parrish* reached the justices' desks a few months later, Elsie Parrish's lawyer, C. B. Conner, placed considerable emphasis on *Nebbia*.

"Everything about the decision is disturbing"

James Giordano, who owned the Bright Light Laundry, believed the Court's decision in *Tipaldo* was "one of the finest things that ever happened to the girls" working at his establishment.[152] In reality, the decision was not kind to either the girls or their immediate boss. Indeed, the legal victory came at an immense cost to Joseph Tipaldo. Yes, the Court had confirmed that he was constitutionally entitled to pay his workers *minimal*, rather than *minimum*, wages. But then, so was every other laundryman, and those competitors did not have to face the negative publicity surrounding the decision that bore Joseph Tipaldo's name. That publicity turned customers away in droves. Tipaldo's laundry facilities attracted protesters from Local 280, the Laundry Workers' International Union, and he reported that his "drivers were beginning to complain that customers told them I shouldn't have fought this case." When one added to these obstacles the $20,000 in legal fees that Tipaldo paid to fight the New York state law (approximately $375,000 in 2020 dollars), financial ruin was just over the horizon. Joseph Tipaldo had fought to underpay his workers; within three months of securing that right, he, himself, was broke and unemployed. When efforts were made to contact him for a September 1936 newspaper article, his wife "reported he was 'out looking for a job.'" The article's title said it all: "Wanted: A Job, by Laundryman Who Upset Minimum Wage Law."[153]

"Without being vindictive," wrote the Cleveland *Plain Dealer*, "many liberally-minded folk will view with a satisfying equanimity the decline in the business fortunes of Joseph Tipaldo."[154] Among "liberally-minded folk" there was a dominant view of the Supreme

Court's decision to hand Tipaldo a *legal* victory. As Dorothy Thompson wrote in the *New York Herald Tribune*, "Everything about the decision is disturbing."[155] Ray Clapper, the FDR-supporting syndicated journalist, captured the criticisms in a *Washington Daily News* column that was published the evening of the Court's decision. He refused to hold back in expressing his contempt and said that the Court's anti–New Deal decisions, culminating in *Tipaldo*, represented a "dead-pan travesty on self-government, second only to Herr Hitler's recent trick election." Clapper struggled to accept this situation as fact rather than fiction: "[T]he Supreme Court now begins its summer breathing spell," he wrote, "ending a winter's performance which leaves the stage, as in the last act of a Shakespearean tragedy, strewn with the gory dead." In telling this particular winter's tale, Clapper drew not only upon the Bard but also upon the words of Nathaniel Hawthorne in *The House of the Seven Gables*: "A dead man sits on all our judgment seats; and living judges do but search out and repeat his decisions."[156]

In a press conference the next day, President Roosevelt was also deeply critical of the Court's actions. "It seems to be fairly clear," he understatedly said, that "as a result of this decision and former decisions . . . the 'no-man's-land' where no Government restate [*sic*] or Federal—can function is being more clearly defined."[157] The polls demonstrated that an overwhelming majority of the nation's laymen agreed with the president that this was something that the government *should* be able to do. A Gallup poll taken before *Tipaldo* (in April 1936) found considerable popular enthusiasm for a broader "pro-labor" addition to the Constitution, "giving Congress the power to limit, regulate, and prohibit the labor of persons under 18." That proposal received the support of 61 percent of respondents.[158] After *Tipaldo*, a Gallup poll revealed that now 70 percent of those surveyed favored "an amendment to the Constitution to regulate minimum wages." Similarly, a *Fortune* magazine survey published in July 1936 showed that over two-thirds of the respondents believed there should be some sort of minimum wage regulation.[159]

Both of the main political parties were keenly aware of this public sentiment. The Republican Party was faced with the dubious distinction of having to respond very quickly and very publicly to *Tipaldo*, because the Republican National Convention was scheduled to begin in Cleveland on June 9, just eight days after the Court's announcement of its judgment in the case. As William Lasser observes, "[A]s disturbing as *Tipaldo* was to the Democrats, it was even more devastating to the Republicans."[160] The Republican Party "had long since committed itself to supporting various New Deal-style initiatives *at the state level* . . . and its leaders had already approved a platform plank calling for '*state laws* and *interstate compacts* to . . . protect women and children with respect to maximum hours, minimum wages and working conditions.'"[161] This official platform expressed the party's belief that "this can be done within the Constitution as it now stands."[162] Justice Butler's uncompromising language in *Tipaldo* threw a mighty constitutional wrench into the works of any plans to try and implement that "belief." When the party's presidential candidate, Alf Landon (who "stood at the central crossroads of the party"), proposed an alternative—a minimum wage amendment that would overturn the decision, Republicans immediately exposed themselves to charges of hypocrisy; in one fell swoop they had gone from defending to attacking the anti–New Deal Court.[163]

As mentioned above, the president's initial public response to *Tipaldo* came at his June 2 press conference. Over the course of his 1936 reelection campaign, Roosevelt actually had much more to say about it, though. He must have relished the opportunity to do so on June 10 in Little Rock, Arkansas, in a speech that came the day after the Republican convention had begun. Landon's endorsement of a constitutional amendment meant that the GOP's position was in flux; it now seemed as though Republicans were ready to change the Constitution rather than the Court. This was a political *volte-face* that made the Republicans very vulnerable. As the *New York Times* observed two days after the president's speech, "To advocate . . . [a constitutional amendment now], merely because public opinion has been disturbed and distressed by a single decision of the Supreme Court, would be inviting Republican orators to swallow their own words."[164] Sensing his opponents' weaknesses, Roosevelt seized upon this political opening in his speech. Reflecting upon the work of the Framers in Philadelphia in 1787, the president now defended the Constitution. Unlike the Republicans, Roosevelt did not believe the Constitution needed to be changed. "Under its broad purposes we intend to and we can march forward, believing, as the overwhelming majority of Americans believe, that the Constitution is intended to meet and to fit the amazing physical, economic and social requirements that confront us in this modern generation." Roosevelt proceeded to make it very clear that he believed the Constitution authorized the "modern generation" to, among other things, enact laws prescribing minimum wages for women:

> If you have been in Washington recently, you will have seen beneath one of the symbolical figures which guard the entrance to our great new Archives Building this quotation from Shakespeare's "Tempest"—"What is past is prologue." Times change but man's basic problems remain the same. He must seek a new approach to their solution when the old approaches fail him. . . .

> These problems, with growing intensity, now flow past all sectional limitations. They extend over the vast breadth of our whole domain. Prices, wages, hours of labor, fair competition, conditions of employment, social security, in short the enjoyment by all men and women of their constitutional guaranties of life, liberty and the pursuit of happiness . . . these problems we are today commencing to solve. It is true that the new approach to these problems may not be immediately discernible; but organization to meet human suffering can never be predicated on the relaxation of human effort.

In closing, the president reminded his audience that:

> We still find inspiration for the work before us, in the old spirit which meant achievement through self-reliance; a willingness to lend a hand to the fellow down in his luck through no fault of his own. Upon those principles our democracy was reborn a century ago; upon those principles alone will it endure today and in the days to come.

These were the principles outlined in the Constitution as it existed in September 1787 *and* June 1936.[165]

There was, however, one problem with this soaring rhetoric. Republicans were not the only ones who believed a constitutional amendment might be necessary to bring about "the enjoyment by all men and women of their constitutional guaranties of life, liberty and the pursuit of happiness." Ten days after the Little Rock speech, Attorney General Homer S. Cummings wrote to inform the president that "[t]here seems to be a growing conviction amongst our friends that the Democratic Platform should contain some affirmative statement dealing with a constitutional amendment." Cummings had "[n]o doubt . . . that the way has been opened up for such a course" by *Tipaldo*.[166] When the Democratic National Convention began a few days later in Philadelphia, the party endorsed a platform that stopped short of calling for an amendment. However, it did not foreclose the possibility that one might be needed in the near future:

> The Republican platform proposes to meet many pressing national problems solely by action of the separate States. We know that drought, dust storms, floods, minimum wages, maximum hours, child labor, and working conditions in industry, monopolistic and unfair business practices cannot be adequately handled exclusively by 48 separate State legislatures, 48 separate State administrations, and 48 separate State courts. Transactions and activities which inevitably overflow State boundaries call for both State and Federal treatment.

> We have sought and will continue to seek to meet these problems through legislation within the Constitution.

> If these problems cannot be effectively solved by legislation within the Constitution, we shall seek such clarifying amendment as will assure to the legislatures of the several States and to the Congress of the United States, each within its proper jurisdiction, the power to enact those laws which the State and Federal legislatures, within their respective spheres, shall find necessary, in order adequately to regulate commerce, protect public health and safety and safeguard economic security. Thus we propose to maintain the letter and spirit of the Constitution.[167]

The overwhelming bipartisan opposition to *Tipaldo* caught Justice Stone off guard. Writing to Justice Cardozo, he commented that the decision was "having many repercussions, some of which I did not foresee, especially the apparent dispositions of the Republican convention to repudiate it. It is good to see that there are some doses too nauseous for even a hidebound Conservative to swallow."[168] As the sarcasm evident in his reply indicated, Cardozo was also surprised, but less so than his colleague. "I think we should be more than human if we failed to sit back in our chairs with a broad grin upon our faces as we watch the response to the minimum wage decision," he wrote. "Is it possible that both political parties hold the view that legislation condemned by the majority of our brethren as an arbitrary and capricious assault upon liberty is so necessary and beneficial that we cannot get along without it? Perish the thought!"[169]

*   *   *

On April 2, 1936, two months before *Tipaldo*, the Washington Supreme Court issued its decision in *Ernest and Elsie Parrish v. West Coast Hotel Company*. In a unanimous opinion written by Chief Justice William J. Millard, the court boldly brushed aside *Adkins* and upheld the Washington State minimum wages for women law. Fred Crollard, the lawyer for the West Coast Hotel Company, sought to try and understand why his client had lost. How, he wondered, could Millard and the other justices have "possibly" produced this judgment "in view of what the U.S. Supreme Court had said in *Adkins*"? Millard is reported to have replied: "Well, let's let the Supreme Court say it one more time."[170] He did not have to wait long because the Supreme Court did indeed "say it one more time" in *Tipaldo*. It therefore came as a great surprise to many observers when that Court announced, in October 1936, that it would hear full arguments in *Parrish* rather than simply summarily reversing the judgment of the Washington Supreme Court. This then begs the following question: to what extent had Elsie Parrish's lawyer presented the justices in Washington, D.C., with arguments that might cause a majority of them finally to have a "change of judicial mind"?[171]

4 Upsetting the Wenatchee Applecart

Wash.–Wenatchee: The Cascadian celebrated its fifth anniversary with the completion, August 9, of an extensive reconditioning program which has put this fireproof house in first class shape thruout [*sic*]. Wenatchee is the "apple capital" of this country and is benefitted also from its neighboring the Grand Coulee Dam, the largest of its kind in U.S.

—Hotel Monthly *magazine (September 1934)*

Although the *Parrish* litigation officially began in June 1935, the events that led up to it began almost two years earlier when, in August 1933, the Cascadian Hotel first hired Elsie Parrish. At that time, the hotel was undergoing an "extensive reconditioning program." As reported by *Hotel Monthly* magazine, this put the building "in first class shape thruout."[1] Although Wenatchee was now feeling the full force of the Great Depression, the hotel's manager, Ray Clark, was determined not to let the nation's financial disaster take down what he had worked so hard to build up. Two years later, when Elsie was let go, Clark's successor, Willard Abel, was equally determined not to let one, now unemployed, chambermaid tarnish the reputation of this important component of the community. After Elsie initiated her lawsuit, Abel (and colleagues from the West Coast Hotel Company) met with Frederick M. Crollard at the Wenatchee offices that the attorney shared with his law partner A. J. O'Connor. Crollard quickly confirmed that decisions made by the U.S. Supreme Court favored the hotel rather than its former employee. Even if that lowly individual, "who was not, by any measure, in a position of influence" in Wenatchee, did dare to seek back pay, she would lose her lawsuit because the state's minimum wage law for women was unconstitutional.[2] The law of the land—as stated by a majority of the nation's highest judicial tribunal—made that very clear.

When Elsie and her husband met with their attorney C. B. Conner, they too sought legal advice about her dismissal from the employ of the Cascadian. Conner sympathized with the couple that sat opposite him; he understood that they were taking a considerable risk. However, unlike Crollard he did not believe that the precedent set in 1923 in *Adkins v. Children's Hospital*[3] stood as an immovable object in the path of his new clients (in part because of the way in which he believed the jurisprudential foundations of that decision had been shaken by the Court's decision in a 1931 case). From the outset, Conner exhibited confidence that he would prevail for the Parrishes, secure a national constitutional validation of the state's progressive legislation, and get Elsie the money she was owed.

This chapter explores and analyzes the way in which *Ernest and Elsie Parrish v. West Coast Hotel Company* wound its way through two lower courts—the Chelan County Superior Court and the Washington Supreme Court. As we will see from the legal filings of Conner and Crollard, both men made various arguments. Some of those arguments stayed consistent across time, while others changed. Myriad factors account for the presence of both consistency and change in the story of *Parrish* at the lower court levels. Formal legal constraints came from within the judicial system (including U.S. Supreme Court precedents—old and new), and informal sociolegal and sociopolitical limits came from the Wenatchee community. All these constraints serve to confirm that by bringing this litigation, Elsie Parrish was very much upsetting the Wenatchee applecart.

C. B. Conner: "Unlike the majority, he had something to think with"

When, in late May 1935, Ernie and Elsie Parrish resolved to sue the Cascadian, they decided to seek help from one of the men who had offices in the Doneen Building. Just like the Cascadian (which is located one block north), the Doneen rose from the dirt of Wenatchee Avenue in 1929, and it too boasted innovative elements of construction (it was the city's first steel and concrete building), and architectural features reflecting the Art Moderne and Beaux Arts styles.[4] In search of assistance from a lawyer who was not afraid to take on the mighty Cascadian, the Parrishes found exactly whom they were looking for when they entered room 312, the third floor office of Charles Burnam (C. B.) Conner. In 1935, the Doneen was home to four different legal practices, but it is very unlikely that the couple sought out the services of any of the other attorneys before they arrived at Conner's door. Conner later observed, "It has been my fortune to be consulted frequently throughout the years by unfortunates, people who were without means, and I have often been told that 'so and so sent me to you and told me that you could help me if anybody could.'" There is no reason to doubt Conner's assessment that "[t]his was [also] true of Elsie Parrish."[5]

Elsie "was entirely without funds," but Conner did not hesitate to take the case pro bono.[6] As Gerry L. Alexander, former chief justice of the Washington Supreme Court, has described it, this was in "the great tradition of Washington lawyers" and represents an "important part of our state's legal history"—the tradition of "provid[ing] legal services at no cost to the economically disadvantaged" in order "to, as the oath of attorneys says, 'never forsake the cause of the defenseless or oppressed.'"[7]

It would not be easy to overcome *Adkins* because, as "any law student in the land could have told" Elsie, "her case" seemed "hopeless" because of that 1923 decision. For Elsie to prevail, "[a] new trail had to be blazed" and "original thinking and planning" was "a necessity." As the prominent Seattle lawyer John P. Hartman observed in his tribute to Conner, "Hundreds were in the same position as Mrs. Parrish. Lawyers generally were advising the clamoring women that they had not a Chinaman's chance." Elsie was "fortunate" because she chose a lawyer who believed in her case (and the greater cause for which it stood), and "unlike the majority," Conner was a lawyer who, in Hartman's view, truly "had something to think with."[8]

C. B. Conner was born in 1876 in Linden, a very small rural village just west of the Appalachian Trail, which straddles the line separating Fauquier County and Warren County in Virginia, approximately sixty-five miles west of Washington, D.C. He was

FIG. 4.1   C. B. Conner. Author's collection.

the second of Thomas and Martha (Pritchard) Conner's seven children. Although there is no record of Civil War military service for
Thomas, there is plentiful evidence that he and Martha made their
children both aware and very proud of their southern heritage. Just
like every other community in the South, Linden was scarred, both
physically and psychologically, by the Civil War. Growing up, C. B.
and his siblings would undoubtedly have been told stories about
the Battle of Manassas Gap. They would have had easy access to
the ground—a mere half a mile from their house—upon which the
battle was fought on July 23, 1863, at the end of the Gettysburg
Campaign.[9] C. B.'s respect for this heritage was just one part of
his abiding cradle-to-grave love of history and country; he read and
wrote extensively about these subjects.[10]

After studying at Shenandoah Normal College in nearby Reliance, Conner again stayed close to home, reading law as an apprentice to Judge Edwin T. Booton in Luray, the county seat of Page County in the Shenandoah Valley.[11] Conner subsequently attended Richmond College School of Law, graduating as a member of the fifteen-person class of 1899.[12] After admission to the Virginia State Bar, he traveled to New Orleans, where he stayed for about a year, taking business classes at a local college, and working as a stenographer. He lived there, with his elder brother Vernon (and Vernon's wife Arabella and the couple's two young sons), but upon Vernon's untimely death in 1901 (at the age of twenty-six) C. B. moved to Oklahoma, the state he would call home for almost fifteen years.

It was there that he found his bride-to-be, Irene T. Grayson, a native of Luray—the same Virginia town wherein C. B. had served his legal apprenticeship. The couple was married in Norman, Oklahoma, on October 16, 1901, at the home of Irene's cousins. The local newspaper's description of the bride was glowing: "Mrs. Conner is a beautiful and accomplished young woman, who will, no doubt, make Mr. Conner a helpmeet indeed." The accompanying account of the groom was no less admiring, describing him as "one of Tecumseh's best young men. He is a christian [sic] gentleman and a prominent lawyer."[13] C. B. established two successful law practices in central Oklahoma, first in Tecumseh, and then in Okemah (approximately fifty-five miles from Tecumseh). "[H]e was considered one of the ablest lawyers" in the area, and his experience, legal acumen, "sound judgment and common sense" led the local Republican Party to endorse him for county judge.[14] Three of the five[15] children born to C. B. and Irene were Oklahomans by birth; the other two were born in Sandpoint, Idaho (1915), and Wenatchee (1916) after a visit to the Pacific Northwest in 1912 eventually spurred C. B. to relocate his family to that region. The family arrived in Wenatchee on March 21, 1915. C. B. and Irene called Wenatchee home for the rest of their lives.

His stellar legal work and his civic engagement earned C. B. the same high level of respect in Wenatchee as he had enjoyed in Okemah and Tecumseh. When he died suddenly in 1941, his obituary in the *Wenatchee Daily World* included a paragraph summarizing many of his civic contributions to the community. "At the time of his death he was secretary of the police commission, a member of the Knights of Pythias lodge, Wenatchee Aerie of Fraternal Order of Eagles and of the State and Chelan County Bar Association" and he was "an active member of the Central Christian church."[16] In 1941 Conner was serving as a justice of the peace, an office to which he had twice been elected, and prior to that he had also served Wenatchee as one of its police judges.

Conner's unpublished memoir describes in detail the cases that he considered the most "important" of his career, cases in which he defended many individuals who stood accused of very serious crimes (primarily during the 1910s and 1920s, long before both *Parrish* and Conner's judicial service). Yet, while his descriptions of those cases are brought together within one chapter of the work, C. B. considered the *Parrish* case worthy of its own dedicated chapter. And it is from that chapter that we learn why Elsie was let go by the Cascadian Hotel—and it had everything to do with the 1913 minimum wage law and Elsie's knowledge that the law existed. "*I think,*" wrote Conner, that "*the real cause of her discharge was the fact that at some time she had thoughtlessly mentioned the fact that in the State of Washington there was supposed to be a minimum wage law, for women, and wondered why the Hotel was paying considerably less,*" and these remarks reached the management and resulted in her discharge."[17] One can easily imagine that the management of the Cascadian took offense at Elsie's temeritous decision to make mention of the law's existence. Not only must they have believed she should be grateful to have a job—especially at the grand and reputable Cascadian, but also they must have been concerned that other employees would learn from her that they too were being illegally underpaid. (As we will see in chapter 6, this concern was justified.)

When Elsie sought out Conner's advice and help after the Cascadian dismissed her, the attorney shrewdly set in course a series of actions designed to generate the lawsuit. As Conner recalls, "I told Mrs. Parrish to go to the Hotel and report for work; that she would not be allowed to work, and that they would give her a check for her wages and would also ask her to sign a receipt and mark the check 'paid in full.'" It was clear to him, from just a short time in her company, that Elsie would willingly comply: "If there ever was a loyal client, this was one."[18] As will become clear both below and in chapter 5, the most important doctrinal element of the arguments that Conner made in his *Parrish* briefs reflected his belief that his client's case—and the defense of the Washington state law—could be distinguished from *Adkins*, and that a ruling in favor of Elsie would not require that Supreme Court decision to be overruled. As Conner observed, "[T]he bar generally throughout the State and the United States had accepted the decision of the Supreme Court of the United States in the Adkins vs Children's Hospital Case as final and regarded the Minimum Wage Law as unconstitutional. I never did take that view."[19] Conner knew full well that when he initiated Elsie's lawsuit, and submitted his first briefs with the clerk of the Chelan County Superior Court in Wenatchee, the principal legal retort from the hotel's lawyers would be "we should win—see *Adkins*." After all, there was every reason to believe that those lawyers were part of "the bar [that] generally throughout the State and the United States had accepted . . . [that 1923] decision." He was right; "[T]he lawyers for the Hotel Company presented the case just as I anticipated they would do."[20]

*　*　*

By now it should be clear that Elsie's decision not to sit back and accept her situation was a very brave one. However, even though she likely knew that when she walked into Conner's office, what she almost certainly did not know is that in deciding to sue the Cascadian, she would be taking on not one, but two Wenatchee landmarks simultaneously—the hotel and the lawyer whose services it retained. This is because the lawyer who "presented the [Cascadian's] case just as" Conner "anticipated" was Frederick M. Crollard.

Fred Crollard: "Filled with a determination to make good"

If there was a civic organization in Wenatchee, at some point Fred Crollard[21] served as one of its leaders. He deliberately avoided running for elected political offices (including judgeships), but even without that line on his résumé his "achievements" certainly did "read like an illustrious page in 'Who's Who.'"[22] From the Wenatchee Chamber of Commerce (president), Chelan County Bar Association, Wenatchee School Board (member for sixteen years, serving two terms as president), the Chelan County Educational Board, the Advisory Board of St. Anthony's Hospital, Community Chest (president), and the Grand Knights of Columbus (organizer of the Wenatchee Knights of Columbus Council and later grand knight), to the Boy Scouts (president of the North Central Washington Council), Wenatchee Golf and Country Club (president), Wenatchee Choir, Community Concert Association (he established the concert series, and was chairman for nine years), and the Elks (exalted ruler of the Wenatchee Lodge and then district deputy grand exalted ruler), until his death in 1968, Fred Crollard was one of the most civically engaged Wenatchee-ites. He was a beloved member of the entire community, a prominent attorney with prominent clients (including the West Coast Hotel Company).[23] In a letter that he wrote to Crollard in 1967, Kirby Billingsley (Manager of the Public Utility District No. 1 of Chelan County) perfectly captured the region's sentiment when he said that "[t]he tributes to you are truly deserving." Crollard, he observed, was one of those people to whom "[a]ll our hats should be raised," for such individuals "have done so much to make this a wonderful community in which to live and raise our families."[24] It was this influential and pioneering Wenatcheeite that Elsie was taking on when she chose to sue the Cascadian.

Like Elsie Parrish, Frederick Michael Crollard was a native of Kansas. He was born in Girard, in the southeastern corner of the state, on May 4, 1885, to Jules and Elizabeth (O'Connor). A "highly educated" Frenchman who "spoke and wrote seven languages," thirty-five-year-old Jules Crollard arrived in New York in January 1879 aboard the Labrador, a ship that had sailed from Le Havre under the operation of the Compagnie Générale Transatlantique.[25] Elizabeth, known to everyone as Lizzie, was Canadian by birth, but immigrated to Kansas with her family in 1869, when she was fourteen. Fate brought Jules and Lizzie together in 1882 in the small town of Socorro in New Mexico. Lizzie was spending time there, in the warm and dry climate, recuperating from consumption, when she met Jules, who was traveling through town. (At the time, Jules lived four hundred miles north, in Leadville, Colorado.) A newly married couple, they soon headed west to San Francisco, where Jules found work as a design engineer on several architectural projects, and where their first child, Louis Joseph, was born in 1883. Frederick was born two years later, by which time the family had returned to Kansas, settling in Girard, which neighbored the town of Brazilton, the first town in the United States that Lizzie's family had called home. It was no coincidence that the move back "home"

FIG. 4.2   Frederick M. Crollard. Wenatchee Valley Museum
and Cultural Center, 005-74-292.

followed the tragic death, at the age of six weeks, of Louis's sister.
Frederick entered this world exactly one year after her passing.[26]

It was in the nation's capital, where they lived with their
mother from 1889 until 1904, that Louis and Fred first took music
lessons; they quickly became accomplished performers, Louis
on the violin, Fred on the cornet (and piano).[27] Playing for the
Gonzaga College High School band, Fred recalls how he and his
brother "marched down Pennsylvania Avenue many times; in the
Triumphal Parade for Admiral Dewey upon his return from Manila,
McKinley's Inaugural Parade, McKinley's Funeral march, Theodore

Roosevelt's Inaugural Parade and on many other occasions."[28] It is widely acknowledged that "[n]o story of the Wenatchee band would be complete without a reference to the work of the Crollard boys," who immediately joined that ensemble upon arriving in Wenatchee. (Their mother moved the family west in 1904, following three of her brothers—Frank, Mike, and Jack—who had already made their homes in the Apple Capital.)[29]

Fred Crollard's musicality defined much of his early involvement in the local community and left a positive legacy that accompanied him throughout his life. (It was also one of the non-work-related ways in which he interacted with the Conner family.)[30] His subsequent civic engagement in the business of the town ensured that his reputation preceded him wherever he went in Wenatchee (and that reputation was overwhelmingly positive). That engagement, and reputation, was in large part driven by the educational path that he started down in 1905, a path that led him to a life of the law.[31] Enrolling at the University of Washington that fall, and graduating with his law degree in 1910 (he stayed home during the spring quarter to look after his ailing mother), Fred Crollard worked his way through college, providing secretarial services (on a full-time basis over the summer) to the university's registrar, president, and law school dean.[32]

Upon graduation, Crollard returned to Wenatchee to practice law with Louis at the firm of Reeves, Crollard, and Reeves. Initially working as their stenographer (and as a court reporter), Louis Crollard subsequently served his legal apprenticeship with Frank and Fred Reeves, two of the town's most prominent attorneys. Passing the state bar exam in 1908, he was made a partner in the firm the following year. By 1915 both of the Reeves brothers had retired, thus leading to a change of name; the business shingle now read "Crollard and Crollard."[33] That family collaboration, however, was tragically cut short when the influenza epidemic came to town in 1918. The first case of the flu was confirmed in Chelan County on October 6, 1918, during what is considered to be the "second wave." Although the survival rate in Wenatchee was much higher than in some of the state's largest cities, Louis succumbed on November 26 of that year.[34] Upon Louis's death Fred entered into partnership first with R. S. Steiner, a retired judge, and then with A. J. O'Connor in 1927.[35] The latter was a partnership that lasted until 1950, when Fred Crollard was joined in practice by his son Frederick M. Crollard Jr., the second of the five children born to Fred and Stella (Zwight), who were married in Wenatchee on June 12, 1912.[36]

It was understandable that it was this firm—Crollard & O'Connor—to which the West Coast Hotel Company turned for legal defense when it was served with the summons in *Parrish*. For, in addition to Crollard's community influence, in 1929 in his capacity as president of the Wenatchee Chamber of Commerce (an organization of which he had been a member for nineteen years), Fred Crollard participated in the groundbreaking ceremony for the Cascadian Hotel.[37]

Parrish, Round 1: Chelan County Superior Court

With no rain in sight, and a forecasted daytime high temperature of seventy-five degrees, Monday, June 10, 1935, was a beautiful start to the workweek for the residents of Wenatchee. C. B. Conner's secretary felt the sun's rays warm her body as she turned west from South Wenatchee Avenue and walked up Palouse Street, across Memorial Park, to the office of the clerk of the Superior Court of the State of Washington for Chelan County. She carried with her the first legal documents filed in *Ernest and Elsie Parrish v. West Coast Hotel Company*. Upon reaching the office occupied by clerk Eugene Bowersox and his deputies, she presented them with copies of the Summons and three-page Complaint that had been sent to the firm of Crollard and O'Connor.[38] Bowersox stamped the documents as "received" on June 10. Elsie and Ernie Parrish's legal journey had formally begun.

Judge William O. Parr

Once docketed, the Parrishes' case was assigned to Judge William O. Parr. Geography tied William Olney Parr to Eugene Bowersox. Like his clerk, the Chelan County Superior Court judge was born and raised in Iowa. (Parr was a few months older than Bowersox.) Parr relocated to Washington State from Kansas, arriving with the Great Northern Railway in June 1892, for which he had worked in the commissary department of one of the company's camps in Montana the previous year. Parr was one of the original

Wenatchee pioneers (just like Bowersox).[39] As the railway forged west, Parr accompanied the construction crews all the way to Wenatchee, where he initially set himself up as a barber. The route had taken them via Spokane, where, having realized along the way that the camp barber was wont to make a good amount of money plying his trade, Parr purchased supplies and successfully sought out someone who would teach him the necessary skills. "They rode into Wenatchee on horses in 1892 and when the Great Northern crew arrived, their barber shop was established in a tent on what is now Wenatchee avenue."[40]

"Undismayed by the many evidences of wild life, which tempted him not," Parr went about his barbering and, in his spare time, taught himself the law. As the *Wenatchee Daily World* wrote upon his death, Parr "studied law between customers and after hours, passed the bar examination with honors and was widely recognized as an able interpreter of the law." Conveniently, Parr passed the bar exam in 1899, the same year that Chelan County was organized, thereby giving new business to both him and the other lawyers in town. From that point onward, Parr embarked upon a long and distinguished legal career in Wenatchee, occupying various different positions.[41] The law became his life.

In March 1907 Parr was one of the first tenants to occupy an office in the new Columbia Valley bank building situated at the corner of Wenatchee and Orondo avenues.[42] Part of the construction boom that significantly changed the landscape of Wenatchee in 1906 to accommodate the ever-growing population, construction began on the bank's new home in July.[43] An impressive three-story building constructed from Tenino sandstone and white brick at a cost of almost $50,000, it was described by the *Wenatchee World* as "by far the handsomest business block in Wenatchee."[44] The bank occupied approximately two-thirds of the first floor, with its customers conducting business in a well-lit, sumptuous environment of black walnut and blue and white marble. By the time the building opened, most of the remaining space, including offices in the basement and on the first and second floors, and boarding rooms on the third floor, had been rented. At least two real estate firms, O. F. Etzkorn's tailoring business, the Wenatchee Heating and Plumbing Company, Daniel Gensinger (the self-proclaimed "East Wenatchee Land Man"), and numerous other businesses joined Parr as tenants of this latest creation of the famed architect W. A. Ritchie.[45] For the first five years that he worked out of the bank building, Parr was a forty-something bachelor. That changed when he met Gwen Beulah Jero. Nineteen years his junior, Gwen became Mrs. William O. Parr in November 1912. Their first child, David, born in January 1914, tragically died ten years later. The couple's second child, Florence Margaret, was born in August 1915.

Parr was first elected to the Chelan County Superior Court in 1924. He served continuously for the next sixteen years until he retired in 1940. The entirety of that career was spent deciding from the bench of the Chelan County Courthouse situated on Orondo Avenue. He was one of the first judges to hear cases at that new building, which opened in 1924 and was dedicated during that year's Apple Blossom Festival.[46] The courthouse is an imposing building. From its location on the edge of Memorial Park, it looks down upon the main streets of the city (including the Cascadian Hotel building) and the mighty Columbia about six blocks to its east. Indeed, just as the Cascadian typified the community meeting place model of a Main Street hotel when it was built, the Chelan County Courthouse no less typified what such an entity meant to the people within its jurisdiction. It was "a venue for county politics and its legal system . . . a hub for city business,"[47] and one more communal obstacle that Elsie Parrish had to navigate.

FIG. 4.3 The Chelan County Courthouse, Wenatchee, Washington. Author's collection.

"A total of 2,504 1/2 hours, or 52 weeks and 8 1/2 hours"

Elsie's case came before Judge Parr on October 17, but not before a
series of motions that delayed the court date several times.[48] Finally,
on that Thursday morning she gathered in the courtroom with her
husband and Conner, Crollard and O'Connor, Ray Clark and his
wife, and Willard Abel. We know very little about what went on
in the courtroom that day. What we do know is that, as was to be
expected, "[w]itnesses were sworn and both oral and documentary
evidence was offered and received." Additionally, we know that, as
Fred Crollard reported to his son (Fred Jr.) who was studying law
at Notre Dame, "I argued for about two and half hours," an "ora-
tion" (that included reading, in full, the decision in *Adkins*) which
he believed "wore the other fellows out."[49]

No one disputed that between August 1933 and Saturday,
May 11, 1935, Elsie (Lee) Parrish labored for 2,504 and a half
hours as a chambermaid at the Cascadian Hotel. The court documents do not indicate the specific dates when she was working in
1933 and in February 1934; however, they do suggest that she was
hired on a temporary basis in order to cope with an anticipated
increased occupancy of rooms over the Labor Day holiday weekend. Beginning on March 16, 1934, the specific hours that Elsie
worked are laid out in detail in the filings. On average she made
beds and cleaned bathrooms for seven and a half hours every day
(including her wedding day, Saturday, July 28, 1934—she and Ernie
were married at 8.15pm), never working more than eight hours in
any one day. Some months brought her leaner employment opportunities than others. However, as graph 4.1 shows, interestingly the
greatest number of hours that she worked came during her last two
full months on the hotel's staff. (In March 1935 she worked 204
hours; in April she worked 208 hours.) Additionally, no one disputed that under the terms of the 1913 Washington State minimum wage law for women, over the course of her employment the
Cascadian should have paid Elsie a total of $754.39. The hotel did
not pay her that amount; instead she received wages in the sum of
$538.20, hence her lawsuit seeking the difference between those
two amounts: $216.19. Finally, no one disputed that she was owed
this money *unless* the 1913 statute was constitutionally null and
void. It was to this final point that Crollard most likely devoted
most of his "two and half hours" of argument.

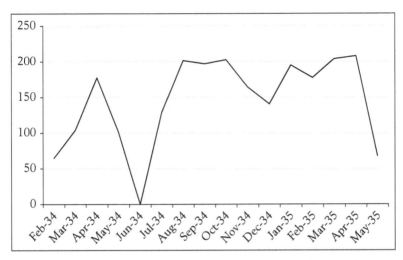

GRAPH 4.1   Hours per month that Elsie Parrish worked at the Cascadian Hotel. Chart compiled using data taken from Ernest Parrish, and Elsie Parrish, his wife vs. West Coast Hotel Company, No. 12215, Amended Complaint, July 12, 1935, pp. 1–4, Superior Court of the State of Washington in and for the County of Chelan.

Judge Parr issued his ruling as soon as the short bench trial (a trial without a jury) ended that day. Elsie walked out of the Chelan County Courthouse a (partial) loser. The ruling amounted to a total victory for the operators of the Cascadian Hotel. It came in two forms—Parr's oral announcement of his judgment in the case (on October 17), and an additional printed document (issued by the court on November 9) summarizing the main "Findings of Fact and Conclusions of Law." Parr concluded that Elsie was legally entitled to a check for seventeen dollars (plus court costs)—so in one respect she was only a partial loser. She would, however, receive no back pay because "any attempt to fix the minimum wage for adult women, as fixed by the Industrial Welfare Commission of the State of Washington, is unsound, is not sustained by the evidence, and . . . [is] as to the defendant in this case a violation of its Constitutional rights."[50] As Parr explained to Conner about his client's case on that Thursday in October, "If the law fixes a minimum wage, then I say she is entitled to her money." However:

If that law is invalid then, of course, she is obligated to accept what she has received from time to time and paid her as full

settlement for what she has done. It seems to me that the decision of the highest court of the land [*in Adkins*] . . . settles
this question absolutely, and beyond all question, for the time
being. . . . I do believe that it [*Adkins*] is in full accord with the
principles on which our order is founded, that it is in accord
with both the letter and the spirit of the Constitutions [of the
United States and of Washington State]; so I believe the decision to be soundly right.[51]

An article in the *Wenatchee Daily World* published two days later
indicated that there was no doubting that Judge Parr "bas[ed] his
opinion" on the U.S. Supreme Court's decision in *Adkins*. As Conner
dryly observed, it was "an extensive and very powerful" opinion.[52]

The *Wenatchee Daily World* article, which represented the newspaper's first reporting on the *Parrish* case, was written by a member
of the paper's news staff. It was longer and more detailed than the
literature leads us to expect from local newspaper coverage of state
and local trial court decisions. It conveyed information about the
case under the headline "Judge W. O. Parr Upholds Constitution,"
and devoted extensive space—twice as much as most of the state's
largest newspapers—to discussing the case. In the article, which
was accompanied by a photograph of Judge Parr, the newspaper
described the ruling "as one of the most momentous decisions ever
handed down" by the Chelan County court. In a way, any decision
by this small court declaring a state law unconstitutional deserves
to be labeled as "momentous"; and perhaps this explains the hometown reporter's choice of word.

However, there are two reasons why the content of the article
counsels a more skeptical view of the veracity of this description of
Parr's decision. First, there is the poor quality of the article's writing (which sets it apart from the average story in the *Wenatchee
Daily World*), and the presence of factual errors (for example, the
Washington Supreme Court upheld the 1913 law in two previous
cases, not three as the article indicates). Second, instead of providing justifications for the label, the paragraphs that followed actually
demonstrated that there was nothing particularly unexpected or
unusual about the decision. Neither the article's detailed recitation
of the facts nor its discussion of the precedential strength of *Adkins*
provided the readers with any significant reason to believe that Parr
had made a historic ruling.[53]

The newspaper was right, however, to say that Parr's ruling was the immediate subject of statewide and national interest. As Crollard reported to his son, "The Associated Press wanted to make special mention of the decision because it in effect is important in many other states that have the same law."[54] Additionally, five of the top ten (in terms of circulation) newspapers in Washington State ran stories about the ruling (although, with the exception of the Spokane *Spokesman-Review*, these publications relied upon almost identical, short, four-paragraph wire service reports).[55] The article in the *Spokesman-Review* serves as an interesting comparison to both these reports and the coverage in the Wenatchee newspaper. First, it is the only article about any aspect of *Parrish* in this Spokane publication that was compiled from neither a wire service report nor a nationally syndicated column. Second, the "interest" of which it spoke—the "interest" it perceived to have been generated by Parr's decision—was "widespread," but was not simply described as statewide and national. Instead, readers of the *Spokesman-Review* were provided with more specific and human-interest details: "The case held the interest of hotel men and their women employees over the state as the so-called minimum wage of $14.50 a week is paid at few, if any places."[56]

*   *   *

When Judge Parr died in 1942, the *Wenatchee Daily World* obituary reported that "[h]is record on the bench is one of the best in the Northwest, very few of his decisions ever being over-ruled by the supreme court."[57] Nine days after he denied C. B. Conner's motion for a new trial, Parr received a copy of the lawyer's notice of intent to appeal the decision to the state's supreme court.[58] When, in April 1936, that higher court rendered its decision, *Ernest and Elsie Parrish v. West Coast Hotel* became one of the rare blemishes on Parr's record.

Parrish, Round 2: The Washington Supreme Court

On December 13, 1935, the same day that he filed his client's appeal of Parr's judgment with the Washington Supreme Court, C. B. Conner penned a letter to Garrison Hamilton. He wanted to call the state attorney general's attention to the case and to request that his office submit an amicus brief (a "friend of the court" brief that is filed by someone other than one of the parties to a case) in support of the appeal.[59] Although the reply that landed upon Conner's desk two weeks later indicated that the attorney general was declining to take the requested action, his staff assured Conner that it was for the best of reasons. First, George G. Hannan wrote that he and another assistant attorney general had "gone over the brief [submitted by Conner] carefully and we believe you have raised all the points of value, and properly analyzed the cases cited in your brief." Consequently, "[t]he attorney general thinks we could not present and file a brief in the case that would add anything to yours, without more research and time than we are at liberty to give it." Second, "[i]n any event," continued Hannan, "I believe that the supreme court will reverse Judge Parr and sustain that act."[60] This prediction was based on prior state rulings. It was an accurate prediction.

In light of the way in which the relevant U.S. Supreme Court jurisprudence unfolded over the preceding half century (as discussed in chapters 2 and 3), it was unsurprising that Judge Parr emphasized the precedent set in *Adkins*. It was entirely reasonable that commentators would view that 1923 decision as spelling "the death of m.w. legislation."[61] Absent any seismic shift in the Court's decision-making, *Adkins* seemed to provide the jurisprudential and doctrinal framework for deciding future minimum wage cases (a state of affairs that *Morehead v. Tipaldo*[62] only appeared to confirm eight months later). And, as noted above, Conner was well aware of this sentiment. He knew things "looked rather dark" for his client.[63]

Sometimes, however, appearances can be very deceptive. Writing in 1935 in the *Kentucky Law Journal*, Norman J. Macbeth Jr. concluded that "[t]he basic premise of the *Adkins*" decision had been "seriously impaired" by the U.S. Supreme Court's 1931 decision in *O'Gorman & Young, Inc. v. Hartford Fire Ins. Co.*, in which the justices upheld a New Jersey law that prohibited insurance agents from receiving commission rates "in excess of a reasonable amount" for selling fire insurance. (The law was designed to ensure that insurance rates were kept "reasonable.")[64] In his brief appealing Elsie Parrish's case to the Washington State Supreme Court, C. B. Conner clearly recognized the potential significance of *O'Gorman & Young*, and indicated (*sub silentio*) his agreement with Macbeth's assessment of the decision and its relationship to *Adkins*. He sought to persuade the justices in Olympia that there were adequate grounds for ignoring the 1923 precedent. As it turns out, they did not need much persuading.

Conner's Brief: "An evil condition should be cured"

The brief that Conner filed appealing Elsie's case to the Washington Supreme Court was dominated by one relatively simple constitutional law syllogism:

1. In *Adkins* the Court confirmed what it had said in *Bunting v. Oregon*[65]—that "in the absence of facts to support the contrary conclusion," it would accept the finding that a minimum wage (or maximum hours) law was "necessary for the preservation of the health of [the] employees" in a particular industry if both the state legislature and state supreme court had so found.
   - In *Adkins* the Court also confirmed that such laws would be upheld only if the business in question were "affected with a public interest."
2. Both the Washington State legislature and the Washington State Supreme Court had found (on multiple occasions) that the 1913 law met the employees' health necessity threshold.
   - And those institutions had also found that the 1913 law addressed the "public interest."
3. Ergo, the 1913 Washington State minimum wage was constitutional under *Adkins*.[66]

While this syllogism was logically solid, the precedent set by *Adkins* suggested that Conner's reasoning was deeply flawed. This is because, as Barry Cushman succinctly observes, "After *Adkins*, it was clear that the *only* available route to sustaining legislation fixing wages was to argue that the business was affected with a public interest."[67] One could argue, as Conner did, that it was plain to see that the public had an interest in alleviating the plight of women forced to work long hours for pitiful wages at the hands of unscrupulous employers:

It would not be going too far to say that in every single community in the state, there are numerous children who are entirely dependent upon the efforts of a tired mother, and they receive their food because of whatever she can earn. **This may be said to have nothing to do with the constitutionality of the law, and yet those are the things that were considered by the legislature and which induced them to enact the law, not for the mere protection of the wage earner, but for the protection of the public.** The welfare of the community generally demands that children eat, have comfortable clothing, blankets to cover them; fuel to warm them, and in the natural course of human events the husband, the father, the man, should be and usually is the bread-winner; but in these more modern times conditions have radically changed, expenses of living are very much heavier, and so thousands and thousands of children throughout the State of Washington would be going hungry and very cold indeed and deprived of the necessities and comforts of life, but for the earnings of a devoted mother. **These are the things which moved the legislature to enact the law to remedy the evil,** not to afford an opportunity for some wage earner to collect certain monies, **but that an evil condition should be cured.**[68]

This was a compelling *social* argument. The *public* did indeed have an *interest* in seeing that female workers were not exploited. And the paragraph appeared on what Conner considered "the most important page that I have ever written or shall ever write," and it was crafted at the behest of one of Conner's Wenatchee colleagues who suggested he put "**more of yourself**" into the brief.[69] However, the *legal* standard for businesses "affected with a public interest" was very different, and after *Adkins* there remained a limited number of categories of businesses designated as such:

Until 1934, most businesses were characterized as private, and the prices at which they sold their goods or provided their services, as well as many aspects of their employment relations, could not be regulated by the state. Only a small group of businesses "affected with a public interest" could be subjected to such control. Grain elevators, railroads, fire insurance, water utilities, certain oil pipelines, public stockyards, the Chicago Board of Trade, and a very few other businesses.[70]

A business did not become "affected with a public interest" simply because it was engaged in transactions that the public should (and perhaps did) care deeply about. And it was self-evident that the Cascadian Hotel in Wenatchee did not fit into any of the afore-mentioned categories. So why, then, did Conner believe that one could plausibly argue that the "public interest" rationale was relevant in *Parrish?*

First, Conner very astutely realized that *Adkins* had not stopped the Court's jurisprudential clock. *Adkins* remained the definitive minimum wage law precedent, and in subsequent cases, challenges to other minimum wage laws had been upheld in perfunctory *per curiam* opinions.[71] However, another post-1923 decision seemed to undermine the doctrinal foundations of *Adkins*. Specifically, Conner believed that *O'Gorman & Young* adequately supported his reasoning. The Court had previously established—in 1914 in *German Alliance Insurance Co. v. Lewis*—that the selling of insurance was a business "affected with a public interest"; consequently premiums could be constitutionally regulated by the state.[72] The appellees in *O'Gorman & Young* believed that *German Alliance Insurance* controlled their case because there was no clear difference between regulating premiums and agent commissions. By contrast, the appellants vehemently contested the relevance of the precedent. In their opinion, the rates of *premiums* could be regulated because the *public* was paying those premiums (and so the business of selling those premiums was "affected with a public interest"), but the *commission rates* were something entirely different—a *private* business transaction internal to the business (and therefore something that would not affect the public). To support this argument, the appellant's brief unveiled a veritable parade of horribles:

> While it must be conceded that the legislature has the right to regulate the rates to be charged to the public, it does not follow therefrom that the detail [*sic*] cost of administration may be fixed and regulated by the government and the management of such business largely assumed by the government. If it be only necessary in order to sustain an act of this character to show that it regulates one of the items of cost entering into the rendition of service to the public, *then there is no detail of the business from the salary of the president to the wages of the charwoman, and the sufficiency of the services rendered by each,*

as well as the price of rent to the price of paper clips, which may not become the ultimate subject of legislative control.[73]

As Cushman observes, were the Court to disregard this argument and find commissions and premiums indistinguishable for constitutional purposes, it would "potentially . . . obliterate . . . the private zone of contractual liberty enjoyed even by businesses affected with a public interest and their employees."[74] In *O'Gorman & Young* the Court did exactly that. The decision in that case seriously undermined the 1917 decision in *Wilson v. New*. Recall, from chapter 3, that in *Wilson* the Court upheld the provisions of the Adamson Act that imposed an "eight-hour day for employees of carriers engaged in interstate and foreign commerce," temporarily prohibited a reduction in railroad workers' wages, and required the payment of overtime "at a rate not less than the *pro rata* rate for" the "standard eight-hour workday." This is because the law affected interstate commerce (which Congress has undeniable constitutional power to regulate), and regulated the actions of the nation's railroads, the paradigmatic businesses "affected with a public interest."[75] In upholding the regulation of the workers' wages, however, the Court had placed great emphasis on the law's temporary status, and the immediate pressing national commercial need to keep the railroads operating. *O'Gorman & Young* suggested that these limitations on the power of the government to regulate internal business practices were no more.[76]

Conner clearly recognized the importance of this, as is confirmed by the emphasis that he placed on one aspect of Justice Louis Brandeis's opinion for the five-justice majority in *O'Gorman & Young*. There was little doubt that the New Jersey law dealt "with a subject clearly within the scope of the police power." However, as Brandeis proceeded to explain, the Court was "asked to declare it void on the ground that the specific method of regulation prescribed is unreasonable, and hence deprives the plaintiff of due process of law."[77] Judicial restraint cautioned against taking that path:

> As underlying questions of fact may condition the constitutionality of legislation of this character, *the presumption of constitutionality must prevail in the absence of some factual foundation of record for overthrowing the statute*. It does not appear upon the

face of the statute, or from any facts of which the court must take judicial notice, that, in New Jersey, evils did not exist in the business of fire insurance for which this statutory provision was an appropriate remedy. *The action of the legislature and of the highest court of the state indicates that such evils did exist.* The record is barren of any allegation of fact tending to show unreasonableness.[78]

Conner used that passage (or the spirit of it) multiple times in his brief.[79] This was an astute move because, in addition to seriously undermining an aspect of the reasoning in *Wilson*, the Court in *O'Gorman & Young* "was now taking the same approach toward statutes regulating compensation that it had toward hours regulation in *Bunting*," the 1917 decision upholding a law prescribing maximum working hours for *all* workers (male and female).[80]

Although Conner's brief is defensible for the reliance that it placed upon *O'Gorman & Young* instead of *Adkins*, it is possible to identify another reason why he believed that the arguments he made would translate into a victory for his client. One needs to remember that the brief was filed with a court that had upheld (or, at the very least, not struck down) the 1913 law on two previous occasions—and, notably, it had done so before *and* after *Adkins*. In 1918, the Washington State Supreme Court ruled that Lillie Larsen was entitled to back pay for her employment as a ticket seller at J. D. Rice's movie theater in Chehalis. In his majority opinion Justice Mark Fullerton cited the U.S. Supreme Court's affirmation (by an equally divided court), the previous year, of the Oregon Supreme Court's decisions in *Stettler v. O'Hara* and *Simpson v. O'Hara*,[81] and wholeheartedly embraced the reasoning of his Beaver State colleagues in support of minimum wage laws.[82] Eight years later, the Washington State Supreme Court was again confronted with a challenge to the 1913 law when elevator operator Elizabeth Sparks sued for the back pay she was owed under the law. Unsurprisingly, the trial court in her case found the law unconstitutional, citing *Adkins*. Writing for the Washington Supreme Court, Justice Oscar Holcomb observed that *Adkins* "probably has the effect of overruling this court in *Larsen*." Rather than actually rule on the question of the constitutionality of the law, however, Holcomb decided to "ignore the question . . . until, if ever, that question is urgently necessary in a proper case for decision."[83]

Chief Justice Millard's Opinion: "rules deemed more
consonant with justice"

Conner's belief in the relevance of *O'Gorman & Young*, and his
deference to and faith in the rulings of the Washington Supreme
Court, was borne out on Thursday, April 2, 1936, when that body
overturned Judge Parr's ruling in a sweeping opinion written by
Chief Justice William J. Millard.

Born in January 1883 in the small western Missouri town of
Bismarck (whose population at the time numbered approximately
300), William James Millard moved to the nation's capital during
the first decade of the twentieth century. Slender, five-foot-nine,
with dark brown hair and piercing blue eyes, Millard cut quite the
dashing figure. While studying for his LLB at Georgetown Law
School, he met and captured the heart of Bertha Newhouser, the
woman who would become his wife and bear him two daughters,
Gertrude (born in 1909) and Alice (born in 1915). After receiving
his law degree in 1910, Millard practiced law in Washington, D.C.,
for four years before relocating his family all the way across the
country to the booming northwest city of Seattle.[84] In 1917 the
opportunity arose to supplement his work as an attorney by moving to Olympia to become the official law librarian for the Washington Supreme Court, the institution to which Governor Roland
Hartley, seeking someone with "no record of political partisanship,"
later appointed him in 1928 in order "to avoid political bickering."[85]
In his biographical history of that court, Charles Sheldon writes
of Millard that he "established himself as a liberal activist, often
opposing the court's conservative majority."[86]

In his unanimous opinion in *Parrish*, Millard made it very
clear that neither he nor his colleagues agreed with the decision
in *Adkins*. He admiringly quoted Chief Justice William Howard
Taft's dissenting opinion in that case *in its entirety*, and then, with an
equal amount of approval, he directly quoted from approximately
75 percent of Justice Oliver Wendell Holmes Jr.'s dissent.[87] Quite
apart from believing that *Adkins* had been wrongly decided, Millard
and his colleagues did not consider themselves bound by that U.S.
Supreme Court decision because they did not view it as controlling
the case at hand.[88] Instead, just as Conner did in his brief, the justices (a) stated that the 1913 minimum wages for women law is
"not wholly a private concern" because it "is protective of the public

FIG. 4.4 Washington State Supreme Court chief justice William J. Millard. Author's collection.

as well as the wage earner,"[89] (b) explained that both the state legislature and their colleagues in *Larsen* had reached this conclusion, and (c) concluded that the holding in *O'Gorman & Young* therefore justified upholding the 1913 law. (On this last point the justices relied on the very same *O'Gorman & Young* paragraph that Conner had emphasized.)[90]

As Millard stated later that year during his reelection campaign, "The law should be used to further progress, not to block it. As long as I'm on the bench I'll continue to give my decisions along the lines that I think will be for the betterment and the greater happiness of the people of Washington."[91] And this is precisely what he believed he and his colleagues had done in *Parrish*. They had "enunciated rules deemed more consonant with justice than the prior rules which had been followed for many years."[92]

Fred Crollard was stunned by the court's decision. He regularly (oftentimes two or three times a week) wrote letters to his son (Fred Jr.) at Notre Dame; in February 1936, the two men corresponded just before and just after Fred Sr. argued before the justices in *Parrish* on the twenty-fifth of that month. In those letters he expressed complete confidence that he would prevail because *Adkins* was the controlling precedent. The decision had "practically settled" the case in favor of the West Coast Hotel Company.[93] When he wrote again six weeks later on April 6, it was to convey his utter disbelief at the ruling handed down four days earlier by the justices in Olympia:

> Well, we received the shock of our lives the other day when the Supreme Court handed down its decision on the Minimum Wage case by holding that it was valid. . . . We were so sure of winning that that [*sic*] it was a great surprise. Even the labor department of the state had ceased to enforce the minimum wage scale since the U.S. Supreme Court's ruling [in *Adkins*], because it was conceded by everyone that our law was clearly unconstitutional.[94]

The Washington Supreme Court's decision brought shock to Fred Crollard, but elation to C. B. Conner and Elsie Parrish. However, it went almost unnoticed by the *Wenatchee Daily World*. The newspaper merely used one AP report to inform its readers of the decision from Olympia. And the article was devoid of the details that a hometown reporter might have used to continue to emphasize the local-interest aspects of the case.[95] The *World*'s coverage of the April 1936 reversal of Judge Parr's decision by the Washington Supreme Court stands in stark contrast to its reporting on the trial court judgment in *Parrish*, and confirms the scholarly consensus of opinion that decisions by state supreme courts typically receive very limited media coverage.[96] Additionally, *Parrish* had now moved two hundred miles from Wenatchee to the state capital (although, as we will see, when *Parrish* moves on to Washington, D.C., the local newspaper coverage of the case is extensive). This suggests that even when a case holds considerable local and human interest for a newspaper's readers, and even when a case involves the fate of a significant state law, coverage of the adjudication of that case by a state supreme court is considered of minimal importance.

When Elsie Parrish and C. B. Conner learned of the June 1, 1936, decision in *Tipaldo*,[97] they were surely disappointed. They were fully aware that it did not bode well for their case. However, perhaps there was some light at the end of the tunnel in the form of the precedent set in *O'Gorman & Young*. Perhaps. Interestingly, however, there was another post-*Adkins* decision that Conner should have—but did not—cite in his Washington Supreme Court brief appealing *Parrish*. That decision is *Nebbia v. New York* (1934), which, when taken together with *O'Gorman & Young*, really does make *Tipaldo* look like a distinct doctrinal anomaly.[98]

Nebbia v. New York: One of "three thunderbolt decisions"

The decision handed down in *Nebbia* on March 5, 1934, was at the time described by the *Washington Post* as "appear[ing] to mark another historic liberalization of the Court's construction of the Constitution, another 'modernization' of judicial interpretation."[99] As professor (and future justice) Felix Frankfurter described it in a letter that he wrote to Justice Owen Roberts, who authored the majority opinion in the case, *Nebbia* was "one of the most important contributions in years to candor and courage."[100] *Nebbia* went unmentioned in Conner's brief appealing Judge Parr's ruling; while Millard referenced it, the chief justice's use of *Nebbia* was minimal, and the passage that he quoted did not speak to the doctrinal heart of the decision.[101] This is despite the fact that it is just as important to the doctrinal story of *Parrish* as *O'Gorman & Young*—important because it meant that by the time Elsie's case came before the U.S. Supreme Court, the principal "analytical impediments to minimum wage regulation" had now "disappear[ed]" from the Court's jurisprudence.[102]

Perhaps, of course, Conner was unaware of the decision in *Nebbia*, but that seems unlikely because his briefs indicate that his legal research was up-to-date in every other respect. It is difficult, then, to explain the lack of attention that he (and Millard) gave to this precedent. As will become clear in the next chapter, though, this is an oversight that Elsie Parrish's counsel corrected when her case was appealed to the highest court in the land. Therefore, the fact that the precedential value of *Nebbia* was ignored at the earlier level of the litigation should not overly concern us.

In this chapter, however, this does not end *our* interest in the neglect of *Nebbia*. This is because of the fact that commentators such as the *Washington Post* and Professor Frankfurter were entirely justified in affixing a "revolutionary" tag to *Nebbia*. *Nebbia* did indeed lay the jurisprudential groundwork for future decisions upholding laws providing minimum wages for women. This generates the following very important question. Why has the standard narrative about the Court's New Deal jurisprudence instead characterized *Parrish* as the truly revolutionary decision? In other words, why does the idea persist that something constitutionally earth-shattering happened on March 29, 1937, rather than March 5, 1934? Before endeavoring to answer that question (by examining the overall treatment that the decision has received), we need to examine what the Court actually said in *Nebbia*, and why commentators considered it such a historic decision.

An Expensive Loaf of Bread

The springtime sun shone down upon Rochester, New York, on April 19, 1933. Residents were used to harsh winters; nevertheless, any meteorological sign that for a few months they could put thoughts of lake-effect snowstorms and bitter temperatures to the backs of their minds was a blessing indeed. On this particular Wednesday, there was some dampness in the air, but it was an otherwise very pleasant morning as Jedo Del Signore walked into the Leo Nebbia Market on Jay Street. Like the forty-year-old proprietor after whom this grocery store was named, Del Signore had emigrated to America from Italy and made his home (as had so many of his fellow countrymen) in this upstate New York city located on the southern shore of Lake Ontario. To these two men, there was nothing particularly special about the business transaction that they engaged in that morning. More than anything else, Leo felt blessed that he could maintain his business during the depths of the Depression, and Jedo felt equally fortunate that he could afford to purchase basic foodstuffs for his family. That Wednesday, the foodstuffs that Nebbia gave Del Signore amounted to two quarts of milk and a loaf of bread; in return, Del Signore handed over the amount that Nebbia charged for this purchase—eighteen cents.[103] Had the milk been unaccompanied by the bread, no one would have much cared about this exchange of goods, and Leo Nebbia would have remained just one more "insignificant little fellow," a "small grocer of upstate New York, of whom nobody outside his immediate neighborhood had ever heard."[104] However, because the loaf of bread was part of the purchase, the transaction triggered a lawsuit that would ultimately have immense constitutional implications for the future of the nation. The loaf of bread ensured that the resulting litigation—*Nebbia v. New York*—would become an important slice of American legal history.

The Nebbia-Del Signore transaction violated the minimum retail price for milk sales that had been fixed, five days earlier, by the newly created Milk Control Board (authorized by the 1933 Agriculture and Markets Law of the State of New York). The board had fixed the minimum retail price of a quart of milk at nine cents.[105] In establishing the board, the legislature was not acting on a whim; it was responding to real economic problems that affected the dairy industry. As graph 4.2 shows, farm prices for milk in New York were unstable throughout the first three years of the 1930s. They were susceptible to seasonable fluctuations in demand and the reality that milk was an unstable item. When sales were lean, one could not simply stockpile the product in the back room of a store or in a distribution warehouse until such time that demand picked back up. "It is an excellent medium for growth of bacteria" which "necessitate[s] safeguards in its production and handling for human consumption," safeguards "which greatly increase the cost of the business."[106] As Justice Roberts further explained in his majority opinion upholding the board's minimum price regulation:

> The fluid milk industry is affected by factors of instability peculiar to itself which call for special methods of control. Under the best practicable adjustment of supply to demand, the industry must carry a surplus of about 20 per cent, because milk, an essential food, must be available as demanded by consumers every day in the year, and demand and supply vary from day to day and according to the season; but milk is perishable and cannot be stored.[107]

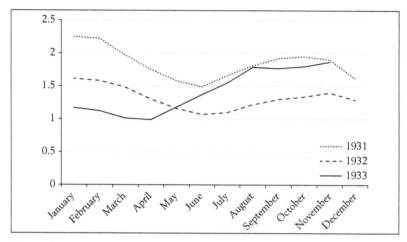

GRAPH 4.2   Farm prices (cents per quart) for milk in New York State, before and after the creation of the New York Milk Control Board in April 1933. Compiled using data from Henry S. Manley, "*Nebbia* Plus Fifteen," *Albany Law Review* 13 (1949): 12n4.

As a result, "the families of dairy producers had become desperate" and now found themselves "call[ing] for state aid similar to that afforded the unemployed, if conditions should not improve."[108]

In one respect, the Milk Board had in its favor that traditionally the milk industry had been heavily regulated. "Save the conduct of railroads," wrote Roberts, "no business has been so thoroughly regimented and regulated by the State of New York as the milk industry."[109] However, there was no escaping the fact that this industry was not one that (under the Court's currents precedents) was "affected with a public interest." The Court had previously upheld price regulations (including those that amounted to price-fixing); however, as long as the formalistic private-public business division remained, most agreed that it was difficult to sustain the Milk Board's actions.[110] Difficult, but not impossible, because had the Court been inclined to take a moderate middle road, it could have done so by latching on to some of the perfectly reasonable arguments that New York made—that "the business of milk distribution was a natural monopoly and a business affected with a public interest" and that "overproduction of milk posed a hazard within the cognizance of the police power."[111] Had it done so, there would have been no reason to describe *Nebbia* as a "historic liberalization" of one aspect "of the Court's" jurisprudence. However, when Justice Roberts announced the decision in that case, it quickly became clear that there was nothing moderate about the reasoning the justices had used. Roberts offered a stunning repudiation of the formalistic concept of a distinction between private businesses and those "affected with a public interest." "It is clear," he wrote, "that there is *no* closed class or category of businesses affected with a public interest."[112] On the one hand, he did not foreclose the possibility that such businesses would exist, because from this point onward he stated that such distinctions would be wholly a matter of judicial interpretation. On the other hand, however, what he wrote next strongly indicated that this was a redundant point. In terms of "due process," he concluded that "in the absence of other constitutional restriction, a state is free to adopt whatever economic policy may reasonably be deemed to promote public welfare, and to enforce that policy by legislation adapted to its purpose." As if this were not bold enough, he went further. "If the laws passed are seen to have a reasonable relation to a proper legislative purpose, and are neither arbitrary nor discriminatory, the requirements of due process are satisfied."[113] This test essentially stated that a law could only be held to violate liberty of contract if there was no "reasonable relation" between it and "a proper legislative purpose" *and* that law was "neither arbitrary nor discriminatory."

As Professor Richard D. Friedman observes, the Court only went so far in O'*Gorman & Young*. In that case, "Brandeis's opinion . . . pointed briefly to the 'presumption of constitutionality' favoring legislation in general, [but] his argument there attempted no new synthesis; he purportedly applied and did not attempt to reshape the doctrine."[114] The doctrinal reshaping came three years later in *Nebbia*. It was therefore unsurprising that in the immediate aftermath of *Nebbia* "a bevy of contemporary Court-watchers" (many of them household names in their fields) took to the pages of law and political science journals to express their belief that *Adkins* would soon fall by the wayside. Roberts's "expansive" reasoning, they concluded, now made it very difficult to strike down minimum wage laws. Difficult, yes; but not impossible (as the decision in *Tipaldo* demonstrated).[115]

*   *   *

After *Tipaldo*, Josephine Goldmark wrote to thank Herbert Rabinowitz for his help in shepherding the case through the courts. They were disappointed that the Court had struck down the New York State minimum wage law for women. However, Goldmark—one of the women who led the National Consumers' League's fight for such laws—was not about to abandon her crusade in the face of this one defeat. Rabinowitz agreed that there was reason to be optimistic but also cautioned against being too hopeful; "the chances of victory would be very small," he wrote. "At the very least," continuing to press the matter "would force a definite statement from the court, and there is always the chance that if the issues were squarely presented, Mr. Justice Roberts might side with the Chief Justice and Justices Brandeis, Stone and Cardozo, on this point, as he did in the *Nebbia* case."[116] Rabinowitz could not have made a more prescient point.

Preserving *Parrish* and *Nebbia*

History, of course, tells us that Rabinowitz's prediction came true on March 29, 1937. That historical fact immediately helps us to understand why, in terms of the *sociopolitical* commentary about the Court during the New Deal, the scholarly literature about the jurisprudence of the time period has for so long focused on that date rather than upon March 5, 1934, the day *Nebbia* was decided. First, it was *Parrish* (rather than *Nebbia*) that explicitly overruled *Adkins*.[117] In other words, the identifiable "switch" in the Court's decision-making came in 1937, not 1934. As we know from chapters 2 and 3, during the waning years of the nineteenth century and opening decades of the twentieth century, much of the relevant jurisprudence unfolded in a direction that made *Parrish* look like a switch. In *Lochner v. New York*,[118] the Court took a strident laissez-faire approach to the subject of contractual liberty; and when for the first time a majority of the Court voted on the fate of a minimum wage law for women, it struck down the law at issue (in *Adkins* in 1923). Yes, the trio of wage and hours regulations cases decided in 1917 gave progressive reformers some hope, but that hope only lasted until *Adkins*. When one combines *Lochner* and *Adkins* with the decision in *Tipaldo*, it seems all but set in stone that the Court suddenly and dramatically switched course on Easter Monday in 1937.

Second, it was *Parrish* (rather than *Nebbia*) that was decided just six weeks after FDR's announcement of his Court-packing plan. We have long since known that the justices voted on *Parrish* in December 1936, six weeks before the president's announcement of his plan to reorganize the judiciary (and this plan was an exceptionally closely guarded secret, so there is absolutely no reason to believe that any of the justices were privy to this executive endeavor). In other words, the idea of *Parrish* as a *Court-packing plan-precipitated* "switch" has long been discredited. However, the perception that partisan political forces nevertheless drove the Court to "switch" in *Parrish* has proven to be a stubborn myth.

Third, and inextricably intertwined with the previous two reasons, is the fact that the general public finds it much easier to understand the complexities of the Court's work by latching on to concrete decisions rather than doctrinal complexities. Writing two years after the Court's spring 1937 decisions, the historians Charles and Mary Beard made the following observation: "Since the decisions and opinions of the Court in these cases seriously affected the general public, the inexpertness of laymen outweighed the panurgy of the legal fraternity in the formation of popular sentiments. . . . Readers of newspapers, unskilled in the technology of the law, could readily assume from the morning headlines that the Court had reversed itself and surrendered."[119] On its own, "the inexpertness of laymen" to which the Beards refer offers a basic explanation as to why the average member of the general public tends to focus upon Supreme Court decisions rather than the doctrines laid out in those decisions. Perhaps Justice Antonin Scalia was being uncharitable toward the American public when he famously argued that the institutional complexities of the Supreme Court served to limit popular understanding of it, and "[t]hat is why the University of Chicago Law Review is not sold at the 7-Eleven."[120] However, his basic point is valid; the public has a limited interest in and understanding of the U.S. Supreme Court and the U.S. Constitution.

However, it is important to look beyond a simple "the public is not sufficiently educated, or sufficiently well versed in the material" explanation. Rather than get bogged down in details, the general public looks at distinctive moments that allow them to connect with and latch on to a timeline and to recognize cause and effect. Focusing on important moments rather than complex details is part of something more demonstrative of how the public looks at history, government, and politics. The U.S. Supreme Court is no exception. In the modern era, the public might view the Court as a valuable institution that significantly influences policies intimately affecting the lives of the American public. Throughout the Court's history, numerous examples abound of impactful decisions, such as *Brown v. Board of Education* (1954), *Miranda v. Arizona* (1966), *Roe v. Wade* (1973), and *Citizens United v. Federal Election Commission* (2010).[121] While other lesser-known decisions have affected the lives of the American public, it is the landmark decisions such as these that the public looks to, often relying upon them for its understanding of the politics and workings of the Court.[122] The public generally knows what these decisions did and what their places in history are; however, they are far less likely to know anything about the doctrinal complexities of the opinions written by the justices who decided those cases.

These three reasons help us to understand why *Parrish* rather than *Nebbia* has traditionally dominated the literature about the relationship between FDR, his New Deal agenda, and the U.S. Supreme Court. They help to explain why the standard socio-political narrative (with varying ideologically driven variations on a single theme) tells us that in one dramatic moment on Monday, March 29, 1937, the relationship between the Court and the other two branches of the federal government changed forever.

As this chapter has suggested, however, and as will become even clearer in the next chapter, if one were to tell the stories of the principal characters involved in the drama of *Elsie and Ernest Parrish v. West Coast Hotel Company* at the expense of a substantive discussion of *Nebbia*, one would be telling incomplete stories. The esteemed judicial politics scholar C. Herman Pritchett once admonished members of his profession to remember that "political scientists who have done so much to put the 'political' in 'political jurisprudence' need to emphasize that it is still 'jurisprudence.'"[123] In other words, the degree to which the American judicial system, and the opinions that its members author, are politicized must not be exaggerated. However, Pritchett's warning similarly informs us that students of American constitutional law should not ignore the political environment out of which cases are born, and within which the justices work. So yes, the larger context of the New Deal and the factors that precipitated the Court-packing plan are important to the story of *Parrish*. We cannot overlook that decision's relationship to the legal and doctrinal evolution that *Parrish* was part of—an evolution of which *Nebbia* is a crucial component. This is because the actors in the *Parrish* story (who were *living* the events that historians can only later analyze) saw the importance of precedents such as *O'Gorman & Young* and *Nebbia*. As historians Andrew R. L. Cayton and Jeffrey P. Brown remind us:

> It is arguable that historians ultimately have a better sense of what was happening in the past than the people we study, lost as they were in multiple sensations of their lives. From our removed perspective we can discriminate among events and organize them into patterns that were imperceptible to people in the middle of them. But we pay a price for this ability. We drain the past of its complexity, particularly the ambiguities and irresolutions of life, in order to prove or disprove our interpretive models. In the end, the words and actions of human beings must remain at the center of our constructions of their lives.[124]

As will become even clearer in the following chapter, *O'Gorman & Young* and (especially) *Nebbia* played important roles in the "words and actions" of the lawyers who shepherded the *Parrish* case up from the Washington Supreme Court to the U.S. Supreme Court.

5 On to Washington (D.C.)

Any way you look at it, the decision in this state's minimum wage law for women, is destined to rank along with
the famous Dred Scott decision and similar important
cases in shaping this nation's future.

—*Editorial in* The Journal *(East Wenatchee, Wash.)*
newspaper (January 1937)

According to at least one newspaper, after the U.S. Supreme Court
issued its decision in *Morehead v. Tipaldo*[1] on June 1, 1936, minimum wage laws immediately sank into a constitutional "twilight zone." This situation only seemed to worsen after the Court
announced, four months later, that it had decided to hear the appeal
in *West Coast Hotel v. Parrish*. There was widespread agreement that
such laws were "a step nearer to the chopping block."[2] As the *New
York Times* reported, in the nation's capital there was "not even the
tiniest echo" of hope that Elsie Parrish would emerge victorious.[3]

Elsie's legal journey from Olympia to Washington, D.C., began
on July 9, 1936, when the West Coast Hotel Company filed its
petition appealing the Washington Supreme Court's ruling in *Parrish*.[4] Six weeks earlier, on May 20, the justices in Olympia had
denied the company's petition for a rehearing. As deflating and
surprising as that ruling was for Fred Crollard, there was never
any doubt—in either his mind or the minds of his clients—that it
would be appealed. This is because *Adkins v. Children's Hospital*[5]

still remained the principal precedent, and the U.S. Supreme Court had treated it far more favorably than had Chief Justice Millard and his colleagues at the Temple of Justice. Admittedly, there were concerns that *Nebbia v. New York*[6] and *O'Gorman & Young, Inc. v. Hartford Fire Ins. Co.*[7] offered the justices in Washington, D.C., a different jurisprudential path to follow if they so chose. However, there were not yet any real signs that a firm *majority* was inclined to tread that new constitutional ground.

And then, of course, there was the pending decision in *Tipaldo*. Crollard was very aware of that case (as would have been any lawyer in his position). On May 12, he wrote to the U.S. Supreme Court to inquire about the status of the case. The clerk informed him that it was "at present under advisement. The Court will probably adjourn for the Term on June 1st, and it is possible that a decision may be rendered in this case before that time."[8] The Court waited until that final day of the Term to hand down its decision. One month later, after the Washington Supreme Court's judgment was formally entered, it came as no surprise to anyone that the West Coast Hotel Company filed its appeals petition with the nation's highest court.

To Hear, or Not to Hear?

Once it was decided that *Parrish* would be appealed to the U.S. Supreme Court, the West Coast Hotel Company asked John W. Roberts and E. L. Skeel, a pair of Seattle-based attorneys, to handle the litigation.[9] In 1936 the rules of the Supreme Court presented Roberts and Skeel with two options. When appealing a final decision by the highest court of a state in a case where that court had held that a state law did not violate the U.S. Constitution, an attorney was permitted to file (a) a petition for a writ of certiorari, or (b) a petition for appeal for a writ of error.[10] Although the Judiciary Act of 1925 (commonly known as the 1925 Judges Bill) significantly increased the Court's discretionary jurisdiction by reducing the types of cases that the justices were legally mandated to hear, these two options for appealing a state court decision were retained. Not until Congress passed the Supreme Court Case Selections Act in 1988 was the Court handed complete discretion over such appeals.

This meant that *Parrish* came to the justices as the type of case that, in theory, they were supposed to agree to hear; however, there was certainly no guarantee that the justices would take the case simply because Roberts and Skeel filed a petition for appeal. As two of Chief Justice Charles Evans Hughes's former clerks explained in a treatise published earlier that year, the justices would only note that they had probable jurisdiction in (and therefore would decide to hear) a case that came to them as a petition for appeal if the case involved a "substantial federal question" *and* as long as the answer to that question was not "foreclosed by well settled principles enunciated in prior decisions."[11] Put another way, "counsel were obliged to 'persuade the Court that the record presents an issue that is not frivolous and is not settled by prior decisions.'"[12]

These were the rules that governed the justices' decision-making about the petition in *Parrish*, but just what did it mean to say that a case involved questions "foreclosed by well settled principles enunciated in prior decisions"? As Howard Gillman astutely observes, "[J]urisprudence operates most effectively on a willing mind, and a judge's willingness to take seriously the imperatives of precedent depends largely on whether she or he is ideologically inclined to agree with the policy implications inherent in the doctrine."[13] This does not mean that the attitudinal model of judicial behavior—which, in its purest form, contends that a judge allows his or her policy preferences to guide their legal decisions—is necessarily an accurate predictor of the way in which a justice will treat a precedent which is consistent or inconsistent with his or her preferred policy views.[14] Rather, Gillman's point is that it would be naïve of us to think of a judge as making a decision about the value of a precedent without *any* consideration of the relationship between the policy values for which that precedent stands and the judge's own policy values. Therefore, when Hughes took a particular position on *Adkins* and/or *Tipaldo*—the two most important precedents—during the two conferences at which *Parrish* was discussed, we can assume that that position was in part driven by his views on the doctrinal value of contractual liberty and, in part, by his views regarding the economic policy implications attached to either constraining (or not) such liberty using minimum wage and/or maximum hours statutes. As Barry Cushman has shown, not until relatively recently, when the docket books of some of the Hughes Court justices became available for scholarly consultation,

FIG. 5.1   U.S. Supreme Court justice Owen J. Roberts relaxing at his
summer home in Kimberton, Pennsylvania, in August 1936. Library
of Congress.

did we know exactly what Hughes's views on these precedents
were when the justices sat down to consider Elsie Parrish's case.[15]
We already know that Hughes clearly disagreed with the policy
outcomes of *Adkins* and *Tipaldo*; however, the docket books tell us
that at the *Parrish* conference he was also concerned with another
aspect of those precedents, particularly another aspect of *Tipaldo*.

If ever there was a case, in the fall of 1936, which should *not*
have been heard by the justices because it was "foreclosed by well
settled principles enunciated in prior decisions," *West Coast Hotel
v. Parrish* was it. *Adkins* and its progeny (especially *Tipaldo*) were

good law. Elsie should have lost, there and then, on October 10, 1936, at the conference table of the justices of the Supreme Court of the United States. Consistent with those precedents, the decision of the Washington State Supreme Court should have been summarily reversed.[16] Yet, that did not happen. From that fact, it is possible to make two important observations. First, there is every reason to believe that at the conference Justice Owen Roberts expressed his desire to uphold the Washington state law and overturn *Adkins*. This is because the Court clearly had jurisdiction in *Parrish*. Indeed, after *Tipaldo* "it would have been ludicrous to reject jurisdiction on the ground that the case did not present a substantial federal question." After *Tipaldo*, of course, it also "would have been ludicrous" to proceed with full briefing and oral arguments in *Parrish* unless the justices did not believe it was "foreclosed by well settled principles enunciated in prior decisions."[17] Second (as Justice Pierce Butler's docket book confirms), at that conference Hughes also seemed to express a desire to see Elsie Parrish prevail, and *Adkins* overturned. "Butler records Hughes as presenting the case to the conference with the statement, 'This case is under Adkins rather than Tipaldo.' *Tipaldo*, he appeared to assert, did not actually settle the precise principles set out in *Adkins*, because the statutes involved in the two cases had differed materially."[18] As we saw in chapter 3 in his dissenting opinion in *Tipaldo*, Hughes, ever cautious about overturning a precedent, sought to distinguish the New York law from the one struck down in *Adkins*. Unlike Justices Harlan Fiske Stone, Louis Brandeis, and Benjamin Cardozo, he was not willing to call for the reversal of the 1923 decision. By October 1936, however, things had clearly changed, and Hughes was painfully aware of this. Making what is the only reference to public opinion that appears in the docket books, Hughes said, "Public mind much disturbed—Campaign." This is an obvious reference to the negative public reaction to (and bipartisan presidential campaign rejection of) *Tipaldo*.[19]

Briefly Stated

Exactly what the implications of this concern would be for *Parrish* would become clearer after the oral argument, which took place on December 16 and 17, 1936. As with every case, the justices headed into that argument after reading the merits briefs prepared and submitted by the two parties.

Appellee's Brief on the Law

The first merits brief filed in *Parrish*—the Appellee's Brief on the Law submitted to the Court on November 9—was brief in both name and nature. It was only four pages long. C. B. Conner was listed as the lead attorney for Ernest and Elsie Parrish. Now, for the first time in the *Parrish* litigation, his name was joined by that of Samuel M. Driver. It is important to note, however, that this did not signal a *change* of counsel—as was the case with Roberts and Skeel *replacing* Crollard. Rather, the *addition* of Driver was for purely procedural reasons. Another Wenatchee attorney, Driver did not take any formal part in *Parrish*. He merely lent the use of his name because, unlike Conner, he had been admitted to the U.S. Supreme Court Bar.[20]

Conner did not give the justices much to go on in his brief, and his legal arguments were quite weak. However, from a historical perspective the approach he took is both interesting and intriguing, its substantive shortcomings and brevity notwithstanding. As in the brief that he submitted to the justices of the Washington Supreme Court (discussed in the previous chapter), Conner made extensive use of *O'Gorman & Young*. This time, however, that analysis was supplemented by significant reliance upon the decision in *Nebbia*. The brief strongly indicates that Conner believed the reasoning in these two cases decisively and unequivocally settled the constitutional issues in *Parrish* and settled them in favor of his client. Indeed, such was the doctrinal reliance that he placed upon those decisions, one cannot help but conclude that Conner stretched the implications of the reasoning in them far beyond those either envisioned or anticipated by Justice Brandeis (in *O'Gorman & Young*) or Justice Roberts (in *Nebbia*) when they wrote the majority opinions in those cases.

Conner looked at the relevant precedents for *Parrish* in the manner outlined in table 5.1. When these decisions are simplified and conveyed in this manner, a clear pattern emerges—a pattern that Conner (just like any other lawman [or layman]) saw. This pattern indicates that until *Parrish* the U.S. Supreme Court had followed the lead of the lower appeals court in every case

TABLE 5.1   Disposition of *Parrish*-related precedents before both
the intermediate appeals courts and the U.S. Supreme Court

Case	Disposition of the case by the intermediate appeals court	Disposition of the case by the U.S. Supreme Court
Bunting v. Oregon (1917)	Statute upheld	Statute upheld
Stettler v. O'Hara (1917)	Statute upheld	Statute upheld
Adkins v. Children's Hospital (1923)	Statute struck down	Statute struck down
Murphy v. Sardell (1925)	Statute struck down	Statute struck down
Donham v. West Nelson Mfg. Co. (1927)	Statute struck down	Statute struck down
Morehead v. Tipaldo (1936)	Statute struck down	Statute struck down

Note: Although C. B. Conner did not cite *Stettler v. O'Hara*, 243 U.S. 629 (1917), he might as well have, because the outcome of the case was consistent with the pattern he saw.

involving a challenge to a minimum wage law. Unfortunately, as clear and simple as this pattern is, it ignores the actual substance of the decisions. Equally unfortunately, in his brief Conner hung his hat on this pattern, and argued that when *any* legislature (state or, as in the case of *Adkins*, Congress) enacted a minimum wage regulation, if that regulation was then upheld by the state's highest court (or, as in the case of *Adkins*, the relevant federal appeals court), it was then "*entitled to approval* by the Supreme Court of the United States."[21] In other words, Conner was asking the Court to rubber-stamp lower court rulings on the constitutionality of any such laws. This was convenient for Conner because it enabled him to distinguish *Parrish* from *Adkins*. In Conner's opinion, in *Adkins* the Court had merely followed the lead of the District of Columbia court in striking down the act of Congress. *Parrish* was therefore distinguishable because the Washington Supreme Court had *upheld* the state law. If one followed this logic, *Parrish* was an easy case with a certain victor.

Why did Conner believe he was justified in grossly oversimplifying these precedents in this manner? The answer to that question is simple: *O'Gorman & Young.* Recall that in that case (decided in 1931), the Court concluded that "*the presumption of constitutionality must prevail in the absence of some factual foundation of record for overthrowing the statute. . . . The action of the legislature and of the highest court of the state indicates that such evils did exist.*"[22] Unlike in his previous brief, Conner did not actually *directly* quote this passage in its *entirety*. Nevertheless, he (albeit without quotation marks) made copious use of its language and spirit in the brief he submitted to the U.S. Supreme Court: "The presumption of constitutionality must prevail in the absence of any factual foundation in the record for declaring the act unconstitutional. . . . [T]here is no indication of anything of the kind, and the act of the Legislature, with the approval of the highest Court of the State . . . conclusively shows that an evil existed for which this act is a proper remedy."[23]

In that brief, Conner also demonstrated that he now saw the relevance and importance of *Nebbia* for his argument. The main "question involved and the issue to be determined" in *Parrish* was whether the 1913 Washington law was "a valid and reasonable exercise of the police power" of that state. Citing *Nebbia*, Conner concluded that the law was valid because states had constitutional free rein to regulate any "matters pertaining to public welfare" as long as "those matters be exercised in a manner reasonably tending to that end."[24] Although Conner neither quoted directly from nor cited any particular page numbers from *Nebbia*, it is evident that this doctrinal argument took its cue from Justice Roberts's opinion.[25] Putting *O'Gorman & Young* and *Nebbia* together, Conner reached the following exceptionally broad conclusion: *the U.S. Supreme Court is duty bound to uphold any regulation that achieves a public welfare goal in a manner reasonably related to that goal (and the reasonableness is determined by both the enacting legislature and an intermediate appeals court)*.

There is no doubt that the test laid out in *Nebbia* encouraged federal judicial deference to the police power decision-making of state legislatures. However, it did not give legislators the kind of freedom that Conner's brief ascribed to it. Over time, the Court would water down the *Nebbia* test (especially as it related to economic liberty) to such an extent that legislators would find themselves with the amount of regulatory liberty (at least with regard to commercial regulations) that Conner envisioned. That development was a number of years away, though.

Appellant's Brief

The brief that John W. Roberts filed in *Parrish* ran to far more pages than Conner's, but it was just as short on substance. This is because the counsel for the West Coast Hotel Company was equally convinced that the precedents favored his client. Indeed, devoting very little discussion to the subject matter, Roberts summarily concluded that the Washington law was indistinguishable from those struck down in *Adkins, Murphy v. Sardell*,[26] and *Donham v. West Nelson Mfg. Co.*;[27] the 1913 statute "contains all of the [same] vices," he wrote.[28] Conveniently ignoring all of the opposition to those decisions, Roberts sought to give even greater strength to his client's case by writing that the fate of those laws (at the hands of the U.S. Supreme Court) had been "generally accepted by the bench, bar and public" alike.[29] Just like Conner, Roberts saw a pattern in the precedents; and just like Conner, Roberts saw a pattern that benefited his arguments.

In one important way, however, the *Parrish* briefs submitted by Conner and Roberts were very different. Although Roberts engaged in a lengthy, critically analytical discussion of Millard's lower court opinion in the case, he recognized that it would be best to do so without mentioning either *O'Gorman & Young* or *Nebbia*.[30] However, in the section that Roberts devoted to exploring the scope of legislative power, he made it clear that he had those two decisions (or, more specifically, Millard and Conner's interpretations of them) very much at the forefront of his mind.[31]

Roberts saw and understood the implications of those broad interpretations of state regulatory power. "If the Washington court's theory is to be accepted," he wrote, "the fact that the state legislature and state court find that a law is a proper exercise of the police power" makes "the Supreme Court of the United States . . . powerless to grant any relief against the legislation. . . . The mere statement of this proposition shows its fallacy. *If it were accepted, then the Constitution would be a nullity.*"[32] And for every precedent that supposedly endorsed this new position of judicial restraint, there existed one that articulated the opposing position, grounded in the importance of reining in regulatory power in order to protect significant constitutional rights.

For Roberts, there were two relevant Fourteenth Amendment due process clause liberty precedents, and they were not *O'Gorman & Young* and *Nebbia*. Instead, in his Appellant's Brief, Roberts quoted admiringly from *Buchanan v. Warley* (1917) and *Meyer v. Nebraska* (1923).[33] Both stood for the principle that "*[t]he state legislature and the State Supreme Court can not deprive a person of his constitutional rights by merely stating that the enactment is made as an exercise of the police power for the correction of an existing evil.*"[34]

In *Buchanan*, the Court struck down a segregationist ordinance enacted by the city of Louisville, Kentucky. The 1914 law made it illegal to sell real estate, located in white neighborhoods, to African Americans. The justices unanimously rejected the contention that this was a legitimate exercise of the police power. It was not a means for achieving a public health, safety, or welfare goal. Rather, it was an interference with contractual liberty, pure and simple. They acknowledged "[t]hat there exists a serious and difficult problem arising from a feeling of race hostility which the law is powerless to control, and to which it must give a measure of consideration. . . . But its solution," wrote Justice William R. Day, "cannot be promoted by depriving citizens of their constitutional rights and privileges."[35] And that is exactly what the ordinance did. As Day emphasized in the passage that Roberts quoted in his *Parrish* brief:

> The authority of the State to pass laws in the exercise of the police power, having for their object the promotion of the public health, safety, and welfare, is very broad, as has been affirmed in numerous and recent decisions of this court. Furthermore, the exercise of this power, embracing nearly all legislation of a local character, is not to be interfered with by the courts where it is within the scope of legislative authority and the means adopted reasonably tend to accomplish a lawful purpose. But it is equally well established that the police power, broad as it is, cannot justify the passage of a law or ordinance which runs counter to the limitations of the Federal Constitution; that principle has been so frequently affirmed in this court that we need not stop to cite the cases.[36]

The excerpts that Roberts chose to use from Justice James C. McReynolds's majority opinion in *Meyer v. Nebraska* reaffirmed this sentiment.

In *Meyer*, by a vote of 7–2 the Court struck down a Nebraska law that prohibited the teaching of any "modern" language, except English, to any elementary or middle school children. Although McReynolds conceded that the Court had "not attempted to define with exactness the liberty . . . guaranteed" by the due process clause of the Fourteenth Amendment, he nevertheless recognized that "the term has received much consideration and some of the included things have been definitely stated." He proceeded to list what, "[w]ithout doubt," that liberty encompasses (beyond "merely freedom from bodily restraint").[37] In a statement that would have far-reaching consequences, he explained that the "liberty" also "denotes . . . the right . . . to contract, to engage in any of the common occupations of life, to acquire useful knowledge, to marry, establish a home and bring up children, to worship God according to the dictates of his own conscience, and generally to enjoy those privileges long recognized at common law as essential to the orderly pursuit of happiness by free men."[38] Two pages later, McReynolds wrote the following paragraphs that Roberts quoted in his brief:

> It is said the purpose of the legislation was to promote civic development by inhibiting training and education of the immature in foreign tongues and ideals before they could learn English and acquire American ideals, and "that the English language should be and become the mother tongue of all children reared in this State." It is also affirmed that the foreign born population is very large, that certain communities commonly use foreign words, follow foreign leaders, move in a foreign atmosphere, and that the children are thereby hindered from becoming citizens of the most useful type, and the public safety is imperiled.

> That the State may do much, go very far, indeed, in order to improve the quality of its citizens, physically, mentally and morally, is clear; but the individual has certain fundamental rights which must be respected. The protection of the Constitution extends to all, to those who speak other languages as well as to those born with English on the tongue. Perhaps it would be highly advantageous if all had ready understanding of our ordinary speech, but this cannot be coerced by methods which conflict with the Constitution—a desirable end cannot be promoted by prohibited means.[39]

In Roberts's mind, these excerpts served to strengthen the judicial limits upon legislative activity that he believed *Buchanan* endorsed, but with one important addition—they suggested that Roberts believed that the right to enter into a contract was a "fundamental" one.

Roberts's decision not to mention either *O'Gorman & Young* or *Nebbia* in this brief was entirely understandable, because both of those precedents had the potential to significantly undercut his main argument. However, this strategy of avoidance was derailed by the amicus brief submitted by the State of Washington, so much so that Roberts felt compelled to write an answer to it. In that answer Roberts ultimately discussed the Court's reasoning in *Nebbia* in such a way as to turn that decision from a thorn in his client's side to a potential problem for his opposing counsel.

With a Little Help from One's Friends

Today it is extremely rare for a U.S. Supreme Court case to find its way to the justices' desks without being accompanied by amicus curiae briefs, and it has been that way for most of the twenty-first century (as shown in graph 5.1). These "friend of the Court" briefs are submitted by entities other than the parties to a case. With the exception of those that are filed by the Office of the Solicitor General of the United States, any entity wishing to file an amicus brief must obtain the permission of both of the parties to the case. Whether submitted by an organization, group, or individual, an amicus brief is typically intended to provide the justices with information about the issues raised in a case (information that reflects the particular body of knowledge or expertise of the amicus) and/ or provides the Court with a different way of looking at the issues (again reflecting the perspective of the amicus). For example, if a case involves a dispute over the meaning of an amendment to the U.S. Constitution, a group of prominent legal historians might come together to coauthor an amicus brief that educates the justices about the different congressional and state-level debates that took place during the adoption of that amendment. Amicus briefs are still used to educate the justices, but over the years many briefs have presented information in a manner more akin to partisan advocacy.[40]

Things were very different when the Court heard and decided *Parrish*. Although the database detailing exactly how many cases have had amicus briefs filed in them only goes back as far as 1946,[41]

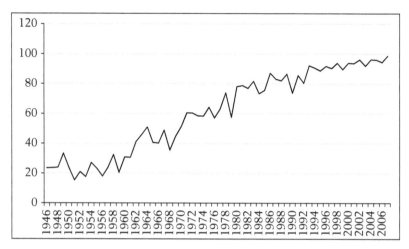

GRAPH 5.1   Percentage of U.S. Supreme Court cases with amicus curiae participation, 1946–2007 Terms. Compiled using data kindly provided to the author by Paul M. Collins Jr.

it is generally accepted that during the 1930s it was unusual for amicus briefs to be filed in a case. One simply could not imagine *Tipaldo* being appealed today without a flood of amicus briefs trailing in its wake; however, in 1936 only three were part of the case filings.

The Washington State Amicus Brief: "The welfare of the whole state is at stake"

The number of amicus briefs filed in *Parrish*—one—also pales in comparison to the number that would be filed in a modern-day minimum wage case. Washington attorney general G. W. Hamilton submitted that lone amicus brief.[42] The state had expressed an interest in entering the *Tipaldo* litigation as an amicus, but it had waited until May 21, 1936, almost one month after oral arguments in the case, to inquire about doing so. Predictably Henry Epstein and John Bennett, New York State's solicitor general and attorney general respectively, agreed that it would be "fruitless to file briefs at this late date."[43] When it became clear that *Parrish* was headed to the nation's highest court, Washington State's formal involvement came at the request of C. B. Conner. Elsie's lawyer contacted the state attorney general's office about the matter less than a week after Chief Justice Millard and his colleagues denied the West Coast Hotel Company's petition for a rehearing. "The hotels," Conner wrote, "are taking this case to the Supreme Court of the United States, and I hope that your office can see its way clear to prosecuting the action." What Conner said next was his polite way of indicating to the state that Elsie Parrish's lawyer was emotionally committed, wholeheartedly, to his client's cause, but having taken on the case pro bono, the financial reality of seeing this case through to its constitutional climax was beginning to set in.[44] "The Plaintiff in this case is a mere laborer in the hotel and entirely without funds, *and the welfare of the whole state is at stake.* Will you please advise me what assistance your department can render, otherwise the matter may go by default."[45] In other words, Conner's question to himself was "how can I afford to take this case forward?" while his question to the Washington attorney general was "how can the State afford *not* to?"

Two days later, he followed this letter with another much longer one, in which he outlined in more detail just what he felt was at stake in the case. It is worth quoting extensively from that piece of correspondence, because in it Conner brings another element into the conversation—what he believed to be the political consequences of the case for the state's elected officials:

> Another thing in this connection which might be quite import-
> ant from a political point of view, the labor people are inter-
> ested very much and it would have a very important bearing
> on their vote upon the question of who should be the Attor-
> ney General. In other words, if the Attorney General's Office
> should decide that it is their business to defend this law, and
> I am in a position to say that information to the labor unions,
> there isn't any question but what [sic] it will have quite a bit of
> weight; while . . . on the contrary, they will of course not feel
> quite so kindly toward any candidate for governor or attorney
> general who is not in favor of supporting this law. It looks to
> me like a place to secure the labor support, and I will be glad
> to cooperate.[46]

Conner was suggesting that if the labor unions were to find out that the state had declined to take up the *Parrish* litigation mantel on behalf of Elsie Parrish (thereby potentially jeopardizing the future of its own minimum wage law for women), there could be severe political repercussions. Although 1936 was an election year—and both Governor Clarence D. Martin and Attorney General Garrison W. Hamilton were up for reelection—there was never any realistic chance that either of them would fail to secure another term in office.⁴⁷ Therefore, it is unlikely that the labor-related concerns that Conner expressed in his letter were shared by Hamilton's office. Instead it seems much more likely that his previous piece of correspondence contained points that struck home, and spurred the attorney general to take up Elsie's case; because, even though it contained hyperbole, there was also much truth to the statement that the *Parrish* litigation concerned the "the welfare of the whole state" of Washington.

Unfortunately, the amicus brief that the state filed with the Court at the end of November⁴⁸ only provided Conner with limited substantive assistance for his case. The brief was disorganized and offered up contradictory approaches to defending the 1913 law, only one of which lent any genuine support to the arguments outlined by Elsie Parrish's lawyer.

The first approach, which consumed much of the first half of the brief (no doubt disappointing Conner), advocated narrowing the focus of the litigation. The state believed that the 1913 law was constitutional in its entirety; however, in this section of its brief it only sought to defend the law as it applied to Elsie Parrish and the West Coast Hotel Company. Indeed, it argued that the case merely involved a "contract between a chambermaid . . . and an inn keeper" and that the "state statute is involved only incidentally."⁴⁹

The state argued that it was "the appellee's contention here that the record is devoid of relevant facts necessary for a full consideration of the question of the validity of the Washington minimum wage statute which the appellant so vigorously assails."⁵⁰ This is a problematic argument for several reasons. If, by "the appellee's contention," Hamilton and his staff meant the contention of Conner, then such a statement is patently false. Conner never made an argument that the record was factually wanting. Indeed, the only reference to the absence of facts that Conner made in his brief came, ironically, in the section where he discussed the importance of *O'Gorman & Young* and loosely quoted from that case: "The presumption of constitutionality must prevail in the absence of any factual foundation in the record for declaring the act unconstitutional."[51] Conner went on to say that "[i]n this case there is no indication of anything of the kind, and the act of the Legislature, with the approval of the highest Court of the State of Washington, conclusively shows that an evil existed for which this act is a proper remedy."[52] As explained above, Conner used these words to defend judicial restraint. Nothing in those words suggested (as the state claimed in its amicus brief) that shortcomings in the factual record required the adoption of a narrow litigation strategy.

If by "the appellee's contention," Hamilton and his staff were referring to themselves, then an even bigger problem arises. On the next page of their brief, they stated: "There are no findings of fact. . . . The supreme court [of Washington] might very properly have reversed the cause because the court below made no findings of fact or conclusions of law in support of his judgment."[53] Once again, this simply was not the case. Judge Parr's ruling in *Parrish* came in two parts—(a) an oral announcement of the judgment (on October 17, the same day as the bench trial), and (b) a printed document (issued by the court on November 9) summarizing the main *"Findings of Fact and Conclusions of Law."*[54] As we saw in the previous chapter, that oral announcement was admittedly short on substance, for it was Parr's contention that "the decision of the highest court of the land [*in Adkins*] . . . settles this question absolutely, and beyond all question, for the time being."[55] What we today know about the content of that oral announcement primarily comes from the "Amended Statement as to Jurisdiction" that Roberts filed with the U.S. Supreme Court when the West Coast Hotel Company made the decision to appeal the decision of the Washington Supreme Court. This is ironic, because in that brief Roberts goes on to quote from Parr's "Findings of Fact."[56] To Hamilton and his staff, however, who contended that there were "no findings of fact," it was as if the opposing counsel had never filed this document.[57]

The second approach that Washington State adopted in its amicus brief stood in complete contrast to the first because it closely followed (admiringly so) the arguments in favor of expansive legislative power made by both Conner and Millard. Extensive quotes supporting a broad conception of the police power were reprinted from Millard's opinion, including one section where the chief justice had noted that this was not the first time that the Washington Supreme

Court had upheld the 1913 law. Admittedly, these quotes appeared below a subheading that read as follows: "The Statute of Washington is Within tee [*sic*] Police Power of the State *When Applied to Fixing a Minimum Wage for Women Employees in a Hotel.*"[58] However, the subsequent section (succeeded only by the document's conclusion) left no doubt about the nature of legislative power that the state was now endorsing. "The courts have always recognized the right of the legislative branch of government to determine when the necessity for protecting the peace, health, safety, morals and the general welfare of the people exists. These are things which by duty and necessity the legislature must inquire into and determine for the purpose of making rules to serve such ends." Continuing, the section said that "[w]here there is no reasonable ground for supposing that the legislature's determination is not supported by the facts, or that its judgment is one of speculation rather than from experience, its findings are not reviewable."[59] In support of this proposition, Hamilton and his staff cited numerous cases. Special attention, however, was paid to *O'Gorman & Young*. That they chose to accompany the citation with the following passage (discussed in the previous chapter) from that decision only serves to support the conclusion that in the second half of the amicus brief the State switched from a narrow to a broad defense of the law:

> The statute here questioned [in *O'Gorman & Young*] deals with a subject clearly within the scope of the police power. We are asked to declare it void on the ground that the specific method of regulation prescribed is unreasonable and hence deprives the plaintiff of due process of law. As underlying questions of fact may condition the constitutionality of legislation of this character, the presumption of constitutionality must prevail in the absence of some factual foundation of record for overthrowing the statute. It does not appear upon the face of the statute, or from any facts of which the court must take judicial notice, that in New Jersey evils did not exist in the business of fire insurance for which this statutory provision was an appropriate remedy. The action of the legislature and of the highest court of the state indicates that such evils did exist. The record is barren of any allegation of fact tending to show unreasonableness.[60]

All that was left for the State to do was to cite and quote from *Nebbia*, which it did on the penultimate page of its brief.[61]

Appellant's Answer to Brief of Amici Curiae

Two-thirds of the "Appellant's Answer to Brief of Amici Curiae," which John Roberts filed with the Court on December 15, was consumed with what E. L. Skeel would say during the oral arguments scheduled to begin the following day. This is because the state's amicus brief landed upon the desk of Roberts and Skeel just before they left for Washington, D.C. "We therefore submit," wrote Roberts, that the reply to that brief represents a "summary of our oral argument."[62] The remaining (and concluding) third of the document, however, did constitute a specific response to the arguments made by Conner and Millard (and, to a much lesser extent, the state in its amicus brief). It was, however, a poorly written response dominated by the following contention: "The argument of appellee and the Washington Supreme Court goes to the full extent of saying that the Supreme Court of the United States has *no* power to protect an individual citizen against the encroachment upon his individual rights by the State under the guise of the police power. That is not the law."[63] Yes, indeed this was not the law. However, neither Conner nor Millard ever contended that it was. Admittedly, as we have seen, they did use the reasoning in *O'Gorman & Young* and *Nebbia* to support an expansive conception of legislative regulatory power, but it was not a conception that envisioned *no* judicial checking and/or balancing.

Roberts and Skeel continued their mischaracterization two pages later when they said that "[t]he real point of appellee's brief . . . is the contention that because the Washington Act received the approval of the Supreme Court of Washington it is . . . entitled to approval by this Court . . . in the absence of any factual foundation in the record for declaring the Act unconstitutional."[64] What is one to make of these mischaracterizations? Perhaps one can attribute them to the zeal of adversarial representation, or to the time constraints faced by counsel. Whatever the reason, the "Conclusion" to the brief made it abundantly clear that neither Roberts nor Skeel considered them to be important elements of their central argument.[65] That does not excuse their presence in the brief. It

simply serves to underscore the only syllogistic point the two lawyers thought that the nine justices really needed to know:

- The 1913 Washington law was no different from the law
  struck down in *Adkins*.
- *Adkins* is still good law.
- Ergo . . . the 1913 Washington law is unconstitutional.

This is the argument that Skeel laid out before the Court on
December 16 and 17.

"Mr. Chief Justice and may it please the Court"

Parrish was the fourth case to come before the justices on December 16, 1936. Consequently, time constraints dictated that the oral
arguments be divided over two days. Representing the West Coast
Hotel Company, Skeel began his argument on December 16, concluding the next day. Our knowledge about the content of oral
arguments from this time period is quite limited; audio record-
ings of the arguments were not made until 1955, which therefore
means that information must be gleaned from disparate sources
such as newspaper articles and legal memoirs.[66] As noted above,
much of what we know about Skeel's argument in *Parrish* comes
from the "Appellant's Answer to Brief of Amici Curiae" filed with
the justices on December 15.

Although that brief professed to engage in a discussion of
Tipaldo without "any view of debating the correctness of the opinions therein filed," it subsequently became clear that a position was
indeed being taken upon that precedent—specifically, upon the
Tipaldo dissent authored by Chief Justice Hughes.[67] Recall from
chapter 3 that in that solo opinion Hughes argued that *Adkins*
was not a relevant precedent because, unlike the New York law,
the minimum wages provided for by the 1918 Act of Congress
struck down in *Adkins* were not related to the fair value of the
services being performed. In his argument before the justices in
Parrish, Skeel emphasized the correctness of that view. Agreeing
with Hughes about the substantive difference between the two
laws, Skeel removed *Tipaldo* from the precedential equation. Only
Adkins "governed" his client's case because only *Adkins* involved a

similar law. "The element of reasonable value of services" was missing from the Washington statute; therefore, "[o]ur case is governed
solely by the *Adkins* case and the subsequent cases in conformity
with its holding."[68] Interestingly, Skeel conceded that *Tipaldo* might
have been wrongly decided because "[a] statute fixing minimum
wages upon the basis of value of services, applicable to all individuals in a given class, permitting reasonable flexibility under
changing conditions, may accomplish a social service and be a reasonable exercise of the police power." *Parrish*, however, presented
the justices with a very different case—a case involving a law
"which looks at one side of the problem only." Foreshadowing later,
explicit references to the standard laid out in *Nebbia*, Skeel emphasized that the Washington statute "attempt[ed] to fix wages upon
the basis of necessity rather than earning power," thus making it an
"arbitrary . . . and improper exercise of the police power."[69] That
power, he continued, "should be upheld in a proper case, but it
accomplishes no social or economic relief to uphold statutes based
on extreme or illogical applications of the police power." The Constitution would become a nullity "[i]f we sustain every act of a legislature because it is within the general range of subjects embraced
by the police power, regardless of how *arbitrary* are the means
employed. . . . If and when such a policy is adopted, and acts with
good purpose but *inappropriate and arbitrary means* are sustained,
the liberties guaranteed by the Constitution are gone."[70]

While Skeel believed that Hughes had been correct in his
dissent in *Tipaldo*, he felt equally strongly that Justice Stone had
engaged in "erroneous reasoning" in his dissent when he issued a
clarion call for placing the vast majority of minimum wage laws
within a "presumptively constitutional" box of protection.[71] In support of that reasoning, Stone had cited numerous cases, including
O'Gorman & Young and *Nebbia*.[72] Skeel (and Roberts) had previously steered well clear of those two decisions in their *Parrish* filings.
Perhaps, upon reading the briefs filed by Conner and the State of
Washington, Skeel felt compelled to discuss these precedents during
oral argument. Although his arguments ultimately did not succeed,
one cannot help but admire the creative use to which he finally put
Nebbia (and, by implication, *O'Gorman & Young*). Skeel's argument
was very simple. In *Nebbia*, the Court said that "[i]f . . . laws passed
are seen to have a reasonable relation to a proper legislative purpose, and are *neither arbitrary nor discriminatory*, the requirements

of due process are satisfied."[73] The statute that authorized the New York Milk Board to fix prices had met these "requirements" because, unlike the 1913 Washington State minimum wage law for women, "[i]t was not a loosely drawn statute" because it empowered the board to "ascertain . . . what prices for milk will best protect the milk industry . . . and insure a sufficient quantity of pure and whole-some milk." By contrast, the 1913 law "makes it mandatory to fix wage price *not based upon value but solely upon the necessities of a living wage.* The element of reasonable return to the producer was included in the Nebbia statute. *The element of fair value received is excluded in the Washington statute.*"[74] For Skeel, that constituted "a complete and conclusive distinction between those cases,"[75] and conveniently reinforced his main point—*Parrish* was an easy case to decide in his client's favor. Why? See *Adkins.*

*   *   *

The amicus brief that Washington State filed in *Parrish* was not the extent of its involvement in the case at the U.S. Supreme Court level; it was, however, the only role that Attorney General Hamilton and his Assistant Wilbur Toner had originally envisioned playing. Ultimately, Toner also assumed the duty of arguing on behalf of Elsie Parrish. This is because it was not possible for Conner to make the long and expensive trip to Washington, D.C.; Toner already had plans to be in the nation's capital on a fortnight-long trip, and therefore agreed to argue the case for Conner.[76] As Conner explains in his memoir:

> Living at this distance from Washington City, it was quite inconvenient for me to be presented and admitted to the bar of the Supreme Court as that has to be done in person. Of course, it would have been a pleasure to have appeared person-ally in the matter, but that was not necessary and I hesitated to spend the considerable amount of money that would have been incident to going to Washington City for that purpose. . . . Toner . . . had a case requiring his presence before the United States Supreme Court at the same time and very kindly agreed to present the oral argument for me. For this I shall always be greatly indebted to him.[77]

Toner was a well-respected attorney who spent much of his legal career working in Walla Walla, Washington, before becoming Washington State assistant attorney general.[78] For his argument in *Parrish*, Toner adopted the first of the two strategies that he had helped to lay out in the state's amicus brief. As he later explained in a letter to Albert Leslie, the secretary of the Central Labor Council of Spokane and Vicinity, "The validity of the whole law was not in issue in the cause, at least we elected to argue it upon that theory and argued it simply as a regulation of hotels for that seemed to be the particular occupation affected by the Parrish case."[79]

Additionally, Toner sought to distinguish the Washington law from that which was struck down in *Adkins*. He attempted to do this by invoking the *Munn v. Illinois* doctrine (which had not been discussed in the briefs). As we saw in chapter 2, in this seminal decision in 1876 the Court stated that businesses "affected with a public interest" could be constitutionally subject to far greater regulation than private property.[80] Toner contended that "the business of an innkeeper was affected with a public interest."[81] It was very clear that in 1936 the only way in which one could argue that the Cascadian Hotel was a business "affected with a public interest" was to adopt the strategy employed by Conner in *his* briefs. This meant that one would have to argue that the plight of working women (a plight alleviated by minimum wage laws) was a subject of general public concern, meaning that all businesses that employed women were automatically "affected with a public interest." This argument, as we know, would only hold sway with the justices if they were committed to reasserting the expansions of regulatory power hinted at in *O'Gorman & Young* and *Nebbia*. However, because Toner chose to defend the Washington law on narrow grounds, this was not the approach that he adopted when invoking *Munn*. Instead, as Hughes explained in his opinion, Toner used the "affected with a public interest" doctrine to try and "distinguish the *Adkins* case." In other words, Toner contended that *Parrish* involved a business "affected with a public interest" and *Adkins* had not. As the chief justice noted, this "effort at distinction" was "obviously futile." This is because one of the parties in *Adkins* was a hotel employee, namely Willie Lyons, who contended that the law had caused her to lose her job as an elevator operator at the Congress Hall Hotel.[82]

"Minimum Wage Law Question Arouses Much Speculation"

Toner's rather esoteric, narrow argument about only defending one specific application of the law proved confusing for the media covering the case. Newspapers generally devote minimal space to analysis of oral arguments, because the structure and substance of these judicial proceedings do not lend themselves to easy and engaging summarizing and contextualizing. The task only gets harder when the arguments that journalists are assigned to cover are themselves far from clear.[83] The *Wenatchee Daily World*'s coverage of the oral arguments in *Parrish* began on December 4, with an article that embodied the newspaper's belief in the importance, to its readers, of the local and human-interest aspects (rather than just the legal issues) of *Parrish*. It reported: "C. B. Conner, counsel for Mrs. Elsie Parrish, 37 year old grandmother, today was informed by the clerk of the Supreme court of the United States that the wage case of the former local chambermaid against the West Coast Hotel company will not be argued before the week beginning December 14 or possibly later. It was to have been argued some time next week."[84] Readers were then reminded about the basic facts of the case, but only the facts that related to why Elsie had initiated the lawsuit. It was important to tell Elsie's story—which included mentioning that upon relocating to Omak, she and her husband gained employment at the Jim Hill Hotel and the Biles-Coleman Mill respectively.

Ten days later, on Monday, December 14, the newspaper informed its readers that the oral arguments in *Parrish* would take place later that week. This time, however, the front-page report was noticeably shorter and far more concerned with the New Deal implications of the case. Elsie was identified as a party to the lawsuit, and mention was made of the fact that she was "a hotel chambermaid." But this time, in part because of the details contained in the December 4 article and also because the report came from Washington, D.C., via the Associated Press (AP) rather than from Wenatchee via the *Daily World*'s staff, no reference was made to the local nature of the case, beyond noting that at issue was the constitutionality of a Washington State law.[85] On December 16, the *Daily World* made no mention of the fact that oral arguments in *Parrish* had begun. However, this was not for lack of interest. Rather, it can be attributed to the fact that the Court only heard a small portion of the arguments that day—too late in the day for even a Pacific time zone newspaper to cover. Therefore, the newspaper recommenced its coverage the next day when the arguments resumed.

The December 17 AP article that the newspaper ran addressed a human-interest aspect of the oral arguments, but its focus was on one of the justices rather than the parties to the case. As evidenced by the first two paragraphs, the wire service was of the opinion that the most noteworthy aspect of that morning's proceedings was the absence of Justice Stone. His vacant seat at oral arguments was widely interpreted as meaning that only eight justices would take part in the judgment of *Parrish*. The article included some brief commentary on the substance of the arguments made by Skeel. However, this paled in comparison to the references to Justice Stone's absence.[86]

The further one got from Wenatchee, the more Stone's absence was emphasized in newspaper coverage of the oral arguments in *Parrish*. The AP article that ran in the *Daily World* also appeared in the *Seattle Post-Intelligencer* and the *Tacoma News-Tribune*.[87] And the *Everett Herald, Spokane Press*, and *Seattle Star* all printed a United Press (UP) report for which the focus of the day's proceedings in *Parrish* was the incomplete bench of justices.[88] The UP article is of additional interest because it identifies a detail that has been overlooked by the literature on the case. It states that *two* members of the Court—Justice Stone *and* Justice McReynolds— were absent from the oral arguments, which "caused fresh speculation today on the outcome of the long debated question which has repeatedly split the court into liberal and conservative ranks." For the Washington law to survive, "a switch of one vote" would have to take place, and the article speculated that this would most likely have to be the action of Justice Roberts. As a "Situation Complicated" subheading indicated, however, this was idle and unnecessary speculation. This is because, as it was reported, Chief Justice Hughes "'vouched' McReynolds into the case" which, as the article explained, involved announcing (presumably in open Court, although this was not stated) that McReynolds would participate in *Parrish*, his "temporary" absence notwithstanding. (In another version of the wire service article he was described as away "on personal business.")[89] The ailing Stone, by contrast, had been kept away from oral arguments since the beginning of the Term in October,[90] and there was genuine doubt that he would be "physically able to participate" in *Parrish*. Whatever one makes of the fact that McReynolds's absence from oral arguments on this day has gone unnoticed by the literature on *Parrish*,[91] the fact remains that this particular article demonstrates an unusually high level of understanding of the Court's legal procedures. This is confirmed by its closing sentences, in which the potential fate of the Washington law is discussed in light of the possible absence, from deliberations, of only Justice Stone. Were "a switch by one conservative member" of the Court to take place, the article observed, the Court "could uphold the Washington law only in this one test case and could influence no future decisions because the alignment would be four to four."[92] It might be *Stettler* all over again.

This wire service report notwithstanding, it is fair to say that in general the AP and UP articles about the oral arguments in *Parrish* were marked by considerable clarity and explanation of the legal issues in layman's language.

December 19, 1936

If his colleagues were not already aware of Hughes's desire to see *Adkins* overruled, when they met in conference at noon on Saturday, December 19 to discuss the case, they were left with no doubt that this had been his intention from the start.[93] He started somewhat coyly, by asking, "Can Adkins be distinguished." This was clearly a rhetorical question because he proceeded to renew the objections about Toner's argument that he had raised while the Washington lawyer had stood at the lectern before him two days earlier. It surely came as no surprise to his colleagues when Hughes proceeded to flat out ask them, "[S]hould Adkins be overruled."[94] As Professor Cushman indicates, we will likely never know exactly why Justice Roberts voted with the majority in *Parrish* (prompting the famed "switch" accusations), but what we do know is that the *Tipaldo* backlash weighed heavily on the chief's mind, ultimately leading to his willingness to take this position regarding *Adkins*.[95]

However, it is important not to jump to the conclusion that *Parrish* was ultimately a public opinion-driven "switch" for the chief justice (or Justice Roberts). Hughes did far more than take the nation's pulse by looking at polling data; he did not simply stick his finger in the air and feel the cold winds of economic change blowing. (After all, they had been blowing for a while and had not had a supremely noticeable effect on the Court's decisions.)[96] Additionally, he did not look at FDR's landslide reelection the previous month and decide to lead the "supreme coort [to] follow . . . th' iliction returns."[97] For, at the December 19 post-oral argument conference Hughes "indicated that he 'Agreed with Taft's [dissenting] op[inion]' in *Adkins*. 'J's opn has more weight now.' Those challenging the statute had 'not shown' that the 'Reasonable value' of the employee's labor was 'less than [a] living wage.'"[98] What this meant would become publicly clear when Hughes read from his opinion for the Court in *Parrish* a few months later. Privately, however, the justices emerged from that conference knowing exactly what the ultimate fate of the case would be.

*   *   *

At that conference only eight justices cast their votes in *West Coast Hotel v. Parrish* because Justice Stone was still hospitalized. In his biography of Chief Justice Hughes, Merlo Pusey reports that "in a private chat" with the chief justice, Justice Roberts "had divulged his intention of voting to sustain the Washington law."[99] Consequently, going into the conference, Hughes knew two things: (a) the justices would be evenly split in *Parrish* and (b) if announcement of the decision in the case were delayed to enable a recuperated Stone to participate, the Washington law would be upheld by a vote of 5–4.[100] That delay did indeed occur.

"Why the delay?"

Just *when* the Court would announce its decision in *Parrish* was the subject of much speculation for a considerable period of time. In his syndicated newspaper column published on Saturday, February 27, 1937, Raymond Clapper reported that the Roosevelt Administration had heard rumors that the Court was poised to hand down its "overdue" decision in the "highly embarrassing" *Parrish* case on Monday. Clapper described the justices' inaction on the case as tardiness because of the fact that *Adkins* and *Tipaldo* were both decided within thirty-five days of their oral arguments, and over two months had now elapsed since arguments were heard in *Parrish*.[101]

In notes that Clapper kept for his files, the Scripps-Howard newspaper editor Walker Stone similarly observed that in the past "[n]either the majority nor the dissenting Justices have found the issues involved in the minimum wage cases so complicated or intricate as to require any long period of time in preparing their opinions." This led him to ask, "Why the delay?":

> Can it be that the Court has special reasons for withholding its decision? Can it be that the Court's action is affected by the criticisms which have been directed towards some of its members? Can it be that the Court is affected by the President's proposal for the reorganization of the judiciary? Can it be that the Court fears the justified public resentment that would be aroused by a reaffirmation of the *Adkin's* [*sic*] case? Can it be that the Court fears to overrule the *Adkin's* case because by doing so it must confess that it has erred in interpreting the Constitution and that the President's complaint—that the present majority in the past has obstructed social and economic legislation by unnecessarily restrictive interpretations of the Constitution—is fully justified. **Can it be that the Court which ought to be above politics is playing politics?**[102]

Of course, such accusations (whether phrased rhetorically or otherwise) were not leveled at the Court merely because it was taking the justices a curiously long time to arrive at their decision in *Parrish*. Something else led commentators to speculate that the justices were "playing politics."

That "something" was the Judicial Procedures Reform Bill, more commonly known as the Court-packing plan. Scholars have sacrificed many trees in their quest to unpack (every pun intended) this famous (and infamous) moment in American constitutional history, and many excellent treatments of the subject have been written.[103] As explained from the outset, this book seeks to bring the stories of individuals such as Elsie Parrish, C. B. Conner, and Fred Crollard out of the enormous FDR-related shadows that have long since been cast upon the *Parrish* case. Therefore, here it is only necessary to provide a very brief overview of the Court-packing plan.

In terms of the U.S. Supreme Court, the winter of 1936–37 was one of bitter discontent for the president as he continued to be frustrated at the way in which a conservative majority of the justices struck down key pieces of his New Deal agenda. He agreed with Professor Edward S. Corwin's assessment that it was "probably Utopian to hope that the Court" would "supply the needed remedy" for this "situation which it has itself created."[104] Therefore, emboldened by his recent landslide reelection, FDR chose to seek his own remedy; the one he settled upon, and the way he defended it, demonstrated a complete and utter presidential desire *not* to compromise on any level.[105]

Unveiled to the public on February 5, 1937, the Court-packing plan called for the passage of legislation that would create one new seat on the U.S. Supreme Court for every justice who reached the age of seventy and did not retire and/or resign from that bench within the next six months. Although Roosevelt contended that the legislation was needed in order to alleviate the workload burden felt by the elder justices, an increasing workload that also negatively affected the American public because it "contribute[d] to the slow rate of speed with which causes move through the Courts," his real motivation was transparently political.[106] He wanted to fill the bench with his own appointees in order to tilt the ideology of that institution in his favor. The proposed bill would permit for a maximum of six new justiceships to be created. It was more than convenient that six was the very number of new seats that Roosevelt would have had the chance to fill had the bill been enacted in 1937, and similarly convenient that a Court of fifteen justices was exactly what his advisers told him was necessary to secure a foolproof pro-New Deal majority on the current Court.[107]

In short, the Court-packing plan was a major political gamble that failed, and it is one that history has been right not to reflect kindly upon. The plan never secured the support of a majority of either the American public or their elected members of Congress, and it brought "into sharp relief the gridlock-related implications of a variety of the features of" American government—"ranging from judicial review to Article V to the congressional committee system to the Senate filibuster."[108] And ultimately, in addition to major *bipartisan* congressional opposition, the plan went down in flames because the anti–New Deal tide began to turn. Most notably, Willis Van Devanter, one of the major conservative voices on the Court, announced his decision to retire in June 1937, and on March 29, the Court decided *West Coast Hotel v. Parrish*.

There is no reason to believe that the Court was playing politics by delaying the announcement of the decision in *Parrish* even though (understandably) this was the widespread conclusion to which people immediately jumped. Although no one knew it at the time, the justices had long since decided what the outcome in the case would be. They were simply waiting for Justice Stone to return so that they could announce a decisive 5–4 judgment in the case rather than have a repeat performance of *Stettler*. However, even in light of this knowledge, the "Why the delay?" question persists because Stone returned to his work in early February, two months before *Parrish* was decided. Again, we *now* know that the Wagner Act cases—three decisions upholding much of the National Labor Relations Act and therefore signaling a pro-New Deal change of course in terms of the Court's commerce clause jurisprudence—could have been handed down on March 29, with *Parrish*, had Justice McReynolds not "dawdled along," seemingly resenting the fact that Van Devanter had asked him to write the three dissents in these cases (and delaying the issuance of the decisions until April 12).[109] However, that cannot have been the delaying factor for *Parrish*. First, Justice Sutherland, not McReynolds, wrote the solitary dissenting opinion. (As we will see in the next chapter, Sutherland was always going to write the main dissent in *Parrish* because of the way in which that decision undid his treasured work in *Adkins*.) Had McReynolds written the dissenting opinion in *Parrish*, maybe he might not have walked out of the courtroom, declining to hear Hughes read from the majority's opinion.[110] Second, it is clear that Hughes chose to announce the *Parrish* decision on March 29 in order to put some temporal distance between the two major ways in which he affected the fate of the Court-packing plan. *Parrish* was the second of those ways; the first came exactly one week earlier, on Monday, March 22.

Senator Burton K. Wheeler (D-MT) was one of the principal congressional opponents of the Court-packing plan, and he sought to persuade members of the Court to testify before the Judiciary Committee. After all, who better than the justices themselves to refute the accusation that they were overworked and in need of additional colleagues? Unwilling to testify in person because Justice Brandeis declined to accompany him, Chief Justice Hughes did the next best thing. He provided Senator Wheeler with a letter to read on his behalf: "The letter, thought two veteran journalists, was 'a masterpiece of exposition.' Roosevelt's original line of attack, the alleged inefficiency of the Court, had struck a chord on which Hughes, the exemplar of efficiency, was particularly sensitive. He responded with his favorite weapon, the facts. . . . Not only was the addition of new Justices unnecessary for efficiency, wrote Hughes, it would positively hamper the Court's operation."[111] Ultimately, the letter probably served as nothing more than powerful confirmation of the already well-aired and increasingly influential views of the plan's opponents. However, it is important to remember that on March 22, 1937, *Parrish* was still pending. That changed one week later, on March 29, when the Court, by a 5–4 vote, decided that Washington State's minimum wage law for women was constitutional. Elsie Parrish had won.

6   1937

"This Is OUR Year"

The end crowns all. But surely it would require the author of *Bleak House* to do justice to a course of litigation whereby it took thirty years for the States to be allowed to deal through minimum wage legislation with some of the deep social problems created by the entry of women in large numbers into industry.

—*Professor Felix Frankfurter,*
"The Orbit of Judicial Power" (1938)

The banner headline emblazoned across the front page of the December 27, 1936, issue of the *Sunday News*—a pro-New Deal labor newspaper published in Seattle—predicted that for labor, 1937 "Is OUR Year." Albert Leslie, the secretary of the Central Labor Council of Spokane and Vicinity, was not as sanguine. In February 1937, he wrote to the Washington State attorney general in order to ask whether the state's minimum wage law for women was unconstitutional. The law was still in effect and enforceable; indeed, it had been this way since its enactment in 1913. Nevertheless, considerable confusion and uncertainty surrounded the status of the nation's minimum wage laws in the spring of 1937.[1] The appeal in *West Coast Hotel v. Parrish* sat on the justices' desks, undecided; and, there could be no guarantee that a final judgment in that case would erase the confusion and uncertainty. What was clear, however, was that not until the nation's highest court resolved this latest

FIG. 6.1   The front cover of the *Sunday News* (Seattle) newspaper, December 27, 1936.

chapter in a decades-long struggle over the constitutionality of such laws could the opponents and advocates of progressive legislation plan their next moves with any degree of clarity and confidence.

That resolution came, in *Parrish*, on Easter Monday, the first day, since the announcement of the Court-packing plan, that the Court had handed down decisions in orally argued cases.[2] The Court's session was scheduled to begin at midday. By 11 A.M., "four thousand visitors had already been admitted to the building, where many lined up two abreast from the courtroom doorway almost to the suite of Justice Stone in the idle hope of getting a peek at the proceedings. 'There isn't room for them,' said a police guard, 'if they stood here all day long.'"[3] When the time came for Chief Justice Charles Evans Hughes to announce the decision in No. 293: *West Coast Hotel v. Parrish*, everyone in the courtroom witnessed, firsthand, a very particular kind of spectacle—Justice James C. McReynolds rose from his seat and walked out of the courtroom.[4] He wanted no part of what was to come.

Chief Justice Hughes's Majority Opinion: "As lasting as a shaft of granite"

Speaking with a tone "of triumph," the chief justice set about announcing a decision that upheld the Washington law and explicitly overruled *Adkins v. Children's Hospital of D.C.*[5] Hughes resigned his associate justiceship in 1916 in order to run for (and very nearly win) the presidency.[6] Consequently, he did not participate in the reargument of and final decision in *Stettler v. O'Hara*, the 1917 decision in which a deadlocked Court automatically affirmed the Oregon Supreme Court's decision upholding that state's minimum wage law.[7] However, during the first round of oral arguments in that case in December 1914 Hughes had seemed more inclined than many of his colleagues to say that a minimum wages law could be a constitutionally permissible exercise of a state's police power.[8] *Parrish* presented him with the opportunity (as chief justice, he got to choose who would write the majority opinion) to make good on that inclination, albeit over two decades later. When he announced the *Parrish* decision, "reversing his Court, but not himself," he did so with bouts of linguistic "eloquence, even passion" that "few thought him capable of."[9]

Giving the Issues "fresh consideration"

However one frames the Court's decision in *Parrish*, it is clear that Hughes and his authorized biographer Merlo Pusey both overstated their cases when concluding that the Court-packing plan "had not the slightest effect" and "no bearing whatever on the outcome."[10] It is equally clear, however, that the justices were neither insulated from

FIG. 6.2   U.S. Supreme Court chief justice Charles Evans Hughes, circa 1940. Library of Congress.

nor ignorant of the enormously negative reaction to their decision in *Morehead v. Tipaldo*,[11] and the endorsement of New Deal policies that was implicit in the landslide reelection of President Roosevelt in November 1936. Recall, from the previous chapter, that when the justices met for their Saturday conference on December 19, 1936, and took up *Parrish*, the chief justice "indicated that he 'Agreed with Taft's [dissenting] op[inion]' in *Adkins*" and coyly remarked that "J's opn has more weight now."[12] What he meant by this became clear when the final judgment in *Parrish* was announced.

In Hughes's opinion, there were four specific reasons why it was "not only appropriate, but we think imperative, that, in deciding the present case, the subject" of minimum wage laws for women, as it was discussed in *Adkins* (and, by implication, *Tipaldo*) "should receive fresh consideration."[13]

1. "The importance of the question"
2. The fact that "many States" had "similar laws" to the 1913 Washington statute
3. "[T]he close division by which the decision in the *Adkins* case was reached"
4. "[T]he economic conditions which have supervened . . . in the light of which the reasonableness of the exercise of the protective power of the State must be considered"[14]

In his dissenting opinion, Justice George Sutherland made it very clear that he considered Hughes's list to be entirely disingenuous. "It is *urged* that the question involved should now receive fresh consideration," he wrote, "among other reasons, because of 'the economic conditions which have supervened.'"[15] Yes, the chief justice had listed "other reasons," but there was only one *real* reason for revisiting (and overturning) *Adkins*. While there are good reasons to downplay Hughes's "other reasons," this does not mean that Sutherland was right to accuse the majority of altering "the meaning of the Constitution . . . with the ebb and flow of economic events."[16] When Hughes's opinion is read in light of the doctrinal patterns and tendencies discussed in the preceding chapters of this book, it becomes clear that the justices in the majority did not perform a "constitutional somersault," let alone "the greatest" such "somersault in history," in *Parrish*.[17]

"[L]iberty in a social organization"

Front and center in this doctrinal discussion is of course the concept of liberty of contract. It is easy to overstate the case that Hughes was making when he sought to offer up a definition of that concept

FIG. 6.3   U.S. Supreme Court justice George Sutherland, 1937.
Library of Congress.

in *Parrish*. He did not deny that it existed. It could not be found in
the explicit language of the Constitution, and it was not an absolute
freedom—all his colleagues nodded in agreement with these two
points.[18] Nevertheless, it was a liberty protected by the Fourteenth
Amendment. More specifically, it was a constitutionally protected
"liberty" that existed "in a social organization." As Hughes proceeded to explain, this meant an "organization which requires the
protection of law against the evils which menace the health, safety,
morals and welfare of the people."[19] Although this allowed for some
restraint of liberty, it was again difficult for the dissenters to disagree
with this point, for it was grounded in basic social contract theory
and the well-established concept, in America, of state police powers.
As we saw in chapter 2, it is necessary for individuals, as members
of a society, to relinquish some of their liberty in order to protect

themselves, and their society, from the aforementioned "evils." So, why was *Parrish* decided by a bitterly divided Court? Disagreement started to creep into the judicial conversation when Hughes tried to establish *how* far state police powers could encroach upon individual (in this case contractual) liberty.

More than once, Hughes emphasized that "the power to provide restrictive safeguards" on contractual liberty needed to be "reasonable" and related to "the interests of the community."[20] And more than once he emphasized that the Court was not breaking any new ground in saying so. Yes, it was departing from "the decision in the *Adkins* case," but that was simply because *Adkins* had itself been "a departure from the true application of the principles governing the regulation by the State of the relation of employer and employed," constitutional principles whose existence and importance "had many illustrations" that predated and succeeded *Adkins*.[21] Those illustrations ran from the grain elevators in post–Civil War Chicago (in *Munn v. Illinois*)[22] through the O'Gorman & Young insurance brokerage (in *O'Gorman & Young v. Hartford Fire Ins. Co.*),[23] to the Leo Nebbia Market in Rochester (in *Nebbia v. New York*).[24] As Hughes observed, in *Nebbia* the Court "*again* declared that, if such laws 'have a reasonable relation to a proper legislative purpose, and are neither arbitrary nor discriminatory, the requirements of due process are satisfied.'"[25]

At this period in American history, when one said that the due process clauses of the Fifth and Fourteenth Amendments had a substantive component, this meant that one viewed them as protecting "life, liberty, and property" through a separation of governmental powers (as discussed in chapter 2). The clauses guaranteed *judicial* process. Consequently, as long as the legislature was not doing something that deprived you of property rights that you were entitled to, your only recourse was legislative, not judicial, action. The Constitution was not there to protect you from silly and unwise laws; should you find that your elected representatives have indeed enacted such laws, you should go running to the ballot box, not the courthouse. This was the prevailing understanding of due process in *Parrish*. As Hughes wrote: "Even if the wisdom of the policy [of enacting minimum wage laws for women] be regarded as debatable" as it surely was, "and its effects uncertain, *still the legislature is entitled to its judgment*"—just as long as that "[l]egislative response . . . cannot be regarded as arbitrary or capricious." In other words, for the Court in *Parrish* this was a straightforward application of the test established three years earlier in *Nebbia*. This, as Hughes said in a matter-of-fact manner that must have been unbearable for the dissenters to read, "is all we have to decide."[26]

In this respect, while "supervening economic conditions" surely influenced the decision that the justices reached in *Parrish*, the test established in *Nebbia* makes it clear that Hughes and his colleagues placed great emphasis on considering "the reasonableness of the exercise of the protective power of the State." And while "supervening economic conditions" might throw *some* "light" on that consideration, the only effect was to, once and for all, bring *Nebbia* out of the shadows of other decisions such as *Tipaldo*.[27]

The Presence of an "Evil"

Nebbia also made it easy for the Court to decide that the 1913 Washington State minimum wages for women law was not an "arbitrary or capricious" law addressing an "evil."[28] This is because of the way in which that 1934 decision eradicated the private-public business distinction. In the absence of that distinction, Hughes was able to ask the following rhetorical question in his opinion in *Parrish*: "What can be closer to the public interest than the health of women and their protection from unscrupulous and overreaching employers?"[29] No longer limited to declaring "[g]rain elevators, railroads, fire insurance, water utilities, certain oil pipelines, public stockyards, the Chicago Board of Trade, and a very few other businesses" as "affected with a public interest,"[30] in *Parrish* Hughes felt free to lead the post-*Nebbia* Court to a wholehearted embrace of a far broader understanding of what could be regulated in the name of the "public interest."

In doing so, he produced an opinion that vindicated the argument that C. B. Conner, Elsie's lawyer, had laid out in the brief he submitted to the Washington Supreme Court appealing Judge William O. Parr's Chelan County Superior Court decision. Here, it is worth revisiting a passage from that brief, a passage discussed in chapter 4:

> It would not be going too far to say that in every single community in the state, there are numerous children who are entirely dependent upon the efforts of a tired mother, and they receive

their food because of whatever she can earn. **This may be said
to have nothing to do with the constitutionality of the law,**
and **yet those are the things that were considered by the legislature and which induced them to enact the law,** not for the
mere protection of the wage **earner, but for the protection of
the public.** The welfare of the community generally demands
that children eat, have comfortable clothing, blankets to cover
them; fuel to warm them, and in the natural course of human
events the husband, the father, the man, should be and usually is the bread-winner; but in these more modern times
conditions have radically changed, expenses of living are very
much heavier, and so thousands and thousands of children
throughout the State of Washington would be going hungry
and very cold indeed and deprived of the necessities and comforts of life, but for the earnings of a devoted mother. **These
are the things which moved the legislature to enact the law to
remedy the evil,** not to afford an opportunity for some wage
earner to collect certain monies, **but** that an **evil condition
should be cured.**[31]

When one compares Conner's words with those of Hughes, there
are distinct similarities. The two men approached the subject matter from the same perspective:

The legislature of the State was clearly entitled to consider the
situation of women in employment, the fact that they are in the
class receiving the least pay, that their bargaining power is relatively weak, and that they are the ready victims of those who
would take advantage of their necessitous circumstances. *The
legislature was entitled to adopt measures to reduce the evils of the
"sweating system,"* the exploiting of workers at wages so low as
to be insufficient to meet the bare cost of living, thus making
their very helplessness the occasion of a most injurious competition. The legislature had the right to consider that its minimum wage requirements would be an important aid in carrying
out its policy of protection. The adoption of similar requirements by many States evidences a deep-seated conviction *both
as to the presence of the evil and as to the means adapted to check
it.* Legislative response to that conviction cannot be regarded as
arbitrary or capricious.[32]

That "[l]egislative response" found constitutional support not only from *Nebbia* but also from *Muller v. Oregon*, the 1908 decision in which the Court upheld a law prescribing maximum working hours for women.[33] In his opinion in *Adkins*, Justice Sutherland placed great stock in the "revolutionary . . . changes . . . in the contractual, political and civil status of women" that had taken place since *Muller*, changes "culminating in the Nineteenth Amendment" and, in his opinion, effectively eradicating the "differences" between the sexes.[34] Without seeing the need to do much more than say "we stand by the decision in *Muller*," Hughes rejected the argument that a woman was no longer in need of governmental protection from "oppression" in the workplace.

In this respect, Hughes's opinion in *Parrish* ensured that, just like *Muller*, it would "lead . . . a double life in constitutional history—as both a step forward on the road to modern labor standards and a step backward away from sexual equality."[35] To the chief justice, however, at this point in American history there was a pressing social condition that necessitated the state taking a "special interest" in the "employment of women."[36]

The Needs and Interests of the Public

It is easy to see why Hughes's opinion secured the wrath of the dissenters, who accused him of amending the Constitution by judicial fiat. In *Adkins*, the Court concluded that the market should determine the value of the services performed by an employee. Allowing the government to make that decision interfered with the contractual liberty of both the employer and the employee. When that interference came in the form of a minimum wage law, "it amount[ed] to a compulsory exaction from the employer" because in the absence of that law, market forces would have generated a contract under whose terms the employee would have accepted a smaller income than the statutorily prescribed minimum. Even worse, there was no relationship between that "compulsory exaction" and the actual amount of work undertaken. The employer is required "to pay at least the sum fixed in any event, because the [state has determined that] the employee needs it, but requires no service of equivalent value from the employee." If an employee was down on their economic luck—for whatever reason—it was not (in the eyes of the *Adkins* majority) the fault of the employer. In *Adkins* the Court therefore concluded that a minimum wages law "in effect, arbitrarily shifts to his [the employer's] shoulders a burden which, if it belongs to anybody, belongs to society as a whole."[37] Cass Sunstein neatly summarizes this in the following way: "In *Adkins*, the Court saw minimum wage legislation as requiring a subsidy to the public from an innocent employer. Such legislation was thus a kind of 'taking' from A to B. According to the Court, if B is needy, it is not A, but the public at large, who should pay."[38]

In *Parrish*, this understanding of a subsidy was "turned on its head."[39] The majority of Hughes's opinion was devoted to explaining why a minimum wage law was a constitutional "exercise of the protective power of the State" because it had sufficient "reasonableness."[40] Although this explanation was dominated by discussions drawing upon *O'Gorman & Young*, *Nebbia*, and *Muller*, in the final two pages of the opinion Hughes switched explanatory gears. "There is an additional and compelling consideration," he wrote, "which recent economic experience has brought into a strong light." This was the undeniable "exploitation of a class of workers who are in an unequal position with respect to bargaining power, and are thus relatively defenceless against the denial of a living wage." This "is not only detrimental to their health and wellbeing, *but casts a direct burden for their support upon the community. What these workers lose in wages, the taxpayers are called upon to pay.*" Continuing, he explained that "*[t]he community is not bound to provide what is, in effect, a subsidy for unconscionable employers.*"[41] In *Adkins*, the Court concluded that the burden for subsidizing the nation's impoverished women workers should be borne by the public. In *Parrish*, the Court concluded that in the absence of minimum wage laws, the public has to bear the burden (in the form of economic support for the downtrodden). However, it is only being compelled to do so because the nation's "unconscionable employers" refused to pay their workers a living wage. Hence the argument that governmental support for underpaid workers actually amounts to a subsidy for those who are doing the underpaying.

Significantly, this aspect of the majority opinion in *Parrish* helped to fuel the "switch in time" thesis. Yes, the opinion spoke directly to the current economic climate, but it was impossible to ignore the fact that *Tipaldo* had also been decided, a mere ten months earlier, during "the recent period of depression" when there similarly existed "unparalleled demands for relief." Hence the remark that came from Attorney General Homer Cummings, who was in favor of minimum wage statutes but nevertheless expressed concern about the way in which the Court had finally arrived at the decision to uphold such laws. "So it happens," observed Cummings two days after *Parrish*, "that the Constitution on Monday, March 29, 1937, does not mean the same thing that it meant on Monday, June 1, 1936."[42]

Further fueling this "switch" conclusion was the fact that Hughes was using the "unparalleled demands for relief" rationale to uphold a law *enacted in 1913*. It was one thing to say that the Great Depression had intensified the need for legislative regulatory action to address exploitative employment practices. It was quite another to say that such an action, taken over two decades earlier, was in fact constitutionally justified because *now* the circumstances showed an *additional* need for the existence of that law. In his Brief of Appellant, John Roberts made note of the fact that the Washington statute, when enacted, did "not represent any effort to meet an emergency or any unusual situation." He made this point as part of his general argument that *Parrish* did not raise any new questions and that *Adkins* was a very solid prevailing precedent. The Washington law, he reminded the Court, was not only "part of the regular statutory laws of the state, without respect to any particular situation, which the legislature may have had before it at the time of the passage of the law," but had also been of doubtful constitutionality ever since 1923.[43] Hughes simply ignored this argument because (a) he did not believe that *Adkins* had been correctly decided, and (b) he considered the vintage of the law irrelevant. The law was still on the books in Washington, and it was being enforced during a time when the need for such protective legislation had never been clearer. As if anyone doubted the sincerity of his belief that this was a constitutionally meritorious argument, Hughes further emphasized that it did not matter that Washington had provided no evidence of the Depression-era needs of its 1913 law. "While, in the instant case, no factual brief has been presented," he wrote, "there is no reason to doubt that the State of Washington has encountered the same social problem that is present elsewhere."[44]

Had a factual brief been submitted, it would have shown that the Depression had hit Washington very hard. Although its unemployment rates were not the highest in the nation, they did exceed the national average.[45] And there was widespread support for change—the kind of change that would be effected by the implementation of Democratic New Deal policies. In 1932 Washingtonians overwhelmingly turned their state blue: 57.5 percent cast their ballots for Roosevelt (almost identical to the national average of 57.4 percent); Democratic candidates unseated five Republican congressmen (four members of the House of Representatives, one senator); the state's only Democratic incumbent in the House was reelected; and a Democrat claimed victory in the election to fill the newly created sixth seat in the House. In 1936 the margins of victory simply increased—as they did across the country. Although he was undoubtedly exaggerating, George F. Yantis (the Speaker of the Washington State House of Representatives) made a valid point when he observed, in a letter to Congressman Martin F. Smith in June 1935, that "[e]very Washingtonian should be a 100 per cent New Dealer."[46]

*　*　*

In his first inaugural address, FDR uttered the following famous words that resounded with so many struggling Americans: "[L]et me assert my firm belief," said the new president, "that the only thing we have to fear is fear itself." This is perhaps the most well-known portion of that March 4, 1933 speech. However, it was one of the later observations from that address that spoke to the heart of the *means* with which the president intended to achieve the *end* of lifting the nation out of its fearful depression.

As he "assume[d] unhesitatingly the leadership of this great army of our people dedicated to a disciplined attack upon our common problems," Roosevelt meant to take "action" by using, rather than dramatically changing, "the *form* of government which we have inherited from our ancestors." This is because that form included a "Constitution . . . so simple and practical that it is possible always to meet extraordinary needs by changes in emphasis and arrangement without loss of essential form."[47] As Gerard Magliocca astutely observes, this "statement" about the Constitution "is true only insofar as lawyers and politicians accept that certain constitutional provisions can be read liberally."[48] Justice Sutherland was not inclined to read the due process clauses of the Fifth and Fourteenth Amendments in this manner.

Justice Sutherland's Dissenting Opinion:
"A defense . . . of his entire judicial career"

You have created "a monument to yourself as lasting as a shaft of granite." This is how Judge Armstead Brown (Supreme Court of Florida) described the *Parrish* majority opinion in his letter to Chief Justice Hughes.[49] Justice Sutherland could not have disagreed more. In his view, Hughes had produced a self-serving monument to judicial hubris. Perhaps the chief justice's opinion would indeed be "as lasting as a shaft of granite." Longevity, however, would come at the expense of the United States Constitution, which now lay in tatters on the courtroom floor.

Sutherland felt that the majority opinion in *Adkins*—his opinion for the majority (and the majority opinion in *Tipaldo*)—provided "[a] sufficient answer" to everything that he wanted to say about *Parrish*.[50] He nevertheless believed it necessary to pen a dissent in *Parrish* because it would serve as a forceful "restate[ment]" of the "reasons and conclusions" reached by himself and his conservative brethren.[51] As Joel Francis Paschal concluded in his biography of Sutherland, the *Parrish* dissent represented "a defense . . . of" Sutherland's "entire judicial career."[52]

An Arbitrary "Declaration"

In *Parrish*, precedents were of equal importance to Hughes and Sutherland. However, the two men relied upon very different prior decisions. Sutherland did not deign to discuss (or even cite) either *O'Gorman & Young* or *Nebbia*. Those two sacrilegious decisions were conspicuous by their absence because they represented everything that had gone wrong at the Court in recent years. *Adkins* and *Tipaldo* took their place as proper precedents because they represented legitimate *judicial* "interpretations" of the Constitution rather than efforts to amend that document "under the guise of interpretation."[53] Indeed, in *Parrish* Sutherland devoted almost three pages of his thirteen-page dissent to reprinting what he clearly considered to be the heart of his writing in *Adkins*, and a further page and a half to pertinent passages from Justice Pierce Butler's opinion in *Tipaldo*.[54]

Although Sutherland could not bring himself to cite *Nebbia*, he made copious, not-so-subtle references to the errors of its way, using the word "arbitrary" eight separate times. Four of the "arbitrary" appearances came in excerpts from other decisions that Sutherland inserted to make his point that *Nebbia* had been a distinct (and unwelcome) diversion from the Court's jurisprudential norm.[55] Unsurprisingly, Sutherland was in complete agreement with the argument made by Roberts in the briefs that the lawyer had submitted for the West Coast Hotel Company (and the points made, from those briefs, by Skeel during oral argument). The attorneys were correct; *Adkins* governed this case, period. "The Washington statute," wrote Sutherland, "admits of the same situation and result" as in the 1923 case. And just like the 1918 federal law struck down in *Adkins*, the 1913 Washington law could not "be justified as a reasonable restraint upon the freedom of contract. On the contrary, it is *essentially arbitrary*" because "[n]either the statute involved in . . . *Adkins* . . . nor the Washington statute . . . has the slightest relation to the capacity or earning power of the employee, to the number of hours which constitute the day's work, the character of the place where the work is to be done, or the circumstances or surroundings of the employment." Instead, "[t]he sole basis upon which the question of validity rests is the *assumption* that the employee is entitled to receive a sum of money sufficient to provide a living for her, keep her in health, and preserve her morals."[56] Sutherland resolutely rejected this "assumption" in *Adkins*, and found it to be no less constitutionally objectionable in *Parrish*.

Sutherland's remaining three discussions of the "arbitrary" nature of both the Washington law and the majority's opinion in *Parrish* came in one specific section of the dissent. This was a section which (a) helped to explain why the aforementioned "assumption" was still very much misguided, and (b) spotlighted another precedent whose name the justice refused to mention—*Muller*. Just as in *Adkins*, Sutherland rejected the argument that the "State has a special interest"[57] in enacting protective legislation directed at the fairer sex. "Women today," he wrote, "stand upon a legal and political equality with men. There is no longer any reason why they should be put in different classes in respect of their legal right to make contracts." Additionally, no one should deny them "the right to compete with men for work paying lower wages which men may be willing to accept . . . it is an *arbitrary* exercise of the legislative power to do so."[58]

The nation's minimum wage laws for women, Sutherland concluded, were acts of "arbitrary discrimination." Seemingly oblivious to the realities of the workplace, he doggedly determined that "a suggestion that the bargaining ability of the average woman is not equal to that of the average man would" of course "lack substance." Why? The answer was simple. "The ability to make a fair bargain, *as everyone knows*, does not depend upon sex."[59] Although Sutherland phrased this as an empirical statement, it was actually a normative pronouncement grounded in both an aspirational understanding of sexual equality and a laissez-faire view of constitutionalism. It would have been more accurate for Sutherland to say: "As everyone knows, the ability to make a fair bargain *should not* depend upon sex." The harsh reality, in 1930s America, was quite different: "The ability to make a fair bargain, as everyone knows, *does* depend upon sex." Workplace discrimination against the *weaker* sex and "unscrupulous employers" made sure of that.

In an incisive article in which he undertook a "reconsideration" of the jurisprudential legacy of Justice Sutherland, Samuel Olken observed that "the principal mistake made by those who have sought to pigeonhole Sutherland is to assume that his was a constitutional jurisprudence devoted to preserving the socioeconomic status quo for a privileged elite and that his judicial motivation reflected an overriding intent to apply an overarching theory of economic determinism to the facts of cases."[60] In his opinions in both *Adkins* and *Parrish*, Justice Sutherland used language, and espoused a theory of constitutionalism that made him an easy and convenient target for the defenders of protective legislation. Even if his critics did *mistakenly* "pigeonhole" Sutherland in the manner that Olken suggests, the justice's own words in these two cases certainly did not do him any favors.

Amenable to Amendable Adaptation

It would be wrong, however, to interpret those words as meaning that Sutherland was completely *unaware* of the world around him or that he had a blatant disregard for the employment conditions faced by the female workforce. As discussed in chapter 3, in the wake of *Adkins* a cartoon ran in the *New York World* famously depicting Sutherland as an intimidating jurist who subjugated the nation's female workers and "affirm[ed]" their "constitutional right to starve." There is, however, an important problem associated with using this handy caption to condemn Sutherland's position. The caption all too easily suggests to its reader that Sutherland was an old, mean-spirited, out-of-touch-with-reality, highly reactionary, misogynistic, and antiquated justice who had little time for women's rights.[61] First, as several scholars have shown, it would be wrong to describe all of Sutherland's jurisprudence as a font of conservative "Four Horsemen" principles.[62] Second, Sutherland cared deeply about women's rights. This was, after all, the same George Sutherland who, while a Republican senator from his adopted home state of Utah, was "the acknowledged leader of the forces fighting in behalf of the women." In 1915 he introduced into the Senate what would become the Nineteenth Amendment, supporting something which "was to him an act of simple justice. 'Any argument which I may use to justify my own right to vote,' he declared, 'justifies the right of my wife, sister, mother, and daughter to exercise the same right.'"[63] This was just one of the numerous contributions that Sutherland made to the feminist cause.[64]

How then do we account for the position that Sutherland took in *Adkins* and *Parrish*, the position that was reduced to "you have a constitutional right to starve"? Ironically, that catchphrase perfectly describes the reason Sutherland was opposed to minimum wage laws for women; but it has nothing to do with him being an anti-woman fuddy-duddy. Instead, it has everything to do with what, in modern constitutional parlance, we would describe as originalism.

Simply put, the emphasis for Sutherland was on the *constitutional* rights that each individual has. He placed the Constitution front and center in his *Parrish* dissent, and concluded that there was a *constitutional* right to freely contract for less than any amount the state deemed preferable as a "minimum wage." Had the caption read "a right to starve," that would have been an entirely unfair characterization of Sutherland's views. "A *constitutional* right to starve" was, however, a very accurate, albeit rather crude, description of the justice's position.

Sutherland concluded that by failing to strike down the unconstitutional Washington statute (and no one could have any "rational doubts" about its unconstitutionality), the justices in the majority had "betray[ed] . . . the trust" given to them by the nation's "supreme law." They had sacrificed their "judicial duty" at the altar of public opinion, which had the disastrous effect of allowing "the meaning of the Constitution" to be "change[d] with the ebb and flow of economic events."[65] This was not a case wherein his colleagues should have exercised judicial "[s]elf-restraint," because that was a phenomenon that "belong[ed] . . . in the domain of will, and not of judgment."[66] This was clearly a reference (albeit implicit) to Alexander Hamilton's famous *Federalist 78* discussion of the powers to be held by the judicial branch of the new federal government. The judiciary would stand in distinct contrast to the other two branches of the government. "The executive," wrote Hamilton, "holds the sword of the community. The legislature not only commands the purse, but prescribes the rules by which the duties and rights of every citizen are to be regulated." By contrast, *"[t]he judiciary on the contrary has no influence over either the sword or the purse,* no direction either of the strength or of the wealth of the society, and can take no active resolution whatever. *It may truly be said to have neither FORCE nor WILL, but merely judgment."*[67] Here, Hamilton contended that applying "judgment" would be the proper duty of the nation's judges. In his *Parrish* dissent, Sutherland built on this, saying that "self-restraint" would have no legitimate role to play when a judge engaged in this exercise of judicial judgment. The only form of "restraint" to which judges would be subject was "constitutional"—they were to be checked not by their "will" but rather by three specific things: (1) their "oath of office," (2) "the Constitution," and (3) their "own conscientious and informed convictions."[68]

At first blush, this third, very subjective constraint seems to be in tension with the first two very objective ones. However, within the context of the entire dissent it actually sends a strong message about the degree of contempt that Sutherland had for the position his colleagues (in the majority) had taken. Admittedly, he acknowledged the "right of those in the minority to disagree." However, if he believed that one should be constrained by one's "own conscientious and informed convictions," *and*—as his dissent indicated—he *also* vehemently disagreed with the outcome in *Parrish*, then this leads to the conclusion that Sutherland believed that the chief justice, and Justices Brandeis, Stone, Roberts, and Cardozo had reached their decision in the case based upon reckless and uninformed convictions.[69] Reckless, uninformed, and *arbitrary* convictions determined by "the ebb and flow of economic events."[70]

Although originalism and "non-originalism" "are conventionally thought to center on the appropriate sources of constitutional interpretation, at bottom they are about something else: the capacity of the Constitution to *adapt* to new conditions, or the question whether the meaning of constitutional provisions can be said to change over time." As G. Edward White persuasively explains, "Ultimately the narrative in which *West Coast Hotel* prominently figures is about the meaning of constitutional adaptivity."[71] Hughes was amenable to adapting the meaning of the Constitution by judicial interpretation, in large part because of the inescapable reality of "the economic conditions which . . . [had] supervened." Sutherland was only amenable to adapting the meaning of the Constitution through the process of formal amendment. Amenable to adaptation versus amenable to amendable adaptation. Therein lay the key difference of constitutional interpretive opinion in *Parrish*.

*   *   *

As we will see in the conclusion, Justice Sutherland's approach to constitutionalism attracted the admiration of a number of feminists who stood opposed to protective legislation. The words of Helen Elizabeth Brown, a Maryland lawyer and founder of the Business and Professional Women's Council, went to the heart of these women's disagreement with the decision in *Parrish*. "Women acquired the protection of the Constitution by means of the two previous minimum wage decisions," wrote Brown. "Now they have been again *excluded from the Constitution* by the Washington case."[72]

On the other side of the country, in Washington State, a good many women begged to differ. In the "Apple Capital of the World," women were quick to file post-*Parrish* minimum wage lawsuits, and there would be many familiar faces as the next chapter of this particular legal story was written. On April 9, 1937, legal proceedings were initiated against the West Coast Hotel Company by Mrs. Jennie Estella Sample, who worked as a chambermaid at the Cascadian Hotel between October 1931 and October 1936. Like Elsie, she was paid less than the weekly minimum wage of $14.50, she sought to recover back pay, she was represented by Conner, and they were opposed by Fred Crollard. In March 1938, almost a year after the decision in *Parrish*, Judge Parr entered a judgment awarding Jennie Sample $292 in back pay and $61.80 in court costs and taxes.[73]

Washington State Newspapers React to *Parrish*

Interviewed by a journalist in the days that followed the Supreme Court's decision in *Parrish*, Elsie Parrish expressed considerable and characteristic humility: "I'm not sure I understand all the things, but I'm glad it's all over," she said.[74] Legally, things were not over. It still remained for Judge Parr to issue a Satisfaction of Judgment in the case. However, this was a mere formality. Four years after Elsie entered into the employment of the Cascadian Hotel, and two years after she and Ernest walked into C. B. Conner's office seeking to sue that Wenatchee landmark, Parr completed this step.[75] On May 24, 1937, Elsie received the sum of $250; the remainder (including court costs)—a total of $151.74—went to her lawyer, C. B. Conner.[76]

When news of the decision in *Parrish* reached Washington, only two of the ten largest circulating newspapers published in the state led with headlines that focused on the decision's implications for Roosevelt's Court-packing plan. The closer one got to Wenatchee, the more the local newspapers led with the local story rather than the national narrative of *Parrish*. On March 29, 1937, the *Wenatchee Daily World* published five articles about the decision. The time difference between Washington, D.C., and Wenatchee enabled the newspaper to cover the case within hours of the justices' announcement of their decision. However, pragmatic considerations of expediency compelled it to rely upon wire service reports. The Associated Press (AP) article that ran on the front page was positioned below a banner proclamation that the "Minimum Wage Law Is Upheld." It detailed the outcome of *Parrish* within a larger discussion of all the decisions issued by the Court that day, but without reference to the political implications of *Parrish*.[77] It did not emphasize the local nature of the decision; however, the newspaper's intent to frame the overall story in that manner was evident from the two photos—of Elsie and her lawyer C. B. Conner—that shared the front page with the article. In what remains the iconographic picture of her, Elsie is posing for the *Wenatchee Daily World*'s photographer who, in November 1936, came to capture her working (making a bed) as a chambermaid at the Jim Hill Hotel in Omak. That photograph was printed beneath the headline "Her Wage Suit Brought Decision." The label "Wins Important Case" headlines the article that accompanied the smaller but similarly conspicuous picture of Conner, who is quoted saying: "It has always been my opinion that the state reserves its right to pass such legislation as should be found necessary to protect its citizens and that is just what was done in this case. I am delighted with the findings of the United States Supreme Court. The decision couldn't have been wiser."[78]

Three other March 29 articles came from AP correspondents reporting out of Seattle and Olympia, a fact that helps to explain their focus on the various local-interest aspects of the Court's decision. A short article emphasized that the justices had upheld a Washington State law; it made the observation that the twenty-four-year-old law had received bipartisan legislative support, and it included quotations from the lower court opinions of Judge Parr and Chief Justice William J. Millard.[79] Two longer articles, both reported from Olympia, examined the immediate local and state influence and impact of the decision. The first consisted almost entirely of quotations from an "elated" Millard, who declared the Supreme Court's decision a "great victory for states' rights." "It is," he observed, "a recognition of the sovereignty of the states and likewise a recognition of human rights."[80] The second reported the reaction of E. Pat Kelly, the Washington State director of labor and industries, who pledged to use the state's "force of field deputies to see that the [1913] law is enforced." No longer, he said, would employers be permitted to "beat down, chisel and pay the women as little as they could possibly get away with."[81]

The following day, the *Omak Chronicle* (a twice-weekly publication that appeared every Tuesday and Friday) also reported the U.S. Supreme Court's decision in *Parrish*. It ran an article that placed even greater emphasis on the local and human-interest elements of the story. In so doing, it provided further support for the argument that geographical proximity was the most important factor influencing local newspaper coverage of this case. That article, written by one of the newspaper's reporters, ran under the headline "Omak Woman Wins Back Wages Case in Supreme Court." The subheading read as follows: "Mrs. Elsie Parrish Notified Yesterday By United Press Of Her Victory." On March 29, when a reporter from the *Omak Chronicle* reached her at the Model Laundry & Cleaners where she was working, and conveyed to her the United Press (UP) report of the Supreme Court's decision, Elsie said, "I am so glad, not only for myself, but for all the women of the state who have been working for just whatever they could get." While the article also devoted a few paragraphs to summarizing the facts and judicial history of the case, the focus was undeniably upon "the local girl made good." From this article we learn about when the Parrishes moved to Omak, and about this thirty-seven-year-old grandmother's place of employment in that town. In other words, the *Omak Chronicle* chose to devote its *first* report of the Supreme Court's decision to Elsie's story (even if the banner headline that day was reserved for informing readers that a "Record Crowd Will Attend Clam Bake").[82]

Many of these details were subsequently conveyed to the readers of the *Wenatchee Daily World*, but not until April 6—a delay seemingly attributable, in part, to the somewhat perplexing difficulty that the newspaper's reporter encountered in locating Elsie. The April 6 article explained that Elsie was "[t]hankful her fight to test the state minimum wage law will now make it possible for the nation's millions of hard-working women to receive just payment for the labor they do." The first paragraph of the article concluded by observing that the former chambermaid was also determined to "continue doing everything in her power to further the cause." However, when one turns to the subsequent and extensive quotations from the reporter's interview with Elsie, a very different picture of her reaction emerges—a picture that, ironically, the article made clear to its readers with the subheading "Not Seeking Notoriety." To be sure, Elsie was very proud of her lawyer's accomplishment, and she accepted that her name would forever be linked to an important legal decision favoring workers' rights. But she was uncomfortable with all the publicity, in no small part because during an earlier stage of the case it had, she believed, negatively affected her employment opportunities.[83]

Upon initiating their lawsuit, Ernest and Elsie became personae non grata in Wenatchee; neither of them wanted the same thing to happen to them in Omak. Across the state, it quickly became clear that they had no reason to be fearful. The tide had turned decisively in favor of the state's female workforce.

The King County Superior Court

At the same time as Jennie Sample began her lawsuit in Wenatchee, "a . . . flood of minimum wage law suits" started "to be filed [elsewhere] in the state of Washington," and often these filings were front-page news.[84] In Seattle the complaints flooded in almost before the ink on the U.S. Supreme Court's decision was dry. When the April 3, 1937, issue of the *Sunday News* went to press, splashed across its front page was a banner headline that read: "Women Sue for Back Pay on Wage Minimum." The publication regaled readers with several short stories of former chambermaids for whom *Parrish* was the gateway to obtaining the considerable amounts of wages to which they now felt they were constitutionally entitled. Their sister-in-arms, Elsie Parrish, went unmentioned, but the importance of her legal triumph was not left to the reader's imagination. "A lot of money is going to change hands within the next few days," observed the newspaper: "The money, representing the difference between virtual peonage and a rock-bottom minimum wage, will be reluctantly transferred from the well-cared for hands of bankers, trust company officials, landlords, apartment house owners, into the work-worn, red hands of chambermaids, domestics, charwomen, janitors, housekeepers, student nurses, switchboard operators, office girls."[85] In reality, it took far longer than a "few days" for these lawsuits to be resolved and, for reasons that will become clear, the women plaintiffs received far smaller amounts of back pay than they initially sought.[86]

Although various newspapers reported that the "flood of minimum wage law suits" filed after *Parrish* numbered into the hundreds in Seattle,[87] the analysis that follows draws on a dataset consisting of sixty-five civil cases filed by female plaintiffs seeking back pay. Many of the records have not survived the ravages of time (and it is possible that the newspaper reports exaggerated the numbers of filings). The dataset represents a sample, not a complete record, of all cases filed, because for the following reasons I cannot be certain that I identified every single minimum wage lawsuit filed by a female plaintiff in King County in 1937. Court documents were located by first using the relevant microfilm records at the Records Office of the King County Superior Court. Unless one has a specific case number, the only way one can search the civil court records index from the 1930s is by name. The *handwritten* alphabetized index provides scant details about the cases—details limited to case number, plaintiffs' names, and the date of filing. The cases were filed with the King County Superior Court in Seattle between April 2 and December 4, 1937. I looked through the entire index for any lawsuits filed after March 29, 1937, that involved female plaintiffs, excluding cases wherein the female plaintiff was suing a male defendant with the same last name (a perusal of the court filings confirms the expectation that these are divorce cases). From a list of female plaintiff lawsuit case numbers, I then looked at the filings for every case to identify which ones involved minimum wage claims.

The women plaintiffs in these sixty-five cases were white, rarely had any years of high school education, and were either married or had at some point been married. Some were native Washingtonians, but the overwhelming majority emigrated to Seattle. Representative of the demographic changes the city had experienced since the turn of the century, they came from across the country and from around the world.[88] Their stories are vivid reminders of the way in which the Great Depression destroyed people's lives, wreaking havoc and disruption, and causing widespread displacement (both economic and social).

As table 6.1 indicates, one firm of lawyers represented 87 percent of the plaintiffs who filed minimum wage cases in 1937 in King County (according to the records that I was able to locate). Indeed, such was the volume of cases they handled, these lawyers created a special boilerplate Complaint form; the only details that needed to be filled in were the parties' names, places and hours of employment, and amount of back wages sought. That firm consisted of Messrs. John C. Stevenson and Sam X. Gershon. Located on the thirty-second floor of the Smith Tower on Second Avenue, their offices were conveniently situated a mere stone's throw from the King County Superior Courthouse on Third Avenue. During

TABLE 6.1   Number of King County 1937 minimum
wage cases handled by plaintiffs' lawyers

	Number of minimum wage cases handled	
Lawyers	Number	Percent
Paul Coughlin	1	1.5
Frank Harrington	1	1.5
Harry C. Hazel	1	1.5
Dwight M. Stevens	1	1.5
Stevenson & Gershon	57	87.7
Identity unknown	4	6.3
Total	65	100

the first two weeks of April 1937 (the height of the minimum wage filings), Stevenson and Gershon found themselves deluged by prospective plaintiffs; as the *Seattle Star* reported as early as April 2, "Scores of complaints . . . were being looked over" by the two lawyers.[89] The two men represented the Building Service Employees Union (BSEU)[90] and had arranged to take the back pay cases of women workers pro bono (with an agreement that the firm would receive 10 percent of any settlement).

The data in table 6.1 stand in stark contrast to the data in table 6.2. The latter table indicates that very few lawyers represented multiple defendants in the minimum wage cases. Two law firms represented the defendants in five different cases each. However, one of those firms—Hartman, Hartman, Simon & Coles—represented a single client in all five cases, and it is reasonable to assume that all the legal matters of the client in question—Calvin Philips and Company—were handled by this firm. Similarly, three of the five cases handled by Skeel, McKelvy, Henks, Evenson & Uhlmann involved the same defendant, the commercial real estate magnate Charles P. Clise.[91] Indeed, although little is known about most of the defendants' lawyers in the minimum wage cases, it is clear that a majority of them worked for some of the largest law firms in the state and were experienced at handling the legal affairs of corporate, financial, and insurance clients.[92]

Stevenson and Gershon's involvement in the minimum wage litigation is unsurprising. Seattle has long been home to a strong, militant union presence,[93] and at the time of the *Parrish* ruling, labor unions in Seattle were nearing the height of their powers. "When the New Deal's National Labor Relations Act [of 1935] codified collective bargaining, millions of Americans joined trade unions. On what truly was the left coast, Seattle was a hotbed of labor unrest. . . . FDR's campaign manager, Postmaster General James A. Farley, famously proposed a droll toast in 1936 'to the American Union—47 states and the Soviet of Washington.'"[94] The BSEU Local 6, which covered many of the maids and apartment workers seeking back pay, was a relatively young union at the time of the *Parrish* ruling, originating in 1933 as an organization of men and women working in apartment houses as managers and janitors seeking better pay and working conditions.[95] However, it quickly expanded, growing to 345 members in 1935 and over 2,000 by the end of 1936.[96] Stevenson had played a central role in facilitating

TABLE 6.2   Number of King County 1937 minimum
wage cases handled by defendants' lawyers

Lawyers	Number of minimum wage cases handled	
	Number	Percent
Allen & Wilkins	1	1.5
Burkheimer & Burkheimer	1	1.5
Dorsey & Seering	1	1.5
Arthur G. Dunn Jr.	1	1.5
Eggerman & Rosling	1	1.5
E. M. Farmer	1	1.5
Clarence A. Hardesty	1	1.5
Thomas Masuda	1	1.5
William Mathewson	1	1.5
M. M. Pixley	1	1.5
Roberts and Skeel, and Harry Henke Jr.	1	1.5
Philip Tworoger	1	1.5
Arthur E. Griffin	2	3.1
Kerr, McCord & Carey	2	3.1
Palmer, Askren, & Brethorst	2	3.1
Edward E. Merges	2	3.1
C. E. Hughes	2	3.1
Hartman, Hartman, Simon & Coles	5	7.8
Skeel, McKelvy, Henks, Evenson & Uhlmann	5	7.8
Unknown	33	50.9
Total	65	100

BSEU negotiations with employer organizations, so the involvement of his law firm in the minimum wage litigation made sense.

On Wednesday, March 31, two days after the decision in *Parrish*,
Stevenson and Gershon took depositions from Ethel Fritz and Mary
Lee Dempsey. Their lawsuits would be the first minimum wages
for women cases, filed that spring, to be decided by the judges of
the King County Superior Court. Both women brought suit against
the executors of the estate of William D. Perkins, who had (up until
his death on September 18, 1936) owned and operated the Oxford
Hotel. They sought back pay for their employment as two of the
hotel's chambermaids from May 1, 1933 (Fritz) and May 5, 1935
(Dempsey) through April 1937. (Ten days after they filed their
lawsuits, both women began to be paid in excess of the minimum

wage.) For the majority of their time working at the hotel, Fritz and Dempsey received $11.50 per week, $3 less per week than the law entitled them to. They both had $2 per week deducted from that base pay in order to cover the costs of rooms for the women to stay in the hotel (regardless of the fact that they "advised the defendants that . . . [they] had no need whatever for any such room"). These two cases were far simpler than many, and this probably explains why they were the first to be decided. After a short bench trial on June 21, Judge James T. Lawler ruled in favor of both women.[97]

Most of the women who worked "full-time" and filed suit for back pay in Seattle were forced into the workforce by the impact of the Depression on their spouses' employment. In April 1930, 11 percent of Seattle's residents were unemployed; five years later, that figure was close to 27 percent.[98] As a 1934 Washington Emergency Relief Commission survey of eleven of the state's cities demonstrated, it was possible to put together a clear description of the average unemployed person. Forty-two, male, an unskilled industrial worker: "He has been employed at his usual occupation for fifteen years. He has not worked at his usual occupation for one year and seven months. He has not had any work for over ten months. He is married and has 2.34 persons dependent upon him. He has received a common school education. He has resided in the state for over twenty years."[99] That picture accurately depicts so many of the husbands of minimum wage case plaintiffs. However, it is important to remember that the Depression did not discriminate; it hit all industries—blue collar and white collar—hard. The following three examples illustrate this fact. In 1929, John Brandt was a salesman for the Hamilton Lumber Company; five years later, he and his wife Frieda could be found working as janitor and housekeeper at the Linda Vista Apartments on East Lynn Street.[100] In 1930, Oscar Elsoe worked as a streetcar operator, a position he had held for over a decade; in 1934 he was still able to put his engineering skills to work, but now it was as a maintenance man at the Keystone Apartments on Terry Avenue, where his wife Mary worked alongside him as a janitress.[101]

Finally, there is the story of the Harrells. In 1929, Selwyn Harrell was the vice president of the Harrell Realty Company, a fixture of the Seattle real estate landscape for many years. The path that Harrell's career subsequently took reflected the way in which the Depression affected the city. In the early 1930s, Harrell briefly worked as a salesman for the Brannen MacFarlane real estate company. After all, initially such skills were still needed (albeit barely). Between 1920 and 1930, Seattle experienced a 16 percent growth in its population, and people needed places to live.[102] As graphs 6.1 and 6.2 show, building construction reflected this growth. Construction during that decade experienced blips, primarily because after World War I the city's economy was hit hard by a decline in shipbuilding. As Richard C. Berner explains in his three-volume history of the city, "Despite strong desires and promotional attempts by the Chamber of Commerce, the Seattle Lighting Department, and their supporters, manufacturing between 1919 and 1929 declined by about 27%."[103] Yet, new construction (residential and commercial) continued and, until the Depression really took hold of the city, realtors were still needed to broker contracts for the occupants and owners of those buildings. However, as graphs 6.1 and 6.2 also show, that demand had all but disappeared in 1931. For example, between 1933 and 1937 the city issued only five permits for apartment house construction.[104] It is little surprise that by 1934 Selwyn and his wife, Josephine, now in their seventies, were employed at the Claytonia Apartment house;

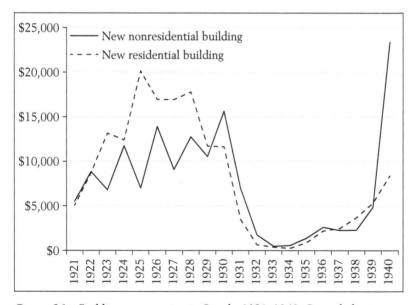

GRAPH 6.1   Building construction in Seattle, 1921–1940. Compiled using data from Richard C. Berner, *Seattle 1921–1940: From Boom to Bust* (Seattle: Charles Press, 1992), 179.

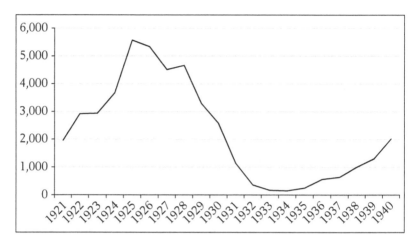

GRAPH 6.2   Number of new family dwelling units in Seattle, 1921–1940.
Compiled using data from Richard C. Berner, *Seattle 1921–1940: From Boom
to Bust* (Seattle: Charles Press, 1992), 179.

Selwyn was working as a janitor instead of selling and renting such
buildings. Although only limited details of their case have survived,
one thing is clear—this former real estate executive and his spouse
were now working for less than minimum wage.[105]

An Unprecedented Legal Procedure

Although the first ruling in a Seattle minimum wage case came
on June 21, 1937, many of the cases dragged on for years, some of
them not being resolved until 1940. This was not an optimal situation, and it was one that the judges of the King County Superior
Court attempted to avoid as much as they could. The stacks of files
that landed on their desks and the articles that appeared in the
Seattle Times told them that the flood of cases filed in the immediate aftermath of *Parrish* would likely not slow to a trickle for
quite some time. The newspaper's reporting of the litigation often
contained factual errors. However, the case files confirm that the
following article, from May 14, 1937, painted a generally accurate
picture of the caseload that the judges quickly began to confront:

> John C. Stevenson, former county commissioner, and Perry and
> Sax X. Gershon, his law partners . . . yesterday filed nineteen
> complaints in Superior Court asking a total of about $200,000

from defendant apartment houses, office buildings and other property owners. "We have at least 100 additional complaints in preparation," Perry Gershon said today. "All ask deficiency wages to bring the earnings of the maids, housekeepers, janitresses and building managers to the standard of the public housekeeping order issued by the Industrial Welfare Commission in 1921."[106]

In accordance with the Special Rules of the Superior Court of King County, adopted in 1929, each judge was in charge of a "judicial department." Cases would be assigned to a judge, sitting in his[107] department, by the presiding judge (one of the thirteen, chosen based upon both seniority and the entire group of judges), and typically each case (civil and criminal) would be heard individually, by one judge sitting on his own.[108] First elected to the bench in 1925, his eleven years of judicial experience told Judge Malcolm Douglas that the wage cases would likely require minimal time in the actual courtroom.[109] Nevertheless, he was also very aware that they would generate considerable paperwork, paperwork that would be exceptionally repetitive because so many of the fact patterns were basically the same, differing only in terms of the identities of the plaintiffs and defendants, and the dates and total hours employed. Consequently, seeking to resolve the minimum wage cases in an expeditious manner, in May 1937 Judge Douglas went to discuss the matter with his colleagues, Judges Howard M. Findley and Hugh C. Todd. Although Todd was fairly new to the bench, Findley was a veteran jurist, appointed to the Superior Court by Governor Roland Hartley in 1925. Both men met Douglas's proposition with enthusiasm; what happened next broke legal ground in King County. Douglas recommended that instead of hearing cases individually, the three men consolidate nineteen of the cases and hear them sitting together as a three-judge panel. All but one of the nineteen plaintiffs was seeking back pay for work as a janitress in one of the city's numerous apartment houses.[110] And the women's cases had several important questions in common, questions that it was essential for the court to address and answer before any rulings could be issued.

The Language, Purpose, and Spirit of a Law

The complete files of fifteen of the nineteen consolidated cases have survived, and from those files we know that three (20 percent) were

settled out of court, and five (one-third) of the judgments were in
favor of the female plaintiffs. This means that almost half (47 percent) of the women workers lost their cases and walked away from
court without any back pay. Similar win/loss statistics can be found
when examining the cases that were not decided as part of the consolidated nineteen. Occasionally there was a rather oddball, case-
specific reason why a plaintiff did not prevail. Take, for example,
Kathryn Daggett's case. She found work as a housekeeper just after
the finalization of her divorce. In reaching its conclusion that she
was not entitled to back pay for her work at the Glenwood Apartments, the court essentially stated that she had worked too hard:

> [O]bviously plaintiff having been accustomed to the keeping
> of her own residence, and being an exceptionally capable and
> efficient housekeeper—apparently one of those characters who
> chase after dirt, looking for something that only the most vigi-
> lant housekeeper will find, and contented only when armed with
> broom and mop, because of which proclivity more than because
> of necessity in such house, together with her natural desire to
> please and to accommodate tenants, and practically to guaran-
> tee an unguaranteed telephone service, and in various and many
> ways to please tenants as well as her employers—*she did assume
> tasks and unrequired duties which, together with her required
> duties,* occupied fully six hours per day on the average.[111]

In other words, the court reasoned that had Daggett not performed
her *assigned* duties in such an excessively meticulous manner, her
work would not have consumed hours in excess of those that constituted part-time employment. Of course, this also ignored the
reality (as discussed below) that the duties expected of a "part-
time" employee typically consumed far more hours of the day than
those for which she would be paid.

It was, however, unusual for a case to be decided upon such
grounds. Generally, the cases all turned on the same issues of law.
And it was here that the value of the single decision in the consolidated cases quickly became apparent. That decision, issued
by Judges Douglas, Findley, and Todd, provided answers to four
important questions.

*First, did the 1913 law apply to women working in apartment
houses?* The "principal point urged by the defendants"[112] was that

the law did not apply in such cases because of the following language in the statute: "It shall be unlawful to employ women or minors in any *industry or occupation* within the state of Washington under conditions of labor detrimental to their health or morals; and it shall be unlawful to employ women workers in any *industry* within the state of Washington at wages which are not adequate for their maintenance."[113] The defendants' interpretation of this language turned on the absence of "or occupation" from the provision relating to minimum wages (and its existence in the provision relating to labor conditions). They argued that this was an important linguistic difference because it indicated that the legislature (a) believed that not all "occupations" were "industries," and (b) specifically intended to confine the minimum wages requirement to employment in "any *industry*." In other words, if the legislature had intended that requirement to extend to "any industry or occupation," it would have said so. They were arguing that the plaintiffs' reading of the law as extending to apartment housework (which was not an "industry") made the "or occupation" language nothing more than mere surplusage.[114] They "confess[ed] that . . . [they had] found no conclusive authority" explaining exactly what was an "occupation" and what was an "industry."[115] They nevertheless believed that it was necessary to "follow . . . the mandate of strict construction" and "adopt the restricted dictionary meaning . . . that an industry is a branch of business which employs much labor and capital, and is a distinct branch of trade."[116] This reading, they contended, had been "judicially approved by our Supreme Court."[117] As Judges Douglas, Findley, and Todd explained, however, the precedent to which the defendants referred actually hurt, rather than helped their cause. This is because the dictionary defined "industry" as: "Any department or branch of art, occupation or business; *esp.*, one which employs much labor and capital and is a distinct branch of trade; as, the sugar *industry*."[118] As the judges noted, "the word 'industry'" in this definition "is all-inclusive and embraces most occupations."[119] When this conclusion was coupled with the important observation that "the broad purpose of the act [had been] to guarantee wages for women workers which are adequate for their maintenance," the judges did not hesitate in rejecting the defendants' desired "narrow definition," which was "predicated" on nothing more than a "finespun distinction between . . . words."[120]

Second, which section of the Statute of Limitations covers the employment back pay claims made by the plaintiffs? The case files indicate that the women who filed post-*Parrish* minimum wage claims had been hired and had begun the work for which they were seeking back pay, in three distinct time periods. A handful of the women's formal Complaints listed hours worked at jobs that began in 1931/1932, the majority sought compensation for employment that began in 1934/1935, and another small group had started at their jobs in 1936. The principal reason why many of the plaintiffs either had their cases dismissed or received far less money than they were seeking was because of the Washington State Statute of Limitations, which stated that such legal actions had to be commenced within a certain period of time.

The Washington State Statute of Limitations included three sections that potentially covered the minimum wage back pay claims. As the court explained, it was easy to reach the conclusion that for cases involving *written* employment *contracts*, an action had to be commenced within six years; and if a contract was not in writing, claims had to be filed within three years. This is what two sections of the law clearly stated.[121] However, the judges felt compelled to consider a third section—Section 165—that said, "[a]n action for relief not hereinbefore provided for shall be commenced within two years after the cause of action shall have accrued."[122] In "able and exhaustive briefs," the defendants' lawyers "urge[d]" that the plaintiffs' back pay claims were not legally grounded in any employment contracts, but instead in the 1913 law. This, they argued, brought Section 165 into play because that section dealt with noncontractual actions.[123] Yet, as the court pointed out, this argument put the proverbial cart before the horse, because the 1913 law only became relevant when a woman had been deprived of the wages she was owed under that law, wages that she could not have been entitled to without an employment contract.[124] "While it is true," wrote the judges, "that the right to sue would be non-existent except for the [1913] statute . . . neither would it exist except for the [contractual] relationship . . . of the parties." One could not operate without the other: "The statute is entirely ineffective and inapplicable unless there exists the relationship of employer and employee, voluntarily entered into between the parties. The statute operates upon the contract and not independently."[125]

Third, for Statute of Limitations purposes, when did the clock start for filing for back pay? Having established that back pay claims had to be commenced within six years (for employment based on a written contract) or three years (for employment based on a verbal contract), the judges next had to determine when exactly the Statute of Limitations clock started. This was not an easy issue to decide, and the judges' work was complicated by the fact that the lawyers made "spirited efforts—on the one side to invoke, and on the other to abjure, the doctrine" of the principal precedent—*Ah How v. Furth* (1896).[126] They sparred over *Ah How*, but also "happily . . . agreed upon one point," namely that the case had turned on the fact that "the agreement for services *did not fix any certain time for payment,*" thus meaning that the Statute of Limitations clock did not start to run until such time that the employment was terminated.[127] It was this aspect of the *Ah How* decision, the judges concluded, that distinguished it from the minimum wage cases. The female plaintiffs' employment contracts did fix "certain times[s] for payment"—they were to be paid by the week or the month. Therefore, they were entitled to claim the statutorily mandated minimum wage at the end of every week or month. This was both the "broad purpose and spirit of the [1913] act."[128]

This, of course, had the effect of ensuring that a large number of the women plaintiffs walked away from their litigation with either no money or far less than they had filed for. The overwhelming majority of these women had entered into unwritten contracts; consequently, the ruling ensured that they could not claim for any back pay from employment that took place prior to 1934. This aspect of the judges' decision in the consolidated cases was deeply ironic. On the one hand, it was the very fact that Elsie Parrish had initiated her lawsuit, and ultimately prevailed, that gave these King County women the legal impetus to file their complaints. On the other hand, the judges' ruling in the consolidated cases suggested that had these women (rather than Elsie) taken the original constitutional initiative as soon as they began to be paid less than the law owed them, then their claims would not have been precluded by the Statute of Limitations. As we have seen, it took a brave woman to take the initiative, and many of the post-*Parrish* plaintiffs were surely just as brave as Elsie. It behooves us to remember, however, that had any of those plaintiffs initiated litigation as soon as their employers failed to pay them what the law said they were entitled to, they would have exhibited bravery far beyond that of Elsie Parrish. This is because in May 1935 Elsie was no longer employed by the Cascadian; she had no job to lose. That would not have been the case for the women that were now losing before the King County Superior Court judges. As Albert Leslie observed in his letter to the Washington State attorney general while *Parrish* was still pending, women had been reluctant to bring cases under the 1913 law "for the reason the complainant must file a sworn statement, thus bringing down the wrath of the employer and causing fear of loss of job."[129] It is little wonder that, at the height of the Depression in Seattle, women were not willing to bring such lawsuits. Yet, it was for this very reason that many of them ultimately failed to get the back pay that *Parrish* had suggested was owed them.

Fourth, could the plaintiffs recover back pay for hours worked in excess of the hours, deemed by the 1913 law, as constituting "full-time" employment? The fourth and final question that the judges addressed in the consolidated King County cases was the easiest for them to answer. Nevertheless, as with the second question—which spoke to the subject of the Statute of Limitations—the briefs the plaintiffs' lawyers submitted made it seem like this was far from a simple and cut-and-dried issue.[130] It was in their clients' interests to press this overtime issue because of the nature of apartment house work, which typically required one to be "on duty" at all hours of the day. Charlotte Roberts's story was typical: "[A]mong other duties, the plaintiff was compelled to light the fires, clean the halls, collect the rentals, dust empty apartments, wash the windows in vacant apartments, give information to tenants whenever inquiries are made, and inspect every burner every few hours."[131]

Everyone knew that these duties would require a woman to work, or be available to work, for more hours in a week/month than the statute defined as constituting "full-time" work. There was, however, no escaping the clarity of the 1913 law, which contained no provisions for overtime pay.[132] The plaintiffs' lawyers conceded this, but nevertheless sought to recover the additional monies. As the court observed, their efforts were not at all convincing. "In asserting the right to recover for overtime," the judges wrote, "counsel for the plaintiffs seem to be *somewhat at sea when it comes to pointing out what rate of pay should govern*, contenting themselves with saying that 'necessarily some basis must be used.'"

The lawyer offered "three alternatives . . . thirty-five cents per hour, thirty-one cents per hour and *quantum meruit* [reasonable pay reflecting the actual value of the services rendered]." The judges were not impressed, observing that the lawyers' "uncertainty in the matter doubtless arises from the fact that the law does not fix a rate for overtime, and either does not contemplate a recovery for overtime in the absence of an agreement for the same between the parties, or does not permit it at all."[133] While the language of the 1913 law gave the defendant landlords a clear victory on the question of overtime back pay, one of the other reasons why they were frequently victorious had nothing to do with statutory language. Instead it had everything to do with the nature of the work that they required of their female workers, and persistent sexual stereotypes.

"Duties which fall within a woman's realm"

It was common for a defendant to contend that a married female plaintiff never engaged in full-time work because she only undertook limited duties (the kind of duties that were suited to her sex) and exclusively served as a part-time assistant to her husband. As one typical affirmative defense brief explained: "[T]he plaintiff wife would perform only such duties which fall within a woman's realm, that is helping to clean up the apartments and helping to sweep the halls, etc., leaving to the plaintiff husband the heavier work."[134] Frequently implicit in these documents was the assumption that "such duties which fall within a woman's realm" would never occupy more than a few hours of a woman's time. This, it was believed, was entirely appropriate because the remainder of a woman's time would, and should be devoted to the "household duties and other [similarly domestic] occupations and pleasures" which "she was privileged and allowed to work at"—in other words, "the duties of an average housewife living in an apartment."[135] Indeed, oftentimes a court did not consider it necessary to "specifically mention . . . the various chores or duties," because "it is *plain from the evidence of a number of owners and operators and keepers, mostly women,* of apartment houses that all the duties required of her and necessary to the proper management of an apartment house . . . could . . . be performed by working at an average of not exceeding three hours per day."[136] Here, it is striking that the court goes out of its way to emphasize that the evidence, which down-plays the duties of the female plaintiffs, was provided by fellow women—albeit the women in charge of assigning those duties to their employees.

* * *

In the wake of *Parrish*, only three minimum wage cases made their way up to the Washington State Supreme Court. However, none of those cases involved any challenge to the constitutional veracity of the 1913 law. Indeed, only one—*Hilda Ferber v. Anna Wisen*—even raised that question. Immediately after the decision in *Parrish*, Hilda Ferber and Hannah Halverson filed suit against Anna Wisen, the operator of the Alhambra Hotel in Seattle. The two women plaintiffs sought back pay for their work as waitresses in 1934 and 1935, work that sometimes found them waiting tables seven days a week for as little as twenty dollars per month. *Parrish* made it easy for the lower court to reject Wisen's counterargument that the law was unconstitutional; so easy, in fact, that Wisen did not raise that question on appeal. Instead, what came to the Washington Supreme Court were primarily factual disputes, including a question as to whether the quantity of work undertaken by Ferber and Halverson amounted to full-time employment.[137] In the only other two cases involving provisions of that law that made it to the state's highest bench, similar factual questions were presented; the constitutional question was nowhere to be found.[138] That matter had been well and truly laid to rest, in a well-made bed, by the Supreme Court of the United States on Monday, March 29, 1937.

Conclusion

"Oh, Elsie! We owe you so much!"

> Generally, change in our society is incremental, I think.
> Real change, enduring change, happens one step at a time.
> —*Ruth Bader Ginsburg, 1993 U.S. Senate Judiciary*
> *Committee hearing on her nomination to*
> *the Supreme Court of the United States*

In 1997, six decades after *West Coast Hotel v. Parrish*, the political scientist Hadley Arkes contended that "in the long sweep of things" the decision had been and "would [continue to] be diminished in its importance" because "[t]he minimum wage . . . [had] become an irrelevance over the years."[1] While the idea of a minimum wage has not always been well received and always will divide the American public and their elected representatives, one simply cannot make the case that it has "become an irrelevance." As graph C.1 demonstrates, the subject is frequently mentioned or discussed by the nation's major newspapers, regardless of the makeup of their intended audiences. And it constantly attracts the academic attention of scholars (from numerous disciplines) around the world.[2]

More important, though, for those workers who make minimum wage and must try to survive upon that income, the subject is by no means an irrelevance. To quote a retired friend of the family upon hearing about this book, "making minimum wage; that's the story of my life." In a 1936 radio address, Elinore Morehouse

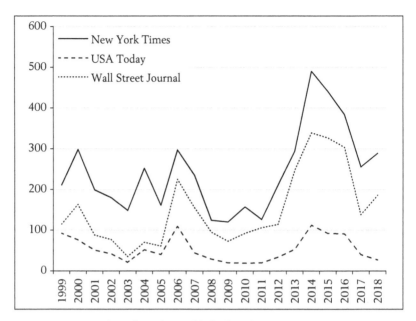

GRAPH C.1   Number of articles, published in three newspapers 1999–2018, that included the phrase "minimum wage." Compiled using data from National Newspapers Premier database.

Herrick, a regional director for the National Labor Relations Board, said that ultimately minimum wage laws are "not an academic question or even a legal one, but [instead] a human problem."[3] That sentiment is as true today as it was over eight decades ago.

It is also impossible to agree with Professor Arkes's conclusion that the decision in *Parrish* has been and "would [continue to] be diminished in its importance." For, as we have seen, to this day *Parrish* is widely considered a landmark U.S. Supreme Court decision worthy of continued attention. *However*, as this book has made clear, much of the attention that the 1937 ruling attracts has been, and remains, the result of its temporal association with President Franklin D. Roosevelt's infamous attempt to "pack" the nation's highest court. This has obscured the stories of the parties involved in *Parrish*, a wrong that *Making Minimum Wage* has sought to right.

*   *   *

In 1990 a local historian writing for the *Okanogan County Heritage* magazine lauded Elsie Parrish's brave actions. "'Oh, Elsie!' she exclaimed, 'We owe you so much!'"[4] The pages that follow briefly outline some of the reasons why that sentiment is true—reasons that demonstrate that neither the decision in *Parrish* nor the story of Elsie's decision to initiate her lawsuit has "diminished in . . . importance." However, to put them in context, it is important to remember that in 1937, just as now, not everyone embraced the decision in *Parrish* and the sociopolitical changes it would bring.

A "tragic set-back to the advancement of women"

In 1937 the decision in *Parrish* enjoyed the admiration of many individuals. However, it also had its fair share of detractors. Much of that opposition came from members of the National Woman's Party (NWP), feminists vehemently opposed to minimum wage laws for women because they viewed those statutes as affording women different rather than equal treatment. Their concern about a potential decision in *Parrish* upholding the Washington state law was laid bare in correspondence between two NWP members in January 1937, correspondence that predicted such a decision would trigger an "avalanche of 'protective' legislation." In their opinion, this would be a disastrous development.[5]

This was a time when "feminists were in *open and often bitter disagreement* with one another," therefore "the movement . . . seemed diffuse and impotent to outside observers."[6] Feminists were united by a belief that the *liberty* of women was of paramount importance. Similarly, they agreed about the need to achieve and maintain women's equality. However, their "open and often bitter disagreement" was over the "*nature*" of equality and liberty.[7] Then, just as now, liberty and equality were universally agreed-upon goals, but only because there was no universally agreed-upon definition of those terms. Nowhere were these disputes more obvious than in debates about the fate of a minimum wage for women— the one subject about which "[n]either side . . . was willing to compromise."[8] This is why "Feminists Divided,"[9] one of the newspaper headlines that appeared in 1936 after *Morehead v. Tipaldo*,[10] might as well have been reprinted after the decision in *Parrish*, when it was just as applicable as it had been one year earlier.

On the one hand, *Parrish* was a victory for female workers because they now had a constitutional right to be paid a fair minimum wage. On the other hand, they had gained this victory by

virtue of a judicial opinion which reiterated the decades-old jurisprudential conclusion that a "woman's physical structure and the
performance of maternal functions place her at a disadvantage in
the struggle for subsistence," thereby necessitating special, paternalistic treatment from the state.[11] As Elaine Zahnd Johnson succinctly
observes, when the Court decided *Parrish*, it did so by "pulling the
cobwebbed *Muller* [*v. Oregon*] patriarchal ideology out of the dusty
closet."[12] Embodied in the Court's opinions in both *Muller* and (to
a lesser extent) *Parrish* was a paternalistic idea that women were
a special class in need of protective governmental action. This idea
was wholeheartedly rejected by the NWP, whose members believed
it was nothing less than "the grinning spectre of Discrimination" that
was "advancing behind a smiling face," a face labeled as "Protection."[13]

As Anna Kelton Wiley, the secretary of the NWP's National
Council, observed in a 1941 article for *Equal Rights* (the party's
official newsletter that was published weekly from 1923 through
1954 and distributed to every dues paying member), the "'alleged'
incapacity" of a woman "and her so-called 'weakness'" was nothing
more than an ignorant "hangover from a traditional taboo." Additionally, the idea that in the 1930s economic times had worsened
(since *Adkins v. Children's Hospital*[14]) and therefore compounded
the contractual misery of women, completely missed the important point that it was during times of hardship and "distress"—such
as the Great Depression—that women had made their greatest
"gains." Of course, the argument could be made that a woman's
ability to achieve those "gains" was significantly enhanced by public
policies like minimum wage laws. However, Wiley and her NWP
compatriots would have none of that argument, because they
believed that women could only achieve things in their lives when
they were free to do so—and that freedom meant being treated as
equal human beings.

The 1936 decision in *Tipaldo* brought the NWP much joy and
relief. Indeed, the party's members were a significant component
of the small but vocal minority of individuals who bucked the
national trend by vigorously defending that decision. In her October 1936 "Equal Rights Report" for the NWP, Alma Lutz proudly
reported that circulation of *Equal Rights* had increased by 250 percent since 1934.[15] This was no coincidence. While FDR looked at
Tipaldo and saw a "no-man's-land" to condemn, the NWP looked
at it and rejoiced at the sight of the "no thoroughfare" sign that the

Court had "placed upon our area of equally reserved liberties." To members of the NWP, *Tipaldo*'s "no man's land" was a sacred area "that the ancestors of many of us crossed the Atlantic two hundred, some of them three hundred, years ago" in order "to find."[16]

This view found expression in the letter that Ruth G. Williams wrote to Justice George Sutherland two days after the decision in *Tipaldo*, praising him for preventing women from "being ruled inferior citizens." While she was rather worried that "it is unethical to write to a Supreme Court Justice," she nevertheless found herself compelled to reach out to Sutherland in order to let him know "how very thankful women are to you and the four justices who concurred with you. . . . It is hair-raising to consider how very close women in America came to being ruled inferior citizens."[17] She described Chief Justice Charles Evans Hughes's dissent as "one long insult to women citizens," and she believed "[e]very self-respecting woman should see red when reading." It was therefore "fortunate for Americans," men and women—she did not discriminate, "that we have at this time enough sane, just, clear thinkers on the Supreme Court to preserve our Constitution against the schemes of the so-called 'liberals.'" In her mind, the dissenters in *Tipaldo* meant to "wreck American principles" and "American morale."[18]

Justice Sutherland cannot have been surprised to receive Williams's letter praising his opinion because the correspondence expressed the same views as the NWP amicus brief submitted in *Tipaldo*. This was a brief that did not hold back in expressing its belief that *Adkins* (a) was correctly decided, and (b) controlled *Tipaldo*. As the authors of the brief forcefully stated in their closing paragraph, which quoted admiringly from *Adkins*, "[T]he Constitution . . . is still supreme . . . and . . . the principles of constitutional liberty apply to women as well as to men . . . The *Adkins* decision . . . gave them assurance that their fundamental liberties are recognized by the Courts. It may be said," continued the brief, "that *their Magna Charta is found in the words of Mr. Justice Sutherland*: 'We cannot accept the doctrine that women of mature age . . . require or may be subjected to restrictions upon their liberty of contract which could not lawfully be imposed in the case of men under similar circumstances.'"[19] A June 6 NWP Press Release joyously proclaimed that after *Tipaldo* "[n]ever again can it be argued that women are helpfully affected by minimum wage laws which fail to apply equally to men."[20]

Anna Kelton Wiley summed up the NWP opposition to minimum wage laws for women in the effusive letter that she wrote
to Justice Sutherland the day after *Parrish* was decided. It is worth
quoting extensively from this piece of correspondence. "My dear
Mr. Justice Sutherland," the letter began:

> I am taking this first opportunity to express to you and to your
> three colleagues [the justices who joined Sutherland in the
> *Parrish* dissent] . . . my gratitude for the display of *character*
> and *wisdom* exhibited in the Minority opinion on the Wash-
> ington State Minimum Wage case. This decision is marked by
> courage and sound thinking, it places a long-time-program of
> justice to women, over a *temporary expedient to grant a few
> women an increased wage*.
>   In the long run the Majority Opinion, in my opinion,
> will hurt the prestige of our splendid Supreme Court, more
> than anything else that could have happene.d. I rejoice that a
> minority stood firm under the terrific pressure of recent events.
>   It is encouraging to know that four eminent justices see the
> point which many woman [*sic*] are now upholding, namely,
> that interference with a woman's right to contract for labor
> (her dearest possiession [*sic*] and sole source of her potential
> wealth) is an interference with her constitutional liberty. The
> strange sight is to view organized labor clamoring for protec-
> tive laws for women *only* but protesting vigorously against such
> laws for themselves. . . . It is strange to realize that the human-
> itarian persons who advocate restrictive laws for women *only*,
> cannot see the greater advantage of welfare laws for *persons* in
> industry.
>   The only hope is that the working out of this *tragic set-
> back to the advancement of women* may serve to awaken more
> women to the position taken by the Natl. Woman's Party for
> an equal rights amendment to the constitution. . . . If this deci-
> sion will hasten the day of the passage of this proposed amend-
> ment, then *this calamity of yesterday*, in God's good time, will
> work out for the good.
>   At the present time we have the spectacle of men and
> women, economically speaking, at each other's throats for jobs.
> And the decision of yesterday will in the long run make wom-
> en's struggle more difficult.

She closed by reiterating that although she felt "*personal* gratitude" for the "wise and courageous stand" that Sutherland took in his *Parrish* dissent, she believed she was also "voicing the gratitude of multitudes of women all over the country."[21]

One of those women was the famed Maryland suffragette Edith Houghton Hooker, who had spent over three decades advocating for equal treatment for women.[22] One week after the decision in *Parrish*, Hooker sent identical letters to the two dissenting justices, offering her full-throated praise of their votes in that case. She had considered writing to them after *Tipaldo*—a decision for which she had "tender[ed] unqualified commendation of [their] majority opinion," but held off doing so because she "thought . . . that the Court was inviolate and that it would be presumptuous on my part either to commend or to condemn action taken by the Justices." The combination of the Court-packing plan (which "assail[ed] the dignity of the Court" and was nothing more than a presidential effort "to bring the opinions of the Court into conformity" with FDR's "personal opinions") and the decision in *Parrish* finally spurred Hooker to put pen to paper.[23]

In Hooker's opinion, Justices Sutherland and Van Devanter had demonstrated great "faith and courage" in voting to strike down the Washington State law.[24] Borrowing the words of William Wordsworth's poem "My Heart Leaps Up," Hooker wrote that "the minority opinion handed down [*in Parrish*] . . . is, to me, what the rainbow was to Mr. Wordsworth." "My heart leaps up at the faith and courage that you demonstrated. Justice is not dead, for she spoke from your lips. . . . You did my sex the honor of regarding women as persons and citizens, in the eyes of the law . . . capable of enjoying the equal protection of the laws guaranteed to all persons under the Fourteenth Amendment." In a quite remarkable closing sentence, she wrote: "In my extremity, I approach you, as one human being who loves liberty to another, but I bow down my head and cover my eyes, for I realize that, in your presence, I am upon holy ground, in the presence of Justice herself, in whose cause I ask your counsel."[25]

Ten days after the announcement of the decision in *Parrish*, the NWP issued a statement outlining a series of talking points about minimum wage laws. It began by identifying—in stark terms—the two different paths that legislators, who were inclined to pass such laws, could now take. Such a law could either protect *only* women and children, or it could protect everyone—man, woman, and child.

The document left the reader in no doubt that the NWP firmly believed that the first option—which relied on the "idea of affording them [women and children] protection against 'unscrupulous employers'" (it was telling, here, that the NWP used language from Chief Justice Hughes's opinion in *Parrish*)—was completely unacceptable. "If minimum wage laws are good for labor," the statement read, "then *apply* them to labor—not just to women. . . . A minimum wage when enacted for women only is *not* solving the problem. It is immeasurably adding to the problem of women, and of their dependents in the struggle for a living."[26]

*　*　*

By contrast, numerous state lawmakers across the nation viewed *Parrish* as vindicating their belief (and that of their Progressive Era predecessors) that laws mandating minimum wages for *women* were both socially necessary and politically appropriate. Indeed, by the end of 1937 twenty-two states, the District of Columbia, and Puerto Rico had minimum wage laws in place for their women workers.[27] After New York's law was struck down in *Tipaldo*, the legislature in Albany began to discuss enacting a new statute as soon as its new session began in January 1937. Concerns about the need to avoid another defeat at the hands of the Supreme Court led to talk rather than action, but that changed after *Parrish*. By April 27 Governor Herbert Lehman had on his desk a bill that he promptly signed into law.[28] Meanwhile, in the Pacific Northwest in the summer of 1937, Oregon's Welfare Commission reduced the maximum permitted working hours for women (from forty-eight to forty-four per week), and concurrently raised the minimum wage for the state's female workers (from 27.5 to 30 cents per hour).[29] On Thursday, October 7, 1937, from its offices in Olympia, the Washington State Department of Labor and Industries Industrial Welfare Committee issued Order No. 36, establishing sixteen dollars as the minimum weekly wage for women and minors working full-time in apartment houses. For any week when the employee worked less than forty-eight hours, she would be compensated at a minimum of 37.5 cents per hour. The order also stated how much an employer could deduct from an employee's pay packet to cover the costs of an on-site apartment when inhabitance of such accommodation was a condition of the employment.[30]

In a *Seattle Times* editorial published one week after *Parrish*, the newspaper's associate editor, James Wood, reminded readers that in 1937 the nation's minimum wage laws were not "in any sense a product of Mr. Roosevelt's political genius." This was an accurate statement because, as we saw in chapters 2 and 3, these laws were borne of *state* governmental innovation.[31] Indeed, of the aforementioned two-dozen minimum wage statutes in place by the end of 1937, ten predated *Adkins* and fourteen were later enactments.[32] Yes, some were enacted in 1933 at the prodding of the new president, but Wood was right, the overwhelming majority of the laws were not the result of either Rooseveltian genesis or genius.

A "far-sighted program for the benefit of [some] workers"

In many ways, however, an important part of the "real" and "enduring change"[33] wrought by *Parrish* did come from the Roosevelt Administration when, in 1938, Congress passed, and FDR signed into law the Fair Labor Standards Act (FLSA). On Monday, May 24, 1937, the president sent to Congress a message advocating passage of *federal* legislation prescribing minimum wages and maximum hours. *Parrish* enabled FDR to describe this initiative as "*further* action to extend the frontiers of social progress"—action beyond which had already been "initiated by the legislative branch . . . administered by the executive, and," crucially, "sustained by the judicial" branch of the government.[34] A year later, on June 28, 1938, the president signed the FLSA into law, accomplishing many of the goals he had outlined in his 1937 message. Of all the laws enacted over the past three years, he described it as second only in importance to the Social Security Act of 1935.[35] As he explained in his June 25 Fireside Chat, with the exception of the 1935 law the FLSA was "the most far-reaching, far-sighted program for the benefit of workers ever adopted here or in any other country. Without question it starts us toward a better standard of living and increases purchasing power to buy the products of farm and factory."[36]

"Mixed implications"

While the FLSA was indeed "far-reaching," a large percentage of the nation's *female* workers (especially those most in need of wages and hours help) simply did not benefit from the statute. In the words of the historian James MacGregor Burns, the FLSA that FDR signed into law in 1938 was "crippled, undersized, and hardly recognizable to its progenitors."[37] Above all else, this is because of basic (and timeless) philosophical differences about the nature and size of the federal government that divided members of Congress (especially in the House). For this particular legislative fight, senators and representatives waged battles (many of them internecine) about the extent to which wages and hours standards should be administratively flexible, bringing a total of ten very different bills to the floor of Congress over thirteen months.[38] As John Forsythe observed in his 1939 study of the FLSA's enactment, ultimately it was "compromises as to flexibility in attaining minima and the inclusion of a provision which could be construed to allow regional differentials" which "paved the way to agreement" on a bill that could be sent to the president for his signature.[39]

It was a far more important characteristic of the law, however, that ensured its coverage would not extend to the vast majority of women workers. *NLRB v. Jones and Laughlin*,[40] decided by the U.S. Supreme Court two weeks after *Parrish*, significantly influenced the decision of FDR and Congress to "anchor . . . [the FLSA] in the Commerce Clause."[41] It was this constitutional "anchor" that significantly limited the law's coverage. Located in Article I, Section 8 of the Constitution, the Commerce Clause empowers Congress "[t]o regulate Commerce with foreign Nations, and among the several States, and with the Indian Tribes."[42] In 1824 the Court's interpretation of this clause provided Congress with broad regulatory power, holding that the power to "regulate Commerce" "means the power to regulate; that is, to prescribe the rule by which commerce is to be governed. This power, like all others vested in Congress, is complete in itself, may be exercised to its utmost extent, and acknowledges no limitations, other than are prescribed in the Constitution."[43] However, a series of late-nineteenth and early-twentieth-century decisions by the justices sharply constricted this power by, among other things, concluding that Congress could not use its commerce power to regulate *manufacturing* because that was distinct from *commerce* (even though it was very clear to a great many people that such a distinction did not reflect the reality of much of the nation's manufacturing).[44] The decision in *Jones and Laughlin* began to change that constitutional tide.

The Commerce Clause justification "had mixed implications for workers, *especially women*."[45] Section 15 (a) (1) of the FLSA made it "unlawful for any person to transport, offer for transportation, ship, deliver, or sell in commerce, or to ship, deliver, or sell with knowledge that shipment or delivery or sale thereof in commerce is intended, any goods in the production of which any employee was employed in violation of section 6 or section 7." Those sections imposed minimum wages and maximum working hours respectively.[46] Neither Elsie Parrish, nor any of the Seattle-based workers discussed in chapter 6, were covered by the law because their work took place within a state's borders, making it intrastate commerce, which did not affect interstate commerce (as understood by the Court at the time). Arguably, those who needed the law the most found their low pay and long working hours completely unaffected by the FLSA. In case anyone thought otherwise, the act specifically "exempted workers in agricultural, retail, and service occupations, along with professional workers, seamen, and fishermen."[47]

By the 1960s, with the civil rights movement in ascendancy and congressional Dixiecrats no longer wielding the legislative clout they once did, and the rise of the women's liberation movement in the 1970s, amendments to the original law ultimately eliminated many of these exemptions.[48] In *1938*, however, if the FLSA really was "the original anti-poverty law," as one commentator has described it, it alleviated the poverty of only a fraction of the nation's workforce.[49] This, of course, meant that in 1938 it was the nation's *state* statutes employing police powers for "health, safety, and welfare" reasons, not the *federal* law grounded in a commerce clause justification, that offered legislative assistance for most of the nation's women workers. State statutes such as that which the West Coast Hotel Company unsuccessfully sought to defeat in *Parrish*. It is therefore problematic to couple the legacy of *Parrish* to the FLSA because implicit in that coupling conclusion is the belief that the state minimum wage laws for women, declared valid by *Parrish*, were surpassed in importance and effect by the federal law in 1938. Nothing could have been further from the truth. It was *Parrish*, not the FLSA, which had the real, lasting impact on women making minimum wage.

Epilogue

Disappearing into History?

> "It was like, whoa . . . cool!"
> —*Debra Parrish Stewart*

In their 1997 *Wenatchee Business Journal* article commemorating the sixtieth anniversary of the *Parrish* decision, Kris Young and Mark Behler informed their readers that "Elsie moved to Omak where she and her husband raised their family and disappeared into history."[1] This was an accurate assessment. In 1937 Elsie Parrish made history when she became the "Minimum Pay Law Joan d'Arc,"[2] but after that, *she and her story* did "disappear into history." "Few Americans," wrote Peter Irons, "can recollect the names of the . . . people who began important Supreme Court cases. Hardly anyone, aside from family and friends, knows anything of their lives."[3] This rings true for the people whose stories have been told in this book. All that remains is for me to tell you what happened to some of those characters after March 29, 1937, a time when most of them did indeed disappear into history.

C. B. Conner

In his memoir, Elsie's lawyer brought the chapter about the *Parrish* case to a close with the following paragraph, which is worth printing in its entirety:

And what did I get for all these hours of labor? I should be very much disappointed if my son should be called upon to perform some heavy task for the welfare of his community and having done it well sit down and consider the amount of his compensation in dollars and cents, overlooking the results of his work. I should want him to be satisfied in the knowledge that his labors had brought comfort to some needy person; that he had rendered a real community service. That is how I should want him to consider his work, and I would be false to myself did I think of compensation from this case as is measured by money—*working women are receiving better wages, children have more food and better clothes. May I not have a reason to hope that I have served my country and in this thought receive a very handsome remuneration indeed?*[4]

This passage captures all the reasons why Conner considered it important to take Elsie's case. He knew exactly what was at stake. He knew that in 1913 the Washington state legislature—"the physician who feels the pulse of the state and is supposed to know whether the system is in proper condition"—had "felt the pulse, examined the heart beats, and being fully advised as to the needs of the State . . . did pass a minimum wage law for women." He also knew that in the mid-1930s the "need" for that law was no less than it had been almost a quarter century earlier.[5]

Conner's role in the *Parrish* case was crucial, and this fact was not lost on the Washington legal community. As the Seattle lawyer John P. Hartman observed: "That done by Mr. Conner is a legacy of great worth to our people, and now bequeathed to coming generations, forming a bright star in the legal constellation of that which shall last."[6] The three of C. B. and Irene's five children that lived beyond the age of twenty[7] all would, in their own particular ways, bequeath important legacies to future generations, just as their father had done. Charles Jr. (Chuck) became a surgeon; Anna (who went by her middle name Louise) graduated with honors from the University of Washington and worked as a music teacher; and Robert E. Conner followed directly in his father's footsteps, taking over C. B.'s law practice in Wenatchee, and serving multiple terms as Chelan County prosecutor and justice of the peace.[8] Robert "had just won the biggest case of his life before he died" in 1978, recalls his daughter Chris.[9]

C. B. lived to see very few of his adult children's accomplishments. In the spring of 1941, he and Irene departed Wenatchee for a long-planned car trip that would take them through twenty-one states as they made their way to the Shenandoah Valley to visit their families. C. B. could not afford to spend a protracted amount of time away from his work, so he completed the eight-thousand-mile round trip on his own, driving back to the Pacific Northwest while Irene stayed on with her family. Her vacation was cut short when word arrived of her husband's death. On May 21, 1941, while on business at a hotel in Seattle, C. B. suffered a sudden and fatal heart attack. Indicative of the way in which the stories of the people closest to *West Coast Hotel v. Parrish* quickly faded from people's memories, references to that decision, the biggest case C. B. ever litigated, were conspicuous by their absence from the obituaries published in the *Wenatchee Daily World*.[10]

Fred Crollard

Fred Crollard outlived his opposing *Parrish* counsel by almost a quarter century, passing away in Wenatchee on June 22, 1968. As we saw in chapter 4, during his lifetime Fred Crollard played important roles in just about every civic organization in town. While one would do well not to accept as gospel some of the tales of community history told by the historian John Gellatly (another of Wenatchee's pioneers and leading lights), he is not overstating his case when he says that "[w]hen one undertakes to talk about self-made men, he dares not pass the name of Fred M. Crollard."[11] For his service Crollard received abundant community awards including, most significantly, the Golden Key to the City, presented at the Pioneer Citizen Award dinner on December 16, 1953. In 1967, one year before his passing, a series of *World* articles honored Crollard's work, including describing the ways in which he had taken "great pride in the success of young lawyers whom he has helped boost up the legal ladder."[12]

Unlike Conner, Fred Crollard lived long enough to enjoy and take pride in the myriad adult accomplishments of the five children that he and Stella raised. Veronica spent over three decades working for the United States Forest Service, principally serving as a "supervisory purchasing agent" for the Wenatchee National

Forest. As one of her colleagues observed about her work in a 1966 newspaper article, Veronica "knows everything there is to know from a business standpoint. . . . If we want something done, we turn it over to Veronica and forget about it."[13] Veronica's brother David "Bud" Crollard was "[a] complicated man, probably with [an] inferiority complex" because he completed only two years of college, which paled in comparison with the academic accomplishments of his siblings. However, he would build or fix just about anything; for example, he constructed an airfield in Alaska during World War II and built custom homes in Wenatchee for his parents and his brother Fred Jr. He outlived all but one of his siblings.[14]

Three years younger than Bud, Louis Joseph (named after his uncle who perished in the 1918 flu pandemic) was a talented musician. After enlisting in the navy during World War II (serving as a radar technician), Louis returned to his studies, and subsequently became one of Wenatchee's most well-known and beloved optometrists for the next forty-five years.[15] Two of Fred's sons—Fred Jr. and Homer—became lawyers. Both served in the military in World War II, but Homer was the only one of the Crollard siblings to see active combat. He earned a Bronze Star for his army service as a mortar squad leader and fought in the Battle of the Bulge (December 1944–January 1945).[16] Jeff and Jonah, Homer's son and grandson, continue the family tradition to this day, both practicing law in Seattle.

Judge W. O. Parr

For the Parr household, there was every reason to believe that January 1942 would be a joyous month. Florence, the only child of the judge and his wife, was heavily pregnant, and expected to bring a bouncing baby boy into the world within days of her father's seventy-third birthday on January 12. Although he still maintained the same office he had occupied since setting up in business in the early twentieth century, Parr had retired from the bench in 1940, and was enjoying being a grandfather. This grandchild would be the baby brother to Ann Elizabeth. When the family gathered on the twelfth, however, any thoughts of celebration had evaporated. Heavy hearts abounded, hearts filled with immeasurable shock and grief from the death in childbirth of both Florence and the baby. Florence's untimely death broke the judge's heart. On Monday, February 16, Judge Parr went into the office to file probate on Florence's will. The following evening, he died of a massive heart attack.[17]

Parr's death deprived Wenatchee of one of its most esteemed residents. As fellow judge Fred Kemp observed in the *Wenatchee Daily World*, Parr "had been lawyer and superior court judge for over 40 years—since Chelan county was organized. And in his passing, we have lost one of our most distinguished and useful citizens."[18] At 11 A.M., on Friday, February 20, 1942, six local attorneys served as the pallbearers carrying Parr's casket into the chapel of the Jones & Jones funeral home. Fred Crollard and Robert Conner were two of those men.[19]

The Cascadian

In 1968, when Crollard passed away, the Cascadian Hotel was living on borrowed time. Seven years earlier, a new Cascadian motor hotel extension opened. Built at a cost of over $300,000, it was "designed," as Clair Van Divort, the president of the corporation overseeing construction, proclaimed, "to be at least five years ahead of the times in motor hotel construction." Operated by the Cascadian, it was connected to the back of the original hotel structure by a third-floor walkway.[20] There was only one problem. Rather than being "five years ahead of the times," the new motor inn was approximately five years *behind* the times. It was a classic example of that type of motel construction and was built toward the tail end of a decade-long boom that, by the mid-1960s, had seen over sixty thousand such motels spring up nationwide.[21] The Seaman Building adjoining the Cascadian was converted into a seven-hundred-person capacity banquet room in 1963, giving the hotel valuable additional conference meeting space.[22] However, behind these developments there had long been unmistakable indications that the Cascadian's heydays were behind her.

The October 1929 stock market crash put the hotel into a precarious economic position almost as soon as it opened. People could not afford to stay in hotels as paying guests. The Cascadian benefited from important regional infrastructure developments, such as the opening (by the Great Northern Railway) of the eight-mile-long Stevens Pass tunnel in 1929 and construction of the Rock Island Dam (about ten miles outside Wenatchee), which brought added business to the hotel through 1933.[23] However, as we saw in chapter 1, the Cascadian survived the Great Depression in large part because of the managerial prowess of Ray Clark who, over a career that lasted three decades, became "one of the leading and best known hotelmen" in the Pacific Northwest and "one of the most enthusiastic boosters of the states of Washington and Oregon."[24] Among other things, in the early 1930s Clark successfully made the Cascadian a go-to place of accommodation for prominent visitors to Wenatchee.

Famous Guests

In May 1933 the famed German Bohemian-American contralto Madame Ernestine Schumann-Heink brought her singing tour to Wenatchee. About to turn eighty-two, she no longer had the stunning voice to which the world of opera had first been introduced in 1878.[25] As the *New York Times* remarked upon the reissue of one of her albums over two decades later, "In her later years Schumann-Heink's voice had lost some of the splendor evident in her early records." However, as the newspaper also noted, "What remained were the singer's vitality, her humor and her power to charm an audience." She "could perform a work like the dialect yodeling song 'I und mei Bua' with such irresistible comedy as to draw gales of laughter from listeners understanding scarcely a word of German."[26] As the *Morning Star* (Long Beach, Calif.) reported, she could delight her listeners with the gift of her voice in such a way that when she sang it was as though she was "talking to people across the footlights in the most beautiful of tones."[27]

The Liberty Theater, across whose footlights she talked to Wenatcheeites in 1933, was built in 1919 and still stands today; much of the Liberty's external majesty has now gone, but it remains a working movie theater. It is located a block away from the Cascadian building, but it was more than proximity that accounted for Schumann-Heink's decision to stay at the Cascadian. Like almost every prominent visitor to Wenatchee in the 1930s, Madame Ernestine stayed at the Cascadian because it was the grandest hotel in town, with an exceptional staff. Importantly for Schumann-Heink, it also offered on-site beautician services. The morning of her scheduled appearance at the Liberty, Madame Ernestine sat in her room, admiring the view of the mighty Columbia River and enjoying a manicure being performed by Miss Taggart, the employee who had been summoned to work on the guest's nails and hair. Later that evening, after being invited backstage, Miss Taggart was thrilled to receive a kiss, a corsage, and a personally autographed photo from the famous singer.[28]

Fourteen years later, another recording artist—ultimately far more famous than Madame Ernestine—made a stop in Wenatchee as part of his national tour and stayed at the Cascadian. However, for him it took the intervention of Eddie Carlson, vice president of Western Hotels, before he would be granted a room at the hotel. The singer in question was Nat King Cole, and on that eventful night he forever "changed Wenatchee."[29]

Although 1940s Wenatchee was home to only a few African American families, in 1947 three members of the Wenatchee music business community—Mark Sorley (KPQ radio), Bob Godfrey (Belmont Radio & Music Store), and Bill VanHoose (Seattle First National Bank)—sensed an important promotional opportunity when they heard that the King Cole Trio wanted to book some Pacific Northwest locations for their national tour. The subsequent "true multicultural" concert was a huge success, as approximately five hundred people—white and black—piled into the Wenatchee Auditorium. However, as significant as the show was, "[t]he memorable events of the evening were still to come." By no means for the first time in their lives, the three men were refused rooms at a place of public accommodation because of their race; not until Cole placed a call to Carlson would he, his two band members, Wesley Prince and Oscar Moore, and their "sizable entourage" be permitted to stay at the Cascadian. It was on that night that "a color line fell in Wenatchee."[30]

As famous as Madame Ernestine and the King Cole Trio were, in the history of the Cascadian they were by no means its most celebrated guests; that honor undoubtedly belongs to two men who stayed at the hotel in October 1931. Earlier that year, after Clyde Pangborn and Hugh Herndon Jr. failed in their attempt to break the speed record for a round-the-world flight, they resolved instead to try and capture the prize for being the first individuals to fly nonstop across the Pacific Ocean, from Japan to the continental

United States. After bad weather prevented them from landing in Seattle, they headed east; the triumphant, record-breaking pair touched down in Wenatchee in their plane the *Miss Veedol*, on October 5, forty-one hours and thirteen minutes after taking off from Misawa.[31] From the aircraft, "[t]he fliers emerged haggard, dirty and tired, mostly wanting a bath and sleep. Wenatchee and East Wenatchee went wild and cars soon plugged the tiny, winding road that led to the airport. Clyde's brother, Percy, sneaked them out a back way to town over fields and through some fences."[32]

They could not escape the crowds, however, and they experienced a true heroes' welcome that "extended for days." Inevitably, that welcome included accommodation at the Cascadian, where they enjoyed much-needed sleep, bathing, and hearty meals.[33] Numerous photographs captured their stay at the hotel (including images of the men lounging in their beds, and meeting with Ray Clark) and were reprinted in newspapers across the nation. For example, the October 9 issue of the New York *Daily News* featured a picture of the pair eating a breakfast that "was served to them hot in Cascadian Hotel"; the photograph ran beneath a heading that read, "Breakfast on Terra Firma."[34] Many of the images have stood the test of time, and several of those that grace the walls of the passenger terminal at Wenatchee's Pangborn Memorial Airport educate visitors about the fact that it was the Cascadian Hotel that hosted these two famous fliers.

Famous Employees

Over the years, numerous dedicated staff members at all levels of the hotel's operation served guests staying at the Cascadian. For some of these individuals, employment at this particular establishment represented the beginning of a long and distinguished career working for—or working their way up the corporate ladder at—Western Hotels. Two such examples are Georgina Tucker and Harry Mullikin.

Gina Tucker (née Petheram) began her career at the Cascadian, where, upon graduation from the State College of Washington in 1933 (the State College became Washington State University in 1959), she joined six other young women cheerfully referred to as the hotel's "popular collegiennes."[35] These young women undertook fourteen months of training aimed at making them "capable of managing a restaurant, tea room or hotel dining room of modern size." As one local newspaper proudly informed its readers, "The Cascadian is the only hotel in the Northwest that is following out this policy of developing American college girls to a point where they are capable of accepting a position of responsibility such as food supervisor which will assure them of a good salary and place them in very responsible positions."[36]

Tucker spent the next forty-two years working for Western Hotels (later Western International Hotels [WIH] Company, and then Westin Hotels) or one of its subsidiaries. Four years after receiving the 1971 Thurston-Dupar Inspirational Award, the company's "highest employee award distinction," she retired, having risen to the prestigious position of executive in charge of housekeeping of the grand Century Plaza Hotel in Los Angeles. Tucker was affectionately known as the "first lady" of WIH.[37]

Harry Mullikin, who "was born into the hotel business," began working at the Cascadian in the early 1940s.[38] Over the course of his life, Harry's father, William, operated several different hotels. When Harry was born in April 1927, William had been the manager of the Greystone Hotel, a two-story establishment in McGehee, Arkansas, for seven years. After the devastating flood of 1927 was followed by more flooding and numerous tornadoes in Arkansas in 1929, and then the drought of 1930–31, "one of the worst in American climatological history," the Mullikins became one of the many Depression-era refugee families that came to Wenatchee seeking to put the memories of the last few years behind them.[39] They were initially housed at the Cascadian, which became a source of income for Harry in the early 1940s as he worked there after school, on the weekends, and during his winter and summer breaks. Originally hired in the spring of 1942, he was primarily an elevator operator, but he also performed bellman, busboy, porter, night janitor, room clerk, and houseman duties, eventually working shifts that lasted up to ten hours as he and the other young men of Wenatchee filled the holes in the town's workforce left by World War II enlistments.[40]

Over the course of his distinguished career Mullikin spent very little time out of the employment of the Western Hotels Company or away from his beloved Pacific Northwest, and he became one of

Seattle's most prominent civic leaders.[41] In 1973 he became president of the company (which was now WIH), and led it through a period of unprecedented growth, leading to a 1977 *New York Times* profile titled "The Man Behind the Megahotels."[42]

After he left the Cascadian in 1934, Ray Clark continued to work in the hospitality industry for another four years, ending his career at the Commercial Hotel in Yakima. Clark left the managerial position there to become the secretary-treasurer and general manager of the Bactericidal Ray Sales Company; instead of selling the merits of hotels, he sold and distributed the Sperti patented Vitamin D sunlamp.[43] So, at the age of forty-six, Ray Clark, who had spent the entirety of his adult life working in the hotel business, abruptly switched occupational gears, leaving behind him an industry that fondly and proudly remembered him for his tireless boostering of hotels across the Pacific Northwest (and not for his hiring and underpaying of Elsie Parrish).

Obituary: The Cascadian Hotel, 1929–71

The Cascadian that Clark left behind in the 1930s proved to be a profitable enterprise for about another twenty-five years. Ann Phillips, who joined the hotel's staff as an assistant housekeeper in 1950 and worked there until its closure in 1971, recalls that in 1951, when Alcoa began construction on a new smelter in Malaga, just southeast of Wenatchee, "It was a busy time. Every room in the hotel was full every night. We had to hold people back in the coffee shop until seats were available."[44] Within a decade the future for the hotel began to look much less positive. During the 1960s it was sold three times in five years. In 1962 new ownership came in the form of a group of investors that included Wilfred R. Woods and James W. Woods of the dynastic *Wenatchee World*-owning Woods family.[45] Led by A. J. "Jerry" Barash, the longtime owner-manager of the Columbia Hotel in Wenatchee, this group had high hopes that it would be able to revive the fortunes of the financially ailing Cascadian. However, as Wilfred Woods ruefully reflected a half century later, within two years the investors "found out that Western Hotels knew better than our group that the Cascadian just could not become profitable, and we bailed out."[46] The Cascadian was sold to a Seattle-based corporation with plans to aggressively market the hotel to organizations that were interested in holding conferences and conventions in Wenatchee.[47] But these plans did not materialize, and the Cascadian once again found itself under new ownership the following year when James D. Ward, a Wenatchee native and Seattle-based restaurateur, purchased the property by establishing the "Cascadian Enterprises" corporation.[48] Tragically, in July 1970 the fifty-year-old Ward died of a heart attack while on a fishing trip in Idaho. It was clear to everyone that Ward had been the last best hope for the Cascadian and that it, too, was coming to the end of its life.[49]

On Monday, July 19, 1971, a group of Delta Kappa Gamma delegates gathered for their scheduled meeting at the hotel. They drove to Wenatchee from across the region and were excited to see one another again and catch up on news. Upon arrival at the Cascadian they were shocked to find themselves greeted by shuttered doors and a sign unequivocally stating that they would have to find somewhere else to meet because effective at four o'clock that day, the hotel was "closed."[50] The next day, what amounted to eviction notices were delivered to the twenty-one permanent residents of the hotel and the motor inn. Dr. Eva Anderson had lived at the Cascadian for the past five years and like so many of the other occupants—both residential and commercial—she had become brutally aware of the downturn in the building's fortunes. Yet, the abrupt shuttering of the building still came as a shock. "I had no warning. I knew business was poor," remarked Anderson, but "[n]ow they say they're going to turn the lights off. I have to find a place to live and get my furniture out. . . . It's like a disturbed ant hill here today. It's not only my own home but I have friends on the staff."[51]

These men and women, primarily retirees, were, as the *World* described them, "hit the hardest" because they were being told to leave the apartments that they had called home for many years.[52] However, the impact of the distribution of the brutal, sudden closure notifications was also felt by all the businesses at the hotel—including a barbershop, bank, travel agency, beauty parlor, cocktail lounge, and restaurant. As with the permanent residents, the proprietors of several of these businesses had been mainstays at the Cascadian for many years. James Stewart had cut hair there for over a decade at his Crown Barber Shop, and working out of a suite of two rooms Harold Faulkner had provided massage services to the townsfolk since 1939.[53]

Even though, in 1971, it was true that "Wenatchee without the Cascadian is a town without a place where major conventions can be fed . . . a downtown without a meeting headquarters," in reality all the major meetings and conventions in the world could not have saved this landmark.[54] Over the years, the pages of the *World* bore numerous announcements and reports of the myriad meetings held at the Cascadian every week. Yet, as a 1971 *World* editorial matter-of-factly observed, the era of the grand dame, downtown hotel had long since passed. "Closure of the hotel is not a reflection of business conditions in Wenatchee"; instead, "[i]t's a reflection on what happens to old, downtown hotels."[55]

The closure notices had barely been posted when speculation about the Cascadian's future began to fill the pages of the *World* and the dinner table and coffee shop conversations of Wenatchee-ites.[56] Wherever its future lay, by the end of 1971 two things were fairly clear. First, the Cascadian would never again be a hotel. Second, the imminent removal of the sky bridge connecting the main building to the motor inn represented much more than a physical separation of the two entities—the plans for redevelopment of the motor inn were entirely separate from plans (if any actually existed) for redevelopment of the hotel.[57]

The transformation of the motor inn happened relatively quickly. The Uptowner Motel opened in April 1972 with a business model that involved selling the refurbished apartments as twenty-three condominiums, which were expected to only be owner-occupied for about one month in the year, allowing them to be rented out to visitors during the rest of the year.[58] The unsightly, weathered, and decidedly incongruous Uptowner sign painted on the side of the Cascadian building remains (much to the disquiet of many of the city's residents),[59] but the motel has long since been converted into apartments. As Molly Elliott, the manager who oversaw the change in 1997, observed, "With so many new places coming in and with us not being on the main road through town, it just wasn't profitable."[60]

At the end of November 1971, four months after the main hotel closed, an application for government funding for subsidized housing for elders was submitted to the U.S. Department of Housing and Urban Development (HUD). The plans called for eighty-four three-room apartments, exclusively available for individuals fifty-five years or older, with $5,000 or less in assets.[61] Remodeling began in January 1973 after confirmation of the federal financing finally came through. An anticipated reopening date to coincide with the spring 1973 apple blossom festival came and went. Finally, the Cascadian Apartments opened in November 1973, with 100 percent occupancy and an eighty-five-person waiting

FIG. E.1   An American Aircraft brand clothes dryer, built by the American Laundry Machinery Company, located in the basement of the Cascadian building. Author photo.

list. The criteria for residency were revised from initial reports; the minimum age was now sixty-two, and applications were opened not only to those on a very limited income, but also to disabled individuals. A new fire escape and fire alarm were added; the elevators remodeled; and the exterior thoroughly cleaned. Accompanying the apartments were lounges on four different flours; a space with a semi-kitchenette that was available for parties to hire out; and two levels (the first and second floors) dedicated to commercial enterprises (including the Central Washington Bank, a former hotel tenant).[62]

Nine months earlier, on Friday, February 23, 1973, at 7:30 in the evening, people gathered at Colonel Jim's Gold Creek Auction House, half a mile south of Gold Creek Park in Woodinville. They were there to bid on items from the Cascadian, including "200 to 300 pillows, countless blankets and sheets, lamps, night stands and other furniture."[63] Many items were left behind in Wenatchee as reminders of the building's former life—such as the mail chute box and the hand-operated elevator.[64] Some such memories are still there—collecting dust in the basement are the seventh-floor swamp cooler, the original American Aircraft clothes dryer, and the original ten-to-twelve-feet-wide clothes mangle. Perhaps Elsie used some of these implements; we can only speculate.

Also preserved are most of the blueprints from the construction of the hotel in 1929. For all of the Cascadian's employees like Elsie Parrish, their day would have begun here in the basement, where the dressing rooms were located. The blueprint shown in figure E.2 shows separate dressing rooms for the men and women. The basement also had a separate men's washroom, with terrazzo flooring, but notably, there was no equivalent for the women.

*   *   *

From the northern banks of the Columbia, if one looks south across the river at the Wenatchee skyline, one's eye is immediately drawn to the Cascadian building, behind which is the dramatic backdrop of the Mission Ridge hills (including the iconic Saddle Rock). While the building's days as a hotel might be long gone, it remains a "primary visual definer . . . integral to people's memory of [Wenatchee's] Main Street."[65] Many storefronts in downtown Wenatchee underwent dramatic reconfigurations in the 1970s, but

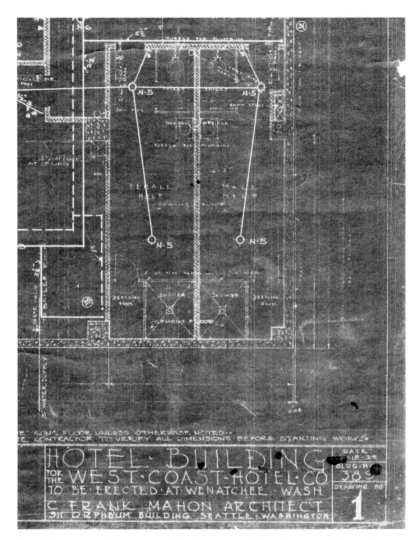

FIG. E.2   Original blueprint of the basement of the Cascadian Hotel. Courtesy Tryg and Barb Fortun.

the Cascadian was spared most of these facial ignominies. In 2008 the National Register of Historic Places approved designating eight blocks as the Downtown Wenatchee National Historic Register District, with all the architectural protections that such a label brings. Future generations will understand what Tracy Warner, a *Wenatchee World* reporter, meant when he wrote, "When we look at the old hotel that still dominates our skyline, we see a place of history."[66]

FIG. E.3 The Cascadian Hotel building today, featuring the "Uptowner Motel" sign painted on the side. Author photo.

Elsie

What of Elsie, "Omak's Minimum Pay Law Joan d'Arc" who played an important part in the history of the Cascadian? Although the lawsuit negatively affected her ability to find employment opportunities in Wenatchee, upon relocating to Omak in early 1936 she found work as a chambermaid at the Jim Hill Hotel. On November 16, 1936, just as King Edward VIII was summoning the British Prime Minister to inform him of his desire to marry the commoner Wallis Simpson, six thousand miles away the manager of the Jim Hill summoned his employee to his office to inform her that a photographer and reporter from the *Wenatchee Daily World* had arrived to capture "the story of her life." Just as the Duke and Duchess of Windsor would become personae non grata in Great Britain after his abdication from the throne, Ernie and Elsie found it impossible to remain in Wenatchee as her minimum wage lawsuit wound its way through the courts. This helped to explain why Elsie was "so flabbergasted" and "thought there must be some mistake" when the reporter and photographer came to see her. She was wont to say "my goodness" as she was interviewed and posed for a photograph as she made a bed at the Jim Hill Hotel.[67]

Little is known about the next few years of Elsie and Ernie's life together. All we know is that in 1938 Elsie headed east for a family reunion at the Murray homestead, and that the 1940 census found the couple living in Roosevelt, a rural Washington community on the banks of the Columbia, from where, looking across the river, one could see Oregon (the middle of the Columbia marks the border between the two states). Ernie's listed occupation was "box maker." From Roosevelt, the Parrish family relocated to Everett, an industrial city north of Seattle, whose population experienced a 12 percent increase over the course of the next decade. Just as the Wenatchee Valley saw a significant decrease in its population during World War II—two-thirds of the residents of Douglas County (neighboring Chelan County) "left for the coast and jobs in defense plants" during the war—it is reasonable to assume that the promise of wartime construction employment attracted the extended Parrish family to Everett.[68] The city directories list Ernie and Elsie living there until 1950 (at the same time as Elsie's daughter Gladys and her husband David Major); and those volumes indicate that Ernie held various jobs as a shipfitter, flaskman, and foundry worker.[69] In 1951, again to be close to their children, Ernie and Elsie moved to Southern California, initially staying with family in Compton and then buying a house in Anaheim, which would be their home for the rest of their lives.[70]

As Debra Parrish Stewart, their great-granddaughter, recalls, "[T]hings were a lot easier" for Elsie "when she married Ernie," and upon moving to Anaheim, Elsie no longer had to work. (Although there was never any doubt that Elsie, just as she had always done, "wore the pants in the family"; Ernie "never had much to say"— it was Elsie who "did all the talking.") For the first time since her marriage to Roy Lee in 1915, Elsie was able to enjoy being a wife, mother, grandmother, and great-grandmother without having to concern herself with living and coping with an alcoholic spouse, caring for a large brood of children, or seeking employment outside of the home so as to keep food on the table. She did, however, provide for one of her extended family. Born in nearby Compton in 1956, Debra lived with Elsie and Ernie on and off for over a decade, until Elsie's death in 1980, sharing their home on South Pepper Street, very close to the gates of Disneyland (which opened in 1955). Elsie was like a mother to Debra, who "misses her all the time"; Debra fondly recalls the dress "grandma" bought her for her junior high graduation; the enticing smell of freshly baked biscuits, dripping with butter and honey; her first job—at Carl's Jr.—that Elsie got her; all the clothes that Elsie made for Debra's dolls; and those times when, the avid gardener that she was, Elsie would take Debra to a local nursery and surreptitiously put clippings of plants into her purse, saying that this ultimately was very good for the shrubs. Elsie raised the teenage Debra at the same time that she focused on the many pleasures of her "retirement" because Ernie brought home a regular income from his work at Knotts Berry Farm—from where Debra got her pet turtle and rabbits.[71]

Los Angeles became Elsie's adopted home—she and Ernie rarely traveled beyond the confines of their neighborhood—and she became an avid fan of the Los Angeles Thunderbirds roller derby team and a devoted follower of the Los Angeles Dodgers beginning in 1958 after the Major League Baseball franchise relocated from Brooklyn. (Recall from chapter 1 that growing up in Kansas, Elsie enjoyed playing baseball with her brothers.) This was a golden age for the Dodgers, and Elsie enjoyed rooting for her "home team" as they captured seven National League pennants between 1959 and 1978 and won the World Series three times during the same time period—in 1959, 1963, and 1965. If the Dodgers hit a home run, Elsie would exclaim, "That's my team!" She did not live to experience the Fernandomania that swept through Los Angeles (named after the pitcher Fernando Valenzuela) in the early 1980s, but she did get to experience the famous teams led by pitchers Sandy Koufax and Don Drysdale. Watching on KTTV channel 11 or listening to the legendary Vin Scully broadcast the games on the radio "was just about the only time she swore."[72]

FIG. E.4   Elsie and Ernest Parrish. Courtesy Wenatchee Valley Museum and Cultural Center, 87-169-2.

FIG. E.5   Barbara K. Roberts, governor of Oregon
(1991–1995). Courtesy of Edmund Keene.

On Monday, March 31, 1980, Elsie and Ernie received the joyous news that Karen, wife of Debra's brother Dwayne, had gone
into labor; Ryan was born that evening. It was a welcomed addition to a family that was still grieving from the untimely death, six
weeks earlier, of Elsie and Roy's daughter Gladys. The family's happiness was short-lived, though. Sometime early in the morning on
Thursday, April 3, Elsie Parrish died peacefully in her sleep.[73] Ernie
survived her by nine years and was buried next to her in the Forest
Lawn Memorial Park in Long Beach.

Baby Ryan's birth came two days after the forty-third anniversary of the Supreme Court decision that bore his great-great-
grandmother's name. In the Parrish household, though, March 29

was never considered an occasion in need of marking or remembering. Debra's observation exemplifies the way in which Elsie's five minutes of legal fame were a mere footnote in the family's history: "I've known about this for years," she says, "but nobody ever paid much attention to it."[74] Members of the family grew up knowing very little about this episode in their relative's life. Barbara Roberts, the former governor of Oregon, only found out about her famous great-aunt when I first contacted her in 2017. Debra only found out about the case when she was a teenager. Her reaction? "It was like, whoa . . . cool!"[75]

*   *   *

There was nothing understated or unemotional about *Some Are Born Great*, the book published in 1974 by Adela Rogers St. Johns. A celebrity "sob sister" journalist and fiction writer (working principally for the Hearst organization), St. Johns portrayed the book as a women-only version of John F. Kennedy's *Profiles in Courage*. The common characteristic of all the women featured was "*gallantry*."[76] Befitting the dramatic nature of the work's prose, St. Johns invoked Prime Minister Winston Churchill's immortal words from his 1940 Battle of Britain speech in order to describe Elsie Parrish, one of the women highlighted in the book. Elsie was "the woman to whom never-have-so-many-owed-so-much, not even to the few but to one. One Woman."[77] Using language that would have been very much at home in one of the Hollywood screenplays she wrote, St. Johns proceeded to turn *West Coast Hotel v. Parrish* into a judicial clash of Biblical David and Goliath proportions. "I saw one woman," she wrote: "Mrs. Elsie Parrish . . . stand alone before Nine Men robed in all the power and glory of the final judgment and accomplish for all women a practical fact of freedom and justice on which we still walk across a chasm that once separated us from equal pay, opportunity and decent working conditions."[78]

There is no evidence that Elsie ever traveled to Washington, D.C., and she certainly never "stood alone" before the justices of the Supreme Court. (Then, as now, laypersons are not authorized to practice law before the Court.)[79] But that is beside the point, because even though St. Johns knew full well—as do we today— that she was writing with a heavy dose of dramatic license, her basic observation is still valid. The constitutional victory achieved by Elsie Parrish in 1937 had monumental sociopolitical and legal implications. With the courage of her convictions, in 1935 when she initiated her lawsuit, Elsie Deliah Parrish set in motion a chain of events that ultimately guaranteed that many women across the United States would finally be making minimum wage.

Notes

ACKNOWLEDGMENTS

1. Jim Sargent, *Too Poor to Move, But Always Rich: A Century on Montana Land* (self-pub., CreateSpace, 2014), 107.
2. Quoted in Nancy McCarthy, "State's Public Records from 1833 to Present Moved to New Home," *Oregonian* (Portland, OR), December 10, 1991.

PROLOGUE

1. Unless otherwise specified, all of the weather information in this book is taken from the NOAA National Centers for Environmental Information, Climate Data Online website: http://www.ncdc.noaa.gov/cdo-web/
2. "Omak Woman Wins Back Wages Case in Supreme Court," *Omak Chronicle* (Omak, WA), March 30, 1937.
3. "Forecast of the Weather Over the Nation," *New York Times*, December 16, 1936; "The Weather Over the Nation and Abroad," *New York Times*, December 17, 1936.
4. Letter from Edward S. Corwin to Homer S. Cummings, December 16, 1936, Box 88, Papers of Homer S. Cummings, MSS 9973, Albert and Shirley Small Special Collections Library, University of Virginia.
5. 300 U.S. 379 (1937).
6. That first case was *Stettler v. O'Hara*, which is discussed in chapter 3.
7. Ernest Parrish, and Elsie Parrish, his wife v. West Coast Hotel Company, Complaint, June 10, 1935, at 1–2; Amended Complaint, July 12, 1935, at

1–4, 6; Answer to Amended Complaint, September 9, 1935, at 2–3, Superior Court of the State of Washington in and for the County of Chelan, No. 12215; Chelan County Marriage Records, reference number cechemarcert0007480, July 28, 1934.

8. Charles C. Kerr, *The World of the World: From Frontier to Community, 1905–1980—A History of Growth and Development in North Central Washington* (Wenatchee, WA: Wenatchee World, 1980), 91; Robert E. Ficken, *Rufus Woods, the Columbia River, & the Building of Modern Washington* (Pullman: Washington State University Press, 1995), 102, 111.

9. Julie Novkov, *Constituting Workers, Protecting Women: Gender, Law, and Labor in the Progressive Era and New Deal Years* (Ann Arbor: University of Michigan Press, 2004), 3.

10. Only very recently has a scholar reached what must be considered the definitive conclusion about the identity of the person to whom we can attribute the New Deal-related "switch in time" quip. See John Q. Barrett, "Attribution Time: Cal Tinney's 1937 Quip, 'A Switch in Time'll Save Nine,'" *Oklahoma Law Review* 73 (2020).

11. Morehead v. New York ex rel. Tipaldo, 298 U.S. 587 (1936).

12. The justices met and voted on the fate of the Washington law on December 19, 1936 (two days after oral argument). They simply delayed the announcement of the decision so that the hospitalized Justice Harlan Fiske Stone could recover and return to cast his vote (which everyone knew would be the fifth vote to uphold the law). Merlo J. Pusey provided this factually accurate account of these events in his authorized biography of Chief Justice Charles Evans Hughes in 1951. Merlo J. Pusey, *Charles Evans Hughes* (New York: Macmillan, 1951), 2:757. Pusey later wrote that it was in this biography that the "true facts" of the *Parrish* timeline first became public. Merlo J. Pusey, "Justice Roberts' 1937 Turnaround," *Yearbook of the Supreme Court Historical Society 1983* (1983), 106. However, a nationally syndicated newspaper column written by David Lawrence, and published three days after the decision in *Parrish*, informed the public of Stone's illness and its relationship to the decision-making in the case. See David Lawrence, "Denies Roosevelt Bill Swayed Supreme Court," *Spokane Daily Chronicle*, April 1, 1937.

13. Walter F. Murphy, *Congress and the Court: A Case Study in the American Political Process* (Chicago: University of Chicago Press, 1962), 57.

14. It has been called the *Wenatchee World* since 1971.

15. *Wenatchee Daily World*, July 31, 1908, quoted in Ficken, *Rufus Woods*, 9.

16. Margie Jones, "Elsie Parrish . . . A Woman History Forgot," *Okanogan County Heritage* (Winter 1990–91): 17.

17. "Women's Constitutional Right to Starve," Radio Address by Elinore Morehouse Herrick, Regional Director, NLRB, Station WEAF, 6:35 P.M., Friday, March 13, 1936, 2, Box 2, Folder 51, National Consumers League Records

#5235, Kheel Center for Labor-Management Documentation and Archives, Cornell University Library.

INTRODUCTION

1. Howard Zinn, foreword to *A People's History of the Supreme Court: The Men and Women Whose Cases and Decisions Have Shaped Our Constitution*, by Peter Irons (New York: Penguin, 2000), v.

2. Peter Irons, preface to *The Courage of Their Convictions: Sixteen Americans Who Fought Their Way to the Supreme Court* (New York: Penguin, 1990), xii. This observation applies regardless of the status of the party (petitioner or respondent; appellant or appellee), and regardless of whether the party is someone with whom the average person might be inclined to sympathize and/or someone about whose life story the average person wishes to know more. For example, Robert D. Johnston suggests that "we have lost Curt Muller"—of Muller v. Oregon (208 U.S. 412 [1908]) fame (this decision is discussed in chapter 2)—because of, in part, "the scholarly instinct to expunge the petite bourgeoisie from the historical record." Robert D. Johnston, *The Radical Middle Class: Populist Democracy and the Question of Capitalism in Progressive Era Portland, Oregon* (Princeton, NJ: Princeton University Press, 2003), 19.

3. Zinn, foreword to *A People's History of the Supreme Court*, v.

4. Irons, preface to *The Courage of Their Convictions*, 4.

5. "Life on the American Newsfront: Supreme Court Reverses Itself on Minimum Wages," *Life*, April 12, 1937, p. 30.

6. One of the most engaging (and hilarious) reads has to be Jay Wexler's book about the road trips he took to find out the stories behind some of the U.S. Supreme Court's most famous religion cases. Jay D. Wexler, *Holy Hullabaloos: A Road Trip to the Battlegrounds of the Church/State Wars* (Boston: Beacon Press, 2009).

7. Michael C. Dorf, "Introduction—Putting the People Back in 'We the People,'" in *Constitutional Law Stories*, 2nd ed., ed. Michael C. Dorf (New York: Foundation Press, 2009).

8. "The courage of their convictions" is the exceptionally appropriate title of one of Peter Irons's books. See Irons, *The Courage of Their Convictions*.

9. 551 U.S. 393 (2007); James C. Foster, *BONG HiTS 4 JESUS: A Perfect Constitutional Storm in Alaska's Capital* (Fairbanks: University of Alaska Press, 2010).

10. Foster, *BONG HiTS 4 JESUS*, 218.

11. 478 U.S. 186 (1986); 539 U.S. 558 (2003).

12. Peter Irons, "Michael Hardwick v. Michael Bowers: I. 'I Saw a Bedroom Door Partially Open,'" in Irons, *The Courage of Their Convictions*; William N. Eskridge Jr., "The Crime against Nature on Trial, *Bowers v. Hardwick*,

1986," in *Civil Rights Stories*, edited by Myriam E. Gilles and Risa L. Goluboff (New York: Foundation Press, 2007); Michael Hardwick, "Michael Hardwick v. Michael Bowers: II. 'What Are You Doing in My Bedroom?,'" in Irons, *The Courage of Their Convictions; Bill Moyers: In Search of the Constitution*, episode 9, "For the People: Defending Constitutional Rights," directed by Wayne Ewing, hosted by Bill Moyers, aired June 11, 1987, on PBS, https://billmoyers .com/content/for-the-people/.

13. Dale Carpenter, *Flagrant Conduct: The Story of* Lawrence v. Texas—*How a Bedroom Arrest Decriminalized Gay Americans* (New York: W. W. Norton, 2012). As Peter Irons explains in his similarly engaging analysis of the three World War II Supreme Court cases upholding the internment of Japanese Americans, the U.S. government deliberately fed the justices false sets of facts. Peter Irons, *Justice at War: The Story of the Japanese-American Internment Cases* (Berkeley: University of California Press, 1983).

14. Take, for example, Justice Anthony M. Kennedy's opinion for the majority in *Obergefell v. Hodges*, 576 U.S. 644 (2015), and Justice Harry A. Blackmun's dissent in *DeShaney v. Winnebago County Department of Social Services*, 489 U.S. 189, 212–13 (1989) (Blackmun, J., dissenting).

15. For example, compared with the Court consisting of justices appointed by President Franklin Delano Roosevelt, the Rehnquist Court (under the leadership of Chief Justice William H. Rehnquist [1986–2005]) was staffed by justices relatively disinclined to write such opinions. Laura Krugman Ray, "Judicial Personality: Rhetoric and Emotion in Supreme Court Opinions," *Washington and Lee Law Review* 59, no. 1 (2002): 222. Ray attributes this, in part, to the increasing role played by law clerks in the opinion-writing process.

16. Beverly Blair Cook, "Justice Brennan and the Institutionalization of Dissent Assignment" (unpublished manuscript, 1995), 19n85. The footnote quoted from here only appeared in an unpublished manuscript. I am very grateful to Larry Baum for informing me about and sharing a copy of the document with me. The manuscript is an extended version of the following published article: Beverly Blair Cook, "Justice Brennan and the Institutionalization of Dissent Assignment," *Judicature* 79, no. 1 (July–August 1995). On the collegial and strategic constraints faced by the justices, see, generally, Walter F. Murphy, *Elements of Judicial Strategy* (Chicago: University of Chicago Press, 1964); Lee Epstein and Jack Knight, *The Choices Justices Make* (Washington, DC: CQ Press, 1998); John Brigham, *The Cult of the Court* (Philadelphia: Temple University Press, 1991).

17. Ernest Parrish, and Elsie Parrish, his wife v. West Coast Hotel Company, Findings of Fact and Conclusions of Law, November 9, 1935, at 1, Superior Court of the State of Washington in and for the County of Chelan, No. 12215.

18. Ernest Parrish et al. v. West Coast Hotel Company, 185 Wash. 581, 582 (1936).

19. 300 U.S. 379, 388 (1937).

20. Peter Irons, preface to *The Courage of Their Convictions*, xii.

21. John T. Noonan Jr., *Persons and Masks of the Law: Cardozo, Holmes, Jefferson, and Wythe as Makers of the Masks*, with a new preface (1976; repr., Berkeley: University of California Press, 2002), 6.

22. Noonan, *Persons and Masks of the Law*, 14.

23. Michael Kammen, *A Machine That Would Go of Itself: The Constitution in American Culture*, with a new introduction by the author (New York: Alfred A. Knopf, 1986; Abingdon, UK: Routledge, 2017).

24. Noonan, *Persons and Masks of the Law*, 4.

25. Noonan, *Persons and Masks of the Law*, 17 (italics added).

26. In *Legally Blonde*, Elle Woods, the movie's principal character, gives the following student address at the end of the film: "On our very first day at Harvard, a very wise professor quoted Aristotle: 'The law is reason free from passion.' Well, no offense to Aristotle, but in my three years at Harvard I have come to find that passion is a key ingredient to the study and practice of law— and of life. It is with passion, courage of conviction, and strong sense of self that we take our next steps into the world, remembering that first impressions are not always correct. You must always have faith in people. And most importantly, you must always have faith in yourself." *Legally Blonde*, directed by Robert Luketic (2001; MGM Home Video, 2004), DVD.

27. William J. Brennan Jr., "Reason, Passion, and 'The Progress of the Law,'" *Cardozo Law Review* 10, no. 3 (1988): 3, 9.

28. William E. Leuchtenburg, "The Case of the Wenatchee Chambermaid," chap. 6 in *The Supreme Court Reborn: The Constitutional Revolution in the Age of Roosevelt* (New York: Oxford University Press, 1995); Gerry L. Alexander, "*Parrish v. West Coast Hotel Company*: A Chelan County Chambermaid Makes History," *Columbia: The Magazine of Northwest History* 27, no. 1 (Spring 2013); Gerry L. Alexander, "*Parrish v. West Coast Hotel Co.*—Did This Washington Case Cause the Famous 'Switch in Time That Saved Nine'?," *Washington State Bar News* 64 (December 2010); L. Darlene Spargo, "Wenatchee's Quiet Warrior—Elsie Parrish," *Good Life*, April 2012; Margie Jones, "Elsie Parrish . . . A Woman History Forgot," *Okanogan County Heritage* (Winter 1990–1991); Kris Young and Mark Behler, "Cascadian Hotel Was Site of Historical Lawsuit," *Wenatchee Business Journal* 11, no. 7 (July 1997).

29. Helen J. Knowles, "'Omak's Minimum Pay Law Joan D'Arc': Telling the Local Story of *West Coast Hotel v. Parrish* (1937)," *Journal of Supreme Court History*, 37, no. 3 (November 2012); Helen J. Knowles, "The Cascadian: An 'Outstanding Small City Hotel,'" *The Confluence* 33, no. 2 (Summer 2017).

30. Unfortunately, some of the limited scholarly iterations of the facts of the case contain errors. For example, Elsie Parrish has been misidentified—see Charles C. Kerr, *The World of the World: From Frontier to Community, 1905–1980—A History of Growth and Development in North Central Washington*

(Wenatchee, WA: Wenatchee World, 1980), 92 (although quite clearly referring to the facts of Elsie's lawsuit, Kerr stated that it was a "Rosa Wilson" who
brought the case). Her age has been misstated—see Burt Solomon, *FDR v.
The Constitution: The Court-Packing Fight and the Triumph of Democracy* (New
York: Walker Books, 2009), 157 (Elsie was thirty-seven, not forty-six, as Solomon states, in 1937). Elsie worked as a chambermaid, not as a custodian, at
the Cascadian—for the custodian error, see G. Edward White, *The Constitution
and the New Deal* (Cambridge: Harvard University Press, 2000), 222. She did
not secure legal victories at both the trial court and Washington State Supreme
Court stages, as one scholar has claimed—see Julie Novkov, *Constituting Work-
ers, Protecting Women: Gender, Law, and Labor in the Progressive Era and New
Deal Years* (Ann Arbor: University of Michigan Press, 2004). The law upheld in
Parrish was enacted in 1913, not 1932, as Shanna Stevenson states—see Shanna
Stevenson, *Women's Votes, Women's Voices: The Campaign for Equal Rights in
Washington* (Tacoma: Washington State Historical Society, 2009), 75. The West
Coast Hotel Company did not "settle . . . in 1937" as Kerr states—Kerr, *The
World of the World*. There was no settlement (in the legal sense of the word),
because the company was not going to give Elsie any back pay until such time
that the U.S. Supreme Court ruled in her favor. And the hotel did not "munif-
icently offer . . . her $17 to drop the suit," as was reported in Jack Beatty, *Age
of Betrayal: The Triumph of Money in America, 1865–1900* (New York: Vintage,
2008), 181. We can lament these errors, because in one sense they are important, considering that "[i]f you don't know the facts, you can't really understand
the case and can't understand the law." Orin S. Kerr, "How to Read a Legal
Opinion: A Guide for New Law Students," *Green Bag 2d* 11 (Autumn 2007):
57. However, in another sense they are trivial; they are not excusable, but they
are also not egregious.

31. 300 U.S. at 388.

32. In his excellent constitutional law textbook Aaron Caplan provides
a far more substantive treatment of the story of *Parrish* than is usual in such
volumes. Nevertheless, he still manages to get the name of the hotel wrong,
stating that Elsie Parrish worked at the West Coast Hotel. Aaron Caplan, *An
Integrated Approach to Constitutional Law* (St. Paul, MN: Foundation Press,
2015), 284.

33. A Westlaw law reviews and journals search, performed July 25, 2018,
found 2,141 articles including the phrases "West Coast Hotel" and "Parrish" in
the same sentence. The search was performed like this, instead of just search-
ing for "West Coast Hotel Co. v. Parrish," to avoid the problems of identifying
some articles that referred to variations of that case title (such as omitting
"Co."). Only three of the articles contained the word "Cascadian": Ashley D.
Jyles, "The Newly Increased Minimum Wage: Congress's Way of Robbing Peter
to Pay Paul," *Southern University Law Review* 37 (Spring 2010): 366; Amanda
Rose Kapur, "A Faulty Federal Standard: A Call for a Federal Minimum Wage

That Is Actually 'Fair' Under the Fair Labor Standards Act," *University of Miami Business Law Review* 25 (Spring 2017): 140n4; William Quigley, "Full-Time Workers Should Not Be Poor: The Living Wage Movement," *Mississippi Law Journal* 70 (Spring 2001): 908.

34. "Omak's Minimum Pay Law Joan d'Arc Would Lecture," *Wenatchee Daily World*, April 6, 1937.

35. Quoted in Barbara Roberts, *Up the Capitol Steps: A Woman's March to the Governorship* (Corvallis: Oregon State University Press, 2011), 233.

36. Associated Press, "Chambermaid in Small Town is Flabbergasted," *Post-Register* (Idaho Falls, ID), November 16, 1936.

CHAPTER 1

1. Before she joined the Sisters of the Holy Names in Marylhurst in 1916, Sister Theresa went by her birth name, Caroline Gleason.

2. Sister Miriam Theresa, *Bulletin of the Women's Bureau, No. 90: Oregon Legislation for Women in Industry* (Washington, DC: Government Printing Office, 1931), 32.

3. Elsie likely gets her middle name from her aunt, Deliah Hannah Sallee (Emma's older sister).

4. "Killed by Thresher: E. H. Murray of Reno County Meets With Horrible Accident," *Wichita Eagle* (Wichita, KS), July 20, 1900.

5. "Killed by Thresher."

6. "Was in Swimming: Sudden Cramp Causes Boy Murray's Death," *Wichita Daily Beacon* (Wichita, KS), June 15, 1901.

7. *Plat Book of Reno County, Kansas. Compiled from County Records and Actual Surveys* (Minneapolis: Northwest Publishing, 1902), 71, accessed November 29, 2019, http://www.kansasmemory.org/item/209395/page/61.

8. Penalosa State Bank v. Murray, 86 Kan. 766 (1912).

9. Richard L. Forstall, ed., *Kansas Population of Counties By Decennial Census: 1909 to 1990* (Washington, DC: Population Division US Bureau of the Census, 1995), accessed November 29, 2019, http://www.census.gov/population/cencounts/ks190090.txt.

10. 1910 Census for Bell Township, Reno County, KS, Sheet 4B.

11. 1910 Census for Langdon Township, Reno County, KS, Sheet 5B.

12. 1910 Census for Coffee Creek, MT.

13. Elsie married when she was under the age of sixteen, and in Montana at that time she needed the written consent of her father. Since he was deceased, she instead needed the written consent of her mother. *The Revised Codes of Montana of 1907: Containing All Laws of a Permanent and General Nature in Force after the Adjournment of the Tenth Legislative Assembly*, vol. 1 (Helena: State Publishing Company, 1908), 1064–66.

14. Michael P. Malone, Richard B. Roeder, and William L. Lang, *Montana: A History of Two Centuries*, rev. ed. (Seattle: University of Washington Press, 1991), 237–38.

15. Malone, Roeder, and Lang, *Montana*, chap. 10.

16. It was a homestead they would call home until 1964. "Murray, Earl E.," *Great Falls Tribune* (Great Falls, MT), March 2, 1965.

17. He subsequently followed his sister Elsie to Washington State in 1942 and then to Southern California. "Murray, E. V. (Stub)," *Great Falls Tribune* (Great Falls, MT), February 26, 1964.

18. Malone, Roeder, and Lang, *Montana*, 232, 236.

19. Mabel Lux, "Honyockers of Harlem, Scissorsbills of Zurich," in *Cowboys and Cattlemen: A Roundup from Montana, The Magazine of Western History*, ed. Michael S. Kennedy (New York: Hastings House, 1964), 333–34.

20. Richard Hofstadter, *The Age of Reform: From Bryan to F.D.R.* (New York: Vintage Books, 1955), 54.

21. For useful discussions of some of the controversies, including labor practices, associated with the Great Northern Railway's acquisition of land in Montana, see Albro Martin, *James J. Hill and the Opening of the Northwest* (New York: Oxford University Press, 1976), especially chaps. 12 and 13; Claire Strom, *Profiting From the Plains: The Great Northern Railway and Corporate Development of the American West* (Seattle: University of Washington Press, 2003), especially chap. 6; Claire Margaret Strom, "Unattainable Edens: James J. Hill, the Great Northern Railway, and Changing Notions of Agricultural Expertise" (PhD diss., Iowa State University, 1998), 45–72, https://lib.dr .iastate.edu/cgi/viewcontent.cgi?article=12811&context=rtd; Lux, "Honyockers of Harlem, Scissorsbills of Zurich."

22. Debra Parrish Stewart, interview with the author, January 16, 2019.

23. Generally, see Malone, Roeder, and Lang, *Montana*, chaps. 10 and 11; Lux, "Honyockers of Harlem, Scissorsbills of Zurich."

24. For an excellent overview of the woman's experience living and farming the Kansas frontier, see Joanna L. Stratton, *Pioneer Women: Voices From the Kansas Frontier* (New York: Touchstone, 1981).

25. Susan Armitage, "Through Women's Eyes: A New View of the West," in *The Women's West*, edited by Susan Armitage and Elizabeth Jameson (Norman: University of Oklahoma Press, 1987), 9, 12.

26. Armitage, "Through Women's Eyes," 12.

27. Debra Parrish Stewart, interview.

28. Bill Murray, interview with the author, August 4, 2016.

29. Debra Parrish Stewart, interview.

30. "Coffee Creek Wins an Exciting Game," *Great Falls Tribune* (Great Falls, MT), June 22, 1915; "Coffee Creek Reds Split the Ravens," *Great Falls Tribune* (Great Falls, MT), June 29, 1915.

31. Lux, "Honyockers of Harlem, Scissorsbills of Zurich," 343.

32. Katherine Harris, "Homesteading in Northeastern Colorado, 1873–1920: Sex Roles and Women's Experience," in *The Women's West*, edited by Susan Armitage and Elizabeth Jameson (Norman: University of Oklahoma Press, 1987), 169.

33. Generally, see Malone, Roeder, and Lang, *Montana*, chaps. 10 and 11; Lux, "Honyockers of Harlem, Scissorsbills of Zurich"; Gayle C. Shirley, *More Than Petticoats: Remarkable Montana Women* (Helena, MT: Falcon Publishing, 1995).

34. Jim Sargent, *Too Poor to Move, But Always Rich: A Century on Montana Land* (self-pub., 2014), 5.

35. Malone, Roeder, and Lang, *Montana*, 253, 281. Also see Sargent, *Too Poor to Move, But Always Rich*, 19–20.

36. Glen's death certificate formally lists the cause of death as a "strangulated hernia left duodenal fossa." I am grateful to my colleague Allison Rank, my contributor to another book Kath Gelber, and my student Nicholas Schmitt, for their help with deciphering the handwriting on the certificate.

37. Malone, Roeder, and Lang, *Montana*, 292.

38. Elsie and Roy were still married in June 1930 when their daughter Vera got married. See Grant County, Washington Marriage Certificate Number 940, J. D. R. Hollingsworth and Vera E. Lee, June 14, 1930 (Roy and Elsie served as the marriage witnesses). In the 1933 Wenatchee city directory, Roy is listed as living on his own and working as a laborer. Neither he nor Elsie appears in the 1931–32 directory. *Polk's Wenatchee City and Chelan County (Washington) Directory, vol. xv (1933)* (R. L. Polk, Seattle, 1933), 122.

39. "Those Who Come and Go: Tales of Folks at the Hotels," *Oregonian* (Portland, OR), January 6, 1930.

40. Chris Rader and Mark Behler, *Images of America: Wenatchee* (Charleston, SC: Arcadia Publishing, 2012), 87; Bruce L. Foxworthy, *Making Do and Hanging On: Growing Up in Apple Country Through the Great Depression* (Bloomington, IN: AuthorHouse, 2008), 169.

41. Rader and Behler, *Wenatchee*, 31.

42. Dorothy O. Johansen, *Empire of the Columbia: A History of the Pacific Northwest*, 2nd ed. (New York: Harper & Row, 1967), 380; Chris Rader, "Wenatchee Is the Apple Capital of the World," *The Confluence* 23, no. 1 (Spring 2007): 4.

43. Johansen, *Empire of the Columbia*, 380; Rader, "Wenatchee is the Apple Capital," 4.

44. Letter from J. H. Auvil, President of the Wenatchee District Co-Operative Association to E. O. Holland, President of Washington State College, January 20, 1926, Box 82, Folder 2474, Office of the President: Ernest O. Holland Records, Manuscripts, Archives, and Special Collections, Washington State

University Libraries, Pullman, WA (hereafter MASC-WSU). This was not the first time the heavily agricultural state had been hit hard by a period of economic downturn. As Howard Allen observes in his biography of the Washington progressive politician Miles Poindexter: "The strength of Populism in Washington reflected serious economic difficulties in the state. In 1890 it was the sixth most heavily mortgaged farm state in the nation—26.8 percent of all farms in the state were mortgaged." Howard W. Allen, *Poindexter of Washington: A Study in Progressive Politics* (Carbondale: Southern Illinois University Press, 1981), 8.

45. Foxworthy, *Making Do and Hanging On*, 121 (the author is quoting his father); Robert E. Ficken, *Rufus Woods, the Columbia River, & the Building of Modern Washington* (Pullman: WSU Press, 1995), 102, 111–12; William E. Leuchtenburg, "The Case of the Chambermaid and the Nine Old Men," *American Heritage* 38, no. 1 (December 1986): 34 (quoting from a WPA guide to Washington State).

46. Richard C. Berner, *Seattle 1921–1940: From Boom to Bust* (Seattle: Charles Press, 1992), 302.

47. "Wenatchee Movement is Making Much Progress," *Washington State Labor News*, August 2, 1935.

48. Foxworthy, *Making Do and Hanging On*, 203–29.

49. John A. Jakle and Keith A. Sculle, *America's Main Street Hotels: Transiency and Community in the Early Auto Age* (Knoxville: University of Tennessee Press, 2009), 66.

50. Jakle and Sculle, *America's Main Street Hotels*, 6.

51. Gerry L. Alexander, "*Parrish v. West Coast Hotel Company*: A Chelan County Chambermaid Makes History," *Columbia: The Magazine of Northwest History* 27, no. 1 (Spring 2013): 2.

52. Jakle and Sculle, *America's Main Street Hotels*, 11.

53. "First 'Swell' Hotel a 'Flop,'" *Wenatchee Daily World* (Wenatchee, WA) (hereafter *World*), August 13, 1929.

54. Rader and Behler, *Wenatchee*, 59.

55. Rader and Behler, *Wenatchee*, 68.

56. "Ferguson Saw His First Hotel Here Just 31 Years Ago," *World*, August 13, 1929.

57. Hu Blonk, "Recollections of Wenatchee's Old Cascadian Hotel," *World*, January 15, 1987. By this time, the spectacle of flagpole climbing/sitting was well established. Bill Bryson, *One Summer: America, 1927* (New York: Doubleday, 2013), 142–3.

58. "Cascadian Pays First Quarter Dividends," *Hotel News of the West* 26, no. 52 (December 28, 1929): 20.

59. "Eleven Story Hotel Prospect Here," *World*, December 24, 1928; "$500,000 Hotel Deal is Consummated," *World*, January 26, 1929; "Hotel Site Ready for Excavators," *World*, February 23, 1929.

60. Quoted in "$500,000 Hotel Deal is Consummated."

61. "Ground Broken For $500,000 Hotel," *World*, February 27, 1929.

62. "'Cascadian' Name Chosen for New Hotel," *World*, April 27, 1929. Somewhat bizarrely, the May 1929 issue of *Hotel Monthly* announced, "The new hotel to be opened by Ray Clark in August will be known as the Clark Hotel, in honor of a Wenatchee pioneer [W. T. Clark], and also the hotel's new manager." "New & Remodeled Hotels," *Hotel Monthly* 37, no. 434 (May 1929): 90. There is no evidence that the two Clark men were related. While Ray Clark was of seminal importance to the Cascadian, it does not make sense that a new hotel's name would partly reflect the last name of its new manager, who was not a household name in Wenatchee in 1929. In February, the *World* reported, "For some time the matter of naming the hotel in honor of W. T. Clark, builder of the high line canal and known as 'the father of the Wenatchee valley,' has been talked up but now that it is planned to name the new junior high in honor of Clark it is believed some other name will be decided upon." "Hotel Site Ready for Excavators." In June 1929, *Hotel Monthly* offered this announcement: "Wash.–Wenatchee: Ray Clark's new hotel, announced as The Clark, will be opened as The Cascadian." "New & Remodeled Hotels," *Hotel Monthly* 37, no. 435 (June 1929): 98.

63. Jakle and Sculle, *America's Main Street Hotels*.

64. This was typical of the time period. As Jakle and Sculle observe: "Expanded self-interest among other businesspeople in the small town or city could turn to the hotel's benefit. This was especially true initially among the numerous local suppliers and tradesmen whom the hotel entrepreneurs employed to build the hotel and who, as standard practice, advertised in the local paper to wish the new business well. News articles routinely accompanied grand openings and named all the local businesses employed in the hotel's construction." Jakle and Sculle, *America's Main Street Hotels*, 56.

65. Also typical of this era, the pages of the newspaper were filled with short paragraphs containing "good luck" messages (often called "bouquets"), primarily from other hoteliers. Photos of the individuals who sent in the greetings sometimes accompanied these. See, for example, the photograph of Harry Gowman, of the Hotel Gowman in Seattle. "'Good Luck' is Messaged to Cascadian," *World*, August 13, 1929. Also see "Some Bouquets," *World*, August 13, 1929, listing some of the congratulatory telegrams received from other hotels, on either the opening Thursday night or Friday morning.

66. This chapter only discusses some of the most important highlights of the Cascadian. For a more complete study of the hotel's history and features, see Helen J. Knowles and L. Darlene Spargo, *Images of America: Cascadian Hotel* (Charleston, SC: Arcadia Publishing, 2020).

67. "And Now We'll Go into the Lobby of the Cascadian," *World*, August 13, 1929; "Cascadian Hotel in Wenatchee Wins Praises of Many Guests," *Hotel News of the West* 26, no. 33 (August 17, 1929): 5; "Complete Change of Air in Cascadian Every Minute," *World*, August 13, 1929.

68. Marsha E. Ackermann, *Cool Comfort: America's Romance with Air-Conditioning* (Washington, DC: Smithsonian Institution Press, 2002), 44, and generally chap. 3.

69. "The Cascadian, 100% Air Conditioned," *Hotel Monthly* 42, no. 498 (September 1934): 53. The magazine invited Clark to submit a letter describing the system.

70. "Complete Change of Air"; "The Cascadian, 100% Air Conditioned," 53, 54.

71. For groups who wished to hold a catered event at the Cascadian, a banquet space was connected to the coffee shop by a door at the rear.

72. "Brilliant Colors Feature Decorations in Hotel," *World*, August 13, 1929; "Cascadian's Coffee Shop is Model One," *World*, August 13, 1929; "And Now We'll Go into the Lobby"; Ben E. Bothun, "Plan 100-Room Addition to Cascadian," *World*, August 13, 1929.

73. Jakle and Sculle, *America's Main Street Hotels*, 131–32, 131.

74. "Bill Dal Bon Superior Chef Came Here From Portland," *World*, August 13, 1929. Kinsella resigned to take a position elsewhere three months after the Cascadian opened. "Kinsella Resigns at Cascadian Hotel," *Hotel News of the West* 26, no. 45 (November 9, 1929): 5.

75. "Popular Collegiennes—Superior Dining Service," *Okanogan Independent* (Okanogan, WA), September 23, 1933.

76. See the Cascadian Hotel menus in Box 5, Folder 67, Georgina Tucker papers, 1920–1997, and Box 371, Folder 371–8, Westin Hotels & Resorts, J. William Keithan archives, 1905–2004 (hereinafter Keithan archives), both MASC-WSU. The Pearce-Young-Angel fruit company ran newspaper advertisements across the country that featured the "Famous Apple Pie Recipe" of the Cascadian Hotel. See, for example, *Asheville Citizen-Times* (Asheville, NC), January 21, 1943; *Times and Democrat* (Orangeburg, SC), October 15, 1942.

77. "New & Remodeled Hotels," *Hotel Monthly* 37, no. 432 (March 1929): 88. The following month the magazine gave more details: "Wash.–Wenatchee: Hyman Harris of San Francisco, promoter, has organized a hotel of 133 rooms at First and Wenatchee ave. Plans are by C. Frank Mahon of Seattle." "New & Remodeled Hotels," *Hotel Monthly* 37, no. 433 (April 1929): 92.

78. "A Hotel That Boosts Local Product," *Hotel Monthly* 42, no. 490 (January 1934): 58.

79. "Clark Started in as Page," *World*, August 13, 1929; "About Hotel Men," *Hotel Monthly* 34, no. 397 (April 1926): 95; "About Hotel Men," *Hotel Monthly* 30, no. 532 (July 1922): 88.

80. Ray W. Clark, "The Get Together Spirit a Winner [Letter to the Editor]," *The Hotel World* 93 (October 29, 1921): 38.

81. "Clark Started in as Page." See Common stock certificate, West Coast Hotel Co., issued to Ray W. Clark, August 1930, Box 66, Stock Certificate

Book 66–9, Keithan archives, MASC-WSU. 1930, Census Place: Wenatchee, Chelan, Washington, Roll 2485, Page 19A, Enumeration District 0046, Image 215.0, FHL microfilm 2342219. Interestingly, the census indicates that in 1940 Ray and Kathryn were living in Portland and that he was working as a hotel manager and she as a chambermaid. We have to assume that in this position, Kathryn was being paid in accordance with Oregon's minimum wage law for women and that, consequently, she was directly benefiting from the decision in *Parrish*. 1940, Census Place: Portland, Multnomah, Oregon, Roll T627_3385, Page 2A, Enumeration District 37–51.

82. Ernest Parrish, and Elsie Parrish, his wife v. West Coast Hotel Company, Superior Court of the State of Washington in and for the County of Chelan, No. 12215—Complaint, June 10, 1935, pp. 1–2; Amended Complaint, July 12, 1935, pp. 1–4, 6; Answer to Amended Complaint, September 9, 1935, pp. 2–3.

83. Edward E. Carlson, *Recollections of a Lucky Fellow* (Seattle: self-pub., 1989), 52; "W. E. Anderson is Toastmaster Head," *World*, October 4, 1935 (describing how Anderson has just taken over the presidency from Abel).

84. "Washington Minimum Wage Law Upheld," *Hotel News of the West* 34, no. 7 (April 1, 1937): 15. The other members of the committee (besides Gowman and Clark) were John O'Rourke (from Bellingham), D. J. Rhind (Wenatchee), Carl Morekm (Aberdeen), William Bonham (Longview), Robert Owen (Spokane), Frank Hickey (Tacoma), and S. W. Thurston, Troy Himmelamn [*sic*], Charles Hunlock, and A. J. Barash (all from Seattle). "Executive Committee Holds First Meeting," *Hotel News of the West* 33, no. 21 (November 2, 1936): 7.

85. "Executive Committee Holds First Meeting," 7.

86. There is only one reference to the "Washington State Hotel Association" in any judicial (federal or state) opinion, court brief, or law review/journal article. That reference came in the majority opinion in Gottstein et al. v. Lister, 88 Wash. 462, 466 (1915). In this case, the appellants were seeking to prevent enforcement of a state law mandating prohibition, a law that the voters in Washington had recently succeeded in passing through the initiative process. The reference to the WSHA was nothing more than an observation that some of the appellants were members of that organization.

87. "Washington Hotel Men Resume Meetings," *Hotel News of the West* 32, no. 18b (October 1, 1935): 5.

88. "Editorial," *Hotel News of the West* 32, no. 20 (November 1, 1935): 8 (italics added).

89. See "Minimum Wage Case Lost," *Hotel News of the West* 33, no. 8 (April 15, 1936): 6; "Editorial," *Hotel News of the West* 33, no. 8 (April 15, 1936): 6; "Washington State Hotel Association: Proposes Reductions in Wine Percentages," *Hotel News of the West* 33, no. 12 (June 15, 1936): 5.

90. 298 U.S. 587 (1936).

91. "Supreme Court Invalidates N.Y. Minimum Wage Law," *Hotel News of the West* 33, no. 11 (June 1, 1936): 19; "Minimum Wage Case to Be Appealed," *Hotel News of the West* 33, no. 11 (June 1, 1936): 19.

92. He continued to serve in that capacity until his death in 1947. Associated Press, "James A. Wood," *New York Times*, February 12, 1947.

93. "Perseverance Won Them Ownership of a Daily Paper," *Editor and Publisher* 51, no. 2 (April 17, 1919): 26.

94. James A. Wood, "Speaking For the *Times*: Everywhere Discussed," *Seattle Times*, April 11, 1937.

95. Quoted in Adela Rogers St. Johns, *Some Are Born Great: Lively and Controversial Tales of Some of the Extraordinary Women of Our Time* (Garden City, NY: Doubleday, 1974), 187.

96. National Consumers' League Meeting Minutes, December 1932, quoted in Robert P. Ingalls, "New York and the Minimum-Wage Movement, 1933–1937," *Labor History* 15, no. 2 (Spring 1974): 179.

97. C. B. Conner, "The Minimum Wage Case," in *From the Blue Ridge to the Cascade Range: Recollections of Boyhood Days in the Mountains of Virginia— and Work as a Lawyer in Oklahoma and in the Shadows of the Cascade Range* (unpublished manuscript, n.d.), 173. I am extraordinarily grateful to C. B.'s granddaughter, Christine (Chris) Conner, for providing me with exclusive access to and permission to use material from this memoir. As C. B. observed at the beginning of the *Parrish* chapter, in the memoir he included a section about the case because he was "asked by several friends to put down in writing the facts connected" with it. Conner, "The Minimum Wage Case," 163. As we will see in chapter 6, the absence of a contract would not stand as a legal obstacle in the path of those Washington women who, post-*Parrish*, made back pay claims under the terms of the 1913 law.

98. 261 U.S. 525 (1923).

99. Conner, "The Minimum Wage Case," 174.

100. Ernest Parrish, and Elsie Parrish, his wife vs. West Coast Hotel Company, No. 12215, Complaint by C. B. Conner and Elsie Parrish, June 10, 1935, pp. 1–2; Amended Complaint, July 12, 1935, pp. 1–4, 6; Answer to Amended Complaint, September 9, 1935, pp. 2–3, Superior Court of the State of Washington in and for the County of Chelan.

101. Parrish, No. 12215, Amended-Complaint, 1–4.

102. Debra Parrish Stewart, interview. According to the census, in 1930 Ernie was a "retail meat salesman" living in Portland, and we know that Wenatchee was the midway point on his regular route between Portland, Oregon, and Colville, Washington. Therefore, one might reasonably conclude that he stayed in Wenatchee (possibly at the Cascadian) and met Elsie there. This is what I noted in my 2012 article. Helen J. Knowles, "'Omak's Minimum Pay Law Joan D'Arc': Telling the Local Story of *West Coast Hotel v. Parrish* (1937)," *Journal of Supreme Court History* 37, no. 3 (November 2012): 301n2.

However, I have since discovered that Ernie was residing in Wenatchee in 1931/1932. He appeared in the Wenatchee city directory for the first time that year, listed as a vulcanizer employed by S. Russell Marlowe. *Polk's Wenatchee City and Chelan County (Washington) Directory, vol. xiv (1931–1932)* (Seattle: R. L. Polk, 1932), 194. The marriage license indicates that in July 1934 Ernie was employed as an orchard worker.

103. Debra Parrish Stewart, interview.

104. Pacific Finance Corporation of California v. Ernest Parrish and Jane Doe Parrish, Superior Court of the State of Washington in and for the County of Chelan, No. 12454; Letter from Ernest Parrish to Washington State Attorney General G. W. Hamilton, April 2, 1936, in 69-11-642: Attorney General's Office, Central Files—General Correspondence, Box 22, Oa-Pe, 1909–1940, Folder: Pa 1929–1940 (hereafter Parrish to Hamilton), Washington State Archives, Central Regional Branch.

105. Pacific Finance Corporation of California v. Parrish, Summons, December 18, 1935; Complaint, December 18, 1935.

106. Pacific Finance Corporation of California v. Parrish, Motion, February 28, 1936; Answer and Cross-Complaint, February 28, 1936.

107. Parrish to Hamilton.

108. Parrish to Hamilton.

109. *Polk's Wenatchee City and Chelan County (Washington) Directory, vol. xvi (1936)* (Seattle: R. L. Polk, 1936), 175.

110. "Sawmill Workers Fight Omak Concern," *Washington State Labor News* (Seattle), June 26, 1936; "Strike Settlement Ends Long Picketing at Biles-Coleman," *Omak Chronicle*, August 2, 1938. More generally, see John E. Lewis, *Biles-Coleman Lumber Company's Reservation Narrow Gauge: The Last Northwest/Washington State Narrow Gauge Logging Railroad, 1928–1948* (self-pub., 1980).

111. "Omak's Minimum Pay Law Joan d'Arc Would Lecture," *World*, April 6, 1937.

112. For an example of a November article accompanied by the bed-making photograph, see "Tests Minimum Wage Law," *Reno Gazette-Journal* (Reno, NV), November 17, 1936. For an example of a November article accompanied by the headshot, see "Women in the News: Tests Wage Law," *Miami Daily News-Record* (Miami, OK), November 24, 1936.

113. Associated Press, "Chambermaid in Small Town is Flabbergasted," *Post-Register* (Idaho Falls, ID), November 16, 1936.

114. "Omak's Minimum Pay Law Joan d'Arc Would Lecture."

CHAPTER 2

1. Irving Dilliard, "A Supreme Court Majority? The Court and Minimum-Wage Legislation," *Harper's Magazine*, November 1936, p. 600.

2. Suzanne Lebsock, "Women and American Politics, 1880–1920," in *Women, Politics, and Change*, edited by Louise A. Tilly and Patricia Gurin (New York: Russell Sage Foundation, 1992), 49.

3. Vivien Hart, *Bound by Our Constitution: Women, Workers, and the Minimum Wage* (Princeton, NJ: Princeton University Press, 1994), 6.

4. Hart, *Bound by Our Constitution*, x (italics added). Also see Theda Skocpol, *Protecting Soldiers and Mothers: The Political Origins of Social Policy in the United States* (Cambridge, MA: Belknap Press of Harvard University Press, 1992); Martha May, "Bread Before Roses: American Workingmen, Labor Unions and the Family Wage," in *Women, Work and Protest: A Century of US Women's Labor History*, ed. Ruth Milkman (Boston: Routledge & Kegan Paul, 1985).

5. This is why slavery is the fundamental antonym of freedom.

6. Civil Rights Act of 1866, 14 Stat. 27–30 (italics added to "contracts" language).

7. U.S. Const., amend. XIV, §1 (italics added).

8. For an excellent discussion of the Civil Rights Act of 1866, see George A. Rutherglen, *Civil Rights in the Shadow of Slavery: The Constitution, Common Law, and the Civil Rights Act of 1866* (New York: Oxford University Press, 2012).

9. Munn v. Illinois, 94 U.S. 113, 130–31 (1876).

10. 94 U.S. at 114, quoting from Article XIII: Warehouses, Section 1, of the 1870 Illinois State Constitution.

11. 94 U.S. at 117, quoting from Section 15 of "An Act to regulate public warehouses and the warehousing and inspection of grain, and to give effect to art. 13 of the Constitution of this State," enacted by Illinois in 1871.

12. The Fifth Amendment's due process clause is limited, in its application, to actions of the federal government and reads, "No person shall . . . be deprived of life, liberty, or property, without due process of law." U.S. Const. amend. V.

13. Roe v. Wade, 410 U.S. 113 (1973).

14. Lawrence v. Texas, 539 U.S. 558 (2003).

15. I offer my profound thanks to Barry Cushman for explaining how substantive due process was thought of before the middle of the twentieth century. Much of the remainder of this paragraph draws heavily from his teachings on the subject during the Institute for Constitutional History "*Lochner* Era" seminar that he led at Stanford University in July 2017.

16. For an excellent and detailed treatment of this, see Nathan S. Chapman and Michael W. McConnell, "Due Process as Separation of Powers," *Yale Law Journal* 121, no. 7 (May 2012).

17. 94 U.S. at 134 (italics added).

18. John Locke, *Second Treatise of Government*, ed. C. B. Macpherson (Indianapolis: Hackett Publishing, 1980); Thomas Hobbes, *Leviathan*, ed.

C. B. Macpherson (New York: Penguin, 1968). For informative discussions of the influence of social contract thinkers on the American founding, see Jason Frank, *Constituent Moments: Enacting the People in Postrevolutionary America* (Durham, NC: Duke University Press, 2010); Walter F. Murphy, *Constitutional Democracy: Creating and Maintaining a Just Political Order* (Baltimore: Johns Hopkins University Press, 2006); Bernard Bailyn, *The Ideological Origins of the American Revolution*, rev. ed. (Cambridge, MA: Belknap Press, 1992); Gordon S. Wood, *The Creation of the American Republic 1776–1787* (Chapel Hill: University of North Carolina Press, 1998); Gordon S. Wood, *The Radicalism of the American Revolution* (New York: A. A. Knopf, 1991).

19. Mark A. Graber, *A New Introduction to American Constitutionalism* (New York: Oxford University Press, 2013), 26.

20. 94 U.S. at 124.

21. 94 U.S. at 124.

22. 94 U.S. at 124, 125.

23. 94 U.S. at 126 (quoting Lord Chief Justice Hale).

24. 94 U.S. at 126 (italics added).

25. 94 U.S. at 131.

26. 94 U.S. at 131–2.

27. 198 U.S. 45 (1905).

28. 198 U.S. at 53.

29. 198 U.S. at 56.

30. 198 U.S. at 54.

31. 169 U.S. 366, 391–2 (1898).

32. 198 U.S. at 59.

33. 198 U.S. at 57 (italics added).

34. 198 U.S. at 56.

35. Ten years later, the importance of the rules established in *Munn* and *Lochner* became clearer in *Coppage v. Kansas*, 236 U.S. 1 (1915). In *Coppage*, a six-justice majority struck down provisions of a 1903 Kansas law that banned so-called "yellow-dog" contracts, contracts that made non-labor-union membership a condition of employment. Under such laws, employers could either refuse to hire someone or could discharge an employee because of his or her membership in a labor union. As Justice Mahlon Pitney wrote, "Included in the right of personal liberty and the right of private property—partaking of the nature of each—is the right to make contracts for the acquisition of property. Chief among such contracts is that of personal employment, by which labor and other services are exchanged for money or other forms of property." Applying the test laid out in *Lochner*, he continued to say that "[i]f this right be struck down or arbitrarily interfered with, there is a substantial impairment of liberty in the long established constitutional sense." For the Court in *Coppage*, this was not even a close case—"[T]here is *no object or purpose, expressed or implied*, that is claimed to have reference to health, safety, morals, or public

welfare *beyond the supposed desirability of leveling inequalities of fortune."* 236 U.S. at 14, 18 (italics added).

36. Conventional, late twentieth, and early twenty-first-century scholarship about *Lochner* has depicted it as the number one Supreme Court bogeyman. However, this morbid infatuation with a jurisprudential enfant terrible is misplaced. Over the course of the first four decades of the twentieth century, the U.S. Supreme Court decided somewhere between two hundred and three hundred cases involving due process of law. Describing these decades as the "*Lochner* era" suggests that (a) the overwhelming percentage of those due process cases involved "liberty of contract" claims, and that (b) those claims were (again overwhelmingly) resolved in favor of the individual's freedom to enter into a contract to work for as long as they wished and for as little money as they wished (and the employer's equivalent freedom to demand long hours and low wages from his/her employees). In fact, as Michael J. Phillips explains:

> [O]nly *fifteen* Supreme Court substantive due process cases striking down government action during the years 1897 to 1937 proceeded on the theory that the challenged law limited contractual liberty. Furthermore, five of these decisions did not contain words "freedom of contract," "liberty of contract," or the like; instead, they merely followed earlier freedom-of-contract cases. By contrast, a relatively informal search unearthed over forty cases in which the Court refused freedom-of-contract challenges to government regulation during the years 1902 to 1932 inclusive. Rather than being central to *Lochner*-era substantive due process, freedom of contract was but one application of a much more general doctrine. (Michael J. Phillips, *The* Lochner *Court, Myth and Reality: Substantive Due Process From the 1890s to the 1930s* [Westport, CT: Praeger, 2000], 58 [also see discussion, in general, in chapters 1 and 2])

Not to mention the fact that in *Lochner* the vote was very close; and although unsubstantiated, there is some thought that Justice John Marshall Harlan, one of the dissenters from the decision, originally prepared a draft majority opinion. Paul Kens, *Judicial Power and Reform Politics: The Anatomy of* Lochner v. New York (Lawrence: University Press of Kansas, 1990), 117, 205n14. Indeed, few commentators paid *Lochner* much attention when it was decided, and legislatures across the country did not generally consider it an impediment to the passage of protective legislation. As Sean Beienburg shows, "Consistent with an interpretation regarding *Lochner* as either a clear outlier or silently overruled, similar protective legislation appeared up and down the legislative journals and statute books of the states." Sean Beienburg, "Progressivism and States' Rights: Constitutional Dialogue Between the States and Federal Courts on Minimum Wages and Liberty of Contract," *American Political Thought* 8 (Winter 2019): 28. *Lochner* had its share of very vocal contemporary critics. For example, beginning with an August 1910 speech to the Colorado legislature, former president Theodore Roosevelt made a concerted effort to turn the decision into "a legal and public icon" by accusing the *Lochner* justices of "ignor[ing] the 'welfare of the general public.'" Victoria F. Nourse, "A Tale of Two *Lochners*: The Untold History of Substantive Due Process and the Idea of Fundamental Rights," *California Law Review* 97 (2009): 779, 780. However, for the most part *Lochner* was "stillborn until its negative canonization by progressive law professors and the political actors who decided to rally against" it many decades later. Beienburg, "Progressivism and States' Rights," 30. To say that there is a voluminous literature discussing the controversies of *Lochner* and its legacy would be a gross understatement. For the purposes of explaining the relationship between that decision, minimum wage laws, and *Parrish*, I am only scratching the surface of that literature's main arguments. For more in-depth studies, see, for example, Howard Gillman, *The Constitution Besieged: The Rise and Demise of Lochner Era Police Powers Jurisprudence* (Durham, NC: Duke University Press, 1993); David E. Bernstein, *Rehabilitating* Lochner: *Defending Individual Rights Against Progressive Reform* (Chicago: University of Chicago Press, 2011); David E. Bernstein, "*Lochner* Era Revisionism, Revised: *Lochner* and the Origins of Fundamental Rights Constitutionalism," *Georgetown Law Journal* 92, no. 1 (2003); Howard Gillman, "De-Lochnerizing *Lochner*," *Boston University Law Review* 85 (2005); Phillips, *The* Lochner *Court, Myth and Reality*; Barry Cushman, "Some Varieties and Vicissitudes of Lochnerism," *Boston University Law Review* 85 (2005).

37. Alice Kessler-Harris, *Out to Work: A History of Wage-Earning Women in the United States* (New York: Oxford University Press, 2003), 180.

38. Such laws met with varying fates in state courts. The California law was struck down, but others in Ohio and Washington were sustained. Kessler-Harris, *Out to Work*, 185.

39. Kessler-Harris, *Out to Work*, 185.

40. This includes generating some important and very consequential court decisions. For example, in 1924 the U.S. Supreme Court upheld a New York law that prohibited women from working at night in restaurants in "large cities." The Court distinguished the law from the minimum wage statute that it struck down the previous year in *Adkins v. Children's Hospital*, 261 U.S. 525 (1923), reasoning that the night work ban was a reasonable exercise of the state police power because it protected the health and welfare of female employees, *Radice v. New York*, 264 U.S. 292 (1924). The National Consumers' League viewed this as a "reaffirmation . . . of the power of *the State to forbid contracts* under which women of any age are to work long hours, or during work periods which experience shows to be harmful." Landon R. Y. Storrs, *Civilizing Capitalism: The National Consumers' League, Women's Activism, and Labor Standards in the New Deal Era* (Chapel Hill: University of North Carolina Press, 2000), 50 (italics in original).

41. Kessler-Harris, *Out to Work*, 180.

42. Elizabeth Brandeis, "Labor Legislation," in *History of Labor in the United States, 1896–1932: Volume III, Working Conditions*, ed. John R. Commons (New York: Macmillan, 1935), 457n1 (for the list of states); also see 457–58 (the quote is on 457).

43. 208 U.S. 412 (1908).

44. Kessler-Harris, *Out to Work*, 187.

45. In terms of official state governmental recognition of Labor Day, Oregon led the way in 1887, becoming the first state to pass a law stipulating that the first Monday in September would be a public holiday (it was therefore unsurprising that Governor George Chamberlain attended and spoke at the 1905 gathering). Elaine Zahnd Johnson, "Protective Legislation and Women's Work: Oregon's Ten-Hour Law and the *Muller v. Oregon Case*, 1900–1913" (PhD diss., University of Oregon, 1982), 237. National observance of Labor Day would be written into the federal statute books in 1894; however, the federal government was very much behind the curve, because by that time thirty of the forty-four states (68 percent) had made the day a public holiday.

46. Quoted in 208 U.S. at 416. Violation of the law constituted a criminal misdemeanor. Significantly, although the bill that became the 1903 law was titled "An act to regulate and limit the hours of employment of females in any mechanical or mercantile establishment, laundry, hotel, or restaurant," the bill could not have passed unless in Section 1 stores (which employed a large number of women) were excluded from its coverage. "In 1907 the law was amended to include mercantile establishments, but a vicious exception in their favor permitted them to employ women not to exceed 12 hours in any one day for one week immediately preceding Christmas Day." Sister Miriam Theresa, *Bulletin of the Women's Bureau, No. 90: Oregon Legislation for Women in Industry* (Washington, DC: Government Printing Office, 1931), 17.

47. Quoted in Ronald K. L. Collins and Jennifer Friesen, "Looking Back on *Muller v. Oregon*," *American Bar Association Journal* 69, no. 3 (March 1983): 294.

48. Theresa, *Bulletin of the Women's Bureau*, 7–8; Johnson, "Protective Legislation and Women's Work," 235.

49. Johnson, "Protective Legislation and Women's Work," 237–41.

50. 208 U.S. at 418.

51. 208 U.S. at 421.

52. 208 U.S. at 420.

53. Johnson, "Protective Legislation and Women's Work," 228. By the time Oregon passed its maximum working hours for women law in 1903, state courts had already upheld similar laws across the country—in Massachusetts: *Commonwealth v. Hamilton Manufacturing Company*, 120 Mass. 383 (1876); Pennsylvania: *Commonwealth v. Beatty*, 15 Pa. Super. 5 (1900); Nebraska: *Wenham v. State*, 65 Neb. 394 (1902); and Washington: *State v.*

Buchanan, 29 Wash. 602 (1902). Additionally, by 1905 at least seventeen other states had such laws in place. Collins and Friesen, "Looking Back on *Muller v. Oregon,*" 295.

54. 208 U.S. at 422 (italics added).

55. 169 U.S. at 391–92. Indeed, in *Holden,* Justice Brown observed, albeit in passing: "In other States, laws have been enacted limiting the hours during which women and children shall be employed in factories; and while their constitutionality, at least as applied to women, has been doubted in some of the States, they have been generally upheld." 169 U.S. at 395.

56. 208 U.S. at 421.

57. 208 U.S. at 421.

58. For an excellent study of how these attitudes affected various aspects of society in 1908, see Jim Rasenberger, *America, 1908: The Dawn of Flight, the Race to the Pole, the Invention of the Model T, and the Making of a Modern Nation* (New York: Scribner, 2007).

59. 83 U.S. 36 (1873); 83 U.S. 130 (1873); Nancy S. Erickson, "*Muller v. Oregon* Reconsidered: The Origins of a Sex-Based Doctrine of Liberty of Contract," *Labor History* 30, no. 2 (1989): 232.

60. The passage of the law, and subsequent creation of the Crescent City Live-Stock Landing and Slaughter-House Company, was an effort to try and clean up this business that caused immense health and safety problems for New Orleans. See Ronald M. Labbe and Jonathan Lurie, *The Slaughterhouse Cases: Regulation, Reconstruction, and the Fourteenth Amendment* (Lawrence: University Press of Kansas, 2003).

61. Erickson, "*Muller v. Oregon* Reconsidered," 232.

62. 83 U.S. at 140, 141 (Bradley, J., joined by Swayne and Field, JJ., concurring).

63. 83 U.S. at 141.

64. Erickson, "*Muller v. Oregon* Reconsidered," 232.

65. The fact that this question remained unanswered also affected the state legislative fate of efforts to enact laws stating *maximum working hours for men.* For example, in 1911 such a bill passed the Oregon state Senate (albeit very narrowly) but resoundingly failed in the House because of concerns about its constitutionality. A revised version of the law was passed during the next session of the legislature. Beienburg, "Progressivism and States' Rights," 29. And in *Bunting v. Oregon,* 243 U.S. 426 (1917), the Supreme Court declined to strike that law down.

66. 261 U.S. at 525.

67. Quoted in Joseph F. Tripp, "Toward an Efficient and Moral Society: Washington State Minimum-Wage Law, 1913–1925," *Pacific Northwest Quarterly* 67, no. 3 (July 1976): 109.

68. Quoted in Dorothy W. Douglas, "American Minimum Wage Laws at Work," *American Economic Review* 9 (December 1919): 703–4.

69. Douglas, "American Minimum Wage Laws," 705–7. Also see Brandeis, "Labor Legislation," 502. By 1917, in Massachusetts minimum wages had only been set for "four industries—retail stores, brushes, laundries, and women's clothing." William Graebner, "Federalism in the Progressive Era: A Structural Interpretation of Reform," *Journal of American History* 64, no. 2 (September 1977): 339. Unsurprisingly, only one state—Nebraska (in 1913)—followed the Massachusetts legislative model when enacting a minimum wage law for women. That law, however, never went into effect because (as the state reported) there were never any minimum wage violation complaints. Douglas, "American Minimum Wage Laws at Work," 710n20.

70. Governor William Spry of Utah signed the nation's third state law providing minimum wages for women on March 18, 1913. The state swiftly sought to ensure compliance with the law; by July it had begun to prosecute employers for failing to pay their workers the mandated minimum wage. Florence Kelley, "The Present Status of Minimum Wage Legislation," Speech delivered at the National Conference of Charities and Correction, Seattle, July 1913, 4, in Box 1, Folder 24, National Consumers League Records (hereafter NCLR) #5235, Kheel Center for Labor-Management Documentation and Archives, Cornell University Library (hereafter Kheel Center).

71. This is Suzanne Lebsock's accurate description of what "social progressivism" sought to address. Lebsock, "Women and American Politics, 1880–1920," 46.

72. For a general overview of the relevant laws passed in New Zealand and Australia, see Mary Katharine Reely, "Introduction," in *Selected Articles on Minimum Wage*, ed. Mary Katharine Reely (White Plains, NY: H. W. Wilson, 1917), 1–2. Also see Paul S. Collier, *Minimum Wage Legislation in Australasia* (Albany, NY: J. B. Lyon, 1915) (this is a reprint of a document that originally appeared as Appendix VIII of the Fourth Report of the New York State Factory Investigating Commission); and Francis G. Castles, *The Working Class and Welfare: Reflections on the Political Development of the Welfare State in Australia and New Zealand, 1890–1980* (Wellington, NZ: Allen & Unwin, 1985). The six industries covered by the Victorian Wage Boards were "furniture-making, baking, boot-making and three branches of the clothing trades." Jenny Lee, "A Redivision of Labour: Victoria's Wages Boards in Action, 1896–1903," *Historical Studies* 22, no. 88 (April 1987): 352.

73. Lee, "A Redivision of Labour," 352.

74. Hart, *Bound by Our Constitution*, chaps. 2 and 3.

75. Louis D. Brandeis, "The Constitution and the Minimum Wage (1915)," in *The Curse of Bigness: Miscellaneous Papers of Louis D. Brandeis*, ed. Osmond K. Fraenkel (New York: Viking Press, 1934), 53; *Report on Condition of Woman and Child Wage-Earners in the United States*, 19 vols. (Washington, DC: Government Printing Office, 1910–1913).

76. Richard Hofstadter, *The Age of Reform: From Bryan to F.D.R.* (New York: Vintage Books, 1955), 133.

77. For an excellent overview of the social sciences during this time period, see Dorothy Ross, *The Origins of American Social Science* (New York: Cambridge University Press, 1991).

78. Quoted in Sar A. Levitan and Richard S. Belous, *More Than Subsistence: Minimum Wages for the Working Poor* (Baltimore: Johns Hopkins University Press, 1979), 52.

79. Allison M. Martens, "Working Women or Women Workers? The Women's Trade Union League and the Transformation of the American Constitutional Order," *Studies in American Political Development* 23 (October 2009); Judith A. Baer, *The Chains of Protection: The Judicial Response to Women's Labor Legislation* (Westport, CT: Greenwood Press, 1978), 19–20.

80. Generally, see May, "Bread Before Roses." Even though at the beginning of the twentieth century women typically played a very minimal role in organized labor, some women's trade unions did exist. Notably, on March 31, 1900, the Seattle Waitresses' Union, Local 240, was the first waitresses' union in the country to be given a charter by the American Federation of Labor (AFL). It began with fifty members in 1900, but by January 1902 that number had quadrupled. The union played important roles in ensuring the passage of Washington's eight-hour workday for women law in 1911, and passage of Senator Piper's wages bill in 1913. Carole L. Davison, "Seattle's 'Restaurant Maids': An Historic Context Document for Waitresses' Union, Local 240 1900–1940" (master's thesis, University of Washington, 1998), 2, 62, 68, 75–8. Also see John C. Putnam, *Class and Gender Politics in Progressive-Era Seattle* (Reno: University of Nevada Press, 2008), chap. 3. The indomitable Alice Lord was the "kingpin" leader of Local 240, and for many years she lobbied constantly for improvements in the working conditions of women in Washington, especially waitresses. Mary Lee Spence, "Waitresses in the Trans-Mississippi West: 'Pretty Waiter Girls,' Harvey Girls, and Union Maids," in *The Women's West*, edited by Susan Armitage and Elizabeth Jameson (Norman: University of Oklahoma Press, 1987), 229 (quotation), and more generally 229–31. "To draw attention to the woes of waitressing," she "walked from Seattle to Olympia in 1900 to testify before the state legislature. 'You give even your horses one day's rest in seven,' she later told the Legislators." Her hard work paid off in 1911 with the passage of the "Waitresses' Bill" setting the eight-hour workday for Washington women. David J. Jepsen and David J. Norberg, *Contested Boundaries: A New Pacific Northwest History* (Hoboken, NJ: Wiley Blackwell, 2017), 204. The example of the Women's Trade Union League is also an instructive reminder that we should not overlook the role that women's unions played. See Martens, "Working Women or Women Workers?"; Colette A. Hyman, "Labor Organizing and Female Institution-Building: The

Chicago Women's Trade Union League, 1904–24," in Milkman, *Women, Work and Protest*. One of the main reasons the Chicago WTUL survived was that it got its message out by using existing social networks and organizational strategies specifically aimed at women.

81. David P. Thelen, "Social Tensions and the Origins of Progressivism," *Journal of American History* 56, no. 2 (September 1969): 341.

82. Dorothy O. Johansen, *Empire of the Columbia: A History of the Pacific Northwest*, 2nd ed. (New York: Harper & Row, 1967), 449.

83. Thelen, "Social Tensions," 338.

84. Robert H. Wiebe, *The Search for Order, 1877–1920* (New York: Hill and Wang, 1967), 45–46 (quotations), but generally the entire book is instructive on this subject.

85. Hofstadter, *The Age of Reform*, 131, 174.

86. William D. P. Bliss, ed., *The Encyclopedia of Social Reform* (New York: Funk & Wagnalls, 1897), 1298.

87. Vivien Hart, "Minimum-Wage Policy and Constitutional Inequality: The Paradox of the Fair Labor Standards Act of 1938," *Journal of Policy History* 1, no. 3 (1989): 321–22. More generally, also see Hart, *Bound by Our Constitution*.

88. Quoted in Skocpol, *Protecting Soldiers and Mothers*, 312.

89. As this book demonstrates, Florence Kelley was absolutely right to observe, in a 1911 speech, that the principal constitutional impediment was not the "eighteenth-century constitution" but rather the "eighteenth-century constitution interpreted by nineteenth-century judges." Quoted in Josephine Goldmark, *Impatient Crusader: Florence Kelley's Life Story* (Urbana: University of Illinois Press, 1953), 135–36.

90. U.S. Const. preamble (italics added).

91. J. Laurence Laughlin, "Monopoly of Labor," *Atlantic Monthly* (October 1913): 451, 452.

92. Goldmark, *Impatient Crusader*, 206.

93. Storrs, *Civilizing Capitalism*, 14–15.

94. Allis Rosenberg Wolfe, "Women, Consumerism, and the National Consumers' League in the Progressive Era, 1900–1923," *Labor History* 16, no. 3 (1975): 378–9 (the quotation is on 379); Kessler-Harris, *Out to Work*, 109–11.

95. Storrs, *Civilizing Capitalism*, 23.

96. Florence Kelley, "Aims and Principles of the Consumers' League," *American Journal of Sociology* 5, no. 3 (November 1899): 299, 298–99.

97. Storrs, *Civilizing Capitalism*, 24.

98. Goldmark, *Impatient Crusader*, 2, 207 (quoting Lillian Wald). For almost the first four decades of its existence the NCL made a conscious effort "to increase its visibility by having famous men as its presidents." However,

they were "[r]arely more than figureheads." The real power was held and exercised by the general secretary. Storrs, *Civilizing Capitalism*, 25.

99. Goldmark, *Impatient Crusader*, 69 (quoting from the tribute given by Paul Kellogg, editor of *Survey* magazine, at Kelley's memorial service in 1932); Norma Smith, *Jeannette Rankin: America's Conscience* (Helena: Montana Historical Society Press, 2002), 146.

100. Felix Frankfurter, foreword to Goldmark, *Impatient Crusader*, v.

101. Storrs, *Civilizing Capitalism*, 14–15.

102. Skocpol, *Protecting Soldiers and Mothers*, 394 (quotation) and more generally 382–95.

103. Smith, *Jeannette Rankin*, 92.

104. Skocpol, *Protecting Soldiers and Mothers*, 376. Also see John J. Dinan, *The American State Constitutional Tradition* (Lawrence: University Press of Kansas, 2006); Emily Zackin, *Looking for Rights in All the Wrong Places: Why State Constitutions Contain America's Positive Rights* (Princeton, NJ: Princeton University Press, 2013).

105. Quoted in Hart, "Minimum-Wage Policy and Constitutional Inequality," 322.

106. On the NCL's influence on the creation and enactment of state minimum wage laws, see Wolfe, "Women, Consumerism, and the National Consumers' League," 386–88.

107. Generally, see Jepsen and Norberg, *Contested Boundaries*, chap. 5; Johansen, *Empire of the Columbia*, 313–17.

108. Jepsen and Norberg, *Contested Boundaries*, 202.

109. Graebner, "Federalism in the Progressive Era," 342 (quotations); Skocpol, *Protecting Soldiers and Mothers*, 413; Tripp, "Toward an Efficient and Moral Society," 99, 101. The minimum wage law that Washington enacted in 1913 did not cover the agricultural or canning industries that accounted for large percentages of workers (male and female). Tripp, "Toward an Efficient and Moral Society," 101.

110. Douglas, "American Minimum Wage Laws at Work," 713.

111. Robert D. Johnston, *The Radical Middle Class: Populist Democracy and the Question of Capitalism in Progressive Era Portland, Oregon* (Princeton, NJ: Princeton University Press, 2003), 123.

112. For a concise overview of these reforms, see Johnston, *The Radical Middle Class*, 123–4. Although, it should be noted that several of the individuals who played important roles in achieving these progressive reforms in Oregon did not achieve their goals without significant criticisms of corruption and betrayals of trust. See, for example, Thomas C. McClintock, "Seth Lewelling, William S. U'ren and the Birth of the Oregon Progressive Movement," *Oregon Historical Quarterly* 68, no. 3 (September 1967); Johnston, *The Radical Middle Class*, chaps. 8 and 9.

113. Jepsen and Norberg, *Contested Boundaries*, 204.

114. *Power for Supremacy: The Pacific Northwest* (Chicago: Chicago Burlington & Quincy Railroad, Great Northern Railway, Northern Pacific Railway, 1923), 15.

115. Quoted in Timothy Michael Dolan, *"Some Seed Fell on Good Ground"—The Life of Edwin V. O'Hara* (Washington, DC: Catholic University of America Press, 1992), 35.

116. Quoted in Dolan, *"Some Seed Fell on Good Ground,"* 40. Information about the ceremony can be found in *Commencement Exercises, University of Notre Dame*, June 11, 1917; University of Notre Dame, "Honorary Degree Recipients, 1844–2016." This information was kindly provided to me by Dwight King, Associate Director for Patron Services, University of Notre Dame Law School Library, email message to author, December 4, 2017.

117. One of the four dissenting legislators subsequently switched his vote. Janice Dilg, "'For Working Women in Oregon': Caroline Gleason/Sister Miriam Theresa and Oregon's Minimum Wage Law," *Oregon Historical Quarterly* 110, no. 1 (Spring 2009): 114–15. At the time, the Oregon House consisted of 5 Democrats, 48 Republicans, and 7 Progressives. The Senate was made up of 2 Democrats and 28 Republicans. Michael J. Dubin, *Party Affiliations in the State Legislatures: A Year by Year Summary, 1796–2006* (Jefferson, NC: McFarland & Company, 2007), 154.

118. Quoted in Gordon Newell, *Rogues, Buffoons & Statesmen* (Seattle: Hangman Press, 1975), 256. The leadership that Lister showed was typical of the role played by governors who sought enactment of socially progressive laws, especially in the West and the South. They "not only had to maintain their coalitions, but they had to do so while directing legislative and administrative programs of unprecedented complexity." Wiebe, *The Search for Order*, 179.

119. Richard C. Berner, *Seattle 1900–1920: From Boomtown, Urban Turbulence, to Restoration* (Seattle: Charles Press, 1991), 126.

120. Mildred Tanner Andrews, *Washington Women as Path Breakers* (Dubuque, IA: Kendall/Hunt, 1989), 17. The Washington State House was comprised of 19 Democrats, 49 Republicans, and 29 Progressives. In the Senate there were 9 Democrats, 27 Republicans, and 6 Progressives. Dubin, *Party Affiliations*, 196.

121. Dubin, *Party Affiliations*, 196; Phil Dougherty, "Croake, Nena Jolidon (1865–1934)," History Link, last modified November 24, 2010, http://www.historylink.org/File/9638.

122. Quoted in "She Fights for Mothers: Woman Enters Politics in Washington to Gain Pensions for Them," *New York Times*, October 11, 1912.

123. Dougherty, "Croake, Nena Jolidon."

124. Editorial, *Seattle Union Record*, January 18, 1913.

125. "Minimum Wage for Women," *Seattle Union Record*, February 1, 1913.

126. The seventeen minimum wage laws were enacted in fifteen states, Puerto Rico, and the District of Columbia.

127. Brandeis, "Labor Legislation," 504.

128. Quoted in "Minimum Pay for Women Given Hearty Support," *Seattle Union Record*, February 15, 1913.

129. Brandeis, "Labor Legislation," 504.

130. "Minimum Pay for Women Given Hearty Support."

131. The newspaper also reprinted Alice Lord's editorial that appeared in one of the city's other newspapers:

> Senator Collins' fight against this bill called forth the following article from Miss Alice Lord, business agent for the Waitresses' Alliance in Seattle, which was published in one of the Seattle papers Monday morning: "To the Editor: In your issue of Saturday morning I noticed that Senator Collins voted against the minimum wage bill for women, his reason for such being that if said bill passed it would prevent manufacturers from coming to our state. Allow me to answer, when fighting for the eight-hour law for women about ten years ago the Chamber of Commerce and Commercial Club, in which Senator Collins is interested, came to Olympia and stated that if the law passed it would eliminate a project they had on to bring manufacturers to our state. The law was defeated. After eight years the bill again came up, and the same Chamber of Commerce and Commercial Club told the same old story about the law preventing the manufacturers from coming to our state. Mr. Editor, those same people had eight years to bring the manufacturers to our state, and they did not under the old law, but they wanted a way to defeat the bill and they fell back on a woman and that woman a working woman, to cover up their inactivity for eight years. Now comes the old story. If the minimum wage law passes it will do the same thing—keep our manufacturers from our state. We citizens of the state of Washington are advancing. We do not want sweat shops nor tenement districts. Now is the time to make laws to prevent such conditions, not wait until said conditions exist and then try to bring about reform. Give a living wage to our working women and there will be no need for charity institutions. If we have to sacrifice the honor of our women for the sake of bringing manufacturers to our state, then do without them. I wonder how much it costs Senator Collins per day to live. That is a different story. Let every citizen, every mother, every working woman in our state use every effort to pass the minimum wage law for women. ALICE M. LORD." ("Minimum Wage Law Passes the Senate," *Seattle Union Record*, March 1, 1913)

132. Journal of the House, State of Washington (1913), 1062–63; Journal of the Senate, State of Washington (1913), 612–13.

133. *Washington State Laws of 1913*, chap. 174, p. 602. As stated above, this was the preamble language in the NCL's model minimum wage law.

134. The only workers exempt (through issuance of a special license by the commission) from the law's coverage were those deemed by the commission to be "physically defective or crippled by age or otherwise" or "an apprentice in such class of employment or occupation as usually requires to be learned by apprentices." *Washington State Laws of 1913*, chap. 174, p. 606. In 1921, administration of the law changed hands from the IWC to the Division of Industrial Relations. Letter from Attorney General G. W. Hamilton to E. Pat Kelly, Director, Department of Labor and Industries, August 26, 1937, 2, AR-20110505–6: Department of Labor & Industries—Employment Standards, AG Correspondence/Policy & Procedures/Rules (1911–1993), Folder: Historical Attorney General Opinions 1911–1974, Washington State Archives, Central Regional Branch (hereafter WASA).

135. *Washington State Laws of 1913*, chap. 174, p. 603 (italics added). Of the nonunion member provision, Florence Kelley said its "obvious aim . . . is that the commission should be disinterested." Kelley, "The Present Status." Apparently unaware of this provision, or unaware of the qualifications of one of his appointees, initially Governor Lister appointed Mrs. N. J. Laumer to the commission, but she had to be replaced because she was "an honorary member of the International Typographical Union." Caroline J. Gleason, *Report of the Industrial Welfare Commission of the State of Washington on the Wages, Conditions of Work and Cost and Standards of Living of Women Wage-Earners in Washington* (Olympia: Frank M. Lamborn, 1914), 5.

136. *Washington State Laws of 1913*, chap. 174, p. 604.

137. *Washington State Laws of 1913*, chap. 174, pp. 605, 607 (italics added).

138. Gleason, *Report of the Industrial Welfare Commission*, 5.

139. Gleason, *Report of the Industrial Welfare Commission*, 6–15.

140. Gleason, *Report of the Industrial Welfare Commission*, 17.

141. Gleason, *Report of the Industrial Welfare Commission*, 9–10.

142. Gleason, *Report of the Industrial Welfare Commission*, 10.

143. Frances K. Headlee, "The Minimum Wage in Washington," *Survey*, January 15, 1916, p. 449.

144. Headlee, "The Minimum Wage in Washington," 449.

145. She submitted similar inquiries to the equivalent authorities in every state that was home to a minimum wage law for women.

146. Letter from Gersha V. Haney to Alma Lutz, April 7, 1933. Washington was not the only state to relay this sort of information to Lutz. See, for example, the letter from Margaret Sinkula to Alma Lutz, March 23, 1932 (reporting on the situation in North Dakota). Both letters are in the Alma Lutz Papers, 1927–1946, A-34, folder 50, Schlesinger Library, Radcliffe Institute, Harvard University, Cambridge, Mass. After the U.S. Supreme Court decision in *Muller*, Curt Muller replaced the female workforce at his Grand Laundry in Portland with more amenable Chinese workers. Jennifer Friesen

and Ronald K. L. Collins, "Looking Back on *Muller v. Oregon* [Part 2]," *American Bar Association Journal* 69, no. 4 (April 1983): 472.

147. Haney to Lutz, April 7, 1933.

148. Letter from Wilbur A. Toner to Sherman W. Child, July 7, 1937 (italics added), in 69-11-642: Attorney General's Office, Central Files—General Correspondence, Box 5, Can-Cok, 1909–1940, Folder: Ce-Ch, 1931–1940, WASA.

149. Jeff Shesol, *Supreme Power: Franklin Roosevelt vs. The Supreme Court* (New York: W. W. Norton, 2011), 222.

CHAPTER 3

1. Stettler v. O'Hara, 243 U.S. 629 (1917).

2. 198 U.S. 45 (1905); 208 U.S. 412 (1908). Technically, there were four cases, but for reasons that will become clear, the Court's decisions in *Stettler* and *Simpson v. O'Hara* are treated and discussed as though they were one case.

3. Glenn W. Miller, *American Labor and the Government* (New York: Prentice-Hall, 1948), 228; 261 U.S. 525 (1923).

4. 298 U.S. 587 (1936).

5. 300 U.S. 379 (1937).

6. Henry's handiwork appears to have languished, untouched, in the files of the NWTUL. Wood's poem describes the conditions faced by a downtrodden seamstress in Victorian England. The original illustrated version, as it appeared in *Punch* magazine, can be seen at the website of the British Library: "Thomas Hood's Poem About Working Conditions, 'The Song of the Shirt,'" British Library, accessed April 20, 2019, https://www.bl.uk/collection-items/thomas-hoods-poem-about-working-conditions-the-song-of-the-shirt.

7. Alice Henry, "Song of the Minimum Wage (With Apologies to Thomas Hood)," manuscript dated May 14, 1921, Microfilm Roll 16, National Women's Trade Union League of America Records, Manuscript Division, Library of Congress, Washington, DC.

8. Elizabeth Brandeis, "Labor Legislation," in *History of Labor in the United States, 1896–1932: Volume III, Working Conditions*, ed. John R. Commons (New York: Macmillan, 1935), 503.

9. Generally, see Brandeis, "Labor Legislation," 504; Dorothy W. Douglas, "American Minimum Wage Laws at Work," *American Economic Review* 9 (December 1919): 708–9n17, 11–13.

10. Will Englund, *March 1917: On the Brink of War and Revolution* (New York: W. W. Norton, 2017).

11. 243 U.S. 332 (1917).

12. 243 U.S. at 346.

13. U.S. Const. art. I, §8.

14. 243 U.S. at 346. The 1819 decision cited is McCulloch v. Maryland, 17 U.S. 316, 421–23 (1819) (cited at 243 U.S. at 346n4).

15. 94 U.S. 113, 131, 126 (1876).

16. 243 U.S. at 347.

17. Quoted in 243 U.S. at 344.

18. 243 U.S. at 388 (McReynolds, J., dissenting).

19. 243 U.S. at 347–8.

20. 243 U.S. at 345–6 (italics added).

21. Barry Cushman, *Rethinking the New Deal Court: The Structure of a Constitutional Revolution* (New York: Oxford University Press, 1998), 63.

22. Janice Dilg, "'For Working Women in Oregon': Caroline Gleason/ Sister Miriam Theresa and Oregon's Minimum Wage Law," *Oregon Historical Quarterly* 110, no. 1 (Spring 2009): 121.

23. Section 2 of the General Laws of Oregon, 1913, c. 102, p. 169, quoted in 243 U.S. 426, 438 (1917).

24. 243 U.S. at 438. Thompson was still in the Oregon Senate when he first argued the case in April 1916. However, by the time of the reargument in January 1917, he was in private practice, having lost reelection in November 1916 by one vote. "Baldwin Wins by One Vote," *Evening Herald* (Klamath Falls, OR), November 13, 1916.

25. 243 U.S. at 436.

26. 243 U.S. at 437.

27. Quoted in 243 U.S. at 438 (italics added).

28. Quoted in 198 U.S. at 65.

29. As we will see below, it is an absence that confounded the dissenting chief justice William Howard Taft six years later when the Court relied upon *Lochner* (which he was certain had been overturned *sub silentio* in *Bunting*) to strike down the minimum wage law in *Adkins*.

30. Barry Cushman, "Some Varieties and Vicissitudes of Lochnerism," *Boston University Law Review* 85 (2005): 937. As Cushman explains, further evidence in support of this conclusion comes from the fact that it was a "pattern [that] was replicated in McKenna's performance in cases concerning the constitutionality of workers' compensation statutes." Cushman, "Some Varieties," 937 (quotation), and discussion on 937–41.

31. State v. Bunting, 139 P. 731 (1914).

32. Stettler v. O'Hara, 139 P. 743 (1914).

33. Jennifer Friesen and Ronald K. L. Collins, "Looking Back on *Muller v. Oregon* [Part 2]," *American Bar Association Journal* 69, no. 4 (April 1983): 473.

34. Thomas Reed Powell, "The Oregon Minimum-Wage Cases," *Political Science Quarterly* 32, no. 2 (June 1917): 297.

35. Philippa Strum, *Brandeis: Beyond Progressivism* (Lawrence: University Press of Kansas, 1993), 59. Hence the title of Roscoe Pound's seminal article

bitterly criticizing such approaches. See Roscoe Pound, "Mechanical Jurisprudence," *Columbia Law Review* 8, no. 8 (December 1908).

36. Felix Frankfurter, "Mr. Justice Brandeis and the Constitution (1932)," in *Felix Frankfurter on the Supreme Court: Extrajudicial Essays on the Court and the Constitution*, ed. Philip B. Kurland (Cambridge, MA: Belknap Press of Harvard University Press, 1970), 251.

37. Felix Frankfurter, "Hours of Labor and Realism in Constitutional Law (1916)," in Kurland, *Felix Frankfurter on the Supreme Court*, 11.

38. Friesen and Collins, "Looking Back on *Muller v. Oregon* [Part 2]," 472.

39. Brandeis took the oath of office to be a Supreme Court justice on June 1, 1916. Although he participated in *Bunting* at the lower court level, his Supreme Court nomination was already pending when the case was first argued before the justices on April 18, 1916. Consequently, he did not participate in that argument or in the reargument of the case on January 19, 1917. Unlike in *Stettler*, the justices in *Bunting* did not deadlock because of McKenna's decision to join four of his colleagues for a 5–3 decision.

40. Quoted in Timothy Michael Dolan, *"Some Seed Fell on Good Ground"—The Life of Edwin V. O'Hara* (Washington, DC: Catholic University of America Press, 1992), 38.

41. Dolan, *"Some Seed Fell on Good Ground,"* 38 (quotation), and 32–33.

42. Dilg, "For Working Women in Oregon," 120.

43. Dilg, "For Working Women in Oregon," 96. Here it is worth keeping in mind that five cents an hour equated to approximately seven cents an hour in 1935 when Elsie Parrish initiated her legislation after losing the job for which she had been receiving twenty-five cents per hour.

44. Quoted in Gladys Turley, "Industry and Sister Miriam," *Sunday Journal Magazine*, May 6, 1951, p. 2-M.

45. Quoted in Turley, "Industry and Sister Miriam," 2-M; Dolan, *"Some Seed Fell on Good Ground,"* 33–34.

46. Dolan, *"Some Seed Fell on Good Ground,"* 34.

47. Quoted in Strum, *Brandeis*, 62 (italics added).

48. Brad Snyder, *The House of Truth: A Washington Political Salon and the Foundations of American Liberalism* (New York: Oxford University Press, 2017), 115. Writing in *The Survey* magazine, Mary Chamberlain offered the following description of the oral argument:

> The scene in the semi-circular courtroom has a touch of irony, almost of the dramatic;—the quiet, stately room so far from the whir of machines and the rush of Christmas shopping; the formality of the proceedings; the inscrutable faces of the eight judges; the attempt of Rome G. Brown of Minneapolis, and ex-Senator Fulton of Oregon, counsel for the plaintiffs, to prove the collapse of constitutional government by the payment of sixty-four cents more a week to a factory girl in Portland; and finally the

earnest appeal of Louis D. Brandeis and Attorney General Crawford of Oregon, representing the defendants, to judge not hypothetical bogies, but the very real terrors of starvation, thin clothing and temptation. (Mary Chamberlain, "The Paper-Box Factory and the Constitution," *The Survey* 33, no. 13 [December 26, 1914], 330)

49. Howard Gillman, *The Constitution Besieged: The Rise and Demise of Lochner Era Police Powers Jurisprudence* (Durham, NC: Duke University Press, 1993), 259n20.

50. Snyder, *The House of Truth*, 115, 158.

51. 243 U.S. at 629.

52. Frankfurter, "The Orbit of Judicial Power (1938)," in Kurland, *Felix Frankfurter on the Supreme Court*, 355.

53. Norma Smith, *Jeannette Rankin: America's Conscience* (Helena: Montana Historical Society Press, 2002), 148.

54. Arkansas: State v. Crowe, 130 Ark. 272 (1917); Minnesota: Williams v. Evans, 139 Minn. 32 (1917); Washington: Larsen v. Rice, 100 Wash. 642 (1918). See Ora L. Marshino and Lawrence J. O'Malley, "Wage and Hour Legislation in the Courts," *George Washington Law Review* 5 (1937): 872.

55. The law was only challenged as it applied to women.

56. Willie's salary had been:

$35 per month and two meals a day. She alleges that the work was light and healthful, the hours short, with surroundings clean and moral, and that she was anxious to continue it for the compensation she was receiving, and that she did not earn more. Her services were satisfactory to the Hotel Company, and it would have been glad to retain her but was obliged to dispense with her services by reason of the order of the board and on account of the penalties prescribed by the act. . . . She . . . could not secure any other position at which she could make a living, with as good physical and moral surroundings, and earn as good wages. (261 U.S. at 542–43)

57. Peter Irons, *A People's History of the Supreme Court: The Men and Women Whose Cases and Decisions Have Shaped Our Constitution* (New York: Penguin, 1999), 263.

58. 261 U.S. at 553.

59. 208 U.S. at 422 (italics added).

60. Quoted in Ronald K. L. Collins and Jennifer Friesen, "Looking Back on *Muller v. Oregon*," *American Bar Association Journal* 69, no. 3 (March 1983): 298.

61. 208 U.S. at 421.

62. Quoted in Alice Kessler-Harris, *A Woman's Wage: Historical Meanings & Social Consequences* (Lexington: University Press of Kentucky, 1990), 33.

63. 261 U.S. at 557. Minimum wage advocates, such as Father John A. Ryan, were often far less sympathetic to the plight of employers. "If the enforced payment of universal living wages would drive any employer or any industry out of existence the contingency should be welcomed, for it is more desirable on every account that the masses of underpaid workers should have the means of living like human beings than that certain *soulless* trades should survive, or certain inefficient employers continue to function as captains of industry." John A. Ryan, "Minimum-Wage Legislation," in *Selected Articles on Minimum Wage; Debaters' Handbook Series*, ed. Mary Katharine Reely (White Plains, NY: H. W. Wilson, 1917), 40–41.

64. 261 U.S. at 546.

65. 208 U.S. at 418.

66. 261 U.S. at 546.

67. 261 U.S. at 554. Sutherland identified four categories of cases in which the Court had previously upheld abridgments of contractual liberty, and then proceeded to explain why the D.C. law did not fall into any of these categories. They were (1) businesses affected with a public interest; (2) contracts for public work; (3) regulations affecting "the character, methods and time for payment of wages"; and (4) working hours. 261 U.S. at 546–55. As Robert C. Post explains, the "affected with a public interest" doctrine "exemplifies the revival of Lochnerism during the Taft Court. . . . Until 1923 there had been an erratic but steady expansion of the kinds of property deemed 'affected with a public interest.'" However, "between 1923 and 1929, the Court both sharply limited the category . . . and held that the state could regulate prices only with respect to such property." Robert C. Post, "Defending the Lifeworld: Substantive Due Process in the Taft Court Era," *Boston University Law Review* 78 (1998): 1505–6.

68. 261 U.S. at 553.

69. Elaine Zahnd Johnson, "Protective Legislation and Women's Work: Oregon's Ten-Hour Law and the *Muller v. Oregon Case*, 1900–1913" (PhD diss., University of Oregon, 1982), 398.

70. 261 U.S. at 554.

71. Quoted in 261 U.S. at 540 and 541–42.

72. 261 U.S. at 555.

73. 261 U.S. at 556.

74. 261 U.S. at 558.

75. Letter from Henry W. Anderson to George Sutherland, April 10, 1923. Also see the letter from Judge Charles H. Robb (Court of Appeals of the District of Columbia) to George Sutherland, April 12, 1923 (describing the logic in Sutherland's *Adkins* opinion as "*irresistible*"), and the letter from Andrew Furuseth (Sailors' Union of the Pacific) to George Sutherland, May 5, 1923. All letters are in Box 4, Folder 1, George Sutherland Papers, Manuscript Division, Library of Congress (hereafter LC), Washington, DC.

76. Irons, *A People's History of the Supreme Court*, 264.

77. 261 U.S. at 562 (Taft, CJ., joined by Sanford, J., dissenting).

78. 261 U.S. at 567 (Taft, CJ., joined by Sanford, J., dissenting).

79. 261 U.S. at 564 (Taft, CJ., joined by Sanford, J., dissenting).

80. 261 U.S. at 564 (Taft, CJ., joined by Sanford, J., dissenting).

81. 261 U.S. at 567 (Taft, CJ., joined by Sanford, J., dissenting).

82. 261 U.S. at 569–70 (Holmes, J., dissenting).

83. 261 U.S. at 568 (Holmes, J., dissenting) (italics added).

84. 261 U.S. at 562 (Taft, CJ., joined by Sanford, J., dissenting).

85. 261 U.S. at 568 (Holmes, J., dissenting).

86. 198 U.S. at 75 (Holmes, J., dissenting).

87. 261 U.S. at 567 (Holmes, J., dissenting).

88. "National Consumers' League. Report of Conference on Minimum Wage Decision of the Supreme Court, April 20, 1923. Cover with cartoon by Rollin Kirby, which the NCL reproduced courtesy of the New York World," *American Women: A Library of Congress Guide for the Study of Women's History and Culture in the United States*, accessed July 1, 2017, https://memory.loc.gov/ammem/awhhtml/awmss5/d10.html.

89. Letter from Florence Kelley to Mrs. John Blair, May 1, 1923, quoted in Vivien Hart, *Bound by Our Constitution: Women, Workers, and the Minimum Wage* (Princeton, NJ: Princeton University Press, 1994), 108.

90. Sean Beienburg, "Progressivism and States' Rights: Constitutional Dialogue Between the States and Federal Courts on Minimum Wages and Liberty of Contract," *American Political Thought* 8 (Winter 2019): 33n26; Alice S. Cheyney, "The Course of Minimum Wage Legislation in the United States," *International Labour Review* 38, no. 1 (July 1938): 28.

91. "Minimum Wage," NCL document, March 10, 1936, in Box 2, Folder 51, National Consumers League Records (hereafter NCLR) #5235, Kheel Center for Labor-Management Documentation and Archives, Cornell University Library (hereafter Kheel Center).

92. Murphy v. Sardell, 269 U.S. 530 (1925); Donham v. West Nelson Manufacturing Company, 273 U.S. 657 (1927).

93. Brandeis, "Labor Legislation," 504–5n14. As Sean Beienburg explains, "While California's Attorney General had feared . . . [the Court] would strike his state's law, California businesses . . . banded together in defense of the state's law immediately after the decision [in *Murphy v. Sardell*]. . . . Even massive companies seemed to refrain from challenging the law: the then-conservative *Los Angeles Times* lamented the 'open secret' behind General Motors' plan to withdraw a plant from California in 1933 rather than contend with Sacramento's supposedly voluntary minimum wage law." Beienburg, "Progressivism and States' Rights," 37. It should be noted that the provision of the Massachusetts law that required newspapers to publicize those who failed to comply with the law was struck down. Brandeis, "Labor Legislation," 505n14.

94. Cheyney, "The Course of Minimum Wage Legislation," 28; Sar A. Levitan and Richard S. Belous, *More Than Subsistence: Minimum Wages for the Working Poor* (Baltimore: Johns Hopkins University Press, 1979), 34; Beienburg, "Progressivism and States' Rights," 33.

95. Kessler-Harris, *A Woman's Wage*, 139n14.

96. Beienburg, "Progressivism and States' Rights," 35–36.

97. Douglas, "American Minimum Wage Laws at Work," 712.

98. Beienburg, "Progressivism and States' Rights," 35; Larsen v. Rice, 100 Wash. 642 (1918); Sparks v. Moritz, 141 Wash. 417, 421 (1926).

99. Brandeis, "Labor Legislation," 505.

100. Brandeis, "Labor Legislation," 506 (italics added).

101. "Congress Profiles: 72nd Congress (1931–1933)," History, Art & Archives, United States House of Representatives, accessed April 23, 2019, https://history.house.gov/Congressional-Overview/Profiles/72nd/; "Congress Profiles: 73rd Congress (1933–1935)," History, Art & Archives, United States House of Representatives, accessed April 23, 2019, https://history.house.gov /Congressional-Overview/Profiles/73rd/; "Party Division," United States Senate, accessed April 23, 2019, https://www.senate.gov/history/partydiv.htm. In the 1934 midterm elections the Democratic Party increased its control of Congress, picking up nine seats in the House and ten in the Senate. "Congress Profiles: 74th Congress (1935–1937)," History, Art & Archives, United States House of Representatives, accessed April 23, 2019, https://history.house.gov /Congressional-Overview/Profiles/74th/; "Party Division."

102. The pre-*Parrish* "Hughes Court" (1930–1936/7) struck down federal laws with a far greater frequency than any of its predecessors (its propensity to strike down local and state laws, by contrast, was far less remarkable). Thomas M. Keck, *The Most Activist Supreme Court in History: The Road to Modern Judicial Conservatism* (Chicago: University of Chicago Press, 2004), 40–41. Here it is important to note, however, that the conservative challenge to the New Deal agenda did not materialize in the form of a consistent and concerted set of hostile judicial rulings until 1935. Between 1935 and 1936, federal judges issued approximately 1,600 injunctions to prevent the enforcement of federal laws. Arthur M. Schlesinger Jr., *The Age of Roosevelt: The Politics of Upheaval* (Boston: Houghton Mifflin, 1960), 447. "At no time in the country's history did the judiciary play a more permeating part in the affairs of the country. At no time in the country's history was there a more voluminous outpouring of judicial rulings in restraint of acts of Congress than the body of decisions in which the lower courts, in varying degree, invalidated every measure deemed appropriate by Congress for grappling with the great depression." Felix Frankfurter and Adrian S. Fisher, "The Business of the Supreme Court at the October Terms, 1935 and 1936," *Harvard Law Review* 51, no. 4 (February 1938): 611.

103. "Inaugural Address, March 4, 1933," American Presidency Project, accessed April 23, 2019, https://www.presidency.ucsb.edu/node/208712.

104. Alfred E. Smith, "Democratic Leadership at the Crossroads," *New Outlook*, March 1933, p. 9.

105. Smith, "Democratic Leadership," 11. This was by no means the first time Smith had advocated for a law providing minimum wages for women workers. In fact, from 1915 onward this was a policy that he "strongly championed . . . year after year." The judgment in *Adkins* made this a problematic policy pursuit from after April 1923, but even though he "grudgingly accepted" that decision, and "guardedly declared it imprudent to explicitly defy the court," he nevertheless felt it was important to have "some legislation on this subject which will pass the test of judicial scrutiny." His subsequent legislative proposals were cautious, but when 1933 rolled around and brought with it a new Democratic president, Smith could afford to "come out for provocative legislation more directly challenging *Adkins*." Beienburg, "Progressivism and States' Rights," 40–41. For a list of the newspaper articles detailing Smith's minimum wage proposals over the years, see Beienburg, "Progressivism and States' Rights," 40n60.

106. The telegram was sent to the following governors: A. Harry Moore, New Jersey; Gifford Pinchot, Pennsylvania; Wilbur L. Cross, Connecticut; Theodore F. Greene, Rhode Island; Henry Horner, Illinois; Paul V. McNutt, Indiana; George White, Ohio; William A. Comstock, Michigan; Albert C. Ritchie, Maryland; C. Douglas Buck, Delaware; J. C. B. Eringhaus, North Carolina; B. M. Miller, Alabama; and John G. Winant, New Hampshire. "Telegram Urging States to Adopt Minimum Wage Legislation, April 12, 1933," American Presidency Project, accessed April 23, 2019, https://www.presidency.ucsb .edu/node/208063. The text of the telegram appeared on the front page of that morning's *New York Times*. See "President Seeks Minimum Pay Acts," *New York Times*, April 13, 1933. To clarify, "approved by Governor Lehman" did not mean the governor had actually signed the minimum wage bill into law. That would not happen until April 29. "Two Bills in Lehman's Hands," *New York Times*, April 13, 1933. For an instructive discussion of the passage of the 1933 law, and the ways in which Governor Lehman "proved a reluctant ally of the minimum-wage movement," see Robert P. Ingalls, "New York and the Minimum-Wage Movement, 1933–1937," *Labor History* 15, no. 2 (1974): 183 (quotation), and more generally 183–87.

107. Editorial, *Call* (Beloit, KS), February 17, 1933.

108. Brandeis, "Labor Legislation," 503n7; Landon R. Y. Storrs, *Civilizing Capitalism: The National Consumers' League, Women's Activism, and Labor Standards in the New Deal Era* (Chapel Hill: University of North Carolina Press, 2000), 94.

109. In 1933 the only state to enact a minimum wage law for women that deviated from the NCL model was Utah. Brandeis, "Labor Legislation," 503n7.

110. §551(7), Chapter 584 of the New York Laws of 1933, quoted in 298 U.S. at 605 (italics added).

111. "The Minimum Wage Bill," *Times-Union* (Albany, NY), March 1, 1933.

112. Letter from Marjorie McFarland to the Organizations in Labor Subcommittee, March 13, 1936, in Box 2, Folder 40, NCLR.

113. Paul Hutchinson, "The Final Verdict on Recovery: Will the Supreme Court Support Mr. Roosevelt?," *Forum and Century* 90, no. 3 (September 1933): 142.

114. Hutchinson, "Final Verdict," 143, 146.

115. "Laundry Women First Affected by Wage Ruling," *Knickerbocker-Press* (Albany, NY), May 17, 1933. See, for example, the letter from H. K. Wilder (secretary of the Laundry Board of Trade of Greater New York) to Elmer F. Andrews (New York State Industrial Commissioner), July 19, 1934, in Box 2, Folder 51, NCLR; and Letter from Herman Brickman (a lawyer who was also an officer of the Brooklyn Laundryowners' Association) to Lucy Mason, January 23, 1936, in Box 2, Folder 64, NCLR.

116. "Women Laundry Workers in Harlem Will Be First to Benefit By New Minimum Wage Law," *Bronx Home News*, May 21, 1933; "Minimum Pay Roll Call," *New York World Telegram*, May 24, 1933.

117. "Laundry Workers Get Pay Increase," *New York Sun*, October 2, 1933. The hourly rate for the rest of the state was 27.5 cents.

118. The other three employees were Salvatore Dallessandro, a realtor who held the laundry's license; James Giordano, who hired Tipaldo and also had the power of attorney for Dallessandro; and Nicoleta Somperisi, the laundry's bookkeeper. "First Criminal Prosecution Under State Minimum Fair Wage Act is Started With Indictment and Arrest of Brooklyn Laundry Operators," Attorney General John J. Bennett Jr. Press Release, November 3, 1934, in Box 2, Folder 60, NCLR; Frederick Woltman, "Girls' Low Pay Helps to Expand Plant of Laundryman Who Upset Wage Law," *New York World-Telegram*, April 9, 1936.

119. In January 1935 the NCL reported that since August 6, 1934, the state had found noncompliance with the law at 488 laundries. However, in the overwhelming majority of those establishments, back wages were paid and the minimum wage was implemented, after state inspections. And it was often no easy task to determine whether laundrymen were complying, especially at the Chinese laundries, where ledgers were in Chinese and age records for minors were frequently nonexistent. After securing in excess of $6,000 in back wages for over 2,500 workers, as of January 1935 the state had only needed to initiate legal proceedings against Tipaldo. Untitled document about laundry minimum wage enforcement in New York, January 30, 1935; "Information, October 13, 1934"—information about New York minimum wage law lack of compliance/difficulty with gathering data from laundries, written by Miss Stubley [?]. Both in Box 2, Folder 60, NCLR.

120. Woltman, "Girls' Low Pay Helps to Expand Plant."

121. Woltman, "Girls' Low Pay Helps to Expand Plant."

122. "New York State Department of Labor Division of Women in Industry and Minimum Wage: Schedule of Hearings on Manditory [sic] Laundry Wage Order," July 1934, in Box 2, Folder 60, NCLR.

123. "First Criminal Prosecution," NCLR.

124. People ex rel. Tipaldo v. Morehead, 156 Misc. 522 (1935).

125. McFarland to the Organizations in Labor Subcommittee, NCLR.

126. People ex rel. Tipaldo v. Morehead, 270 N.Y. 233, 237–38, 238 (1936) (quoting from the brief of the New York State attorney general).

127. People ex rel. Tipaldo v. Morehead, at 238–39 (1936).

128. Quoted in Ingalls, "New York and the Minimum-Wage Movement," 191. Tipaldo's principal lawyer was Nathan L. Miller, who served one term as the governor of New York State (January 1921–December 1922), preceded and succeeded by Al Smith.

129. NCL Press Release, March 5, 1936, in Box 2, Folder 64, NCLR.

130. See, for example, McFarland to the Organizations in Labor Subcommittee, NCLR.

131. "The Week," *New Republic*, March 18, 1936, p. 151.

132. Letter from Jane Norman Smith to Alma Lutz, March 24, 1936, Alma Lutz Papers, 1921–1961, MC182, folder 98, Schlesinger Library, Radcliffe Institute, Harvard University, Cambridge, Mass.

133. Morehead v. New York ex rel. Joseph Tipaldo, 297 U.S. 702 (1936).

134. Letter from Willis Van Devanter to Mrs. Scott E. Welker (of Winter Park, Florida), April 21, 1936, Box 19, Letterbook 52, Page 75, Willis Van Devanter Papers, LC.

135. Heywood Broun, "It Seems to Me," *New York World-Telegram*, September 18, 1936.

136. 298 U.S. at 604, 606–8.

137. 298 U.S. at 609.

138. 298 U.S. at 613 (italics added).

139. Kermit L. Hall and John J. Patrick, *The Pursuit of Justice: Supreme Court Decisions That Shaped America* (New York: Oxford University Press, 2006), 88.

140. Marian C. McKenna, *Franklin Roosevelt and the Great Constitutional War: The Court-Packing Crisis of 1937* (New York: Fordham University Press, 2002), 213.

141. Quoted in Jeff Shesol, *Supreme Power: Franklin Roosevelt vs. The Supreme Court* (New York: W. W. Norton, 2011), 222.

142. Shesol, *Supreme Power*, 222.

143. Shesol, *Supreme Power*, 222. Shesol is referring to "Liberty to Starve," *New Republic*, June 10, 1936, p. 116.

144. This language comes from *Baker v. Carr*, 369 U.S. 186, 270 (1962) (Frankfurter, J., joined by Harlan, J., dissenting).

145. 298 U.S. at 631 (Stone, J., joined by Brandeis and Cardozo, JJ., dissenting).

146. 298 U.S. at 631.

147. 298 U.S. at 633 (italics added).

148. 298 U.S. at 634–35 (quoting from *Nebbia v. New York*, 291 U.S. 502, 537 [1934]).

149. Memo from Harlan Fiske Stone to the Court, May 29, 1936, Box 38, Folder 4, Personal Correspondence 1936 L-Z, Willis Van Devanter Papers, LC. See also Letter from Harlan Fiske Stone to Charles Evans Hughes, May 26, 1936; Letter from Charles Evans Hughes to Harlan Fiske Stone, May 26, 1936. Both in Box 62, Supreme Court File, Case File, *Morehead v. Tipaldo*, Harlan Fiske Stone Papers, LC.

150. 298 U.S. at 636 (Stone, J., joined by Brandeis and Cardozo, JJ., dissenting) (emphasis added).

151. 298 U.S. at 634–35 (quoting from 291 U.S. at 537).

152. Quoted in John W. Chambers, "The Big Switch: Justice Roberts and the Minimum-Wage Cases," *Labor History* 10, no. 1 (1969): 54.

153. Frederick Woltman, "Wanted: A Job, by Laundryman Who Upset Minimum Wage Law," *New York World-Telegram*, September 15, 1936. Also see "'New Deal Shockers' Shun Publicity Now," *Brooklyn Daily Eagle*, September 16, 1936.

154. "He Won But Lost," *Plain Dealer* (Cleveland, OH), September 17, 1936.

155. Dorothy Thompson, "On the Record: Liberty or Anarchy?," *New York Herald Tribune*, June 4, 1936.

156. Raymond Clapper, "High Court Offers Dead-Pan Travesty on Self-Government," *Washington Daily News*, June 1, 1936.

157. "Excerpts from the Press Conference, June 2, 1936," American Presidency Project, accessed April 24, 2019, https://www.presidency.ucsb.edu/documents/excerpts-from-the-press-conference-121.

158. Quoted in Barry Cushman, "Mr. Dooley and Mr. Gallup: Public Opinion and Constitutional Change in the 1930s," *Buffalo Law Review* 50 (2002): 39.

159. Quoted in Cushman, "Mr. Dooley and Mr. Gallup," 40.

160. William Lasser, *Benjamin V. Cohen: Architect of the New Deal* (New Haven, CT: Yale University Press, 2002), 159.

161. Lasser, *Benjamin V. Cohen*, 159 (italics added).

162. "Republican Party Platform of 1936, June 9, 1936," American Presidency Project, accessed November 11, 2020, https://www.presidency.ucsb.edu/documents/republican-party-platform-1936.

163. Lasser, *Benjamin V. Cohen*, 159; William E. Leuchtenburg, "Election of 1936," in *History of American Presidential Elections, 1789–1968*, edited by

Arthur M. Schlesinger Jr., Fred L. Israel, and William P. Hansen (New York: Chelsea House, 1971), 2813.

164. Quoted in Lasser, *Benjamin V. Cohen*, 159.

165. "Address at Little Rock, Arkansas. June 10, 1936," *American Presidency Project*, accessed April 23, 2019, https://www.presidency.ucsb.edu /documents/address-little-rock-arkansas.

166. Letter from Attorney General Homer S. Cummings to President Franklin D. Roosevelt, June 20, 1936, quoted in Lasser, *Benjamin V. Cohen*, 158, 159.

167. "1936 Democratic Party Platform, June 23, 1936," American Presidency Project, accessed April 24, 2019, https://www.presidency.ucsb.edu /documents/1936-democratic-party-platform (italics added).

168. Letter from Harlan Fiske Stone to Benjamin N. Cardozo, June 8, 1936, Box 74, Supreme Court File, Correspondence, Cardozo, Benjamin N. 1936–38 and undated, Harlan Fiske Stone Papers, LC.

169. Letter from Benjamin N. Cardozo to Harlan Fiske Stone, June 9, 1936, Box 74, Supreme Court File, Correspondence, Cardozo, Benjamin N. 1936–38 and undated, Harlan Fiske Stone Papers, LC.

170. Quoted in William E. Leuchtenburg, "The Case of the Chambermaid and the Nine Old Men," *American Heritage* 38, no. 1 (December 1986): 36.

171. Attorney General Homer Cummings, quoted in Leuchtenburg, "Case of the Chambermaid and the Nine Old Men," 40.

CHAPTER 4

1. "New & Remodeled Hotels," *Hotel Monthly* 42, no. 498 (September 1934): 64.

2. Gerry L. Alexander, "*Parrish v. West Coast Hotel Company*: A Chelan County Chambermaid Makes History," *Columbia: The Magazine of Northwest History* 27, no. 1 (Spring 2013): 2.

3. 261 U.S. 525 (1923).

4. Chris Rader, "Wenatchee Avenue Block Brims with History," *The Confluence* 29, no. 3 (Fall 2013): 7.

5. C. B. Conner, "The Minimum Wage Case," in *From the Blue Ridge to the Cascade Range: Recollections of Boyhood Days in the Mountains of Virginia—and Work as a Lawyer in Oklahoma and in the Shadows of the Cascade Range* (unpublished manuscript, n.d.), 163. It is clear that of the four lawyers with offices in the Doneen, only Conner would have been willing to take on their case. Twenty-five-year-old Richard G. Jeffers had only one year of legal experience under his belt; Robert F. Murray, one year younger than Jeffers, served in the state legislature in 1935; and Niles M. Sorensen was an attorney for the city of Wenatchee. *Capitol's Who's Who for Washington: The State Encyclopedia, Including a Number*

of Prominent Idaho Citizens Who Are to a Greater or Lesser Degree Linked With Washington Progress, 1949–50 (Portland, OR: Capitol Publishing, 1949), 367, 451, 526. These men were not about to jeopardize their careers by waging what seemed like a hopeless legal battle against the city's institutional elite.

6. Conner, "The Minimum Wage Case," 164. Conner considered it important to mention in his memoir "that at no time did any person or any organization contribute one single cent to Mrs. Parrish or to me for the purpose of obtaining a final determination of this great question." Conner, "The Minimum Wage Case," 187.

7. Alexander, "A Chelan County Chambermaid Makes History," 4.

8. William E. Leuchtenburg, "The Case of the Chambermaid and the Nine Old Men," *American Heritage* 38, no. 1 (December 1986): 35; John P. Hartman, "A Tribute to Charles B. Conner, of Wenatchee, Washington," in Conner, *From the Blue Ridge to the Cascade Range*, 193. Although the phrase "not a Chinaman's chance" obviously and justifiably strikes us today as expressing a deeply racist sentiment, it would be wrong to remove it from Hartman's sentence because it is of its time.

9. For more details about the significance of the Battle of Manassas Gap, see John S. Salmon, *The Official Virginia Civil War Battlefield Guide* (Mechanicsburg, PA: Stackpole Books, 2001), 214–16; Frances H. Kennedy, *The Civil War Battlefield Guide*, 2nd ed. (Boston: Houghton Mifflin, 1998), 213–14.

10. Chris Conner, interview by the author, January 12, 2019.

11. "Judge Booton was a most lovable man, socially and as a citizen. . . . He was nothing of the demagogue or cheap politician, and in his retiring and modest nature he rather shrank from, than courted, public preferment." Robert F. Leedy, "Memorials of Deceased Members: Judge Edwin T. Booton," in *Report of the Twentieth Annual Meeting of the Virginia State Bar Association*, ed. John B. Minor (Richmond: Richmond Press, 1908), 110.

12. James R. Sipe, "A History of the T. C. Williams School of Law" (honors thesis, Richmond College, 1955), 60, https://scholarship.richmond.edu/cgi/viewcontent.cgi?article=1759&context=honors-theses.

13. "A Quiet Wedding," *People's Voice* (Norman, OK), October 18, 1901. Thirteen years later, C. B. was described in another local newspaper as one of "those who are heart and soul for a greater and better Okemah and community." "Okemah's Second Annual Chautauqua," *Sledge Hammer* (Okemah, OK), June 11, 1914.

14. "C. B. Conner For Judge," *Weleetka American* (Weleetka, OK), April 1, 1910.

15. Four lived to adulthood; the first child, Tom, born in 1902, died in 1910. The couple's second child, Eleanor, also died at an early age; born in 1907, she passed away in 1928, never seeing her twenty-first birthday. "Heart Attack in Seattle is Fatal to C. B. Conner," *Wenatchee Daily World* (Wenatchee, WA) (hereafter *World*), May 22, 1941.

16. "Heart Attack in Seattle." In 1924, C. B. also became one of the founding members of the Wenatchee Kiwanis Club. John A. Gellatly, *A History of Wenatchee: "The Apple Capital of the World"* (self-pub., 1962), 225. Irene was also a civic-minded and community-engaged member of the Conner family. For example, she served as the regent of the John Kendrick Chapter of the Daughters of the American Revolution in Wenatchee, 1939–41. Gellatly, *A History of Wenatchee*, 253.

17. Conner, "The Minimum Wage Case," 163.

18. Conner, "The Minimum Wage Case," 164. Recall from chapter 1 that Elsie and Ernie again sought out Conner's services later in 1935, when an auto financing company sued the couple.

19. Conner, "The Minimum Wage Case," 163 (italics added).

20. Conner, "The Minimum Wage Case," 167.

21. The quote in the heading attributed to Crollard is from R. T. Congdon, quoted in Ralph Wood, "Crollard is Named 'Honor Pioneer Citizen' of 1953," *World*, December 17, 1953.

22. Eva G. Anderson, *Pioneers of North Central Washington* (Wenatchee, WA: Wenatchee World, 1980), 179.

23. Chris Rader, "Fred & Louis Crollard: Musical Wenatchee Lawyers," *The Confluence* 26, no. 2 (Summer 2010): 9–10; Anderson, *Pioneers*, 172, 78; Wood, "Crollard is Named 'Honor Pioneer Citizen' of 1953"; "Crollard New Scout Council President," *World*, n.d. (see Sydney Crollard Ranney, email message to author, November 8, 2017); Frederick M. Crollard family album, 31, in the author's possession (quoted from, and cited with permission of Ross Crollard and Sydney Crollard Ranney).

24. Letter from Kirby Billingsley to Frederick M. Crollard, February 14, 1967 (see Ranney, email, November 8, 2017). In the 1930s Billingsley worked as the managing editor at the *World* and played an important role in helping the paper's owner, Wilfred Woods, to campaign for the Grand Coulee Dam to be built, a project that transformed the region. John C. Hughes, *Pressing On: Two Family-Owned Newspapers in the 21st Century* (Olympia: Washington State Legacy Project, 2015), 269.

25. Crollard family album, 2.

26. Crollard family album, 3–6.

27. Crollard family album, 6–9. Lizzie purchased a piano for the boys, at the cost of $175, from Fred W. Helbig, a piano dealer in Washington, D.C., on January 16, 1899. Ranney email, November 8, 2017.

28. Crollard family album, 10–11.

29. "Elks' Band to Give Concert at Liberty Theatre April 27," *World*, n.d. (see Ranney email, November 8, 2017); Crollard family album, 13–15. Louis was the director of the band from 1910 until his death in 1918. Eva G. Anderson, "Hard Work and Music Filled Attorney's Day," *World*, January 26, 1967. The boys joined the Musicians' Mutual Protective Union in Seattle in

1906. Receipt for initiation dues, October 6, 1906, Ranney email, November 8, 2017. Jack O'Connor was the first of Lizzie's brothers to come to the Wenatchee Valley; he arrived in 1892 with the railroad. "Pioneer Attorney Sees Need for New School," *World*, January 25, 1967.

30. Charles E. Conner, C. B.'s son (born 1913), was an accomplished trumpet player and often performed to great acclaim (with repeated requests for encores) at the Wenatchee summer band concerts. See, for example, the following newspaper articles from Labor Day weekend in 1933. "Trumpet Solo to Feature Concert at Park Friday," *World*, August 31, 1933; "Band Concerts End Next Week," *World*, September 2, 1933.

31. An article in the magazine published by the Wenatchee Valley Museum and Cultural Center was appropriately titled "Fred & Louis Crollard: Musical Wenatchee Lawyers." Rader, "Musical Wenatchee Lawyers."

32. Crollard family album, 15–21.

33. Crollard family album, 14–15, 21.

34. Bruce Mitchell, *Apple City U.S.A.: Stories of Early Wenatchee* (Wenatchee, WA: The Wenatchee World, 1992), 31–32. Generally, see Sandra Opdycke, *The Flu Epidemic of 1918: America's Experience in the Global Health Crisis* (New York: Routledge, 2014).

35. Ross Crollard, email message to author, April 15, 2012; "Fred M. Crollard," *World*, June 24, 1968; Crollard family album, 22.

36. The first child, Veronica, was born on April 6, 1913; Fred Jr. arrived on January 31, 1917; David (Bud) was born on April 12, 1918; Louis on April 29, 1921; and finally, Homer on December 17, 1923. The Wenatchee Band played for Fred and Stella as they departed the train depot on their honeymoon. "Young Attorney Takes Bride," *World*, June 12, 1912.

37. Crollard family album, 29.

38. Ernest Parrish, and Elsie Parrish, his wife vs. West Coast Hotel Company, No. 12215, Summons to the West Coast Hotel Company from C. B. Conner, June 10, 1935; Complaint by C. B. Conner and Elsie Parrish, June 10, 1935, Superior Court of the State of Washington in and for the County of Chelan. Eugene C. Bowersox came to Wenatchee at the end of the nineteenth century and was therefore considered part of the city's pioneer generation. And like the majority of the men and women who built the town, Bowersox had migrated west. In 1899 he and his new bride Ione packed up their belongings and, together with Ione's parents, left their native Iowa, bound for Chelan County. A college man with a liberal arts degree from the University of Iowa, Eugene chose to settle in Wenatchee, where he and Ione would live and raise their three sons for the next five decades.

39. Put his pioneer status together with his long tenure as a county court judge, and it was inevitable that Parr would be a contributing writer for Lindley Hull's history of the area. See W. O. Parr, "The Creation of Chelan County," in *A History of Central Washington: Including the Famous Wenatchee, Entiat,*

Chelan and the Columbia Valleys with an Index and Eighty Scenic-Historical Illustrations, ed. Lindley M. Hull (Spokane, WA: Shaw & Borden, 1929).

40. "Judge W. O. Parr Stricken Suddenly," *World*, February 18, 1942.

41. Hull, *A History of Central Washington*, 180; "Judge W. O. Parr Stricken Suddenly."

42. "Personal Mention," *World*, March 18, 1907.

43. "Chelan County, Washington," *The Coast: Wilhelm's Magazine* 12, no. 4 (October 1906): 196; "Construction and Contract News," *Improvement Bulletin* 33, no. 2 (June 9, 1906): 20.

44. "Columbia Valley Bank Has Elegant New Home," *World*, April 3, 1907.

45. "Columbia Valley Bank Has Elegant New Home," *World*, April 3, 1907; "Personal Mention," *World*, March 15, 1907; "Personal Mention," *World*, March 18, 1907; "Notice," *World*, March 27, 1907.

46. "Judge W. O. Parr Stricken Suddenly"; Chris Rader and Mark Behler, *Images of America: Wenatchee* (Charleston, SC: Arcadia Publishing, 2012), 77, 84.

47. Karl B. Raitz and John Paul Jones III, "The City Hotel as Landscape Artifact and Community Symbol," *Journal of Cultural Geography* 9, no. 1 (Fall/Winter 1988): 17. This second Wenatchee courthouse was arguably less a "hub" than the first one because the initial courthouse (which served as such from the formal organization of Chelan County in 1899 until the new building was constructed in 1924) was a brick building, a former hotel, situated downtown at the corner of Wenatchee Avenue and Kittitas Street. In Wenatchee's early years the principal town did not extend much beyond Wenatchee Avenue and its intersecting streets. Parr, "The Creation of Chelan County," 552–53.

48. These were filed by Crollard & O'Connor, who (a) requested an amended version of the Complaint, one that laid out in more detail the hours that Elsie had worked at the Cascadian, and included a more precise breakdown of the terms of her employment (Conner duly provided this information; Judge Parr denied the motion that Crollard & O'Connor subsequently filed against that amended complaint); and (b) requested that the trial be delayed from its originally scheduled court date of September 9 because (i) Judge Parr had not ruled on their Demurrer, where they had attempted to have the case thrown out of court because of what they believed was still a lack of detail on the part of the plaintiffs, and (ii) Ray Clark and his wife would not be able to travel from Seattle to Wenatchee in time for the trial. See Parrish, No. 12215, Motion by Crollard & O'Connor, June 22; Amended-Complaint filed by Conner, July 12; Order Overruling Defendants' Motion Against Amended Complaint, August 1; Demurrer filed by Crollard & O'Connor, August 8; Motion to Strike Case from Setting filed by Crollard & O'Connor.

49. See Parrish, No. 12215, Findings of Fact and Conclusions of Law, November 9, 1935; Letter from Fred M. Crollard to Frederick M. Crollard Jr.,

October 1935 (see Crollard email, March 19, 2012). For the reference to Crollard reading the entire decision in *Adkins*, see "Minimum Wage Case Dismissed," *Hotel News of the West* 32, no. 20 (November 1, 1935): 8.

50. See Parrish, No. 12215, Judgment and Decree, November 9, 1935, 2.

51. Judge Parr's oral announcement of the judgment in Parrish, October 17, 1935, quoted in John W. Roberts, "Amended Statement as to Jurisdiction (1936)," in *Landmark Briefs and Arguments of the Supreme Court of the United States: Constitutional Law*, edited by Philip B. Kurland and Gerhard Casper (Washington, DC: University Publications of America, 1975), 33:87–88.

52. "Judge W. O. Parr Upholds Constitution," *World*, October 19, 1935; Conner, "The Minimum Wage Case," 167.

53. "Judge W. O. Parr Upholds Constitution."

54. Crollard to Crollard Jr., October 1935.

55. Associated Press, "Minimum Wage Law Is Unconstitutional," *Everett Herald* (Everett, WA), October 19, 1935; "Wage Law Invalid: Woman Loses Suit for Minimum," *Seattle Post-Intelligencer*, October 18, 1935; Associated Press, "Minimum Wage Suit Dismissed," *Seattle Times*, October 18, 1935; United Press, "Women's Wage Law Held Invalid," *Tacoma News-Tribune* (Tacoma, WA), October 18, 1935.

56. "Minimum Wage of Women Loses," *Spokesman-Review* (Spokane, WA), October 18, 1935.

57. "Judge W. O. Parr Stricken Suddenly."

58. See Parrish, No. 12215, Notice of Appeal filed by C. B. Conner, November 18, 1935.

59. Ernest Parrish, and Elsie Parrish, his wife vs. West Coast Hotel Company, No. 26038, Appearance Docket, Supreme Court State of Washington; Letter from Conner to Washington State Attorney General G. W. Hamilton, December 13, 1935, in 69-11-642: Attorney General's Office, Central Files—General Correspondence, Box 6, Col-Cz, 1909–1940, Folder: Con-Coo, 1909–1940 (hereafter "Folder Con-Coo"), Washington State Archives, Central Regional Branch (hereafter WASA).

60. Letter from Washington State Assistant Attorney General George G. Hannan to Conner, December 27, 1935, in "Folder Con-Coo," WASA.

61. "Minimum Wage," NCL document, March 10, 1936, in Box 2, Folder 51, National Consumers' League Records (hereafter NCLR) #5235, Kheel Center for Labor-Management Documentation and Archives, Cornell University Library (hereafter Kheel Center).

62. 298 U.S. 587 (1936).

63. Conner, "The Minimum Wage Case," 167.

64. Norman Macbeth Jr., "Note: Present Status of the *Adkins* Case," *Kentucky Law Journal* 24 (1935): 65; 282 U.S. 251, 255 (1931).

65. 243 U.S. 426 (1917).

66. Brief of Appellant at 11–17 (quoting from 261 U.S. at 550; Conner added the "the" reprinted here in square brackets), Ernest Parrish et al. v. West Coast Hotel Company, 185 Wash. 581 (1936) (No. 26038).

67. Barry Cushman, *Rethinking the New Deal Court: The Structure of a Constitutional Revolution* (New York: Oxford University Press, 1998), 72 (quotation; italics added), 72–78.

68. Brief of Appellant at 27–28, Ernest Parrish et al. v. West Coast Hotel Company, 185 Wash. 581 (1936) (emphasis in original).

69. Conner, "The Minimum Wage Case," 176 (emphasis in original). Upon reading the revised draft, that colleague, J. A. Adams, said to Conner: "That settles the matter. You will win the case." Judge Parr's reaction, when reading a copy given to him by Conner, was: "Well, you might win that case." Conner, "The Minimum Wage Case," 176, 177.

70. Barry Cushman, "Formalism and Realism in Commerce Clause Jurisprudence," *University of Chicago Law Review* 67 (2000): 1128.

71. See Murphy v. Sardell, 269 U.S. 530 (1925); Donham v. West Nelson Manufacturing Company, 273 U.S. 657 (1927).

72. 233 U.S. 389 (1914).

73. Brief for Appellant in O'Gorman at 32, quoted in Cushman, *Rethinking the New Deal Court*, 75–76 (italics added).

74. Cushman, *Rethinking the New Deal Court*, 75.

75. 243 U.S. 332 (1917).

76. Cushman, *Rethinking the New Deal Court*, 76–77.

77. 282 U.S. at 257.

78. 282 U.S. at 257–8 (italics added).

79. Brief of Appellant at 8–9, 14–15, 35–36, Ernest Parrish et al. v. West Coast Hotel Company, 185 Wash. 581 (1936).

80. Cushman, *Rethinking the New Deal Court*, 77.

81. 243 U.S. 629 (1917).

82. Larsen v. Rice, 100 Wash. 642, 646 (1918).

83. Sparks v. Moritz, 141 Wash. 417, 421 (1926). On this issue, scholars often also cite *Spokane Hotel Company v. C. H. Younger et al.*, 113 Wash. 359 (1920), that also upheld the 1913 law. However, in this case the Spokane Hotel Company conceded the constitutionality of the law as an exercise of the state's police power and instead challenged (unsuccessfully) the validity of its notification provisions. Spokane Hotel Company v. C. H. Younger et al., at 362–63.

84. Charles H. Sheldon, *The Washington High Bench: A Biographical History of the State Supreme Court, 1889–1991* (Pullman: Washington State University Press, 1992), 250–53.

85. Phil Roberts, *A Penny for the Governor, $ A Dollar for Uncle Sam: Income Taxation in Washington* (Seattle: University of Washington Press, 2002), 89.

86. Sheldon, *The Washington High Bench*, 250.

87. 261 U.S. at 562–7 (Taft, CJ., dissenting) and 261 U.S. at 567–71 (Holmes, J., dissenting), quoted in Ernest Parrish et al. v. West Coast Hotel Co., 185 Wash. 581, 585–89 and 590–92 (1936). For reasons why lower courts may choose to ignore/disregard a decision of the U.S. Supreme Court, see Michael P. Fix, Justin T. Kingsland, and Matthew D. Montgomery, "The Complexities of State Court Compliance with U.S. Supreme Court Precedent," *Justice System Journal* 38, no. 2 (2017); Matthew E. K. Hall, "The Semiconstrained Court: Public Opinion, the Separation of Powers, and the U.S. Supreme Court's Fear of Nonimplementation," *American Journal of Political Science* 58, no. 2 (April 2014); Sarah C. Benesh and Wendy L. Martinek, "State Supreme Court Decision Making in Confession Cases," *Justice System Journal* 23, no. 1 (2002). Fix, Kingsland, and Montgomery posit that "precedent is merely a means to achieve an end result of desired policy." Consistent with the basic principles of the attitudinal model of judicial behavior, this suggests that while a court may, in theory, be constrained by precedent handed down by higher courts, the personal preference of a judge may matter greatly, as well as his or her political prospects (for example, chances of reelection—a pressing concern for state and local judges). Since Millard was up for reelection at the time *Parrish* was decided, this explanation for his decision to ignore *Adkins* might be of relevance. Fix et al. also refer to the "vitality of a precedent": "the degree to which the high court of a specific state has positively treated a U.S. Supreme Court precedent." They discuss the way in which "each state is responsible for implementing U.S. Supreme Court precedent in a way that is compatible with the state's own legal traditions." This element of precedential "vitality" might help to explain the Washington Supreme Court's decision. Fix, Kingsland, and Montgomery, "The Complexities of State Court Compliance," 152, 150, 152.

88. 185 Wash. at 597.

89. 185 Wash. at 596, 597.

90. 185 Wash. at 593.

91. Quoted in Sheldon, *The Washington High Bench*, 251. His ruling in *Parrish* was one of the principal things for which Millard would be known and recognized. For example, when the *Seattle Times* announced in April 1937 that Millard would be giving a talk to the King County Democratic Club, it said nothing more about the judge than that he was "Justice William J. Millard of the State Supreme Court, who wrote the majority opinion in the Washington State Women's Minimum Wage Law case before it went to the United States Supreme Court." "Democrats to Hear Justice W. J. Millard," *Seattle Times*, April 23, 1937. "The publicity surrounding the case [*Parrish*] led to speculation that Millard might be in line for appointment to the federal circuit court of appeals," but it did not have a negative effect upon his standing with the electorate; Millard was reelected in 1936. Sheldon, *The Washington High Bench*, 251; Associated Press, "William J. Millard Dies at 87," *Seattle*

Times, December 14, 1970. This "speculation" seems to have been just that. The relevant file at the Franklin D. Roosevelt Presidential Library (the *President's Official File* #209, "U.S. Circuit Court of Appeals—Judgeships," sub-file #209-i, "9th Circuit, 1933–1945") does not contain any correspondence that mentions Millard. Virginia Lewick, archivist, Franklin D. Roosevelt Presidential Library, email message to author, December 8, 2017.

92. Marjorie Weiss v. Swedish Hospital, 16 Wash. 2d 446, 457 (1943) (Millard, J., dissenting).

93. Letters from Fred M. Crollard to Frederick M. Crollard Jr., February 26, February 22, and March 11, 1936 (see Crollard, email, March 19, 2012); Sydney Crollard Ranney and Ross Crollard, interview by the author, July 16, 2017. For the date of the oral argument, see Letter from Washington State Assistant Attorney General Browder Brown to New York State Solicitor General Henry Epstein, January 14, 1936. In 69-11-642: Attorney General's Office, Central Files—General Correspondence, Box 8, Ea-Fe, 1909–1940, Folder: El-Eq, 1932–1940, WASA.

94. Letter from Fred M. Crollard to Frederick M. Crollard Jr., April 6, 1936 (see Crollard, email, March 19, 2012).

95. Associated Press, "Local Court Reversed in Hotel Case," *World*, April 2, 1936.

96. Works examining the limited coverage of state supreme court decisions include Richard L. Vining Jr. and Teena Wilhelm, "Explaining High-Profile Coverage of State Supreme Court Decisions," *Social Science Quarterly* 91, no. 3 (September 2010); Alixandra B. Yanus, "Full-Court Press: An Examination of Media Coverage of State Supreme Courts," *Justice System Journal* 30, no. 2 (2009); and F. Dennis Hale, "Newspaper Coverage Limited For State Supreme Court Cases," *Newspaper Research Journal* 27, no. 1 (Winter 2006). These works build upon F. Dennis Hale, "The Court's Perception of the Press," *Judicature* 57, no. 5 (December 1973); F. Dennis Hale, "How Reporters and Justices View Coverage of a State Appellate Court," *Journalism & Mass Communication Quarterly* 52, no. 1 (March 1975); F. Dennis Hale, "Press Releases vs. Newspaper Coverage of California Supreme Court Decisions," *Journalism & Mass Communication Quarterly* 55, no. 4 (December 1978); and F. Dennis Hale, "Factors Associated With Newspaper Coverage of California Supreme Court Decisions," *Orange County Bar Journal* 6, no. 1 (1979).

97. 298 U.S. at 587.

98. 291 U.S. 502 (1934). It is important to note that scholars, such as Barry Cushman, are disinclined to view *Parrish* as *revolutionary*. Instead, they view the Court's 1930s doctrine that led up to that decision as *evolutionary*. As Richard Friedman reminds us, in addition to O'*Gorman & Young*, "Between early 1934 and early 1935 . . . the Court issued three thunderbolt decisions, all by five-to-four votes on the liberal side and with either Hughes or Roberts writing for the majority over the dissent of the conservative foursome."

Richard D. Friedman, "Switching Time and Other Thought Experiments: The Hughes Court and Constitutional Transformation," *University of Pennsylvania Law Review* 142, no. 6 (June 1994): 1892. The three decisions to which he is referring were *Nebbia*; *Home Building & Loan Assoc. v. Blaisdell*, 290 U.S. 398 (1934); and the Gold Clause Cases—*Perry v. United States*, 294 U.S. 330 (1935); *Nortz v. United States*, 294 U.S. 317 (1935); and *United States v. Bankers' Trust Co.* and *Norman v. Baltimore & Ohio R.R. Co.*, 294 U.S. 240 (1935).

Blaisdell was decided eight weeks before *Nebbia*. In this case the Court upheld Minnesota's Mortgage Moratorium Law, which gave homeowners struggling with the financial pressure of the Great Depression longer to pay back their mortgages. Recognizing the emergency necessity of the law, the Court concluded that the statute did not violate Article I, Section 10 of the Constitution, which prohibits states from "impairing the Obligation of Contracts." The Gold Clause Cases were another instance of emergency governmental action upheld by the Court in response to the financial woes of the nation. In these cases the Court concluded that Congress's Article I, Section 8 power to regulate money permitted it to place regulations on the ownership of gold, even if such regulations interfered with existing contracts. *Nebbia* and *O'Gorman & Young* are the two most important ones for the story that this book tells.

99. Quoted in James F. Simon, *FDR and Chief Justice Hughes: The President, the Supreme Court, and the Epic Battle Over the New Deal* (New York: Simon & Schuster, 2012), 248.

100. Letter from Professor Felix Frankfurter to Justice Owen Roberts, March 15, 1934, quoted in John W. Chambers, "The Big Switch: Justice Roberts and the Minimum Wage Cases," *Labor History* 10, no. 1 (1969): 64n97.

101. See 185 Wash. at 593–94, quoting 291 U.S. at 538–39.

102. Cushman, *Rethinking the New Deal Court*, 65.

103. Brief of Appellant at 3, Nebbia v. New York, 291 U.S. 502 (1934) (No. 531), 1933 WL 63319 (U.S.).

104. "Leo Nebbia v. The State of New York," *Cornell Daily Sun* 54, no. 115 (March 7, 1934).

105. Nebbia was aware of the Milk Board's order. Previously he had been charging six cents per quart; when the new regulation went into effect, he raised the price by one-third, bringing it up to the mandated minimum. It is not obvious whether or not he purposefully violated the law. On the one hand, Henry S. Manley (one of the lawyers for the Milk Board during the *Nebbia* case) suggests that although "[j]ust how Leo Nebbia" got himself involved in this litigation "and provided himself with a first-class constitutional lawyer to present his issue, is not entirely clear," there is evidence that "[t]he diligence of the Rochester milk dealers association, and its attorney, Smith O'Brien, must have been an important factor." He also states that Nebbia unlawfully sold milk and bread to "two persons acting for the dealers' association" (he does not say

whether Del Signore was one of the two men). Henry S. Manley, "*Nebbia* Plus Fifteen," *Albany Law Review* 13 (1949): 14. This would tend to suggest that Nebbia's actions were designed to generate litigation that would test the constitutionality of the Milk Board's order. However, on the other hand, a letter that Nebbia wrote to Hugh S. Johnson, Administrator of the National Recovery Administration (NRA), four days after the Supreme Court's decision indicates that he supported the work of the NRA and had a genuine concern not for his own individual contractual liberty but rather for the welfare of his customers. Indeed, in Nebbia's mind he had never actually sold Del Signore the bread: "I gave one loaf of bread [a]way with the purchase of 2 Qrt. of milk." This is because Nebbia had promised to do "good, to the welfare of the people"—*his* people, his fellow Depression-starved Italian American immigrants. Yes, in his letter he did acknowledge a reality that every businessman faced—"[I]f I don't cut prices I can't stay in business." And in this respect, it would have benefited him personally to see the Milk Board minimums eradicated; it would have enhanced his personal contractual liberty. However, in closing he wrote: "I like to say[,] if not out of order[,] to help more[,] the NRA [ought] to have all stores, large and small[,] and all neighborhood stores to be closed at six o'clock in the evening." Currently, Nebbia was struggling "to compe[t]e with the chain stores, [where?] even today the price of milk is chiseled"—competition that all but required the small business owner (who could not afford to stay open all hours of the day like the chain stores) to undercut by violating the Milk Board regulation. His proposal that the milk sales playing field be leveled (at least in one respect) by requiring all stores to close at 6pm suggested he was not simply looking out for number one. Quoted by Dan Ernst, "Leo Nebbia on the NRA," *Legal History Blog*, February 10, 2016, http://legalhistoryblog.blogspot .com/2016/02/leo-nebbia-on-nra.html.

106. 291 U.S. at 516–17.

107. 291 U.S. at 517.

108. 291 U.S. at 515.

109. 291 U.S. at 521.

110. 291 U.S. at 529–31.

111. Cushman, *Rethinking the New Deal Court*, 79.

112. 291 U.S. at 536 (italics added).

113. 291 U.S. at 537.

114. Friedman, "Switching Time," 1919.

115. Cushman, *Rethinking the New Deal Court*, 82, 258n80.

116. Letter from Herbert Rabinowitz to Josephine Goldmark, June 2, 1936, in Box 2, Folder 64, NCLR #5235, Kheel Center. As Barry Cushman observes, one Court commentator writing after *Adkins* also "looked into the future with preternatural clairvoyance" when he wrote: "I am instructed that Mr. Hughes is extremely reluctant to overrule a case expressly, especially when such action would result, as it almost certainly would here, in a five to

four decision. Therefore, in order to placate the minority and to save the face of the court, it is my prediction that the *Adkins* case will be distinguished rather than directly overruled." Cushman, *Rethinking the New Deal Court*, 83 (quoting from Macbeth, "Present Status of the *Adkins* Case," 66).

117. 300 U.S. 379, 400 (1937).

118. 198 U.S. 45 (1905).

119. Charles A. Beard and Mary R. Beard, *America in Midpassage*, vol. 3, *The Rise of American Civilization* (New York: Macmillan, 1939), 361.

120. Quoted in Tony Mauro, "The Right Legislation for the Wrong Reasons," *Michigan Law Review First Impressions* 106 (2007): 8.

121. 347 U.S. 483 (1954); 384 U.S. 436 (1966); 410 U.S. 113 (1973); 558 U.S. 310 (2010).

122. An additional concern relating to lack of knowledge about Court complexities is the propensity of the public to reduce these decisions to politicized rather than legal components. This has many unintended consequences. For some examples, see Keith J. Bybee, ed., *Bench Press: The Collision of Courts, Politics, and the Media* (Stanford, CA: Stanford University Press, 2007).

123. C. Herman Pritchett, "The Development of Judicial Research," in *Frontiers of Judicial Research*, edited by Joel B. Grossman and Joseph Tanenhaus (New York: John Wiley, 1969), 42.

124. Andrew R. L. Cayton and Jeffrey P. Brown, "Introduction," in *The Pursuit of Public Power: Political Culture in Ohio, 1787–1861*, edited by Andrew R. L. Cayton and Jeffrey P. Brown (Kent, OH: Kent University Press, 1994), xi–xii.

CHAPTER 5

1. 298 U.S. 587 (1936).

2. "Still in the Twilight." Newspaper clipping dated October 13, 1936 (newspaper unknown), in Box 232, Reference File, Supreme Court 1936–38, Raymond Clapper Papers, 1908–1962, Manuscript Division, Library of Congress, Washington, DC (hereafter RCP-LOC).

3. Lewis Wood, "Wage Law Issue Puts Amendment to Fore," *New York Times*, October 20, 1936.

4. John W. Roberts, "Amended Statement as to Jurisdiction (1936)," in *Landmark Briefs and Arguments of the Supreme Court of the United States: Constitutional Law*, edited by Philip B. Kurland and Gerhard Casper (Washington, DC: University Publications of America, 1975), 33:79; Appearance Docket, Supreme Court of the State of Washington, No. 26038, Ernest Parrish and Elsie Parrish vs. West Coast Hotel Company.

5. 261 U.S. 525 (1923).

6. 291 U.S. 502 (1934).

7. 282 U.S. 251 (1931).

8. Letter from E. P. Cullinn, Assistant to Charles Elmore Cropley, Clerk of the Supreme Court of the United States, to Crollard and O'Connor, Esqs., May 16, 1936. The attorneys shared a copy of this letter with Chief Justice Millard. See Letter from Crollard and O'Connor to William J. Millard, May 20, 1936. Both letters are in 69-11-642: Attorney General's Office, Central Files— General Correspondence, Box 6, Col-Cz, 1909–1940, Folder: Con-Coo, 1909– 1940, Washington State Archives, Central Regional Branch (hereafter WASA).

9. For the U.S. Supreme Court litigation for the West Coast Hotel Company, Roberts primarily wrote the briefs, and Skeel undertook the oral argument. Skeel was a prominent member of the Seattle legal and business communities. Charles W. Taylor Jr., *Eminent Judges and Lawyers of the Northwest, 1843–1955* (Palo Alto, CA: C. W. Taylor, Jr., 1954), 183. Out of the law firm of Roberts & Skeel grew the current Seattle- and Portland-based firm Betts, Patterson, Mines. "Betts, Patterson, Mines: History," Betts, Patterson, Mines, Attorneys, accessed October 3, 2018, http://www.bpmlaw.com/our-firm/history. As Roberts and Skeel indicated, Rule 46 of the U.S. Supreme Court's rules authorized the filing of the appeal. Appellant's Answer to Brief of Amici Curiae at 4, West Coast Hotel v. Parrish, 300 U.S. 379 (1937) (No. 293), 1936 WL 40058.

10. See Sections 237 (a) and (b) of the Judiciary Act of 1925. Section 237 (a) reads as follows:

A final judgment or decree in any suit in the highest court of a State in which a decision in the suit could be had, where is drawn in question the validity of a treaty or statute of the United States, and the decision is against its validity; or where is drawn in question the validity of a statute of any State, on the ground of its being repugnant to the Constitution, treaties, or laws of the United States, and the decision is in favor of its validity, may be reviewed by the Supreme Court upon a writ of error. The writ shall have the same effect as if the judgment or decree had been rendered or passed in a court of the United States. The Supreme Court may reverse, modify, or affirm the judgment or decree of such State court, and may, in its discretion, award execution or remand the cause to the court from which it was removed by the writ.

Section 237 (b) reads as follows:

It shall be competent for the Supreme Court, by certiorari, to require that there be certified to it for review and determination, with the same power and authority and with like effect as if brought up by writ of error, any cause wherein a final judgment or decree has been rendered or passed by the highest court of a State in which a decision could be had where is drawn in question the validity of a treaty or statute of the United States; or where is drawn in question the validity of a statute of any State on the ground of its being repugnant to the Constitution, treaties, or laws of the United States; or where any title, right, privilege, or immunity is specially set up or claimed by either party under the Constitution, or any treaty or statute of, or commission held or authority exercised under, the United States; and the power to review under this paragraph may be exercised as well where the Federal claim is sustained as where it is denied. Nothing in this paragraph shall be construed to limit or detract from the right to a review on a writ of error in a case where such a right is conferred by the preceding paragraph; nor shall the fact that a review on a writ of error might be obtained under the preceding paragraph be an obstacle to granting a review on certiorari under this paragraph. ("Revised Rules of the Supreme Court of the United States, Adopted June 8, 1925. Effective July 1, 1925," Appendix [Judiciary Act of 1925], 3–4, accessed October 11, 2018, https://www.supremecourt.gov/ctrules/rules/Rules_1925.pdf)

11. Reynolds Robertson and Francis R. Kirkham, *Jurisdiction of the Supreme Court of the United States: A Treatise Concerning the Appellate Jurisdiction of the Supreme Court of the United States, Including a Treatment of the Principles and Precedents Governing the Exercise of the Discretionary Jurisdiction on Certiorari* (St. Paul, MN: West Publishing, 1936), 96. The language that Roberts used in the "Amended Statement as to Jurisdiction"—filed in August 1936—suggests that he was well aware of these rules. See Roberts, "Amended Statement as to Jurisdiction (1936)," 90–91.

12. Felix Frankfurter and James M. Landis, "The Business of the Supreme Court at October Term, 1929," *Harvard Law Review* 44, no. 1 (November 1930): 12, quoted in Barry Cushman, "Inside the 'Constitutional Revolution' of 1937," *Supreme Court Review* 2016, no. 1 (2017): 375.

13. Howard Gillman, "De-Lochnerizing *Lochner*," *Boston University Law Review* 85 (2005): 864.

14. The classic works are Jeffrey A. Segal and Harold J. Spaeth, *The Supreme Court and the Attitudinal Model* (Cambridge: Cambridge University Press, 1993); and Jeffrey A. Segal and Harold J. Spaeth, *The Supreme Court and the Attitudinal Model Revisited* (Cambridge: Cambridge University Press, 2002).

15. Cushman, "Inside the 'Constitutional Revolution' of 1937," 374–78.

16. It would not have been unusual for the Hughes Court to summarily reverse and remand a case. See Richard D. Friedman, "Switching Time and Other Thought Experiments: The Hughes Court and Constitutional Transformation," *University of Pennsylvania Law Review* 142, no. 6 (June 1994): 1948n290.

17. Friedman, "Switching Time," 1948.

18. Cushman, "Inside the 'Constitutional Revolution' of 1937," 376 (quoting from Justice Butler's October Term 1936 Docket Book).

19. Cushman, "Inside the 'Constitutional Revolution,'" 377 (quoting from Justice Butler's October Term 1936 Docket Book).

20. C. B. Conner, "The Minimum Wage Case," in *From the Blue Ridge to the Cascade Range: Recollections of Boyhood Days in the Mountains of Virginia— and Work as a Lawyer in Oklahoma and in the Shadows of the Cascade Range* (unpublished manuscript, n.d.), 187. Driver was prosecuting attorney for Chelan County between 1935 and 1937 and went on to become a justice on the Washington State Supreme Court, and then a federal district court judge for the Eastern District of Washington State (as a Truman appointee). Taylor, *Eminent Judges and Lawyers of the Northwest*, 43.

21. C. B. Conner and Sam M. Driver, "Appellee's Brief on the Law (1936)," in *Landmark Briefs and Arguments of the Supreme Court of the United States: Constitutional Law*, edited by Philip B. Kurland and Gerhard Casper (Washington, DC: University Publications of America, 1975), 33:128 (and generally 128–29).

22. 282 U.S. at 257–8 (italics added).

23. Conner and Driver, "Appellee's Brief on the Law," 128.

24. Conner and Driver, "Appellee's Brief on the Law," 126–27.

25. See 291 U.S. at 537.

26. 269 U.S. 530 (1925).

27. 273 U.S. 657 (1927).

28. Brief of Appellant at 13, West Coast Hotel v. Parrish, 300 U.S. 379 (1937) (No. 293), 1936 WL 40056.

29. Brief of Appellant at 12. This point was repeated in "Appellant's Answer to Brief of Amici Curiae," 7.

30. One might have expected him to refer to those two precedents had he sought to respond directly to points made by opposing counsel. However, because his brief was filed with the Court only one week after Conner's, it is unlikely that he had advanced access to the appellee brief.

31. Brief of Appellant, Parrish, 300 U.S. 379 (No. 293), at 23–26.

32. Brief of Appellant, Parrish, 23–24 (italics added).

33. 245 U.S. 60 (1917); 262 U.S. 390 (1923). Roberts also included the following quote from the 1890 decision in *Minnesota v. Barber*:

> The presumption that this statute was enacted in good faith for the purpose expressed in the title, namely, to protect the health of the people of Minnesota, cannot control the final determination of the question whether it is not repugnant to the Constitution of the United States. There may be no purpose upon the part of a legislature to violate the provisions of that instrument, and yet a statute enacted by it, under the forms of law, may, by its necessary operation, be destructive of rights granted or secured by the Constitution. In such cases, the courts must sustain the supreme law of the land by declaring the statute unconstitutional

and void. This principle of constitutional interpretation has been often announced by this court. (136 U.S. 313, 319 [1890], Brief of Appellant, Parrish, 300 U.S. 379 [No. 293], at 25)

Although this quotation definitely supports Roberts's overall point about the importance of restraining legislative power, the case involves the states' power to regulate commerce and does not involve the due process clause of the Fourteenth Amendment. Hence the fact that, for the purposes of this book, it has been relegated to a footnote. As Barry Cushman explains, however, analyses of decisions like *Barber* make important contributions to our overall understanding of the jurisprudence of this time period. See Barry Cushman, "Formalism and Realism in Commerce Clause Jurisprudence," *University of Chicago Law Review* 67 (2000): 1101–26.

34. Brief of Appellant, Parrish, 300 U.S. 379 (No. 293), at 23.

35. 245 U.S. at 80–81.

36. 245 U.S. at 74, quoted in Brief of Appellant, Parrish, 300 U.S. 379 (No. 293), at 25–26.

37. 262 U.S. at 399.

38. 262 U.S. at 399.

39. 262 U.S. at 401, quoted in Brief of Appellant, Parrish, 300 U.S. 379 (No. 293), at 24–25.

40. Generally, see Paul M. Collins Jr., *Friends of the Supreme Court: Interest Groups and Judicial Decision Making* (New York: Oxford University Press, 2008).

41. See the U.S. Supreme Court Amicus Curiae Database compiled by Paul M. Collins Jr. "Data," Paul M. Collins Jr., Professor of Political Science & Director of Legal Studies, UMass Amherst, accessed October 17, 2018, https://blogs.umass.edu/pmcollins/data.

42. Publicly, the National Consumers' League (NCL) was upbeat about the possibility that *Parrish* would bring a reversal of fortunes for minimum wage laws in the United States. This optimism was clear in the press release issued after the announcement that the Court would not rehear *Tipaldo*:

While the refusal of the United States Supreme Court yesterday to grant a rehearing of the New York minimum wage case is a disappointment, the National Consumers' League through its executives, Lucy R. Mason and Emily Sims Marconnier, expressed the hope that the minimum wage issue now beclouded by technicalities would be cleared through the state of Washington's case which is pending before the highest court. . . . It is the hope of the National Consumers' League that in view of changed economic conditions since 1923 that the U.S. Supreme Court will reverse its decision of that date. (NCL Press Release, October 12, 1936, in Box 2, Folder 64, National Consumers League Records #5235, Kheel Center for Labor-Management Documentation and Archives, Cornell University Library)

Behind closed doors, however, most members of the NCL took the *Parrish* certiorari petition grant as an ominous sign that their campaign was being set up for another legal fall. As Josephine Goldmark observed in a letter to Lucy Mason two days later, "I don't see that there is anything to expect from the Washington case." Letter from Josephine Goldmark to Lucy Mason, October 14, 1936, Box 2, Folder 56, NLCR. Indeed, for the next two weeks the NCL mulled over the possibility of submitting an amicus brief in *Parrish*. After all, there was no disputing the organization's authority on the matter. Ultimately, however, the decision was made to stay out of the case because Benjamin Cohen and Felix Frankfurter were both "rather pessimistic regarding its outcome" and thought the effect of a brief would be minimal unless it were accompanied with amicus participation in the oral argument, something the justices were unlikely to agree to. Letter from Benjamin V. Cohen to Lucy R. Mason, October 23, 1936. Also see the letter from Mason to Cohen, October 9, 1936, and the letter from Mason to Solomon Portnow (secretary of the Lawyers' Committee in charge of drafting a new New York minimum wage law), October 30, 1936; all in Box 2, Folder 56, NLCR.

43. See Letter from New York State Solicitor General Henry Epstein to Washington State Assistant Attorney General George G. Hannan, May 26, 1936. Also see Telegram from Epstein to Hannan, May 21, 1936. Both in 69-11-642: Attorney General's Office, Central Files—General Correspondence, Box 6, Col-Cz, 1909–1940, Folder: Con-Coo, 1909–1940, WASA.

44. It is not possible to know exactly how much the appeal would have cost Conner. As Catherine Romano, Research Librarian for the Supreme Court of the United States, explains:

> The *Revised Rules of the Supreme Court* (adopted June 5, 1928, amended to May 25, 1936) give the amount of fees required, but the typical cost of printing briefs and other documents which must be filed is not mentioned in the Rules nor in an old practice book in use at the time, Reynolds Robertson's 1928 *Appellate Practice and Procedure in the Supreme Court of the United States*. It was more than twenty years later in 1950 that a more current work was published. Robert L. Stern and Eugene Gressman's classic treatise *Supreme Court Practice* does mention printing costs, but that is 13 years after *West Coast Hotel* was decided. (Catherine Romano, email message to author, October 6, 2017)

The *Revised Rules of the Supreme Court* to which Romano refers simply tells us the following about the Supreme Court rules (pertaining to filing fees) that were in existence at the time.

Number of copies of record printed by Clerk of Supreme Court on petition for certiorari; cost thereof; formal papers omitted from printed records.—Where the entire record is in manuscript or typewritten form when application for certiorari is to be made, and it is, therefore, necessary for the Clerk of the Supreme Court to print it in its entirety, he prints 50 copies (unless a greater number be ordered) to the end that an ample number of copies will be available for use at the hearing on the merits, if the writ be granted. Of this number six are sent to counsel for petitioner. More may be ordered if required. Fifty copies of the petition and brief are printed, of which 40 are filed with the Clerk, and 10 are sent to counsel for petitioner. The present cost of 50 copies of the record is slightly in excess of $2 per page of plain matter of 420 words, inclusive of Clerk's and printing costs. The petition and brief cost about $2 per page of 300 words at the present time. Indices and cover pages are additional in both instances, and tabular matter, etc., is charged at a higher rate. In all such cases the Clerk adds to the estimate, an amount considered to be sufficient to cover all filing, docket fees correspondence, etc., by both petitioner and respondent in the case. If the writ be denied there is sometimes a refund; if the writ be granted, usually no additional fees are required. The $35 deposit mentioned on pp. 42, 43, supra, is not in addition to those fees, but is merely a preliminary deposit, and is deducted from the later estimate of costs given to counsel.

The deposit referenced here is discussed using the following language:

Part IV.—Prior to the Docketing of the Case, the Clerk Must Be "Satisfied" as to the Payment of Fees. The fourth, and last, of the "requirements upon docketing a case in the Supreme Court on petition for a writ of certiorari" (discussed supra, p. 17) is that the Clerk of the Supreme Court of the United States shall be "satisfied" as to the payment of his fees, before the docketing of the case. This requirement is explained and discussed in this, Part IV. 1. The rule.—Rule 11, paragraph 1, reads as follows: In all cases the plaintiff in error or appellant, on docketing a case and filing the record, shall make such cash deposit with the Clerk for the payment of his fees as he may require or otherwise satisfy him in that behalf. This rule also applies, by virtue of Rule 41, to cases on petition for writ of certiorari. 2. In all cases, except as herein noted, the Clerk requires that thirty-five dollars ($35) be deposited with him before he will docket case or file petition and accompanying papers. The Clerk of the Supreme Court of the United States requires that a deposit of $35 be made with him prior to the docketing of any case in the Supreme Court. This requirement of the Clerk's office is made under authority of Rule 11, paragraph 1, and Rule 41; and it is inoperative only where an affidavit in forma pauperis is filed, or where a case is docketed under the Seamen's Statute. Therefore, it may be said that, with the two exceptions just noted, no petition for certiorari may be filed in the Supreme Court of the United States until a deposit of $35 has been made with the Clerk of that Court. 3. Purpose of deposit.—The $35 is not a fee charged by the Clerk for the docketing of the case and the filing of the papers, but it is a sum which, in the estimation of the Clerk, will suffice to cover Clerk's costs on all filings and docketing by both petitioner and respondent up to the time when the Court enters an order on the petition for the writ. When costs are taxed at the end of the case any balance remaining is returned to the depositor, or he is called upon to make up any deficit.

Reynolds Robertson, *Appellate Practice and Procedure in the Supreme Court of the United States: A Chronological Outline of Proceedings Necessary Both in the Supreme Court and in the Lower Courts on Petition for a Writ of Certiorari, Writ of Error, or Appeal, to Review a Decision in the Supreme Court of the United States; and of Steps Necessary to be Taken to File and Conduct, or Defend, a Case in the Supreme Court Upon the Granting of a Writ of Certiorari, Writ of Error, or Appeal, or Upon Certified Questions With Forms and Citations to the Applicable Statutes, Rules of Court, and Decisions* (New York: Prentice-Hall, 1928), 38–39, 42–43.

45. Letter from C. B. Conner to the Washington State Attorney General, May 26, 1936 (italics added), in 69-11-642: Attorney General's Office, Central Files—General Correspondence, Box 6, Col-Cz, 1909–1940, Folder: Con-Coo, 1909–1940, WASA.

46. Letter from Conner to the Washington State Attorney General, May 28, 1936, in 69-11-642: Attorney General's Office, Central Files—General Correspondence, Box 6, Col-Cz, 1909–1940, Folder: Con-Coo, 1909–1940, WASA.

47. Governor Martin was reelected in 1936 with 69.4 percent of the vote, which was a greater percentage of the statewide vote than President Roosevelt (66.4 percent) received. Michael J. Dubin, *United States Gubernatorial Elections, 1932–1952: The Official Results by State and County* (Jefferson, NC: McFarland & Company, 2014), 248; "Election of 1936," The American Presidency Project, accessed November 11, 2020, https://www.presidency.ucsb .edu/statistics/elections/1936.

In 1932 Attorney General Hamilton became the first Democrat elected to the position of attorney general in Washington history. In that election he received 54.40 percent of the vote. He was reelected in 1936 and received 66.94 percent of the vote. "Brief History of the Office of the Attorney General: New Roles and the Monopoly Statute," Washington State Office of the Attorney General, accessed October 17, 2018, http://www.atg.wa.gov/brief-history -office-attorney-general; "Elections Search Results: November 1932 General," Washington Secretary of State, accessed October 17, 2018, http://www.sos

.wa.gov/elections/results_report.aspx?e=102&c=&c2=&t=&t2=&p=&p2=&y=; "Elections Search Results: November 1936 General," Washington Secretary of State, accessed October 17, 2018, http://www.sos.wa.gov/elections/results _report.aspx?e=69&c=&c2=&t=&t2=&p=&p2=&y=.

48. Washington State submitted its motion asking for permission to file an amicus brief in *Parrish* on November 21. The brief landed on the justices' desks nine days later. See G. W. Hamilton, W. A. Toner, and George G. Hannan, "Motion for Leave to File Brief and to Participate in Argument as Amici Curiae in West Coast Hotel Company vs. Ernest Parrish and Elsie Parrish, No. 293 (1936)," in *Landmark Briefs*, edited by Kurland and Casper, 33: 131–35.

49. Brief for Attorney General G. W. Hamilton et al. as Amici Curiae at 8, West Coast Hotel v. Parrish, 300 U.S. 379 (1937) (No. 293), 1936 WL 40057.

50. Brief for Attorney General G. W. Hamilton et al. as Amici Curiae, at 10.

51. Conner and Driver, "Appellee's Brief on the Law," 128. What the Court *actually* said in *O'Gorman & Young* was "the presumption of constitutionality must prevail in the absence of some factual foundation of record for overthrowing the statute." 282 U.S. at 257–8.

52. Conner and Driver, "Appellee's Brief on the Law," 128.

53. Brief for Attorney General G. W. Hamilton et al. as Amici Curiae, *Parrish*, 300 U.S. 379 (No. 293), at 11.

54. Ernest Parrish, and Elsie Parrish, his wife v. West Coast Hotel Company, Judgment and Decree, November 9, 1935, at 2, Superior Court of the State of Washington in and for the County of Chelan, No. 12215.

55. Judge Parr's oral announcement of the judgment in *Parrish*, October 17, 1935, quoted in Roberts, "Amended Statement as to Jurisdiction (1936)," 87–88.

56. Judge Parr's oral announcement of the judgment in *Parrish*, October 17, 1935, quoted in Roberts, "Amended Statement as to Jurisdiction (1936)," 88.

57. John Roberts drew this error to the Court's attention, without substantive analysis or discussion, in his brief written and filed in response to the state's amicus brief. See "Appellant's Answer to Brief of Amici Curiae," 4, 16.

58. Brief for Attorney General G. W. Hamilton et al. as Amici Curiae, *Parrish*, 300 U.S. 379 (No. 293), at 16–17 (italics added).

59. Brief for Attorney General G. W. Hamilton et al. as Amici Curiae, *Parrish*, 300 U.S. 379 (No. 293), at 18.

60. 282 U.S. at 257–58, quoted in Brief for Attorney General G. W. Hamilton et al. as Amici Curiae, *Parrish*, 300 U.S. 379 (No. 293), at 19.

61. Brief for Attorney General G. W. Hamilton et al. as Amici Curiae, *Parrish*, 300 U.S. 379 (No. 293), at 22.

62. "Appellant's Answer to Brief of Amici Curiae," 1.

63. "Appellant's Answer to Brief of Amici Curiae," 13 (italics added).

64. "Appellant's Answer to Brief of Amici Curiae," 15.

65. "Appellant's Answer to Brief of Amici Curiae," 18.

66. David M. O'Brien, *Storm Center: The Supreme Court in American Politics*, 10th ed. (New York: W. W. Norton, 2014), 124.

67. "Appellant's Answer to Brief of Amici Curiae," 8 (quotation), and 8–11 (analysis of *Tipaldo*).

68. "Appellant's Answer to Brief of Amici Curiae," 9.

69. "Appellant's Answer to Brief of Amici Curiae," 8 (italics added).

70. "Appellant's Answer to Brief of Amici Curiae," 8 (italics added).

71. "Appellant's Answer to Brief of Amici Curiae," 10.

72. 298 U.S. at 634 (Stone, J., dissenting), quoted in "Appellant's Answer to Brief of Amici Curiae," 10–11.

73. 291 U.S. at 537 (italics added).

74. "Appellant's Answer to Brief of Amici Curiae," 12 (italics added).

75. "Appellant's Answer to Brief of Amici Curiae," 12.

76. Telegram from Washington State Attorney General C. W. Hamilton to Loomis Baldrey (Counsel for Port of Bellingham), December 8, 1936, in 69-11-642: Attorney General's Office, Central Files—General Correspondence, Box 2, At-Bek, 1909–1940, Folder: Bal-Baq, 1909–1940, WASA.

77. Conner, "The Minimum Wage Case," 187. Although neither Conner's memoir nor the files of the Office of the Attorney General in the Washington State Archives tell us which case Toner was overseeing in Washington, D.C., in December 1936, all the evidence points to it being *Great Northern Railway Company v. State of Washington*, 300 U.S. 154 (1937), which was argued on December 7 and 8, 1936. In particular, see Telegram from Hamilton to Baldrey, December 8, 1936.

78. "High Court Hears Women Wage Case," *New York Times*, December 17, 1936; "Wilbur A. Toner," *Walla Walla Union-Bulletin* (Walla Walla, WA), July 7, 1950.

79. Letter from Hamilton and Toner, February 16, 1937, in 69-11-642: Attorney General's Office, Central Files—General Correspondence, Box 5, Can-Cok, 1909–1940, Folder: Ce-Ch, 1931–1940, WASA. In response to a letter from a newspaper editor in Oklahoma, a state that was considering the merits of enacting its own minimum wages for women statute, Toner suggested that such a law would be more likely to pass constitutional muster (remember that he was writing before the decision in *Parrish*) if it only applied to a limited number and specific types of occupations. Letter from Toner to Jim G. Lucas (*Muskogee Daily Phoenix*, Muskogee, OK), January 4, 1937, in 69-11-642: Attorney General's Office, Central Files—General Correspondence, Box 18, Lo-McF, 1909–1940, Folder: Lu, 1909–1940, WASA.

80. Munn v. Illinois, 94 U.S. 113, 126 (1876) (italics added).

81. West Coast Hotel v. Parrish, 300 U.S. 379, 388 (1937).

82. 300 U.S. at 388.

83. William Haltom, *Reporting on the Courts: How the Mass Media Cover Judicial Actions* (Chicago: Nelson-Hall, 1998), 101–3.

84. "Wage Case in Highest Court," *Wenatchee Daily World* (Wenatchee, WA) (hereafter *World*), December 4, 1936.

85. Associated Press, "Local Wages Case Argued," *World*, December 14, 1936.

86. "Wage Case Argument Up Today," *World*, December 17, 1936.

87. "State Wage Law May Be Illegal," *Seattle Post-Intelligencer*, December 18, 1936; "Out of Wage Act Hearing," *Tacoma News-Tribune* (Tacoma, WA), December 17, 1936.

88. United Press, "Minimum Wage Law Question Arouses Much Speculation," *Everett Herald* (Everett, WA), December 17, 1936; "State Attorney Defends Wage Law," *Spokane Press* (Spokane, WA), December 17, 1936; John A. Reichmann, "2 Jurists Absent for Arguments," *Seattle Star*, December 17, 1936.

89. Reichmann, "2 Jurists Absent"; United Press, "Minimum Wage Law Question Arouses Much Speculation."

90. On October 12, Stone came down with "a devastating attack of bacillary dysentery" that left him dangerously ill for many weeks. Alpheus Thomas Mason, *Harlan Fiske Stone: Pillar of Law* (New York: Viking Press, 1956), 440.

91. This was not the last time that McReynolds was absent from the Court's bench on "personal" and/or family business. In late May 1939 McReynolds left Washington for a long-planned family reunion before the Court announced its remaining decisions at the end of that month/beginning of June. This is in large part because the October 1938 Term had originally been scheduled to conclude at the beginning of May. As Barry Cushman explains, it is misleading to suggest, as Bennett Boskey has done (Boskey clerked for Justice Stanley Reed and Chief Justice Stone in the 1940s—*after* McReynolds's retirement), that such behavior was the norm rather than the exception. Barry Cushman, "The Missing Justice in *Coleman v. Miller*," *Journal of Supreme Court History* 42, no. 1 (March 2017) (for the specific discussion of Boskey's suggestion, see page 69). Boskey's suggestion appears in Gregory L. Peterson et al., "Recollections of *West Virginia Board of Education v. Barnette*," *St. John's Law Review* 81, no. 4 (Fall 2007): 787 (Boskey: "Justice McReynolds, who was a very ornery Justice, used to go off a little bit early before the end of the Term on vacation.")

92. Reichmann, "2 Jurists Absent."

93. It was standard procedure for the Court, under the leadership of Chief Justice Hughes, to discuss and vote upon a case on the Saturday immediately following oral argument. Edwin McElwain, "The Business of the Supreme Court as Conducted by Chief Justice Hughes," *Harvard Law Review* 63, no. 1 (November 1949): 17.

94. Cushman, "Inside the 'Constitutional Revolution' of 1937," 376 (quoting from Justice Butler's October Term 1936 Docket Book).

95. Cushman, "Inside the 'Constitutional Revolution' of 1937," 377.

96. Barry Cushman, "The Place of Economic Crisis in American Constitutional Law: The Great Depression as a Case Study," in *Constitutions in Times of Financial Crisis*, edited by Tom Ginsburg, Mark D. Rosen, and Georg Vanberg (New York: Cambridge University Press, 2019).

97. Finley Peter Dunne, *Mr. Dooley's Opinions* (New York: R. H. Russell, 1901), 26. Dunne's humorous fictitious creation, Mr. Dooley, famously said, "no matther whether th' constitution follows th' flag or not, th' supreme coort follows th' iliction returns."

98. Cushman, "Inside the 'Constitutional Revolution' of 1937," 376 (quoting from Justice Butler's October Term 1936 Docket Book).

99. Merlo J. Pusey, *Charles Evans Hughes* (New York: Macmillan, 1951), 2:757.

100. "The Washington Minimum Wage case was argued in Stone's absence . . . but his vote was necessary to a majority as the judges were otherwise divided 4 to 4. 'He did participate in the decision, and it is not uncommon for a Justice who did not hear the arguments to participate in the decision of the case.' (E. P. Cullinn, Assistant to Clerk of Supreme Court, to A.T.M. [Alpheus Thomas Mason], July 14, 1951.)" Mason, *Harlan Fiske Stone*, 456n*.

101. Raymond Clapper, "Wage Law Decision Has Court 'On Spot,'" *Pittsburgh Press* (Pittsburgh, PA), February 27, 1937. Interestingly, as a handwritten note atop a clipping of a Clapper column that ran in the *Washington Daily News* indicates, the *New York World-Telegram* declined to print this article. See clipping of Raymond Clapper, "Justices May Decide Embarrassing Wage Law Suit Monday," *Washington Daily News*, February 27, 1937, p. 2, in Box 59 "1937," Article, Book, and Speech File, 1911–1944, RCP-LOC.

102. "The Court, Politics and Minimum Wage Legislation" with "Walker Stone" handwritten at top and date-stamped March 1, 1937 (emphasis added), in Box 232, Reference File, Supreme Court 1936–38, RCP-LOC.

103. See, for example, Marian C. McKenna, *Franklin Roosevelt and the Great Constitutional War: The Court-Packing Crisis of 1937* (New York: Fordham University Press, 2002); Burt Solomon, *FDR v. The Constitution: The Court-Packing Fight and the Triumph of Democracy* (New York: Walker Books, 2009); Jeff Shesol, *Supreme Power: Franklin Roosevelt vs. the Supreme Court* (New York: W. W. Norton, 2010); William Leuchtenburg, "Franklin D. Roosevelt's Supreme Court 'Packing' Plan," in *Essays on the New Deal*, edited by Harold F. Hollingsworth and William F. Holmes (College Station: Texas A&M University Press, 1969).

104. Letter from Edward S. Corwin to Homer S. Cummings, December 16, 1936, Box 88, Papers of Homer S. Cummings, MSS 9973, Albert and Shirley Small Special Collections Library, University of Virginia.

105. Barry Cushman, "Court-Packing and Compromise," *Constitutional Commentary* 29, no. 1 (Summer 2013).

106. "Franklin D. Roosevelt: Press Conference, February 5, 1937," The American Presidency Project, accessed November 11, 2020, https://www .presidency.ucsb.edu/documents/press-conference-22.

107. Chief Justice Hughes, and Justices Van Devanter, McReynolds, Brandeis, Clarke, and Sutherland were all over the age of seventy in 1937. Cushman, "Court-Packing and Compromise," 11.

108. Barry Cushman, "The Court-Packing Plan as Symptom, Casualty, and Cause of Gridlock," *Notre Dame Law Review* 88, no. 5 (2013): 2106.

109. Dennis J. Hutchinson and David J. Garrow, eds., *The Forgotten Memoir of John Knox: A Year in the Life of a Supreme Court Clerk in FDR's Washington* (Chicago: University of Chicago Press, 2002), 204 (quotation), and 189. The three decisions were *NLRB v. Jones & Laughlin Steel Corp.*, 301 U.S. 1 (1937); *NLRB v. Fruehauf Trailer Corp.*, 301 U.S. 49 (1937); and *NLRB v. Friedman-Harry Marks Clothing Co.*, 301 U.S. 58 (1937).

110. Chesly Manly, "Wage, Debt Holiday and Rail Labor Laws Validated," *Chicago Daily Tribune*, March 30, 1937.

111. Richard D. Friedman, "Chief Justice Hughes' Letter on Court-Packing," *Journal of Supreme Court History* 22, no. 1 (1997): 79–80, 81.

CHAPTER 6

1. Letter from Albert Leslie to Washington State Attorney General G. W. Hamilton, February 8, 1937, in 69-11-642, Attorney General's Office, Central Files—General Correspondence, Box 5, Can-Cok, 1909–1940, Folder: Ce-Ch, 1931–1940, Washington State Archives, Central Regional Branch.

2. William E. Leuchtenburg, "The Case of the Chambermaid and the Nine Old Men," *American Heritage* 38, no. 1 (December 1986): 37.

3. Leuchtenburg, "Case of the Chambermaid," 37.

4. Chesly Manly, "Wage, Debt Holiday and Rail Labor Laws Validated," *Chicago Daily Tribune*, March 30, 1937.

5. Robert H. Jackson, *The Struggle for Judicial Supremacy: A Study of a Crisis in American Power Politics* (New York: Alfred A. Knopf, 1941), 207–8; 261 U.S. 525 (1923).

6. The ticket of Hughes and Charles W. Fairbanks received 254 Electoral College votes; the incumbent president and vice president, Woodrow Wilson and Thomas R. Marshall, won reelection with 277 Electoral College votes.

7. 243 U.S. 629 (1917).

8. At one point during the 1914 oral argument in *Stettler*, Hughes asked Charles W. Fulton, one of the lawyers for the plaintiffs challenging the Oregon minimum wage law, about *Hawley v. Walker*, 232 U.S. 718 (1914). That case involved a challenge to the constitutionality of Ohio's law prescribing maximum working hours for women; the law was upheld through

a per curiam opinion citing the authority of *Muller v. Oregon*. Fulton contended that there was a fundamental difference between wages and hours laws. "Long hours," he said, "break down women so that they become public charges, it is a condition growing *out of* employment. The amount of wages has no relation to health and morals." Hughes tellingly responded: "But . . . suppose it has, suppose this court finds that these evils are in consequence of wages paid in employment?" Quoted in Mary Chamberlain, "The Paper-Box Factory and the Constitution," *The Survey* 33, no. 13 (December 26, 1914): 331. Also see James F. Simon, *FDR and Chief Justice Hughes: The President, the Supreme Court, and the Epic Battle Over the New Deal* (New York: Simon & Schuster, 2012), 51–52.

9. Jackson, *The Struggle for Judicial Supremacy*, 207–8; William E. Leuchtenburg, "The Case of the Wenatchee Chambermaid," in *The Supreme Court Reborn: The Constitutional Revolution in the Age of Roosevelt* (New York: Oxford University Press, 1995), 172.

10. David J. Danelski and Joseph S. Tulchin, eds., *The Autobiographical Notes of Charles Evans Hughes* (Cambridge, MA: Harvard University Press, 1973), 312; Merlo J. Pusey, *Charles Evans Hughes* (New York: Macmillan, 1951), 2:703.

11. 298 U.S. 587 (1936).

12. Barry Cushman, "Inside the 'Constitutional Revolution' of 1937," *Supreme Court Review* 2016, no. 1 (2017): 376 (quoting from Justice Butler's docket books).

13. 300 U.S. 379, 390 (1937).

14. 300 U.S. at 390.

15. 300 U.S. at 402 (Sutherland, J., joined by Van Devanter, McReynolds, and Butler, JJ., dissenting) (italics added).

16. 300 U.S. at 402 (Sutherland, J., joined by Van Devanter, McReynolds, and Butler, JJ., dissenting).

17. Congressman Maury Maverick, quoted in Leuchtenburg, "The Case of the Wenatchee Chambermaid," 176.

18. 300 U.S. at 391–92.

19. 300 U.S. at 391.

20. 300 U.S. at 392 (quoting from *Chicago, Burlington, & Quincy Railroad Company v. McGuire*, 219 U.S. 549, 567 [1911]).

21. 300 U.S. at 397, 392.

22. 94 U.S. 113 (1876).

23. 282 U.S. 251 (1931).

24. 291 U.S. 502 (1934).

25. 300 U.S. at 398 (italics added), quoting from 291 U.S. at 537.

26. 300 U.S. at 399 (italics added).

27. 300 U.S. at 390.

28. 300 U.S. at 399.

29. 300 U.S. at 398.

30. Barry Cushman, "Formalism and Realism in Commerce Clause Jurisprudence," *University of Chicago Law Review* 67, no. 4 (May 2000): 1128.

31. Brief of Appellant at 27–28, Ernest Parrish et al. v. West Coast Hotel Company, 185 Wash. 581 (1936) (emphasis in original).

32. 300 U.S. at 398–99 (italics added).

33. 208 U.S. 412 (1908).

34. 261 U.S. at 553.

35. Nancy Woloch, *Muller v. Oregon: A Brief History With Documents* (Boston: Bedford/St. Martin's, 1996), 4.

36. 300 U.S. at 394.

37. 261 U.S. at 557–8.

38. Cass Sunstein, "*Lochner's* Legacy," *Columbia Law Review* 87, no. 5 (1987): 876.

39. Sunstein, "*Lochner's* Legacy," 876.

40. 300 U.S. at 390.

41. 300 U.S. at 399–400 (italics added).

42. Carl Brent Swisher, ed., *Selected Papers of Homer Cummings, Attorney General of the United States 1933–1939* (New York: Charles Scribner's Sons, 1939), 155 (from the statement that Cummings issued on March 31, 1937).

43. Brief of Appellant at 8, West Coast Hotel v. Parrish, 300 U.S. 379 (1937) (No. 293), 1936 WL 40056.

44. 300 U.S. at 399.

45. James Gregory, "Economics and Poverty," The Great Depression in Washington State: Pacific Northwest Labor & Civil Rights Projects—University of Washington, accessed May 28, 2019, http://depts.washington.edu /depress/economics_poverty.shtml.

46. Letter from George F. Yantis to Congressman Martin F. Smith (D-WA), June 7, 1935—in Series II: Incoming Correspondence, Box 1, Folder 20 (Jan.–June 1935), MS001-06-01, Rufus Woods Papers. Archives and Special Collections, Brooks Library, Central Washington University. In 1933 Smith unseated Representative Albert Johnson, who had served in Congress for two decades.

47. "Franklin D. Roosevelt: Inaugural Address, March 4, 1933" (italics added), American Presidency Project, accessed May 28, 2019, https://www .presidency.ucsb.edu/node/208712.

48. Gerard N. Magliocca, "Constitutional Change," in *The Oxford Handbook of the U.S. Constitution*, edited by Mark Tushnet, Mark A. Graber, and Sanford Levinson (New York: Oxford University Press, 2015), 916.

49. Letter from Armstead Brown to Charles Evans Hughes, April 20, 1937, Reel 87, Charles Evans Hughes Papers, Manuscript Division, Library of Congress, Washington, DC (hereafter LC).

50. 300 U.S. at 401 (Sutherland, J., joined by Van Devanter, McReynolds, and Butler, JJ., dissenting).

324 NOTES TO CHAPTER 6

51. Sutherland concluded his opinion by saying: "A more complete discussion may be found in the *Adkins* and *Tipaldo* cases cited *supra*." 300 U.S. at 414 (Sutherland, J., joined by Van Devanter, McReynolds, and Butler, JJ., dissenting).

52. Joel Francis Paschal, *Mr. Justice Sutherland: A Man Against the State* (New York: Greenwood Press, 1969), 202.

53. 300 U.S. at 404 (Sutherland, J., joined by Van Devanter, McReynolds, and Butler, JJ., dissenting).

54. 300 U.S. at 409–11, quoting from 261 U.S. at 557–59 (Sutherland, J., joined by Van Devanter, McReynolds, and Butler, JJ., dissenting); 300 U.S. at 412–13 (Sutherland, J., joined by Van Devanter, McReynolds, and Butler, JJ., dissenting), quoting from 298 U.S. at 615–17.

55. See 300 U.S. at 406 (quoting from *Adair v. United States*, 208 U.S. 161, 175 [1908]), at 410 and 411 (quoting from Adkins, 261 U.S. at 558, 559), and at 412 (quoting from Tipaldo, 298 U.S. at 616), all from Sutherland, J., joined by Van Devanter, McReynolds, and Butler, JJ., dissenting.

56. 300 U.S. at 408 (Sutherland, J., joined by Van Devanter, McReynolds, and Butler, JJ., dissenting) (italics added).

57. 300 U.S. at 394.

58. 300 U.S. at 411–12 (Sutherland, J., joined by Van Devanter, McReynolds, and Butler, JJ., dissenting) (italics added).

59. 300 U.S. at 413 (Sutherland, J., joined by Van Devanter, McReynolds, and Butler, JJ., dissenting) (italics added). Sutherland's one other use of the word "arbitrary" came in a passage where he described the statute struck down in *Tipaldo*. See 300 U.S. at 412 (Sutherland, J., joined by Van Devanter, McReynolds, and Butler, JJ., dissenting).

60. Samuel R. Olken, "Justice Sutherland Reconsidered," *Vanderbilt Law Review* 62, no. 2 (2009): 641.

61. It is instructive here to consider the student Editorial Board–authored two-page "Note" that appeared in the *Yale Law Journal* in 1937. The article listed a multitude of characteristics of all of the judges who had ruled on the constitutionality of minimum wage laws in seventeen cases primarily at the U.S. Supreme Court or state supreme court level. The article identified fifty-five judges who had voted in favor of the constitutionality of such laws, and twenty who had voted against them, and the authors wondered, out loud, whether "the inner springs of judicial preference [are] to be found in the facts of life." Charts listed the birthplace, college alma mater, law school alma mater, marital status, religion, political affiliation, "clubs, etc.," type of legal practice engaged in, previous public office, age at time when vote was cast in the relevant case(s), average number of years serving on the relevant court, and average number of years as a judge (on all courts). "With the constitutionality of minimum wage laws for women established, a chapter in American constitutional 'law' has closed. The record of that chapter has brought

abundant vindication," the editors declared, "to those who urge that the judge often translates 'his tiny stock of scattered and uncoordinated philosophies . . . with all his weaknesses and unconscious prejudices,' into 'objective truth.'" "Judicial Statistics and the Constitutionality of Minimum Wage Legislation," *Yale Law Journal* 46, no. 7 (May 1937): 1227. Whatever merit there might be in analyzing the minimum wage decisions from this behavioralist perspective, these statistics should be used with caution, because appearances can be deceiving. Justice Sutherland, for example, bucks the trend for the overwhelming majority of the statistical categories in the article. Only the "age at time of decision" accurately describes Sutherland. However, even then the bigger picture offers no support to the "aging, nineteenth century" explanation for Sutherland's views in *Parrish*. This is because in that case, a mere five years separated the average age of the justices in the majority (sixty-nine), from that of the dissenters (seventy-four).

62. See, for example, Barry Cushman, "The Secret Lives of the Four Horsemen," *Virginia Law Review* 83 (1997); Olken, "Justice Sutherland Reconsidered"; Samuel R. Olken, "George Sutherland and the Business of Expression," in *Judging Free Speech: First Amendment Jurisprudence of US Supreme Court Justices*, edited by Helen J. Knowles and Steven B. Lichtman (New York: Palgrave Macmillan, 2015).

63. Paschal, *Mr. Justice Sutherland*, 92.

64. For a good overview, see David E. Bernstein, "The Feminist 'Horseman,'" *Green Bag 2d* 10 (Spring 2007).

65. 300 U.S. at 401, 402 (Sutherland, J., joined by Van Devanter, McReynolds, and Butler, JJ., dissenting).

66. 300 U.S. at 402 (Sutherland, J., joined by Van Devanter, McReynolds, and Butler, JJ., dissenting).

67. Alexander Hamilton, "Seventy-Eight, May 28, 1788: A View of the Constitution of the Judicial Department, in Relation to the Tenure of Good Behaviour," in *The Federalist*, ed. J. R. Pole (Indianapolis: Hackett Publishing, 2005), 412 (italics added).

68. 300 U.S. at 402 (Sutherland, J., joined by Van Devanter, McReynolds, and Butler, JJ., dissenting).

69. 300 U.S. at 402 (Sutherland, J., joined by Van Devanter, McReynolds, and Butler, JJ., dissenting).

70. 300 U.S. at 402 (Sutherland, J., joined by Van Devanter, McReynolds, and Butler, JJ., dissenting).

71. G. Edward White, "*West Coast Hotel*'s Place in American Constitutional History," *Yale Law Journal Online* 122 (September 2012), http://www.yalelawjournal.org/forum/west-coast-hotels-place-in-american-constitutional-history.

72. Letter from Helen Elizabeth Brown to George Sutherland, March 30, 1937 (italics added), Box 4, Folder 5, George Sutherland Papers, LC.

73. William R. Sample and Jennie Estella Sample, his wife v. West Coast Hotel Company, Complaint, April 9, 1937; Amended Complaint, June 5, 1937; Judgment, March 8, 1938. Superior Court of the State of Washington in and for the County of Chelan, No. 13086.

74. Quoted in "Talk of the Week (Compiled by Ollie M. James)," *Enquirer* (Cincinnati, OH), April 4, 1937.

75. Ernest Parrish, and Elsie Parrish, his wife v. West Coast Hotel Company, Satisfaction of Judgment, May 24, 1937. Superior Court of the State of Washington in and for the County of Chelan, No. 12215.

76. See Assignment of Judgment, April 3, 1937; Assignment of Judgment, April 6, 1937, Parrish v. West Coast Hotel Company, No. 12215; Judgment on Mandate from Supreme Court of the United States, May 14, 1937, Ernest Parrish, and Elsie Parrish, his wife v. West Coast Hotel Company, No. 26038, Chelan County No. 12215, Supreme Court of the State of Washington; Satisfaction of Judgment. I am exceptionally grateful to Mark Graber for helping me to decipher these documents.

77. Associated Press, "Minimum Wage Law Is Upheld," *Wenatchee Daily World* (Wenatchee, WA) (hereafter *World*), March 29, 1937.

78. "Wins Important Case," *World*, March 29, 1937. The photo of Elsie can be dated by consulting "Hotel Chambermaid Surprised by Interest Caused by Suit," *Morning Olympian* (Olympia, WA), November 17, 1936.

79. "Decision Affirms 29-Year Old Law," *World*, March 29, 1937. The text of the article got the age of the 1913 law correct even though the headline did not.

80. "Great Victory for State's Rights," *World*, March 29, 1937. It is interesting to note that while the quotation from Millard pluralizes the states, the headline does not; taken in their entirety, Millard's comments suggest that he did not intend for his quotation to suggest that the "rights" he was referring to were anything other than the "rights" of Washington State. Millard's term as chief justice ended on January 11, 1937. Charles H. Sheldon, *The Washington High Bench: A Biographical History of the State Supreme Court, 1889–1991* (Pullman: Washington State University Press, 1992), 250–53.

81. Associated Press, "Minimum Wage Law Will Be Enforced," *World*, March 29, 1937. Also see "Minimum Wage Law to Be Enforced," *Daily Olympian* (Olympia, WA), March 29, 1937; "State to Crack Down on Wage Law Violators," *Seattle Post-Intelligencer*, March 30, 1937.

82. "Omak Woman Wins Back Wages Case in Supreme Court," *Omak Chronicle* (Omak, WA), March 30, 1937.

83. "Omak's Minimum Pay Law Joan d'Arc Would Lecture," *World*, April 6, 1937.

84. "Another Minimum Wage Suit Filed," *World*, April 10, 1937. For example, see "Wages Over Five Years Are Sought," *Walla Walla Union* (Walla

Walla, WA), July 3, 1937. This article ran beneath a banner headline that read "WAITRESS SUES FOR $1,832 IN SALARY CASE."

85. "Union Will Seek to Collect Under U.S. Court Ruling," *Sunday News* (Seattle), April 3, 1937.

86. This section of this chapter draws heavily on the research that I conducted with Emma Rodman in Seattle in March 2018. For an initial draft of some of our findings, see Helen J. Knowles and Emma Rodman, "Legal Mobilization and the Politics of Economic Enforcement after *West Coast Hotel v. Parrish*" (paper presentation, Western Political Science Association Annual Meeting, San Diego, CA, April 18, 2019).

87. "Another Minimum Wage Suit Filed"; "200 Women File for Back Wages on Court Ruling," *Sunday News* (Seattle), April 10, 1937.

88. In 1940 approximately 25 percent of the foreign-born population of Seattle was from Scandinavia; another 20 percent was from Canada. Richard C. Berner, *Seattle 1921–1940: From Boom to Bust* (Seattle: Charles Press, 1992), 207. On the migration to Seattle of Scandinavians during the 1910s and 1920s, see Dana Frank, *Purchasing Power: Consumer Organizing, Gender, and the Seattle Labor Movement, 1919–1929* (New York: Cambridge University Press, 1994), 17.

89. "Women to Demand Pay," *Seattle Star*, April 2, 1937.

90. Which became the Service Employees International Union, or SEIU, in 1970.

91. Recall from chapter 5 that E. L. Skeel was no stranger to minimum wage litigation. Once it was decided that *Parrish* would be appealed to the U.S. Supreme Court, the West Coast Hotel Company asked John W. Roberts and Skeel to handle the litigation. For the U.S. Supreme Court litigation for the West Coast Hotel Company, Roberts primarily wrote the briefs, and Skeel undertook the oral argument.

92. See, for example, information about Burkheimer and Burkheimer (consisting of John E. Burkheimer, Dean Burkheimer, and Clark M. Burkheimer) in Joseph A. Lynch, ed., *Hubbell's Legal Directory 1924* (New York: Hubbell Publishing, 1924), 580.

93. Harvey O'Connor, *Revolution in Seattle: A Memoir* (New York: Monthly Review Press, 1964); Frank, *Purchasing Power*; Robert L. Friedheim, *The Seattle General Strike* (Seattle: University of Washington Press, 1964).

94. John C. Hughes, *Pressing On: Two Family-Owned Newspapers in the 21st Century* (Olympia: Washington State Legacy Project, 2015), 34.

95. "One Alone: An Interview with H. L. Upton," *Union Guardian* 1, no. 3 (September 1937).

96. King County Council Records, 1889–2012, Accession: 1940-001, Box 18: Subseries G Minutes, 1928–1947, 796, Labor Archives of Washington, University of Washington Special Collections.

97. Ethel Fritz v. Russell C. Perkins; Cora E. Perkins; and the National Bank of Commerce, a corporation, individually and as executors of the Estate of William D. Perkins, deceased, No. 297864, Complaint, April 2, 1937, 1–2; Findings of Facts and Conclusions of Law, June 21, 1937, King County Superior Court, Seattle, WA (hereafter KCSC). Mary Lee Dempsey v. Russell C. Perkins; Cora E. Perkins; and the National Bank of Commerce, a corporation, individually and as executors of the Estate of William D. Perkins, deceased, No. 297865, Complaint, April 2, 1937, 1–2; Findings of Facts and Conclusions of Law, June 21, 1937, KCSC.

98. Berner, *Seattle 1921–1940*, 302.

99. Quoted in Berner, *Seattle 1921–1940*, 301.

100. John J. Brandt and Frieda A. Brandt, his wife v. Charles Horn and Lillian Horn, No. 299339, Complaint, May 20, 1937, KCSC.

101. Oscar Elsoe and Mary Elsoe, his wife v. Calvin Phillips & Co., a corporation, No. 299760, Complaint, June 9, 1937, 1–2, KCSC.

102. Berner, *Seattle 1921–1940*, 205.

103. Berner, *Seattle 1921–1940*, 172.

104. Berner, *Seattle 1921–1940*, 183.

105. S. F. Harrell and Josephine Harrell, his wife v. Wm. D. Perkins, a corporation, No. 300008, Motion to Strike, June 21, 1937, 1, KCSC.

106. "$200,000 Wage Suits Planned," *Seattle Times*, May 14, 1937.

107. No female jurist served on any Superior Court in Washington State until 1970, when Nancy Holman became a member of the King County Superior Court. She was appointed by Governor Daniel J. Evans and then won her retention election in 1972 and every reelection thereafter. She retired from the bench in 1997. Mike Roarke, "Pioneering Jurist Nancy Holman Dies at 66," *Seattle Post-Intelligencer*, April 10, 2002, accessed May 28, 2019, https://www.seattlepi.com/news/article/Pioneering-jurist-Nancy-Holman-dies-at-66-1084897.php.

108. In accordance with Special Rule XII, the judges would occasionally sit *en banc* (as a complete group of thirteen) for some issues of law such as, for example, the drawing of a grand jury.

109. Douglas served on the King County Superior Court for a total of thirty-nine years, retiring on December 31, 1963. "Judge Malcolm Douglas, King County Superior Court, Seattle, October 15, 1958," University of Washington Digital Collections: Portraits Collection, accessed May 29, 2019, http://digitalcollections.lib.washington.edu/cdm/ref/collection/portraits/id/700.

110. "Janitress" was generally considered a catchall term. However, as the court explained in its opinion, this work typically required the employee to perform multiple different duties that could be characterized as different types of jobs: "These nineteen suits . . . are brought by women who have been employed as housekeepers, managers, janitresses, caretakers, maids, or in other similar capacities, in various apartment houses in the city of Seattle." William

Walsh and Mae Walsh, his wife v. T. M. Donahoe, as Receiver of The Home Savings & Loan Association, Insolvent, No. 298659, Memorandum Opinion in Minimum Wage Cases, October 5, 1937, 3, KCSC. A rare exception to the *apartment house* janitress plaintiffs was Augusta Ellerson, who between 1930 and 1936 worked intermittently as an office building cleaner. Augusta Ellerson v. Vance Lumber, a corporation, No. 299008, Complaint, May 10, 1937, 1–2, KCSC.

111. Kathryn Daggett v. E. B. Simonton and Jane Doe Simonton, his wife, No. 298680, Memorandum Decision, October 26, 1938, 2 (italics added), KCSC.

112. Memorandum Opinion, 7.

113. Section 2 of the 1913 law (italics added).

114. Memorandum Opinion, 7.

115. Evelyn Pandos, a widow, and Olive Morrison, a single woman, v. John Davis & Co., a corporation, No. 298714, Opening Brief of Defendants in Minimum Wage Cases in Support of Demurrers, Motions to Strike, Motions to Make More Definite and Certain, and Motions to Separately State, July 10, 1937, 8, KCSC.

116. *Pandos and Morrison*, Opening Brief of Defendants, 8.

117. *Pandos and Morrison*, Opening Brief of Defendants, 8.

118. *Webster's New International Dictionary*, 2nd ed. (italics added), quoted in Memorandum Opinion, 7.

119. Memorandum Opinion, 7. The Washington State Supreme Court case to which the defendants referred and which used this dictionary definition was *Dessen v. Department of Labor and Industries of Washington*, 190 Wash. 69, 74 (1937).

120. Memorandum Opinion, 8.

121. Memorandum Opinion, 9, 12.

122. Washington revised statutes, Section 165, quoted in Memorandum Opinion, 9.

123. Memorandum Opinion, 11, 10–11.

124. Memorandum Opinion, 11.

125. Memorandum Opinion, 12.

126. 13 Wash. 550 (1896).

127. Memorandum Opinion, 15 (emphasis in original).

128. Memorandum Opinion, 16.

129. Leslie to Hamilton, February 8, 1937.

130. Memorandum Opinion, 19 (italics added).

131. George Roberts and Charlotte Roberts, his wife v. Seattle Federal Savings & Loan Association, Inc., a corporation; and William Duncan and Stella E. Duncan, his wife, No. 298446, Complaint, April 22, 1937, 2, KCSC.

132. Memorandum Opinion, 21.

133. Memorandum Opinion, 25 (italics added).

134. Joseph and Marian Willi, Husband and Wife v. Alec Hanna and Agatha F. Hanna, his wife, No. 298450, Answer and Affirmative Defense, December 28, 1938, 2, KCSC.

135. Ema Swingen, a widow v. E. E. Powell, No. 298667, Answer and Affirmative Defense, April 27, 1939, 2, KCSC. The majority of the women plaintiffs in the minimum wage cases were provided with accommodation in the apartment houses wherein they worked; the Swingen case was one of the rare instances when a defendant sought to evict his janitress (for failure to pay rent) during the course of the litigation. In August 1937 Judge Allen imposed a restraining order, preventing Powell from evicting Swingen. "Eviction Halted by Judge Allen," *Seattle Times*, September 1, 1937.

136. Memorandum Decision, 2, Daggett v. Simonton (italics added).

137. Hilda Ferber v. Anna Wisen, 195 Wash. 603 (1938).

138. See McDonald v. Goddard, 2 Wn. 2d 553 (1940); Dorothy Evans v. Rudolf Hartmann, 5 Wn. 2d 434 (1940).

CONCLUSION

1. Hadley Arkes, *The Return of George Sutherland: Restoring a Jurisprudence of Natural Rights* (Princeton, NJ: Princeton University Press, 1997), 142.

2. It would, however, be wholly inappropriate here to examine current minimum wage controversies (and the accompanying voluminous cottage industry of literature—academic or otherwise—that they spawn). As this book has shown, the story of *West Coast Hotel v. Parrish* helps us to understand the *historical* foundations of the constitutional aspects of those controversies. But they are just that, *historical*. It would be perilously problematic to wade into the twenty-first century after telling a story rooted in the previous millennium. I have addressed this issue elsewhere. See Helen J. Knowles and Julianne A. Toia, "Defining 'Popular Constitutionalism': The Kramer Versus Kramer Problem," *Southern University Law Review* 42 (Fall 2014). In that article, my coauthor and I criticize two scholars who allowed ideological, contemporary commentary to intrude upon (and tarnish) their otherwise historical scholarship. The first scholar is Scott D. Gerber—principally, see Scott Douglas Gerber, *A Distinct Judicial Power: The Origins of an Independent Judiciary, 1606–1787* (New York: Oxford University Press, 2011). That book contains a decidedly incongruous "Appendix" (which is actually an epilogue). For our critique, see Knowles and Toia, "Defining 'Popular Constitutionalism,'" 44–45 (and 47n55, where we reference other Gerber works that fall prey to the same intellectual problem). The second scholar is Larry D. Kramer—principally see Larry D. Kramer, "The Supreme Court 2000 Term Foreword: We the Court," *Harvard Law Review* 115 (January 2001); Larry D. Kramer, *The People Themselves: Popular Constitutionalism and Judicial Review* (New York:

Oxford University Press, 2004). For our critique of the inclusion of incongruous sentences in the article, and an incongruous final chapter in the book, see
"Defining 'Popular Constitutionalism,'" 40–43.

3. "Women's Constitutional Right to Starve," Radio Address by Elinore
Morehouse Herrick, Regional Director, NLRB, Station WEAF, 6:35 P.M., Fri-
day, March 13, 1936, 2, Box 2, Folder 51, National Consumers League Records
#5235, Kheel Center for Labor-Management Documentation and Archives,
Cornell University Library.

4. Margie Jones, "Elsie Parrish: A Woman History Forgot," *Okanogan
County Heritage* 29, no. 1 (Winter 1990–91): 14.

5. Letter from Jane Norman Smith to Alma Lutz, January 5, 1937, Alma
Lutz Papers, 1921–1961 (hereafter Lutz Papers, 1921–1961). MC182, folder
98. Schlesinger Library, Radcliffe Institute, Harvard University, Cambridge,
Mass. (hereafter Schlesinger Library).

6. Julie Novkov, *Constituting Workers, Protecting Women: Gender, Law, and
Labor in the Progressive Era and New Deal Years* (Ann Arbor: University of
Michigan Press, 2004), 197 (italics added), 187, and generally chap. 5.

7. Novkov, *Constituting Workers*, 197 (italics added).

8. Novkov, *Constituting Workers*, 187.

9. Dorothy Thompson, "Feminists Divided," *New York Herald Tribune*,
June 6, 1936.

10. 298 U.S. 587 (1936).

11. Muller v. Oregon, 208 U.S. 412, 421 (1908).

12. Elaine Zahnd Johnson, "Protective Legislation and Women's Work:
Oregon's Ten-Hour Law and the *Muller v. Oregon Case*, 1900–1913" (PhD
diss., University of Oregon, 1982), 398.

13. National Woman's Party Press Release, June 6, 1936, 1, Lutz Papers,
1921–1961, A-34, folder 51, Schlesinger Library.

14. 261 U.S. 525 (1923).

15. Alma Lutz, "Equal Rights Report," October 24, 1936, Lutz Papers,
1921–1961, MC182, folder 72, Schlesinger Library.

16. "Thank God for the Supreme Court," National Woman's Party Press
Release, June 6, 1936, 7, Alma Lutz Papers, 1927–1946 (hereafter Lutz Papers,
1927–1946), A-34, folder 51, Schlesinger Library.

17. Letter from Ruth G. Williams to George Sutherland, June 3, 1936,
Box 4, Folder 4, George Sutherland Papers, Manuscript Division, Library of
Congress, Washington, DC (hereafter GSP-LC).

18. Williams to Sutherland.

19. Brief for National Woman's Party et al. as Amici Curiae Supporting
Respondent, Morehead v. People ex rel. Joseph Tipaldo at 34 (italics added),
298 U.S. 587 (1936) (No. 838), 1936 WL 64946 (quoting from 261 U.S. at
553). The brief was coauthored by two very accomplished NWP lawyers,
Burnita Shelton Matthews and Rebekah Scandrett Greathouse, who both

pursued myriad changes to law and policy that would further women's rights and equality as those concepts were understood by the NWP. See Richard F. Hamm, "Mobilizing Legal Talent For a Cause: The National Woman's Party and the Campaign to Make Jury Service For Women a Federal Right," *Journal of Gender, Social Policy & the Law* 9, no. 1 (2001): 101. In 1949 President Harry S. Truman appointed Matthews to the United States District Court for the District of Columbia. She was the nation's first female United States district judge and only the second woman to hold an Article III federal judgeship. On Matthews's career, see Kate Greene, "Burnita Shelton Matthews (1894–1988): The Struggle for Women's Rights," in *Mississippi Women: Their Histories, Their Lives*, edited by Martha H. Swain, Elizabeth Anne Payne, and Marjorie Julian Spruill (Athens: University of Georgia Press, 2003). It is an interesting quirk of the history of minimum wage laws for women in the U.S. that the first female Article III judge—Florence Ellinwood Allen, whom President Roosevelt appointed to the Sixth Circuit Court of Appeals in 1934 (she previously served for eleven years on the Ohio Supreme Court)—was also a staunch defender of women's rights, but not as they were understood and advocated for by the NWP. This can be seen, in part, in the unanimous per curiam opinion that she joined, in November 1936, upholding Ohio's 1933 minimum wage law for women. In that case—*Walker v. Chapman*—the Sixth Circuit concluded that, like the New York law struck down in *Tipaldo*, the Ohio law was distinguishable from the federal statute struck down in *Adkins*. This is an unremarkable conclusion given that the Ohio and New York laws, enacted in 1933, were both based on the language of the NCL's model law (as discussed in chapter 3). It is therefore interesting that the Sixth Circuit panel of judges (including Allen) *upheld* the Ohio law, stating that "the decision in the Morehead Case strengthens our view." 17 F. Supp. 308, 309 (1936). Recall that in *Tipaldo*, the U.S. Supreme Court deferred to the New York Court of Appeals construction of the language of the New York law even though it was plain to most people that that court had erred in seeing no substantive and legally meaningful difference between that law and the one in *Adkins*. In essence, in *Walker* this allowed the Sixth Circuit to say that it was not "bound to follow the construction placed upon the statutes of any other state by the courts of such state," thus leaving it free (per the decision in *Tipaldo*) to conclude that its statute was distinguishable from the one struck down in *Adkins*. 17 F. Supp. at 311. On Allen's career, see Jeanette E. Tuve, *First Lady of the Law: Florence Ellinwood Allen* (Lanham, MD: University Press of America, 1984); Sarah Wilson, "Florence Ellinwood Allen," in *Women in Law: A Bio-Bibliographical Sourcebook*, edited by Rebecca Mae Salokar and Mary L. Volcansek (Santa Barbara: ABC-Clio, 1996).

20. National Woman's Party Press Release, 1.

21. Letter from Anna Kelton Wiley to George Sutherland, March 30, 1937, Box 4, Folder 5, GSP-LC.

22. For a short but informative biographical vignette of Hooker, see Lauren R. Silberman, *Wild Women of Maryland: Grit & Gumption in the Free State* (Charleston, SC: History Press, 2015), 77–82.

23. Letter from Edith Houghton Hooker to George Sutherland, April 5, 1937, Box 4, Folder 5, GSP-LC; and Letter from Edith Houghton Hooker to Willis Van Devanter, April 2, 1937, Box 38, Folder 5, Willis Van Devanter Papers, Manuscript Division, Library of Congress, Washington, DC. Technically, the two letters were not identical, because there is an extra sentence in the one to Van Devanter; however, that sentence is inconsequential and does not change the substance of the letter.

24. Hooker to Sutherland; and Hooker to Van Devanter.

25. Hooker to Sutherland; and Hooker to Van Devanter.

26. "For Your Use in Connection with Editorial and Other Comment on Minimum Wage Situation," National Woman's Party Press Release/Talking Points, April 9, 1937, Lutz Papers, 1927–1946, A-34, folder 49.

27. Alice S. Cheyney, "The Course of Minimum Wage Legislation in the United States," *International Labour Review* 38, no. 1 (July 1938): 38. Further legislative developments followed in 1938 and 1939. For example, in 1938 Arizona imposed a new "fair" minimum wage law for women, replacing its sixteen dollar weekly wage that had been applied across the board. *Seattle Times*, February 17, 1938. And in 1939 the Territory of Alaska raised its weekly minimum wage for women. Associated Press, "Alaskan Senate Passes Wage Bill," *Seattle Times*, February 25, 1939; "Women's Wages Made $22 by Alaska House," *Seattle Times*, March 6, 1939.

28. Robert P. Ingalls, "New York and the Minimum-Wage Movement, 1933–1937," *Labor History* 15, no. 2 (Spring 1974): 195–97.

29. Associated Press, "Oregon Cuts Women's Hours," *Seattle Times*, July 19, 1937.

30. I.W.C. Order No. 36, Department of Labor and Industries Industrial Welfare Committee of the State of Washington, October 7, 1937.

31. James A. Wood, "Speaking For the *Times*: Not New Deal Laws," *Seattle Times*, April 7, 1937.

32. Cheyney, "The Course of Minimum Wage Legislation," 38.

33. Confirmation hearings of Ruth Bader Ginsburg, Day 1, Part 2, July 20, 1993, at 36:30, https://www.c-span.org/video/?45747-1/ginsburg-confirmation-hearing-day-1-part-2&start=2039.

34. "Message to Congress on Establishing Minimum Wages and Maximum Hours, May 24, 1937," American Presidency Project, accessed December 7, 2019, https://www.presidency.ucsb.edu/node/209566 (italics added).

35. "Excerpts from the Press Conference in Hyde Park, June 28, 1938," American Presidency Project, accessed December 7, 2019, https://www.presidency.ucsb.edu/node/208993.

36. "Fireside Chat, June 24, 1938," American Presidency Project, accessed December 7, 2019, https://www.presidency.ucsb.edu/node/208978.

37. James MacGregor Burns, *Congress on Trial: The Legislative Process and the Administrative State* (New York: Harper, 1949), 69.

38. John S. Forsythe, "Legislative History of the Fair Labor Standards Act," *Law and Contemporary Problems* 6, no. 3 (Summer 1939): 474, 478, 478n79. One of the main arguments that Forsythe makes throughout the entirety of this article is that the drafting of the FLSA was dominated by battles over flexibility.

39. Forsythe, "Legislative History," 473.

40. 301 U.S. 1 (1937).

41. Robert N. Willis, "The Evolution of the Fair Labor Standards Act," *University of Miami Law Review* 26, no. 3 (1972): 608.

42. U.S. Const. art. I, 8.

43. Gibbons v. Ogden, 22 U.S. 1 (1824).

44. See, for example, United States v. E. C. Knight Co., 156 U.S. 1 (1895); Hammer v. Dagenhart, 247 U.S. 251 (1918).

45. Landon R. Y. Storrs, *Civilizing Capitalism: The National Consumers' League, Women's Activism, and Labor Standards in the New Deal Era* (Chapel Hill: University of North Carolina Press, 2000), 183 (italics added).

46. Section 6 provided an hourly minimum wage of 25 cents for the first year of the law's existence, then 30 cents per hour until October 1945, at which point there would be a further increase to 40 cents per hour. Section 7 capped permissible weekly working hours at 44 for the first year, 42 for the second year, and then 40 after that; it was legal for employees to work overtime, but the law required their employers to pay them one and one-half for any overtime.

47. Storrs, *Civilizing Capitalism*, 197 (and generally chap. 7). For other discussions of these exemptions, see Forsythe, "Legislative History"; Ira Katznelson, *Fear Itself: The New Deal and the Origins of Our Time* (New York: Liveright, 2014).

48. Vivien Hart, "Minimum-Wage Policy and Constitutional Inequality: The Paradox of the Fair Labor Standards Act of 1938," *Journal of Policy History* 1, no. 3 (1989): 339.

49. Willis, "The Evolution of the Fair Labor Standards Act," 607.

EPILOGUE

1. Kris Young and Mark Behler, "Cascadian Hotel Was Site of Historical Lawsuit," *Wenatchee Business Journal* 11, no. 7 (July 1997): 65.

2. "Omak's Minimum Pay Law Joan d'Arc Would Lecture," *Wenatchee Daily World* (Wenatchee, WA) (hereafter *World*), April 6, 1937.

3. Peter Irons, *The Courage of Their Convictions: Sixteen Americans Who Fought Their Way to the Supreme Court* (New York: Penguin, 1990), 3.

4. C. B. Conner, "The Minimum Wage Case," in *From the Blue Ridge to the Cascade Range: Recollections of Boyhood Days in the Mountains of Virginia— and Work as a Lawyer in Oklahoma and in the Shadows of the Cascade Range* (unpublished manuscript, n.d.), 192 (italics added).

5. Conner, "The Minimum Wage Case," 168.

6. John P. Hartman, "A Tribute to Charles B. Conner, of Wenatchee, Washington," in Conner, *From the Blue Ridge to the Cascade Range*, 195.

7. Tom, born in 1902, died in 1910; Eleanor, born in 1907, passed away in 1928, aged twenty. "Heart Attack in Seattle is Fatal to C. B. Conner," *World*, May 22, 1941.

8. When born, Robert was given the name "Robert E. Lee Conner" because of his parents' love of the general. Robert later chose to remove "Lee" and just go by "Robert E. Conner." Chris Conner, email message to author, January 29, 2019.

9. Conner, email.

10. The majority of the information contained in this paragraph is taken from a family timeline shared with me by Chris Conner (C. B.'s granddaughter). It is supplemented by information from "Heart Attack in Seattle is Fatal"; "Conner Rites Tuesday," *World*, May 26, 1941; "Services for C. B. Conner," *World*, May 28, 1941. The problematic nature of the omission of references to *Parrish* in the obituaries of Conner is compounded by the presence, in the *World*'s obituary of Fred Crollard, of the following two very misleading sentences: "One of Crollard's cases made legal history with regard to the minimum wage law. He was responsible for the United States Supreme Court decision to declare that state legislature be empowered to set up minimum wage laws." "Fred Crollard Dies; Long-Time Civic Leader," *World*, June 23, 1968.

11. John A. Gellatly, *A History of Wenatchee: "The Apple Capital of the World"* (self-pub., 1962), 310.

12. Eva Anderson, "Young Attorneys Felt His Guiding Hand," *World*, January 31, 1967.

13. Sydney Crollard Ranney, email message to author, June 11, 2019; "Business Women in Many Fields," *World*, October 16, 1966.

14. Sydney Crollard Ranney, email message to author, February 10, 2019.

15. Ranney, email; "Dad's Memories of World War II"—transcript of December 26, 2003 interview between Jeff Crollard and Homer Crollard— kindly shared with me by Sydney Crollard Ranney.

16. "Dad's Memories of World War II."

17. "Judge W. O. Parr Stricken Suddenly," *World*, February 18, 1942; "Parr Services to be Friday, 11 A.M.," *World*, February 19, 1942.

18. Quoted in "Judge W. O. Parr Stricken Suddenly."

19. "Parr Services to be Friday, 11 A.M."

20. "Plans Announced for Deluxe Downtown Motel," *World*, February 17, 1961.

21. John A. Jakle, Keith A. Sculle, and Jefferson S. Rogers, *The Motel in America* (Baltimore: Johns Hopkins University Press, 1996), 43–51.

22. The pages of the *World* are replete with announcements of meetings and conventions that were held at the Cascadian.

23. Andy Dappen, *Buckle of the Power Belt: Recollections of* The Wenatchee World*'s First 100 Years* (Wenatchee: World Publishing, 2005), 336; Hu Blonk, "Recollections of Wenatchee's Old Cascadian Hotel," *World*, January 15, 1987.

24. "Ray Clark, Booster of the Far Northwest," *Hotel Monthly* 46, no. 538 (January 1938). At the same time as managing and promoting the Cascadian, Clark served as the treasurer for the developers promoting construction of the Grand Coulee Dam, and he enthusiastically dedicated time to serving as one of Rufus Woods's boosters for the project. Wilfred Woods, "Talking It Over: Cascadian—A Building With Many Stories," *World*, October 26, 2007. Also see, for example, Letter from Rufus Woods to the Officers of the Columbia River Development League, February 1, 1936 (mentioning, in glowing terms, Clark's involvement) in Series I: Outgoing Correspondence, Box 1, Folder 15 (1936), MS001-06-01, Rufus Woods Papers, Archives and Special Collections, Brooks Library, Central Washington University.

25. Her first professional appearance, as a seventeen-year-old, was in Verdi's *Il Trovatore* in Dresden, Germany. Richard W. Amero, "Madame Schumann-Heink: San Diego's Diva," *Southern California Quarterly* 73, no. 2 (Summer 1991): 158.

26. John Briggs, "Schumann-Heink in an LP Reissue," *New York Times*, April 6, 1958.

27. Quoted in Amero, "Madame Schumann-Heink," 174.

28. Communication Artifacts Document, 004–35–1, Wenatchee Valley Museum and Cultural Center, Wenatchee, WA.

29. Tracy Warner, "The Night Nat King Cole Changed Wenatchee," *World*, March 10, 2000.

30. Warner, "The Night Nat King Cole Changed Wenatchee." Also see Chris Rader, "Bob Godfrey Played for Wenatchee Dancers," *The Confluence* 27, no. 4 (Winter 2011–12).

31. Jake Lodato, "Pangborn, Herndon Undertake World-Famous Flight," *The Confluence* 32, no. 4 (Winter 2016–17).

32. Lodato, "Pangborn, Herndon," 12.

33. Lodato, "Pangborn, Herndon," 12.

34. "Breakfast on Terra Firma," *Daily News* (New York), October 9, 1931.

35. "Gina Tucker Retires After Nearly 30 Years With WIH," *The Have a Nice Day: A Newsletter By and For Century Plaza Employees*, September 1975, 1, in Box 15, Scrapbook, Folder 126, Georgina Tucker Papers, 1920–1997, Manuscripts, Archives, and Special Collections, Washington State University Libraries, Pullman, WA (hereafter Tucker Papers); "Popular Collegiennes—Superior Dining Service," *Okanogan Independent* (Okanogan, WA), September 23, 1933.

36. "Popular Collegiennes."

37. "Gina Tucker Wins Thurston-Dupar Honors," *Front! Western International Hotels*, February 1971, in Box 1, Folder 1, Tucker Papers. An article about her life indicates that when Gina Tucker got married in 1940, she "interrupted her hotel career for a period of some 13 years." However, the same article and other sources consistently state that she gave forty-two years of service (1933–75) to Western Hotels, Inc. "Gina Tucker—WIH's Active 'First Lady' Retires," *Front! Western International Hotels*, October 1975, in Box 15, Scrapbook, Folder 126, Tucker Papers.

38. "Former Elevator Operator Earns Alumni Recognition," in Box 1, Folder 3, Tucker Papers.

39. Gail S. Murray, "Forty Years Ago: The Great Depression Comes to Arkansas," *Arkansas Historical Quarterly* 29, no. 4 (Winter 1970): 292–95; Nan Elizabeth Woodruff, *As Rare as Rain: Federal Relief in the Great Southern Drought of 1930–31* (Urbana: University of Illinois Press, 1985), 4–5.

40. "Former Elevator Operator Earns Alumni Recognition"; Erik Lacitis, "Hotelier Harry Mullikin Got Big Things Done," *Seattle Times*, May 5, 2011; Harriet King, "The Man Behind the Megahotels," *New York Times*, May 8, 1977.

41. Ray Sylvester, email message to author, November 18, 2017; Harry Mullikin, "Obituary," accessed June 2, 2019, http://www.legacy.com/obituaries /seattletimes/obituary.aspx?pid=150773351; Edward E. Carlson, *Recollections of a Lucky Fellow* (Seattle: Edward E. Carlson, 1989), 152.

42. Lacitis, "Hotelier Harry Mullikin"; Carlson, *Recollections*, 128–29; King, "The Man Behind the Megahotels."

43. "About Hotel Men," *Hotel Monthly* 46, no. 546 (September 1938).

44. Quoted in Vern Matthews, "'Permanents' Hit the Hardest," *World*, July 21, 1971.

45. "Cascadian Hotel Sold to Local Men For $790,000," *World*, December 2, 1962. It came as no surprise to anyone that Wilf Woods would at some point become involved in trying to maintain the Cascadian.

46. Quoted in Nancy McMinn, "Wilf Woods: Cascadian Hotel, a Lesson Learned," *World*, May 26, 2012.

47. "Seattle Firm Buys Cascadian Hotel," *World*, September 3, 1965; "Cascadian Owners Seek Conventions," *World*, September 7, 1965.

48. "Ward Buys Cascadian," *World*, November 1, 1967.

49. "Cascadian Hotel Closes Doors," *World*, July 20, 1971.

50. "Cascadian Hotel Closes Doors."

51. Quoted in "Cascadian Hotel Closes Doors."

52. Matthews, "'Permanents' Hit the Hardest."

53. "Cascadian Hotel Closes Doors."

54. "Cascadian Will Need a Subsidy," *World*, July 22, 1971.

55. "Cascadian Will Need a Subsidy."

56. "Cascadian Will Need a Subsidy."

57. "Cascadian Stirring? Condominiums Studied," *World*, December 2, 1971.

58. "New Owners Plan Three-Part Cascadian Revival," *World*, March 7, 1972.

59. Mike Irwin, "Uptown Funk? Some Have Reservations About Defunct Motel Sign," *World*, March 4, 2016.

60. "Switch to Apartments an Uptown Decision," *Wenatchee Business Journal* 12, no. 3 (March 1998): B11.

61. "Cascadian Stirring?"; "New Owners Plan Three-Part Cascadian Revival"; "Cascadian Awaits Support," *World*, June 20, 1972; "Planners Turn Down Cascadian Proposal," *World*, October 27, 1972.

62. "Cascadian Remodeling Start Due in January," *World*, November 22, 1972; "$670,000 Cascadian Job Permit Asked," *World*, January 24, 1973; "Next Cascadian Move Expected," *World*, February 21, 1973; "Cascadian to Reopen Within Next Two Weeks," *World*, October 30, 1973.

63. "Cascadian Furnishings to Be Sold Off," *World*, February 22, 1973.

64. Hu Blonk, "Recollections of Wenatchee's Old Cascadian Hotel," *World*, January 15, 1987.

65. Jakle and Sculle, *America's Main Street Hotels*, 58.

66. Chris Rader, "Wenatchee Avenue Block Brims with History," *The Confluence* 29, no. 3 (Fall 2013): 3; Tracy Warner, "The Maid Who Made History," *World*, February 2, 2007.

67. Associated Press, "Hotel Chambermaid Surprised by Interest Caused by Suit," *Morning Olympian* (Olympia, WA), November 17, 1936.

68. Robert E. Ficken, *Rufus Woods, the Columbia River, & the Building of Modern Washington* (Pullman: Washington State University Press, 1995), 195–6.

69. *Polk's Everett (Washington) City Directory, vol. XXXIII (1944)* (Seattle: R. L. Polk, 1944), 565; *Polk's Everett (Washington) City Directory, vol. XXXV (1948)* (Seattle: R. L. Polk, 1948), 513, 419; *Polk's Everett (Washington) City Directory, vol. XXXVI (1950)* (Seattle: R. L. Polk, 1950), 575.

70. *Pacific Directory Company's Compton City Directory 1951* (Arcadia, CA: Pacific Directory Company, 1951), 172.

71. Debra Parrish Stewart, interview with the author, January 16, 2019. In 1961, at the age of seventy-one, Roy Lee remarried (his bride, Annette, was eighty-one). Roy died two years later. He is buried in the same cemetery as Elsie. Debra recalls that on numerous occasions her mother and her grandmother took her to visit the couple (who were living in the greater Los Angeles area). Stewart, interview.

72. Stewart, interview.

73. Stewart, interview.

74. Stewart, interview.

75. Stewart, interview.

76. Adela Rogers St. Johns, *Some Are Born Great: Lively and Controversial Tales of Some of the Extraordinary Women of Our Time* (Garden City, NY: Doubleday, 1974), 1; Dennis McLellan, "Writer Adela Rogers St. Johns Dies at 94," *Los Angeles Times*, August 11, 1988.

77. St. Johns, *Some Are Born Great*, 10. Coincidentally, Elsie Parrish and Adela St. Johns have a final resting place in common.

78. St. Johns, *Some Are Born Great*, 185.

79. As the Supreme Court's 1925 Rules stated:

It shall be requisite to the admission of attorneys or counsellors to practice in this court, that they shall have been such for three years past in the highest courts of the State, Territory, District, or Insular Possession to which they respectively belong, and that their private and professional characters shall appear to be good. . . . Admissions will be granted only upon oral motion by a member of the bar in open court, and upon his assurance that he knows, or after reasonable inquiry believes, the applicant possesses the necessary qualifications and has filed with the clerk the required certificate and statement. ("Revised Rules of the Supreme Court of the United States, Adopted June 8, 1925. Effective July 1, 1925" [Act of February 13, 1925, printed as appendix], 1–2, accessed June 2, 2019, https://www.supremecourt.gov/ctrules/rules/Rules_1925.pdf)

Bibliography

CASES CITED

Adair v. United States, 208 U.S. 161 (1908)

Adkins v. Children's Hospital, 261 U.S. 525 (1923)

Ah How v. Furth, 13 Wash. 550 (1896)

Augusta Ellerson v. Vance Lumber, a corporation, No. 299008, King County Superior Court, Seattle, WA (1937)

Baker v. Carr, 369 U.S. 186 (1962)

Bowers v. Hardwick, 478 U.S. 186 (1986)

Bradwell v. Illinois, 83 U.S. 130 (1873)

Brown v. Board of Education of Topeka, Kansas, 347 U.S. 483 (1954)

Buchanan v. Warley, 245 U.S. 60 (1917)

Bunting v. Oregon, 243 U.S. 426 (1917)

Chicago, Burlington, & Quincy Railroad Company v. McGuire, 219 U.S. 549 (1911)

Citizens United v. Federal Election Commission, 558 U.S. 310 (2010)

Commonwealth v. Beatty, 15 Pa. Super. 5 (1900)

Commonwealth v. Hamilton Manufacturing Company, 120 Mass. 383 (1876)

Coppage v. Kansas, 236 U.S. 1 (1915)

DeShaney v. Winnebago County Department of Social Services, 489 U.S. 189 (1989)

Dessen v. Department of Labor and Industries of Washington, 190 Wash. 69 (1937)

Dorothy Evans v. Rudolf Hartmann, 5 Wn. 2d 434 (1940)

Ema Swingen, a widow v. E. E. Powell, No. 298667, King County Superior Court, Seattle, WA (1939)

Ernest Parrish, and Elsie Parrish, his wife v. West Coast Hotel Company, Superior Court of the State of Washington in and for the County of Chelan, No. 12215 (1935; 1937)

Ernest Parrish et al. v. West Coast Hotel Company, 185 Wash. 581 (1936)

Ethel Fritz v. Russell C. Perkins; Cora E. Perkins; and the National Bank of Commerce, a corporation, individually and as executors of the Estate of William D. Perkins, deceased, No. 297864, King County Superior Court, Seattle, WA (1937)

Evelyn Pandos, a widow, and Olive Morrison, a single woman, v. John Davis & Co., a corporation, No. 298714, King County Superior Court, Seattle, WA (1937)

George Roberts and Charlotte Roberts, his wife v. Seattle Federal Savings & Loan Association, Inc., a corporation; and William Duncan and Stella E. Duncan, his wife, No. 298446, King County Superior Court, Seattle, WA (1937)

German Alliance Insurance Company v. Lewis, 243 U.S. 332 (1917)

Gibbons v. Ogden, 22 U.S. 1 (1824)

Gottstein et al. v. Lister, 88 Wash. 462 (1915)

Great Northern Railway Company v. State of Washington, 300 U.S. 154 (1937)

Hammer v. Dagenhart, 247 U.S. 251 (1918)

Hawley v. Walker, 232 U.S. 718 (1914)

Hilda Ferber v. Anna Wisen, 195 Wash. 603 (1938)

Holden v. Hardy, 169 U.S. 366 (1898)

Home Building & Loan Assoc. v. Blaisdell, 290 U.S. 398 (1934)

John J. Brandt and Frieda A. Brandt, his wife v. Charles Horn and Lillian Horn, No. 299339, King County Superior Court, Seattle, WA (1937)

Joseph and Marian Willi, Husband and Wife v. Alec Hanna and Agatha F. Hanna, his wife, No. 298450, King County Superior Court, Seattle, WA (1938)

Kathryn Daggett v. E. B. Simonton and Jane Doe Simonton, his wife, No. 298680, King County Superior Court, Seattle, WA (1938)

Larsen v. Rice, 100 Wash. 642 (1918)

Lawrence v. Texas, 539 U.S. 558 (2003)

Lochner v. New York, 198 U.S. 45 (1905)

Marjorie Weiss v. Swedish Hospital, 16 Wash. 2d 446 (1943)

Mary Lee Dempsey v. Russell C. Perkins; Cora E. Perkins; and the National Bank of Commerce, a corporation, individually and as executors of the Estate of William D. Perkins, deceased, No. 297865, King County Superior Court, Seattle, WA (1937)

McCulloch v. Maryland, 17 U.S. 316 (1819)

McDonald v. Goddard, 2 Wn. 2d 553 (1940)

Meyer v. Nebraska, 262 U.S. 390 (1923)

Minnesota v. Barber, 136 U.S. 313 (1890)

Miranda v. Arizona, 384 U.S. 436 (1966)

Morehead v. New York ex rel. Tipaldo, 298 U.S. 587 (1936)

Morse v. Frederick, 505 U.S. 393 (2007)

Muller v. Oregon, 208 U.S. 412 (1908)

Munn v. Illinois, 94 U.S. 113 (1876)

Murphy v. Sardell, 269 U.S. 530 (1925)

Nebbia v. New York, 291 U.S. 502 (1934)

NLRB v. Friedman-Harry Marks Clothing Co., 301 U.S. 58 (1937)

NLRB v. Fruehauf Trailer Corp., 301 U.S. 49 (1937)

NLRB v. Jones & Laughlin Steel Corp., 301 U.S. 1 (1937)

Obergefell v. Hodges, 576 U.S. 644 (2015)

O'Gorman & Young v. Hartford Fire Insurance Company, 282 U.S. 251 (1931)

Oscar Elsoe and Mary Elsoe, his wife v. Calvin Phillips & Co., a corporation, No. 299760, King County Superior Court, Seattle, WA (1937)

Pacific Finance Corporation of California v. Ernest Parrish and Jane Doe Parrish, Superior Court of the State of Washington in and for the County of Chelan, No. 12454 (1936)

Penalosa State Bank v. Murray, 86 Kan. 766 (1912)

People ex re. Tipaldo v. Morehead, 156 Misc. 522 (1935)

People ex re. Tipaldo v. Morehead, 270 N.Y. 233 (1936)

Perry v. United States, 294 U.S. 330 (1935)

Nortz v. United States, 294 U.S. 317 (1935)

Radice v. New York, 264 U.S. 292 (1924)

Roe v. Wade, 410 U.S. 113 (1973)

S. F. Harrell and Josephine Harrell, his wife v. Wm. D. Perkins, a corporation, No. 300008, King County Superior Court, Seattle, WA (1937)

Slaughter-House Cases, 83 U.S. 36 (1873)

Sparks v. Moritz, 141 Wash. 417 (1926)

Spokane Hotel Company v. C. H. Younger et al., 113 Wash. 359 (1920)

State v. Buchanan, 29 Wash. 602 (1902)

State v. Bunting, 139 P. 731 (1914)

State v. Crowe, 130 Ark. 272 (1917)

Stettler v. O'Hara, 139 P. 743 (1914)

Stettler v. O'Hara, 243 U.S. 629 (1917)

Walker v. Chapman, 17 F. Supp. 308 (1936)

Wenham v. State, 65 Neb. 394 (1902)

West Coast Hotel Company v. Parrish, 300 U.S. 379 (1937)

West Nelson Manufacturing Company, 273 U.S. 657 (1927)

William R. Sample and Jennie Estella Sample, his wife v. West Coast Hotel Company, Superior Court of the State of Washington in and for the County of Chelan, No. 13086 (1938)

Williams v. Evans, 139 Minn. 32 (1917)

William Walsh and Mae Walsh, his wife v. T. M. Donahoe, as Receiver of The Home Savings & Loan Association, Insolvent, No. 298659, Memorandum Opinion in Minimum Wage Cases, King County Superior Court, Seattle, WA (1937)

Wilson v. New, 243 U.S. 332 (1917)

United States v. Bankers' Trust Co. and *Norman v. Baltimore & Ohio R.R. Co.*, 294 U.S. 240 (1935)

United States v. E. C. Knight Co., 156 U.S. 1 (1895)

LEGAL MATERIALS

Appellant's Answer to Brief of Amici Curiae, *West Coast Hotel v. Parrish*, 300 U.S. 379 (1937) (No. 293), 1936 WL 40058.

Brief for Attorney General G. W. Hamilton et al. as Amici Curiae, *West Coast Hotel v. Parrish*, 300 U.S. 379 (1937) (No. 293), 1936 WL 40057.

Brief of Appellant, *West Coast Hotel v. Parrish*, 300 U.S. 379 (1937) (No. 293), 1936 WL 40056.

Brief on Behalf of the National Woman's Party et al. as Amici Curiae, *Morehead v. Tipaldo*, 298 U.S. 587 (1936) (No. 838), 1936 WL 64946.

Conner, C. B., and Sam M. Driver. "Appellee's Brief on the Law (1936)." In *Landmark Briefs and Arguments*, edited by Kurland and Casper, 33:125–29.

Hamilton, G. W., W. A. Toner, and George G. Hannan. "Motion for Leave to File Brief and to Participate in Argument as Amici Curiae in West Coast Hotel Company vs. Ernest Parrish and Elsie Parrish, No. 293 (1936)." In Kurland and Casper, *Landmark Briefs and Arguments*, 33:131–35.

House Journal of the Thirteenth Legislature of the State of Washington. Olympia: Frank M. Lamborn, 1913.

Kurland, Philip B., and Gerhard Casper, eds. *Landmark Briefs and Arguments of the Supreme Court of the United States: Constitutional Law*. Vol. 33. Washington, DC: University Publications of America, 1975.

The Revised Codes of Montana of 1907: Containing All Laws of a Permanent and General Nature in Force after the Adjournment of the Tenth Legislative Assembly. Vol. 1. Helena: State Publishing Company, 1908.

Roberts, John W. "Amended Statement as to Jurisdiction (1936)." In Kurland and Casper, *Landmark Briefs and Arguments* 33:75–91.

Senate Journal of the Thirteenth Legislature of the State of Washington. Olympia: Frank M. Lamborn, 1913.

"West Coast Hotel Co. v. Parrish, 300 U.S. 379." In *Landmark Briefs and Arguments*, edited by Kurland and Casper, 33:73–180.

BOOKS, ARTICLES, AND THESES

"About Hotel Men." *Hotel Monthly* 30, no. 532 (July 1922): 88.

"About Hotel Men." *Hotel Monthly* 34, no. 397 (April 1926): 95.

"About Hotel Men." *Hotel Monthly* 46, no. 546 (September 1938): 66.

Ackermann, Marsha E. *Cool Comfort: America's Romance with Air-Conditioning.* Washington, DC: Smithsonian Institution Press, 2002.

Alexander, Gerry L. "*Parrish v. West Coast Hotel Company*: A Chelan County Chambermaid Makes History." *Columbia: The Magazine of Northwest History* 27, no. 1 (Spring 2013): 2–4.

———. "*Parrish v. West Coast Hotel Co.*—Did This Washington Case Cause the Famous 'Switch in Time That Saved Nine'?" *Washington State Bar News* 64 (December 2010): 22–27.

Allen, Howard W. *Poindexter of Washington: A Study in Progressive Politics.* Carbondale: Southern Illinois University Press, 1981.

Amero, Richard W. "Madame Schumann-Heink: San Diego's Diva." *Southern California Quarterly* 73, no. 2 (Summer 1991): 157–82.

Anderson, Eva G. *Pioneers of North Central Washington.* Wenatchee, WA: Wenatchee World, 1980.

Andrews, Mildred Tanner. *Washington Women as Path Breakers.* Dubuque, IA: Kendall/Hunt, 1989.

Arkes, Hadley. *The Return of George Sutherland: Restoring a Jurisprudence of Natural Rights.* Princeton, NJ: Princeton University Press, 1997.

Armitage, Susan. "Through Women's Eyes: A New View of the West." In Armitage and Jameson, *The Women's West*, 9–18.

Armitage, Susan, and Elizabeth Jameson, eds. *The Women's West.* Norman: University of Oklahoma Press, 1987.

Baer, Judith A. *The Chains of Protection: The Judicial Response to Women's Labor Legislation.* Westport, CT: Greenwood Press, 1978.

Barrett, John Q. "Attribution Time: Cal Tinney's 1937 Quip, 'A Switch in Time'll Save Nine.'" *Oklahoma Law Review* 73 (2020): 229–43.

Bailyn, Bernard. *The Ideological Origins of the American Revolution.* Rev. ed. Cambridge, MA: Belknap Press, 1992.

Beard, Charles A., and Mary R. Beard. *America in Midpassage.* Vol. 3, *The Rise of American Civilization.* New York: Macmillan, 1939.

Beatty, Jack. *Age of Betrayal: The Triumph of Money in America, 1865–1900.* New York: Vintage, 2008.

Beienburg, Sean. "Progressivism and States' Rights: Constitutional Dialogue between the States and Federal Courts on Minimum Wages and Liberty of Contract." *American Political Thought* 8 (Winter 2019): 25–53.

Benesh, Sarah C., and Wendy L. Martinek. "State Supreme Court Decision Making in Confession Cases." *Justice System Journal* 23, no. 1 (2002): 109–33.

Berner, Richard C. *Seattle 1900–1920: From Boomtown, Urban Turbulence, to Restoration*. Seattle: Charles Press, 1991.

———. *Seattle 1921–1940: From Boom to Bust*. Seattle: Charles Press, 1992.

Bernstein, David E. "The Feminist 'Horseman.'" *Green Bag 2d* 10 (Spring 2007): 379–91.

———. "*Lochner* Era Revisionism, Revised: *Lochner* and the Origins of Fundamental Rights Constitutionalism." *Georgetown Law Journal* 92, no. 1 (2003): 1–60.

———. *Rehabilitating* Lochner*: Defending Individual Rights Against Progressive Reform*. Chicago: University of Chicago Press, 2011.

Bliss, William D. P., ed. *The Encyclopedia of Social Reform*. New York: Funk & Wagnalls, 1897.

Brandeis, Elizabeth. "Labor Legislation." In *History of Labor in the United States, 1896–1932*, edited by John R. Commons, 397–697. New York: Macmillan, 1935.

Brandeis, Louis D. "The Constitution and the Minimum Wage." In *The Curse of Bigness: Miscellaneous Papers of Louis D. Brandeis*, edited by Osmond K. Fraenkel, 52–69. New York: Viking Press, 1934.

Brennan, William J., Jr. "Reason, Passion, and 'The Progress of the Law.'" *Cardozo Law Review* 10, no. 3 (1988): 3–23.

Brigham, John. *The Cult of the Court*. Philadelphia: Temple University Press, 1991.

Bryson, Bill. *One Summer: America, 1927*. New York: Doubleday, 2013.

Burns, James MacGregor. *Congress on Trial: The Legislative Process and the Administrative State*. New York: Harper, 1949.

Bybee, Keith J., ed. *Bench Press: The Collision of Courts, Politics, and the Media*. Stanford, CA: Stanford University Press, 2007.

Capitol's Who's Who for Washington: The State Encyclopedia, Including a Number of Prominent Idaho Citizens Who Are to a Greater or Lesser Degree Linked with Washington Progress, 1949–50. Portland, OR: Capitol Publishing, 1949.

Caplan, Aaron. *An Integrated Approach to Constitutional Law*. St. Paul, MN: Foundation Press, 2015.

Carlson, Edward E. *Recollections of a Lucky Fellow*. Seattle: self-published, 1989.

Carpenter, Dale. *Flagrant Conduct: The Story of* Lawrence v. Texas—*How a Bedroom Arrest Decriminalized Gay Americans*. New York: W. W. Norton, 2012.

"The Cascadian, 100% Air Conditioned." *Hotel Monthly* 42, no. 498 (September 1934): 53–54.

"Cascadian Hotel in Wenatchee Wins Praises of Many Guests." *Hotel News of the West* 26, no. 33 (August 17, 1929): 5.

"Cascadian Pays First Quarter Dividends." *Hotel News of the West* 26, no. 52 (December 28, 1929): 20.

Castles, Francis G. *The Working Class and Welfare: Reflections on the Political Development of the Welfare State in Australia and New Zealand, 1890–1980*. Wellington, NZ: Allen & Unwin, 1985.

Cayton, Andrew R. L., and Jeffrey P. Brown. "Introduction." In *The Pursuit of Public Power: Political Culture in Ohio, 1787–1861*, edited by Andrew R. L. Cayton and Jeffrey P. Brown, vii-xii. Kent, OH: Kent University Press, 1994.

Chamberlain, Mary. "The Paper-Box Factory and the Constitution." *The Survey* 33, no. 13 (December 26, 1914): 330–31.

Chambers, John W. "The Big Switch: Justice Roberts and the Minimum Wage Cases." *Labor History* 10, no. 1 (1969): 44–73.

Chapman, Nathan S., and Michael W. McConnell. "Due Process as Separation of Powers." *Yale Law Journal* 121, no. 7 (May 2012): 1672–1807.

"Chelan County, Washington." *The Coast: Wilhelm's Magazine* 12, no. 4 (October 1906): 193–201.

Cheyney, Alice S. "The Course of Minimum Wage Legislation in the United States." *International Labour Review* 38, no. 1 (July 1938): 26–43.

Clark, Ray W. "The Get Together Spirit a Winner (Letter to the Editor)." *The Hotel World* 93 (October 29, 1921): 38.

Collier, Paul S. *Minimum Wage Legislation in Australasia*. Albany, NY: J. B. Lyon, 1915.

Collins, Paul M., Jr. *Friends of the Supreme Court: Interest Groups and Judicial Decision Making*. New York: Oxford University Press, 2008.

Collins, Ronald K. L., and Jennifer Friesen. "Looking Back on *Muller v. Oregon*." *ABA Journal* 69, no. 3 (March 1983): 294–98.

Conner, C. B. "The Minimum Wage Case." In *From the Blue Ridge to the Cascade Range: Recollections of Boyhood Days in the Mountains of Virginia— and Work as a Lawyer in Oklahoma and in the Shadows of the Cascade Range*. Unpublished manuscript, n.d.

"Construction and Contract News." *Improvement Bulletin* 33, no. 2 (June 9, 1906): 16–26.

Cook, Beverly Blair. "Justice Brennan and the Institutionalization of Dissent Assignment." *Judicature* 79, no. 1 (July–August 1995): 17–23.

———. "Justice Brennan and the Institutionalization of Dissent Assignment." Unpublished manuscript, 1995.

Cushman, Barry. "Court-Packing and Compromise." *Constitutional Commentary* 29, no. 1 (Summer 2013): 1–30.

———. "The Court-Packing Plan as Symptom, Casualty, and Cause of Gridlock." *Notre Dame Law Review* 88, no. 5 (2013): 2089–2106.

———. "Formalism and Realism in Commerce Clause Jurisprudence." *University of Chicago Law Review* 67, no. 4 (May 2000): 1089–1150.

———. "Inside the 'Constitutional Revolution' of 1937." *Supreme Court Review* 2016, no. 1 (2017): 367–409.

———. "The Missing Justice in *Coleman v. Miller.*" *Journal of Supreme Court History* 42, no. 1 (March 2017): 67–76.

———. "Mr. Dooley and Mr. Gallup: Public Opinion and Constitutional Change in the 1930s." *Buffalo Law Review* 50 (2002): 7–101.

———. "The Place of Economic Crisis in American Constitutional Law: The Great Depression as a Case Study." In *Constitutions in Times of Financial Crisis*, edited by Tom Ginsburg, Mark D. Rosen, and Georg Vanberg, 95–116. New York: Cambridge University Press, 2019.

———. *Rethinking the New Deal Court: The Structure of a Constitutional Revolution.* New York: Oxford University Press, 1998.

———. "The Secret Lives of the Four Horsemen." *Virginia Law Review* 83 (1997): 559–645.

———. "Some Varieties and Vicissitudes of Lochnerism." *Boston University Law Review* 85 (2005): 881–1000.

Danelski, David J., and Joseph S. Tulchin, eds. *The Autobiographical Notes of Charles Evans Hughes.* Cambridge, MA: Harvard University Press, 1973.

Dappen, Andy. *Buckle of the Power Belt: Recollections of* The Wenatchee World*'s First 100 Years.* Wenatchee: World Publishing, 2005.

Davison, Carole L. "Seattle's 'Restaurant Maids': An Historic Context Document for Waitresses' Union, Local 240, 1900–1940." Master's thesis, University of Washington, 1998.

Dilg, Janice. "'For Working Women in Oregon': Caroline Gleason/Sister Miriam Theresa and Oregon's Minimum Wage Law." *Oregon Historical Quarterly* 110, no. 1 (Spring 2009): 96–129.

Dilliard, Irving. "A Supreme Court Majority? The Court and Minimum-Wage Legislation." *Harper's Magazine*, November 1936, pp. 598–601.

Dinan, John J. *The American State Constitutional Tradition.* Lawrence: University Press of Kansas, 2006.

Dolan, Timothy Michael. *"Some Seed Fell on Good Ground"—The Life of Edwin V. O'Hara.* Washington, DC: Catholic University of America Press, 1992.

Dorf, Michael C. "Introduction—Putting the People Back in 'We the People.'" In *Constitutional Law Stories*, 2nd ed., edited by Michael C. Dorf, 1–12. New York: Foundation Press, 2009.

Douglas, Dorothy W. "American Minimum Wage Laws at Work." *American Economic Review* 9 (December 1919): 701–38.

Dubin, Michael J. *Party Affiliations in the State Legislatures: A Year by Year Summary, 1796–2006.* Jefferson, NC: McFarland & Company, 2007.

———. *United States Gubernatorial Elections, 1932–1952: The Official Results by State and County.* Jefferson, NC: McFarland & Company, 2014.

Dunne, Finley Peter. *Mr. Dooley's Opinions.* New York: R. H. Russell, 1901.

"Editorial." *Hotel News of the West* 32, no. 20 (November 1, 1935): 8.

"Editorial." *Hotel News of the West* 33, no. 8 (April 15, 1936): 6.

Englund, Will. *March 1917: On the Brink of War and Revolution*. New York: W. W. Norton, 2017.

Epstein, Lee, and Jack Knight. *The Choices Justices Make*. Washington, DC: CQ Press, 1998.

Erickson, Nancy S. "*Muller v. Oregon* Reconsidered: The Origins of a Sex-Based Doctrine of Liberty of Contract." *Labor History* 30, no. 2 (1989): 228–50.

Eskridge, William N., Jr. "The Crime against Nature on Trial, *Bowers v. Hardwick*, 1986." In *Civil Rights Stories*, edited by Myriam E. Gilles and Risa L. Goluboff, 151–83. New York: Foundation Press, 2007.

Ewing, Wayne, dir. *Bill Moyers: In Search of the Constitution*. Episode 9, "For the People: Defending Constitutional Rights." Aired June 11, 1987, on PBS, https://billmoyers.com/content/for-the-people/.

"Executive Committee Holds First Meeting." *Hotel News of the West* 33, no. 21 (November 2, 1936): 7.

Ficken, Robert E. *Rufus Woods, the Columbia River, & the Building of Modern Washington*. Pullman: Washington State University Press, 1995.

Fix, Michael P., Justin T. Kingsland, and Matthew D. Montgomery. "The Complexities of State Court Compliance with U.S. Supreme Court Precedent." *Justice System Journal* 38, no. 2 (2017): 149–63.

Forsythe, John S. "Legislative History of the Fair Labor Standards Act." *Law and Contemporary Problems* 6, no. 3 (Summer 1939): 464–90.

Foster, James C. *BONG HiTS 4 JESUS: A Perfect Constitutional Storm in Alaska's Capital*. Fairbanks: University of Alaska Press, 2010.

Foxworthy, Bruce L. *Making Do and Hanging On: Growing Up in Apple Country Through the Great Depression*. Bloomington, IN: AuthorHouse, 2008.

Frank, Dana. *Purchasing Power: Consumer Organizing, Gender, and the Seattle Labor Movement, 1919–1929*. New York: Cambridge University Press, 1994.

Frank, Jason. *Constituent Moments: Enacting the People in Postrevolutionary America*. Durham, NC: Duke University Press, 2010.

Frankfurter, Felix. Foreword to Goldmark, *Impatient Crusader*, v–ix.

———. "Hours of Labor and Realism in Constitutional Law (1916)." In Kurland, *Felix Frankfurter on the Supreme Court*, 8–21.

———. "The Orbit of Judicial Power (1938)." In Kurland, *Felix Frankfurter on the Supreme Court*, 338–57.

———. "Mr. Justice Brandeis and the Constitution (1932)." In Kurland, *Felix Frankfurter on the Supreme Court*, 247–70.

Frankfurter, Felix, and Adrian S. Fisher. "The Business of the Supreme Court at the October Terms, 1935 and 1936." *Harvard Law Review* 51, no. 4 (February 1938): 577–637.

Frankfurter, Felix, and James M. Landis. "The Business of the Supreme Court at October Term, 1929." *Harvard Law Review* 44, no. 1 (November 1930): 1–40.

Friedheim, Robert L. *The Seattle General Strike*. Seattle: University of Washington Press, 1964.

Friedman, Richard D. "Chief Justice Hughes' Letter on Court-Packing." *Journal of Supreme Court History* 22, no. 1 (1997): 76–86.

———. "Switching Time and Other Thought Experiments: The Hughes Court and Constitutional Transformation." *University of Pennsylvania Law Review* 142, no. 6 (June 1994): 1891–1984.

Friesen, Jennifer, and Ronald K. L. Collins. "Looking Back on *Muller v. Oregon* [Part 2]." *American Bar Association Journal* 69, no. 4 (April 1983): 472–77.

Gellatly, John A. *A History of Wenatchee: "The Apple Capital of the World."* Self-published, 1962.

Gerber, Scott D. *A Distinct Judicial Power: The Origins of an Independent Judiciary, 1606–1787*. New York: Oxford University Press, 2011.

Gillman, Howard. *The Constitution Besieged: The Rise and Demise of Lochner Era Police Powers Jurisprudence*. Durham, NC: Duke University Press, 1993.

———. "De-Lochnerizing *Lochner*." *Boston University Law Review* 85 (2005): 859–65.

Gleason, Caroline J. *Report of the Industrial Welfare Commission of the State of Washington on the Wages, Conditions of Work and Cost and Standards of Living of Women Wage-Earners in Washington*. Olympia: Frank M. Lamborn, 1914.

Goldmark, Josephine. *Impatient Crusader: Florence Kelley's Life Story*. Urbana: University of Illinois Press, 1953.

Graber, Mark A. *A New Introduction to American Constitutionalism*. New York: Oxford University Press, 2013.

Graebner, William. "Federalism in the Progressive Era: A Structural Interpretation of Reform." *Journal of American History* 64, no. 2 (September 1977): 331–57.

Greene, Kate. "Burnita Shelton Matthews (1894–1988): The Struggle for Women's Rights." In *Mississippi Women: Their Histories, Their Lives*, edited by Martha H. Swain, Elizabeth Anne Payne, and Marjorie Julian Spruill, 144–59. Athens: University of Georgia Press, 2003.

Hale, F. Dennis, "The Court's Perception of the Press." *Judicature* 57, no. 5 (December 1973): 183–89.

———. "Factors Associated With Newspaper Coverage of California Supreme Court Decisions." *Orange County Bar Journal* 6, no. 1 (1979): 28–38.

———. "How Reporters and Justices View Coverage of a State Appellate Court." *Journalism & Mass Communication Quarterly* 52, no. 1 (March 1975): 106–10.

————. "Newspaper Coverage Limited For State Supreme Court Cases." *Newspaper Research Journal* 27, no. 1 (Winter 2006): 6–17.

————. "Press Releases vs. Newspaper Coverage of California Supreme Court Decisions." *Journalism & Mass Communication Quarterly* 55, no. 4 (December 1978): 696–702, 710.

Hall, Kermit L., and John J. Patrick. *The Pursuit of Justice: Supreme Court Decisions That Shaped America.* New York: Oxford University Press, 2006.

Hall, Matthew E. K. "The Semiconstrained Court: Public Opinion, the Separation of Powers, and the U.S. Supreme Court's Fear of Nonimplementation." *American Journal of Political Science* 58, no. 2 (April 2014): 352–66.

Haltom, William. *Reporting on the Courts: How the Mass Media Cover Judicial Actions.* Chicago: Nelson-Hall, 1998.

Hamilton, Alexander. "Seventy-Eight, May 28, 1788: A View of the Constitution of the Judicial Department, in Relation to the Tenure of Good Behaviour." In *The Federalist*, edited by J. R. Pole, 411–18. Indianapolis: Hackett Publishing, 2005.

Hamm, Richard F. "Mobilizing Legal Talent For a Cause: The National Woman's Party and the Campaign to Make Jury Service For Women a Federal Right." *Journal of Gender, Social Policy & the Law* 9, no. 1 (2001): 97–117.

Hardwick, Michael. "Michael Hardwick v. Michael Bowers: II. 'What Are You Doing in My Bedroom?'" In Irons, *The Courage of Their Convictions*, 392–403.

Harris, Katherine. "Homesteading in Northeastern Colorado, 1873–1920: Sex Roles and Women's Experience." In Armitage and Jameson, *The Women's West*, 165–78.

Hart, Vivien. *Bound by Our Constitution: Women, Workers, and the Minimum Wage.* Princeton, NJ: Princeton University Press, 1994.

————. "Minimum-Wage Policy and Constitutional Inequality: The Paradox of the Fair Labor Standards Act of 1938." *Journal of Policy History* 1, no. 3 (1989): 319–43.

Hartman, John P. "A Tribute to Charles B. Conner, of Wenatchee, Washington." In Conner, *From the Blue Ridge to the Cascade Range*, 193–95.

Headlee, Frances K. "The Minimum Wage in Washington." *Survey*, January 15, 1916.

Hobbes, Thomas. *Leviathan.* Edited by C. B. Macpherson. New York: Penguin, 1968.

Hofstadter, Richard. *The Age of Reform: From Bryan to F.D.R.* New York: Vintage Books, 1955.

"A Hotel That Boosts Local Product." *Hotel Monthly* 42, no. 490 (January 1934): 58.

Hughes, John C. *Pressing On: Two Family-Owned Newspapers in the 21st Century.* Olympia: Washington State Legacy Project, 2015.

Hull, Lindley M., ed. *A History of Central Washington: Including the Famous Wenatchee, Entiat, Chelan and the Columbia Valleys with an Index and Eighty Scenic-Historical Illustrations.* Spokane, WA: Shaw & Borden, 1929.

Hutchinson, Dennis J., and David J. Garrow, eds. *The Forgotten Memoir of John Knox: A Year in the Life of a Supreme Court Clerk in FDR's Washington.* Chicago: University of Chicago Press, 2002.

Hutchinson, Paul. "The Final Verdict on Recovery: Will the Supreme Court Support Mr. Roosevelt?" *Forum and Century* 90, no. 3 (September 1933): 141–47.

Hyman, Colette A. "Labor Organizing and Female Institution-Building: The Chicago Women's Trade Union League, 1904–24." In Milkman, *Women, Work and Protest*, 22–41.

Ingalls, Robert P. "New York and the Minimum-Wage Movement, 1933–1937." *Labor History* 15, no. 2 (Spring 1974): 179–98.

Irons, Peter. *The Courage of Their Convictions: Sixteen Americans Who Fought Their Way to the Supreme Court.* New York: Penguin, 1990.

———. *Justice at War: The Story of the Japanese-American Internment Cases.* Berkeley: University of California Press, 1983.

———. "Michael Hardwick v. Michael Bowers: I. 'I Saw a Bedroom Door Partially Open.'" In Irons, *The Courage of Their Convictions*, 379–91.

———. *A People's History of the Supreme Court: The Men and Women Whose Cases and Decisions Have Shaped Our Constitution.* New York: Penguin, 1999.

Jackson, Robert H. *The Struggle for Judicial Supremacy: A Study of a Crisis in American Power Politics.* New York: Alfred A. Knopf, 1941.

Jakle, John A., and Keith A. Sculle. *America's Main Street Hotels: Transiency and Community in the Early Auto Age.* Knoxville: University of Tennessee Press, 2009.

Jakle, John A., Keith A. Sculle, and Jefferson S. Rogers. *The Motel in America.* Baltimore: Johns Hopkins University Press, 1996.

Jepsen, David J., and David J. Norberg. *Contested Boundaries: A New Pacific Northwest History.* Hoboken, NJ: Wiley Blackwell, 2017.

Johansen, Dorothy O. *Empire of the Columbia: A History of the Pacific Northwest.* 2nd ed. New York: Harper & Row, 1967.

Johnson, Elaine Zahnd. "Protective Legislation and Women's Work: Oregon's Ten-Hour Law and the *Muller v. Oregon Case*, 1900–1913." PhD diss., University of Oregon, 1982.

Johnston, Robert D. *The Radical Middle Class: Populist Democracy and the Question of Capitalism in Progressive Era Portland, Oregon.* Princeton, NJ: Princeton University Press, 2003.

Jones, Margie. "Elsie Parrish . . . A Woman History Forgot." *Okanogan County Heritage* (Winter 1990–1991): 14–17.

"Judicial Statistics and the Constitutionality of Minimum Wage Legislation." *Yale Law Journal* 46, no. 7 (1938): 1227–28.

Jyles, Ashley D. "The Newly Increased Minimum Wage: Congress's Way of Robbing Peter to Pay Paul." *Southern University Law Review* 37 (Spring 2010): 353–70.

Kammen, Michael. *A Machine That Would Go of Itself: The Constitution in American Culture.* New York: Alfred A. Knopf, 1986. Reprinted with a new introduction by the author. Abingdon, UK: Routledge, 2017.

Kapur, Amanda Rose. "A Faulty Federal Standard: A Call for a Federal Minimum Wage That Is Actually 'Fair' under the Fair Labor Standards Act." *University of Miami Business Law Review* 25 (Spring 2017): 137–70.

Katznelson, Ira. *Fear Itself: The New Deal and the Origins of Our Time.* New York: Liveright, 2014.

Keck, Thomas M. *The Most Activist Supreme Court in History: The Road to Modern Judicial Conservatism.* Chicago: University of Chicago Press, 2004.

Kelley, Florence. "Aims and Principles of the Consumers' League." *American Journal of Sociology* 5, no. 3 (November 1899): 289–304.

Kennedy, Frances H. *The Civil War Battlefield Guide.* 2nd ed. Boston: Houghton Mifflin, 1998.

Kens, Paul. *Judicial Power and Reform Politics: The Anatomy of* Lochner v. New York. Lawrence: University Press of Kansas, 1990.

Kerr, Charles C. *The World of the World: From Frontier to Community, 1905–1980—A History of Growth and Development in North Central Washington.* Wenatchee, WA: Wenatchee World, 1980.

Kerr, Orin S. "How to Read a Legal Opinion: A Guide for New Law Students." *Green Bag 2d* 11 (Autumn 2007): 51–63.

Kessler-Harris, Alice. *Out to Work: A History of Wage-Earning Women in the United States.* New York: Oxford University Press, 2003.

———. *A Woman's Wage: Historical Meanings & Social Consequences.* Lexington: University Press of Kentucky, 1990.

"Kinsella Resigns at Cascadian Hotel." *Hotel News of the West* 26, no. 45 (November 9, 1929): 5.

Knowles, Helen J. "The Cascadian: An 'Outstanding Small City Hotel.'" *The Confluence* 33, no. 2 (Summer 2017): 13–15.

———. "'Omak's Minimum Pay Law Joan D'Arc': Telling the Local Story of *West Coast Hotel v. Parrish* (1937)." *Journal of Supreme Court History* 37, no. 3 (November 2012): 283–304.

Knowles, Helen J., and Emma Rodman. "Legal Mobilization and the Politics of Economic Enforcement after *West Coast Hotel v. Parrish.*" Paper presented at the Western Political Science Association Annual Meeting, San Diego, CA, April 18, 2019.

Knowles, Helen J., and L. Darlene Spargo. *Images of America: The Cascadian.* Charleston, SC: Arcadia Press, 2020.

Knowles, Helen J., and Julianne A. Toia. "Defining 'Popular Constitutionalism': The Kramer Versus Kramer Problem." *Southern University Law Review* 42 (Fall 2014): 31–59.

Kramer, Larry. *The People Themselves: Popular Constitutionalism and Judicial Review.* New York: Oxford University Press, 2004.

———. "The Supreme Court 2000 Term Foreword: We the Court." *Harvard Law Review* 115 (2001): 4–169.

Kurland, Philip B., ed. *Felix Frankfurter on the Supreme Court: Extrajudicial Essays on the Court and the Constitution.* Cambridge, MA: Belknap Press of Harvard University Press, 1970.

Labbe, Ronald M., and Jonathan Lurie. *The Slaughterhouse Cases: Regulation, Reconstruction, and the Fourteenth Amendment.* Lawrence: University Press of Kansas, 2003.

Lasser, William. *Benjamin V. Cohen: Architect of the New Deal.* New Haven, CT: Yale University Press, 2002.

Laughlin, J. Laurence. "Monopoly of Labor." *Atlantic Monthly* (October 1913): 444–53.

Lebsock, Suzanne. "Women and American Politics, 1880–1920." In *Women, Politics, and Change,* edited by Louise A. Tilly and Patricia Gurin, 35–62. New York: Russell Sage Foundation, 1992.

Lee, Jenny. "A Redivision of Labour: Victoria's Wages Boards in Action, 1896–1903." *Historical Studies* 22, no. 88 (April 1987): 352–72.

Leedy, Robert F. "Memorials of Deceased Members: Judge Edwin T. Booton." In *Report of the Twentieth Annual Meeting of the Virginia State Bar Association,* edited by John B. Minor, 108–11. Richmond: Richmond Press, 1908.

Leuchtenburg, William E. "The Case of the Chambermaid and the Nine Old Men." *American Heritage* 38, no. 1 (December 1986): 34–41.

———. "The Case of the Wenatchee Chambermaid." Chap. 6 in *The Supreme Court Reborn: The Constitutional Revolution in the Age of Roosevelt.* New York: Oxford University Press, 1995.

———. "Election of 1936." In *History of American Presidential Elections, 1789–1968.* Edited by Arthur M. Schlesinger Jr., Fred L. Israel, and William P. Hansen, 2809–2913. New York: Chelsea House, 1971.

———. "Franklin D. Roosevelt's Supreme Court 'Packing' Plan." In *Essays on the New Deal,* edited by Harold F. Hollingsworth and William F. Holmes, 69–115. College Station: Texas A&M University Press, 1969.

Levitan, Sar A., and Richard S. Belous. *More Than Subsistence: Minimum Wages for the Working Poor.* Baltimore: Johns Hopkins University Press, 1979.

Lewis, John E. *Biles-Coleman Lumber Company's Reservation Narrow Gauge: The Last Northwest/Washington State Narrow Gauge Logging Railroad, 1921–1948.* Self-published, 1980.

"Liberty to Starve." *New Republic,* June 10, 1936.

"Life on the American Newsfront: Supreme Court Reverses Itself on Minimum Wages." *Life,* April 12, 1937.

Locke, John. *Second Treatise of Government.* Edited by C. B. Macpherson. Indianapolis: Hackett Publishing, 1980.

Lodato, Jake. "Pangborn, Herndon Undertake World-Famous Flight." *The Confluence* 32, no. 4 (Winter 2016–17): 7–12.

Luketic, Robert, dir. *Legally Blonde*. 2001; MGM Home Video, 2004, DVD.

Lux, Mabel. "Honyockers of Harlem, Scissorsbills of Zurich." In *Cowboys and Cattlemen: A Roundup from Montana, The Magazine of Western History*, edited by Michael S. Kennedy, 333–48. New York: Hastings House, 1964.

Lynch, Joseph A., ed. *Hubbell's Legal Directory 1924*. New York: Hubbell Publishing, 1924.

Macbeth, Norman J., Jr. "Note: Present Status of the *Adkins* Case." *Kentucky Law Journal* 24 (1935): 59–68.

Magliocca, Gerard N. "Constitutional Change." In *The Oxford Handbook of the U.S. Constitution*, edited by Mark Tushnet, Mark A. Graber, and Sanford Levinson, 909–20. New York: Oxford University Press, 2015.

Malone, Michael P., Richard B. Roeder, and William L. Lang. *Montana: A History of Two Centuries*. Rev. ed. Seattle: University of Washington Press, 1991.

Manley, Henry S. "*Nebbia* Plus Fifteen." *Albany Law Review* 13 (1949): 11–19.

Marshino, Ora L., and Lawrence J. O'Malley. "Wage and Hour Legislation in the Courts." *George Washington Law Review* 5 (1937): 865–78.

Martens, Allison M. "Working Women or Women Workers? The Women's Trade Union League and the Transformation of the American Constitutional Order." *Studies in American Political Development* 23 (October 2009): 143–70.

Martin, Albro. *James J. Hill and the Opening of the Northwest*. New York: Oxford University Press, 1976.

Mason, Alpheus Thomas. *Harlan Fiske Stone: Pillar of Law*. New York: Viking Press, 1956.

Mauro, Tony. "The Right Legislation for the Wrong Reasons." *Michigan Law Review First Impressions* 106 (2007): 8–11.

May, Martha. "Bread Before Roses: American Workingmen, Labor Unions and the Family Wage." In Milkman, *Women, Work and Protest*, 1–21.

McClintock, Thomas C. "Seth Lewelling, William S. U'ren and the Birth of the Oregon Progressive Movement." *Oregon Historical Quarterly* 68, no. 3 (September 1967): 196–220.

McElwain, Edwin. "The Business of the Supreme Court as Conducted by Chief Justice Hughes." *Harvard Law Review* 63, no. 1 (November 1949): 5–26.

McKenna, Marian C. *Franklin Roosevelt and the Great Constitutional War: The Court-Packing Crisis of 1937*. New York: Fordham University Press, 2002.

Milkman, Ruth, ed. *Women, Work and Protest: A Century of US Women's Labor History*. Boston: Routledge & Kegan Paul, 1985.

Miller, Glenn W. *American Labor and the Government*. New York: Prentice-Hall, 1948.

"Minimum Wage Case Dismissed." *Hotel News of the West* 32, no. 20 (November 1, 1935): 8.

"Minimum Wage Case Lost." *Hotel News of the West* 33, no. 8 (April 15, 1936): 6.

"Minimum Wage Case to Be Appealed." *Hotel News of the West* 33, no. 11 (June 1, 1936): 19.

Mitchell, Bruce. *Apple City U.S.A.: Stories of Early Wenatchee.* Wenatchee, WA: Wenatchee World, 1992.

Murphy, Walter F. *Congress and the Court: A Case Study in the American Political Process.* Chicago: University of Chicago Press, 1962.

———. *Constitutional Democracy: Creating and Maintaining a Just Political Order.* Baltimore: Johns Hopkins University Press, 2006.

———. *Elements of Judicial Strategy.* Chicago: University of Chicago Press, 1964.

Murray, Gail S. "Forty Years Ago: The Great Depression Comes to Arkansas." *Arkansas Historical Quarterly* 29, no. 4 (Winter 1970): 291–312.

Newell, Gordon. *Rogues, Buffoons & Statesmen.* Seattle: Hangman Press, 1975.

"New & Remodeled Hotels." *Hotel Monthly* 37, no. 432 (March 1929): 82, 84, 86, 88.

"New & Remodeled Hotels." *Hotel Monthly* 37, no. 433 (April 1929): 86, 90, 92.

"New & Remodeled Hotels." *Hotel Monthly* 37, no. 434 (May 1929): 86, 88, 90.

"New & Remodeled Hotels." *Hotel Monthly* 37, no. 435 (June 1929): 96, 98.

"New & Remodeled Hotels." *Hotel Monthly* 42, no. 498 (September 1934): 64.

Noonan, John T., Jr. *Persons and Masks of the Law: Cardozo, Holmes, Jefferson, and Wythe as Makers of the Masks.* With a new preface. 1976; repr. Berkeley: University of California Press, 2002.

Nourse, Victoria F. "A Tale of Two *Lochners*: The Untold History of Substantive Due Process and the Idea of Fundamental Rights." *California Law Review* 97 (2009): 751–99.

Novkov, Julie. *Constituting Workers, Protecting Women: Gender, Law, and Labor in the Progressive Era and New Deal Years.* Ann Arbor: University of Michigan Press, 2004.

O'Brien, David M. *Storm Center: The Supreme Court in American Politics.* 10th ed. New York: W. W. Norton, 2014.

O'Connor, Harvey. *Revolution in Seattle: A Memoir.* New York: Monthly Review Press, 1964.

Olken, Samuel R. "George Sutherland and the Business of Expression." In *Judging Free Speech: First Amendment Jurisprudence of US Supreme Court Justices.* Edited by Helen J. Knowles and Steven B. Lichtman, 49–73. New York: Palgrave Macmillan, 2015.

———. "Justice Sutherland Reconsidered." *Vanderbilt Law Review* 62 (2009): 639–93.

"One Alone: An Interview with H. L. Upton." *Union Guardian* 1, no. 3 (September 1937): 14.

Opdycke, Sandra. *The Flu Epidemic of 1918: America's Experience in the Global Health Crisis.* New York: Routledge, 2014.

Pacific Directory Company's Compton City Directory 1951. Arcadia, CA: Pacific Directory Company, 1951.

Parr, W. O. "The Creation of Chelan County." In *A History of Central Washington: Including the Famous Wenatchee, Entiat, Chelan and the Columbia Valleys with an Index and Eighty Scenic-Historical Illustrations,* edited by Lindley M. Hull, 546–55. Spokane, WA: Shaw & Borden, 1929.

Paschal, Joel Francis. *Mr. Justice Sutherland: A Man Against the State.* New York: Greenwood Press, 1969.

"Perseverance Won Them Ownership of a Daily Paper." *Editor and Publisher* 51, no. 2 (April 17, 1919): 26.

Peterson, Gregory L., E. Barrett Prettyman Jr., Shawn Francis Peters, Bennett Boskey, Gathie Barnett Edmonds, Marie Barnett Snodgrass, and John Q. Barrett. "Recollections of *West Virginia Board of Education v. Barnette.*" *St. John's Law Review* 81, no. 4 (Fall 2007): 755–96.

Phillips, Michael J. *The Lochner Court, Myth and Reality: Substantive Due Process From the 1890s to the 1930s.* Westport, CT: Praeger, 2000.

Polk's Everett (Washington) City Directory, Vol. XXXIII (1944). Seattle: R. L. Polk, 1944.

Polk's Everett (Washington) City Directory, Vol. XXXV (1948). Seattle: R. L. Polk, 1948.

Polk's Everett (Washington) City Directory, Vol. XXXVI (1950). Seattle: R. L. Polk, 1950.

Polk's Wenatchee City and Chelan County (Washington) Directory. Vol. XIV (1931–1932). Seattle: R. L. Polk, 1932.

Polk's Wenatchee City and Chelan County (Washington) Directory, Vol. XV (1933). R. L. Polk, Seattle, 1933.

Polk's Wenatchee City and Chelan County (Washington) Directory, Vol. XVI (1936). Seattle: R. L. Polk, 1936.

Post, Robert C. "Defending the Lifeworld: Substantive Due Process in the Taft Court Era." *Boston University Law Review* 78 (1998): 1489–1545.

Pound, Roscoe. "Mechanical Jurisprudence." *Columbia Law Review* 8, no. 8 (December 1908): 605–23.

Powell, Thomas Reed. "The Oregon Minimum-Wage Cases." *Political Science Quarterly* 32, no. 2 (June 1917): 296–311.

Power for Supremacy: The Pacific Northwest. Chicago: Chicago Burlington & Quincy Railroad, Great Northern Railway, Northern Pacific Railway, 1923.

Pritchett, C. Herman. "The Development of Judicial Research." In *Frontiers of Judicial Research,* edited by Joel B. Grossman and Joseph Tanenhaus. New York: Wiley, 1969.

Pusey, Merlo J. *Charles Evans Hughes*. 2 vols. New York: Macmillan, 1951.

———. "Justice Roberts' 1937 Turnaround." *Yearbook of the Supreme Court Historical Society 1983* (1983): 102–7.

Putnam, John C. *Class and Gender Politics in Progressive-Era Seattle*. Reno: University of Nevada Press, 2008.

Quigley, William. "Full-Time Workers Should Not Be Poor: The Living Wage Movement." *Mississippi Law Journal* 70 (Spring 2001): 889–944.

Rader, Chris. "Bob Godfrey Played for Wenatchee Dancers." *The Confluence* 27, no. 4 (2011–12): 4–7.

———. "Fred & Louis Crollard: Musical Wenatchee Lawyers." *The Confluence* 26, no. 2 (2010): 9–10.

———. "Wenatchee Avenue Block Brims with History." *The Confluence* 29, no. 3 (2013): 3–9.

———. "Wenatchee Is the Apple Capital of the World." *The Confluence* 23, no. 1 (Spring 2007): 4–6.

Rader, Chris, and Mark Behler. *Images of America: Wenatchee*. Charleston, SC: Arcadia Publishing, 2012.

Raitz, Karl B., and John Paul Jones III. "The City Hotel as Landscape Artifact and Community Symbol." *Journal of Cultural Geography* 9, no. 1 (Fall/Winter 1988): 17–36.

Rasenberger, Jim. *America, 1908: The Dawn of Flight, the Race to the Pole, the Invention of the Model T, and the Making of a Modern Nation*. New York: Scribner, 2007.

Ray, Laura Krugman. "Judicial Personality: Rhetoric and Emotion in Supreme Court Opinions." *Washington and Lee Law Review* 59, no. 1 (2002): 193–234.

"Ray Clark, Booster of the Far Northwest." *Hotel Monthly* 46, no. 538 (January 1938): 36.

Reely, Mary Katharine. "Introduction." In *Selected Articles on Minimum Wage*, edited by Mary Katharine Reely, 1–6.

Reely, Mary Katharine, ed. *Selected Articles on Minimum Wage; Debaters' Handbook Series*. White Plains, NY: H. W. Wilson, 1917.

Report on Condition of Woman and Child Wage-Earners in the United States. 19 vols. Washington, DC: Government Printing Office, 1910–1913.

Roberts, Barbara. *Up the Capitol Steps: A Woman's March to the Governorship*. Corvallis: Oregon State University Press, 2011.

Roberts, Philip J. *A Penny for the Governor, $ A Dollar for Uncle Sam: Income Taxation in Washington*. Seattle: University of Washington Press, 2002.

Robertson, Reynolds. *Appellate Practice and Procedure in the Supreme Court of the United States: A Chronological Outline of Proceedings Necessary Both in the Supreme Court and in the Lower Courts on Petition for a Writ of Certiorari, Writ of Error, or Appeal, to Review a Decision in the Supreme Court of the United States; and of Steps Necessary to be Taken to File and Conduct, or Defend, a Case in the Supreme Court Upon the Granting of a Writ of Certiorari, Writ of Error, or Appeal, or Upon Certified Questions With Forms and Citations to the Applicable Statutes, Rules of Court, and Decisions.* New York: Prentice-Hall, 1928.

Robertson, Reynolds, and Francis R. Kirkham. *Jurisdiction of the Supreme Court of the United States: A Treatise Concerning the Appellate Jurisdiction of the Supreme Court of the United States, Including a Treatment of the Principles and Precedents Governing the Exercise of the Discretionary Jurisdiction on Certiorari.* St. Paul, MN: West Publishing, 1936.

Ross, Dorothy. *The Origins of American Social Science.* New York: Cambridge University Press, 1991.

Rutherglen, George A. *Civil Rights in the Shadow of Slavery: The Constitution, Common Law, and the Civil Rights Act of 1866.* New York: Oxford University Press, 2012.

Ryan, John A. "Minimum-Wage Legislation." In Reely, *Selected Articles on Minimum Wage,* 38–42.

Salmon, John S. *The Official Virginia Civil War Battlefield Guide.* Mechanicsburg, PA: Stackpole Books, 2001.

Sargent, Jim. *Too Poor to Move, But Always Rich: A Century on Montana Land.* Self-published, CreateSpace, 2014.

Schlesinger, Arthur M., Jr. *The Age of Roosevelt: The Politics of Upheaval.* Boston: Houghton Mifflin, 1960.

Segal, Jeffrey A., and Harold J. Spaeth. *The Supreme Court and the Attitudinal Model.* Cambridge: Cambridge University Press, 1993.

———. *The Supreme Court and the Attitudinal Model Revisited.* Cambridge: Cambridge University Press, 2002.

Sheldon, Charles H. *The Washington High Bench: A Biographical History of the State Supreme Court, 1889–1991.* Pullman: Washington State University Press, 1992.

Shesol, Jeff. *Supreme Power: Franklin Roosevelt vs. the Supreme Court.* New York: W. W. Norton, 2010.

Shirley, Gayle C. *More Than Petticoats: Remarkable Montana Women.* Helena, MT: Falcon Publishing, 1995.

Silberman, Lauren R. *Wild Women of Maryland: Grit & Gumption in the Free State.* Charleston, SC: History Press, 2015.

Simon, James F. *FDR and Chief Justice Hughes: The President, the Supreme Court, and the Epic Battle Over the New Deal.* New York: Simon & Schuster, 2012.

Sister Miriam Theresa. *Bulletin of the Women's Bureau, No. 90: Oregon Legislation for Women in Industry.* Washington, DC: Government Printing Office, 1931.

Skocpol, Theda. *Protecting Soldiers and Mothers: The Political Origins of Social Policy in the United States.* Cambridge, MA: Belknap Press of Harvard University Press, 1992.

Smith, Alfred E. "Democratic Leadership at the Crossroads." *New Outlook*, March 1933, pp. 9–12.

Smith, Norma. *Jeannette Rankin: America's Conscience*. Helena: Montana Historical Society Press, 2002.

Snyder, Brad. *The House of Truth: A Washington Political Salon and the Foundations of American Liberalism*. New York: Oxford University Press, 2017.

Solomon, Burt. *FDR v. The Constitution: The Court-Packing Fight and the Triumph of Democracy*. New York: Walker Books, 2009.

Spargo, L. Darlene. "Wenatchee's Quiet Warrior—Elsie Parrish." *Good Life* (April 2012): 8–9.

Spence, Mary Lee. "Waitresses in the Trans-Mississippi West: 'Pretty Waiter Girls,' Harvey Girls, and Union Maids." In *The Women's West*, edited by Susan Armitage and Elizabeth Jameson, 219–34. Norman: University of Oklahoma Press, 1987.

Stevenson, Shanna. *Women's Votes, Women's Voices: The Campaign for Equal Rights in Washington*. Tacoma: Washington State Historical Society, 2009.

St. Johns, Adela Rogers. *Some Are Born Great: Lively and Controversial Tales of Some of the Extraordinary Women of Our Time*. Garden City, NY: Doubleday, 1974.

Storrs, Landon R. Y. *Civilizing Capitalism: The National Consumers' League, Women's Activism, and Labor Standards in the New Deal Era*. Chapel Hill: University of North Carolina Press, 2000.

Stratton, Joanna L. *Pioneer Women: Voices From the Kansas Frontier*. New York: Touchstone, 1981.

Strom, Claire. *Profiting From the Plains: The Great Northern Railway and Corporate Development of the American West*. Seattle: University of Washington Press, 2003.

Strom, Claire Margaret. "Unattainable Edens: James J. Hill, the Great Northern Railway, and Changing Notions of Agricultural Expertise." PhD diss., Iowa State University, 1998.

Strum, Philippa. *Brandeis: Beyond Progressivism*. Lawrence: University Press of Kansas, 1993.

Sunstein, Cass. "*Lochner's* Legacy." *Columbia Law Review* 87, no. 5 (1987): 873–919.

"Supreme Court Invalidates N.Y. Minimum Wage Law." *Hotel News of the West* 33, no. 11 (June 1, 1936): 19.

Swisher, Carl Brent, ed. *Selected Papers of Homer Cummings, Attorney General of the United States 1933–1939*. New York: Charles Scribner's Sons, 1939.

"Switch to Apartments an Uptown Decision." *Wenatchee Business Journal* 12, no. 3 (March 1998).

Taylor, Charles W., Jr. *Eminent Judges and Lawyers of the Northwest, 1843–1955*. Palo Alto, CA: C. W. Taylor Jr., 1954.

Thelen, David P. "Social Tensions and the Origins of Progressivism." *Journal of American History* 56, no. 2 (September 1969): 323–41.

Tripp, Joseph F. "Toward an Efficient and Moral Society: Washington State Minimum-Wage Law, 1913–1925." *Pacific Northwest Quarterly* 67, no. 3 (July 1976): 97–112.

Turley, Gladys. "Industry and Sister Miriam." *Sunday Journal Magazine*, May 6, 1951.

Tuve, Jeanette E. *First Lady of the Law: Florence Ellinwood Allen.* Lanham, MD: University Press of America, 1984.

Vining, Richard L., Jr., and Teena Wilhelm. "Explaining High-Profile Coverage of State Supreme Court Decisions." *Social Science Quarterly* 91, no. 3 (September 2010): 704–23.

"Washington Hotel Men Resume Meetings." *Hotel News of the West* 32, no. 18b (October 1, 1935).

"Washington Minimum Wage Law Upheld." *Hotel News of the West* 34, no. 7 (April 1, 1937): 15.

"Washington State Hotel Association: Proposes Reductions in Wine Percentages." *Hotel News of the West* 33, no. 12 (June 15, 1936): 5.

"The Week." *New Republic*, March 18, 1936.

Wexler, Jay D. *Holy Hullabaloos: A Road Trip to the Battlegrounds of the Church/State Wars.* Boston: Beacon Press, 2009.

White, G. Edward. *The Constitution and the New Deal.* Cambridge: Harvard University Press, 2000.

Wiebe, Robert H. *The Search for Order, 1877–1920.* New York: Hill and Wang, 1967.

Willis, Robert N. "The Evolution of the Fair Labor Standards Act." *University of Miami Law Review* 26, no. 3 (1972): 607–34.

Wilson, Sarah. "Florence Ellinwood Allen." In *Women in Law: A Bio-Bibliographical Sourcebook,* edited by Rebecca Mae Salokar and Mary L. Volcansek, 17–24. Santa Barbara: ABC-Clio, 1996.

Wolfe, Allis Rosenberg. "Women, Consumerism, and the National Consumers' League in the Progressive Era, 1900–1923." *Labor History* 16, no. 3 (1975): 378–92.

Woloch, Nancy. *Muller v. Oregon: A Brief History With Documents.* Boston: Bedford/St. Martin's, 1996.

Wood, Gordon S. *The Creation of the American Republic 1776–1787.* Chapel Hill: University of North Carolina Press, 1998.

———. *The Radicalism of the American Revolution.* New York: A. A. Knopf, 1991.

Woodruff, Nan Elizabeth. *As Rare as Rain: Federal Relief in the Great Southern Drought of 1930–31.* Urbana: University of Illinois Press, 1985.

Yanus, Alixandra B. "Full-Court Press: An Examination of Media Coverage of State Supreme Courts." *Justice System Journal* 30, no. 2 (2009): 180–95.

Young, Kris, and Mark Behler. "Cascadian Hotel Was Site of Historical Law-suit." *Wenatchee Business Journal* 11, no. 7 (July 1997).

Zackin, Emily. *Looking for Rights in All the Wrong Places: Why State Constitutions Contain America's Positive Rights.* Princeton, NJ: Princeton University Press, 2013.

Zinn, Howard. Foreword to *A People's History of the Supreme Court: The Men and Women Whose Cases and Decisions Have Shaped Our Constitution,* by Peter Irons, v–vii. New York: Penguin, 2000.

Index

Lord, Alice, 281n80, 285n131. *See
also* Seattle Waitresses' Union
Local 240
Loughran, John T. See *Morehead v.
New York ex rel. Tipaldo* (1936):
lower court opinions in
Lutz, Alma, 79–80, 113, 228. *See
also* National Woman's Party
Lyons, Willie, 97, 290n56, 179. See
also *Adkins v. Children's Hospital*
(1923)

Macbeth, Norman J., Jr., 140–41,
308n116
Magliocca, Gerard, 200
Major, David, 252
Major, Gladys (née Parrish), 252
Malarkey, Dan J. *See* Oregon:
minimum wage law for women
(1913)
Marconnier, Emily Sims, 313n42
Martin, Clarence D., 172, 316n47
Mason, Lucy R., 313n42
Massachusetts: minimum wage law
for women (1912), 63–65, 72,
105, 280n69, 292n93
Masuda, Thomas. *See* post-*Parrish*
litigation in Seattle: lawyers
involved in
Mathewson, William. *See* post-
Parrish litigation in Seattle:
lawyers involved in
Matthews, Burnita Shelton, 331n19
maximum working hours laws. *See*
protective legislation: maximum
working hours laws as examples of
McFarland, Marjorie, 108–9, 111
McKenna, Joseph, 45, 82, 90–92. See
also *Bunting v. Oregon* (1917)
McReynolds, James C., 45, 88, 167–
68, 181–82, 186, 190, 319n91
Meyer v. Nebraska, 166–68
minimum wage laws for women,
46, 57, 63–67, 74–75, 84–85, 97,
106, 188, 232, 285n131. *See also
individual countries, states, and
territories*

Minnesota: minimum wage law for
women (1913), 86, 96, 105
Minnesota v. Barber (1890),
312n33
Miranda v. Arizona (1966), 156
Montana: 21–27; Murray homestead
in Coffee Creek, 21–24, 26,
27. *See also* Desert Land Act
(1877); Enlarged Homestead Act
(1909); Homestead Act (1862);
homesteading
Moore, Avery, 59. See also *Muller v.
Oregon* (1908)
Moore, Oscar. *See* Cascadian Hotel:
famous guests of
Morehead v. New York ex rel. Tipaldo
(1936), 5, 39, 83, 110–11, 117,
140, 153–54, 158–59; amicus
brief filed by the National
Woman's Party in, 229, 331n19;
Chief Justice Hughes's dissenting
opinion in 115, 116, 162, 176–77,
229; consideration of by justices
while voting in *Parrish*, 182–83;
defense of decision in, 227–29,
231 (*see also* National Woman's
Party); and granting of certiorari
in *Parrish*, 160–62; Justice Butler's
majority opinion in, 113–14;
Justice Stone's dissenting opinion
in, 115–17, 177; lower court
opinions in, 111–15; New York
legislative response to, 232 (*see
also* New York: minimum wage
law for women [1937]), public
criticism of, 114–15, 117–19,
121–22, 162, 190–92 (*see also*
1936 elections); reasoning rejected
in *Parrish*, 192–98
Morse, Deborah. See *Morse v.
Frederick* (2007)
Morse v. Frederick (2007), 9–10
Moyers, Bill, 10
Muller, Curt. See *Muller v. Oregon*
(1908)
Muller v. Oregon (1908), 57–60, 63,
71, 72, 74, 82, 85, 89, 261n2,

CPSIA information can be obtained
at www.ICGtesting.com
Printed in the USA
LVHW031310141221
706153LV00005B/492